THE NEW
SHOP FLOOR
MANAGEMENT

The above Kanji characters are pronounced as *Gen Ba Kan Ri* or, in short, *Genba Kanri*. Here, the first symbol, "Gen," means "reality" as well as symbolizes the movement of "appearing"; whereas "Ba," the second symbol, means "space." Thus, "Genba" represents the place where the reality exists or shows up—whether good or bad. Then, the following symbol, "Kan," means "to administer," and "Ri" means "natural law." Thus, "Kanri" is to administer by following the law of nature.

Recognizing that all of us will be better off if we squarely face and deal with the issues at where the action is, i.e., the shop floor, this book addresses the importance of shop floor management from a new, fresh viewpoint.

(Calligraphy by the author.)

THE NEW
SHOP FLOOR
MANAGEMENT

EMPOWERING PEOPLE FOR
CONTINUOUS IMPROVEMENT

Kiyoshi Suzaki

THE FREE PRESS
New York

The Free Press
A Division of Simon & Schuster Inc.
1230 Avenue of the Americas
New York, N.Y. 10020

Printed in the United States of America

printing number

8 9 10

Library of Congress Cataloging-in-Publication Data

Suzaki, Kiyoshi.
    The new shop floor management: empowering people for continuous
improvement/Kiyoshi Suzaki.
      p. cm.
    Includes bibliographical references and index.
    ISBN 0–02–932265–0
    1. Industrial management. 2. Production management. I. Title.
HD31.S775 1993
658.5—dc20   92–42549
                                                  CIP

*For those who light up
the corners of the world.*

CONTENTS

PREFACE

As the world's business climate changes, it is getting more difficult for us to remain competitive. Customers demand changes, technology changes, and competitive forces change. In a word, our environment has become very turbulent.

Even though the challenges we face today are enormous, we can still address issues that are within our control—from the shop floor up. Keys to meeting today's challenges for any organization include:

- Shared vision
- Customer orientation
- Ownership by people
- Problem solving at the source
- Self-management
- Quality in all business processes

This book will address these topics by:

- Sharing the importance of shop floor management
- Providing the ideas, techniques, concepts, and philosophy necessary to practice better shop floor management
- Illustrating how these are applied in different companies
- Encouraging readers to take significant steps toward continuous improvement that involve everybody
- Upgrading skills and deepening the insights for self-management to maximize everybody's potential

In other words, rather than viewing the shop floor only from the top down, this book attempts to address the organization's needs from shop floor up, presenting a new perspective of the shop floor and its linkage to the total organization. It also points out that just as doctors need to see their patients to make accurate diagnoses, today's managers need to be directly involved in shop floor activities in order to maximize their employees' self-managing abilities.

Also, expanding the "people-friendly techniques" of continuous improvement that were described in my previous book, *The New Manufacturing Challenge* (The Free Press, 1987), the focus of this book is on people and management at the shop floor level. While the traditional specialist orientation may seek intellectual and sophisticated solutions, the emphasis here is on practice and integration of people-friendly techniques by making use of the collective wisdom of the people.

Critiques, questions, or suggestions about the book should be addressed to the author c/o Suzaki & Company, 1137 El Medio Avenue, Suite 101, Pacific Palisades, California 90272.

INTRODUCTION:
RETHINKING OUR SHOP FLOOR

Early this century, Frederick Taylor published a book titled *Shop Management* in which he recommended segregating the planning of work from its execution. As experts with skills such as time-and-motion studies proliferated, a big gap was eventually created between management and workers. Taylor's intention was to find ways to give high wages to workers while maintaining low labor costs for the company, but his theories would later be challenged.

Many argue that Taylor's belief that workers should be considered simply as extensions of machinery has strongly influenced Western management practices for many decades. Taking a look at such beliefs from a fresh vantage, this book will take a much more humanistic as well as holistic viewpoint in addressing the critical elements of shop floor management.

Most of us agree that if we can upgrade people's skills, everyone is better off. As the skill level improves, there should be less fire fighting. More problems will be solved at the source, and smoother communication among people makes it possible to get things done more quickly. Only limited layers of management will be required to oversee activities on the shop floor.

In this book, we view the shop floor as the place where the most fundamental value-added activities take place, whether they are in manufacturing, services, or construction. Looking around, however, we still find many Tayloristic organizations. Even though more managers seem to believe in utilizing people to their maximum potential, the degree of their contribution is still very limited. Specific approaches for maximizing the potential of people at the shop floor have not yet been initiated.

This book will explore such potential by focusing attention on

1

the shop floor. By taking a fresh view of the shop floor and trying to figure out ways to address problems there, we can develop an organization based on actual needs, rather than on a predetermined point of view. This enables us to focus on value-added activities and to empower people, thereby upgrading the foundation of the organization. By clarifying our vision, streamlining the process, and letting people manage themselves, we can realize tremendous improvements in quality, cost, delivery, safety, morale, and the organization's competitive position.

The existing gap between top management and the shop floor can also be narrowed. The company will benefit from the tremendous power of people with this new shop floor management, but it is my hope that people on the shop floor will also find this experience rewarding and exciting, leading to their own personal growth. Accordingly, even though we find ourselves living in a very turbulent world, I feel confident that each of us will find a clear path through it.

REVISITING OUR SHOP FLOOR

One of the major focuses of this book is self-management of people on the shop floor. The shop floor is a foundation of our thinking; it provides a base for our society's growth. The Japanese call shop floor management *genba kanri*. The shop floor (genba) is revered as the place where people ultimately add value to their society and strengthen its foundation.

Whether the activities are in manufacturing (tightening nuts), construction (hammering nails), or service (processing information), each step is crucial (see Exhibit 1). Without them, our society will simply disintegrate. Furthermore, since people who are engaged in activities on the shop floor make up a very large part of our society, they represent not only the producers of value but the customers as well.

We can also see that the shop floor is where many of us start our careers by learning to get things done, to solve problems, and to work with others. Furthermore, many of us spend the majority of our working careers on the shop floor or dealing with issues relating to the shop floor.

Yet, as the world's business environment changes, people on the

Exhibit 1. Adding Value at the Shop Floor

Construction   Manufacturing   Processing Information

Delivery   Research and Development   Service

Sales   Warehouse   Information Sharing

shop floor and their families are often the most vulnerable ones in terms of the impact of change on their livelihood.

In order to address these concerns from both managers' and shop floor people's points of view and to manage the shop floor more effectively, this book attempts to share new perspectives on shop floor management, and provide pragmatic approaches for increasing people's self-managing capabilities. (Exhibit 2 summarizes the important characteristics of shop floor activities.)

By understanding that our work on the shop floor adds value to our society, and at the same time realizing that we are affected by the changes we create, we should be able to define a clear course into the future.

Exhibit 2. Rethinking the Importance of the Shop Floor

- Shop floor activities are crucial to the organization's progress.
- People engaged in shop floor activities represent a majority of working people in our society.
- People on the shop floor are not only producers of value to society but also customers.
- The shop floor provides a critical environment for people's career development.
- Many people spend the majority of their working careers on the shop floor.
- Developing self-managing capability on the shop floor will help people to chart a course in today's turbulent business environment.

BEYOND TAYLORISM

In contrast to such thinking, traditional views toward the shop floor have not been very positive (see Exhibit 3). Konosuke Matsushita, the founder of Matsushita Electric Industries, a Japanese sixty-billion-dollar consumer electronics firm, had a different view. Of the traditional shop floor view he said,

> . . . You firmly believe that good management means executives on one side, and workers on the other; on one side, men who think, and on the other side, men who can only work. For you, management is the art of smoothly transferring the executives' ideas to the workers' hands.
>
> We have passed the Taylor stage. We are aware that business has become terribly complex. Survival is very uncertain in an environment increasingly filled with risk, the unexpected, and competition. Therefore, a company must have the constant commitment of all of its employees to survive. For us, management is the entire workforce's intel-

Exhibit 3. Traditional Shop Floor Views

- Mundane work is done on the shop floor.
- Because management controls all activities, people on the shop floor are not asked their opinions.
- As long as they can do the job, there is no need to educate people on the shop floor.
- Since muscle is all that is needed on the shop floor, it is better to do the work where the labor is cheapest.
- Since people on the shop floor will change jobs for even very little pay differences, it is better not to use any resources to educate them.
- The simpler people's jobs are, the easier it is to hire and fire them.

lectual commitment to the service of the company without self-imposed functional or class barriers.

We have measured the new technological and economic challenges. We know that the intelligence of a few technocrats—even very bright ones—has become totally inadequate to face these challenges. Only the intellect of all employees can permit a company to live with the ups and downs and meet the requirements of its new environment.

—Konosuke Matsushita, from a speech
to U.S. business executives, 1988

MAKING PEOPLE BEFORE MAKING PRODUCTS

While Matsushita is now known by brand names such as Panasonic, Technics, and Quasar, it is worth noting that Konosuke Matsushita started his career at age nine as an apprentice because of his family's financial problems. Though his statement quoted above may sound harsh, his intent was not to be negative. He meant that we may find ourselves in a very undesirable situation if we do not see the flaw in treating people as extensions of machinery.

On one occasion, he asked an employee, "What does Matsushita Electric make?" Answered the employee, "We make TVs, radios, and vacuum cleaners." "No, no, no!" Konosuke Matsushita pointed out, "We make people! We make people first before making products. Matsushita Electric is the place to make people. Our company should be known as such."

As we talk about assuring quality in the product we make, we learn the principles of quality control. Yet the ultimate process control may be achieved by "making people before making products."

ADDRESSING THE INDIVIDUAL'S NEEDS

What we are addressing here is a way in which management can instill in each individual a belief that as he or she grows, the company grows as well. In other words, if each person has self-managing or autonomous capabilities while linked to the total organization, we can create a system that is more humane, addressing the minds of people as opposed to simply viewing the business only in terms of financial position.

As our society progresses and competition intensifies, addressing individuals' needs, as both internal and external customers to the company, becomes critical. Furthermore, such thinking leads to a genba (shop floor) within an organization in which attention to detail is practiced in relation to each person (man), each machine, each specific method, each material, and environment.

GENBA-ORIENTED THINKING (THREE REALS)

As we address each of these issues, we need to be reality oriented rather than concept oriented. Here, we may familiarize ourselves with three basics of shop floor management. In Japanese, they are *genba* (real scene or shop floor), *genbutsu* (real thing), and *genjitsu* (real fact). Here we will call them the "Three Reals." (See Exhibit 4 for illustration.)

To practice the Three Reals, we need to go to the "real scene or shop floor," to see the "real thing" in front of our eyes and understand the "real fact" to address the real problems for improvement. (Please note that in service-related businesses their products are in fact services.) Here, each of the three reals is described in detail:

Exhibit 4. Genba, Genbutsu, Genjitsu (Three Reals)

Genba (Real Place or Shop Floor)

Genbutsu (Real Thing)

Genjitsu (Real Fact)

Genba (real place or shop floor). Whenever we deal with shop floor problems, we typically find many interrelated factors, such as the changes in products or processes. Especially when human factors are involved, the assessment of problems becomes very complex. It almost requires a detective's skill.

In such an environment, pure theory cannot function by itself. And no matter how great our intellect and how extensive our knowledge, if that knowledge is not tied with reality, we simply get more confused, perhaps even resulting in totally different hypotheses to address the same problem.

An important exercise, then, is for us to emphasize substance rather than form. The shop floor is a place to practice pragmatic problem-solving. It may be even viewed as an experimental laboratory. Books, lectures, and intellectual exercises in the office, away from the action, can never bring such experiences by themselves.

Genbutsu (real thing). Here, "thing" may mean products, parts, machinery, or material. If there is a problem with our product, we need to see the "real thing" for ourselves to understand the nature of the problem rather than someone else's interpretation of the problems. If we are sensitive to customer satisfaction and the elimination of waste in our shop, we should not debate the problem away from the shop floor. Rather, we should see for ourselves the nature of the problem, so that we can take action.

If we go into this point a bit deeper, when we provide products for customers, whether they are the persons working in the next processes or they are external to the company, those products represent the producer in the customers' eyes. They may even embody in themselves the philosophy of the company.

In the customers' hands, products do not make any excuses nor do they lie, unlike words and concepts which may contain biases, errors, or even outright lies, as in the case of overrated advertising. Making excuses about a product does not change its value for the customer. Our products are everything. Similarly, when we think of problems, we always need to be objective, see genbutsu in our hands, and identify ourselves with the problem.

Genjitsu (real fact). Visiting the "real scene," and looking at the "real thing," we need to check each potential cause with "real facts" in addressing the problem. We need to constantly ask ourselves "Why?" and behave like detectives who question even measuring instruments to make certain that data has been accurately derived.

As we discover a problem, we need to put the convict (problem) into prison (standardized countermeasures) and make sure that the convict does not escape (process control). To be effective, however, these measures should be applied by everybody.

DEVELOPING A GENBA-ORIENTED MIND

In many ways, therefore, our challenge is to move away from a biased and conceptually oriented mindset and to discipline ourselves to practice reality-based thinking. The following examples may illustrate this shift in thinking.

When we look at a mountain, we think there is a "mountain." But we may not think of it as a "MOUNTAIN." Here, "mountain" represents the thought or concept that our brain has developed over the years through pattern recognition. In contrast, "MOUNTAIN" represents the real object, with different shades of rocks and the smell of trees—this is not the conceptual mountain.

As another example, we may imagine "flower" as something like a red tulip. And we may associate this image with the pictures children draw. This is, however, not the "FLOWER" that actually grows in our garden. When our mind is occupied with something, therefore, we see only the "tulip" but not the "TULIP."

The impressionist painter Monet is known to have explained to his disciples that when we see trees and houses, we should not see them by their names, but by dots or triangles or squares of colors. The point is that if we can identify ourselves with an object, then

Exhibit 5. A Mountain is a "MOUNTAIN," but it is not a "mountain"

with concentration and persistence we can come to understand the real nature of the object. In other words, we may learn to "SEE" instead of "see," and even possibly "LIVE" and "WORK," instead of "live" and "work."

In the context of shop floor management (SFM) we may work on a "problem" but not the "PROBLEM." In the worst case, we may be studying the "problem" in the office instead of attacking the "PROBLEM" with the real product and real facts at the real scene.

The late Taiichi Ohno, who is known as the father of the Toyota Production System, often stated that if we do not understand a problem, we should spend time—a full day if need be—on the shop floor (genba), observing the problem so as to figure out what is wrong. Such an exercise teaches us to reach the core of a problem rather than looking at it conceptually. Ohno even drew a circle on the floor for his subordinate to stand on until he could figure out a certain operation's problem. If today's managers were to visit him, however, I wonder how many of them would understand his point.

When we study management, for example, we try to understand it with words, models, concepts, and the like. However, what we are looking for is the truth, a pragmatic solution instead of an intellectual abstraction. If we are not careful, we may start to think that the model or concept is the reality and not a representation of reality. Thus, even though we need to understand principles and theories from schools and textbooks, we also need to develop reality-oriented minds. Especially in our increasingly complex society, it may be necessary to go back to the basics and practice even housekeeping and workplace organization before we grapple with sophisticated management concepts.

LEARNING FROM THE GENBA EXPERIENCE

To gain an immediate sense of shop floor activities and reality-oriented thinking, it is a Japanese custom for everyone, including those from accounting and marketing, or those with engineering backgrounds, to receive training at the front line of the company before they are assigned to their regular jobs. When I started at Toshiba, fresh from the university, I spent the first few months on the assembly line next to veteran operators, being amazed at their skills. I also spent time selling TVs at the department store, competing against Matsushita's salesman who had an amazing knowledge of products and excellent interpersonal skills. For Westerners, such experiences are rare. Yet Bob Miner, a manager at NUMMI (New United Motor Manufacturing, Inc.), a joint venture between General Motors and Toyota, shared with me his experience on the assembly line at Toyota before starting his assignment as a manager.

> The first day, my trainer, Mr. Sata, gave me my assignment. I said, "No problem," since the work did not seem difficult to me. Mr. Sata simply smiled at the time. The next day, as I was working, he approached me and asked, "No problem?" and smiled. Can you imagine me working up a hard sweat, hitting my head six times over a six-minute period, and feeling as though my hands had five thumbs? I promised myself that I would no longer say, "No problem." . . .
>   Even though the work was difficult for me, this training was the best training I have had in my life. Anyone engaged in the automobile industry should go through such an experience.
>   —K. Suzaki, *JIT Kakumei No Shogeki*, pp. 8–9.

I have also heard that even the legal staff at McDonald's learn how to sell hamburgers and fix milkshake machines at McDonald's University. At Honda's Ohio factory, I saw a human resource representative being trained on the assembly line so as to understand how people experience their work. At Robert Bosch in Germany, I noticed engineers spending time on the production floor a few days a month to improve communication between design and manufacturing.

When we go through these experiences, they tend to have a lasting influence on us. The typical feedback is: (1) these experiences make us feel humble, (2) they make us appreciate the work done by the people on the shop floor, (3) they remind us to look at things from other people's viewpoints, (4) they broaden our knowledge base, and (5) they teach us that concepts do not work by themselves, people have to make them work.

TRANSFORMING AN ORGANIZATION

In today's business, competitive challenge is everywhere. Thanks to the free market system and the principle of survival of the fittest, businesses that offer obsolete or uncompetitive products, services, concepts, or systems will become extinct. The same is true for management concepts. There are many fashionable concepts, but competition will weed out the ones without much substance.

Just looking around, we see that more seminars, books, and video courses become available every day, each promoting new concepts and techniques. Yet we should realize that it is ultimately our responsibility to digest these ideas. If we are not producing results, then, whether we can detect the problem or not will make a difference, as opposed to changing concepts or techniques every now and then, in the hope that things will work someday.

Some of the symptoms of lack of coordination or poor management concepts in traditionally run companies may be easily detected at the shop floor as listed in Exhibit 6. Here, if we can practice the three reals, we should be able to see with our own eyes that things are not functioning well and find the reasons why. In one company in the Midwest, for example, I found soft drink cans scattered underneath the machines. Also, I noticed an operator collecting information regarding defects and feeding this quality information into the computer. But though there was a tremendous amount of information on the computer, no feedback was given to operators. The quality staff was busy, yet not much of the operators' potential was utilized. An operator commented to me, "It worked much better when I was charting the data manually."

In another part of the factory, it had taken many years before one operator's suggestion was listened to about changing the structure of a machine so that comfortable toe-room space was created (see Exhibit 7). And in yet another corner of the factory, people were straining their backs with tremendous effort while handling parts.

Exhibit 6. Symptoms of Traditionally Run Companies Found on the Shop Floor

- Trash on the floor
- People doing troublesome work
- People doing very monotonous work
- Too much inventory
- Parts stored directly on the floor
- Dirty bathrooms
- Management information not shared
- People's desire to improve is neglected

Exhibit 7. Small Improvement for One Person may be Quite Big for Someone Else

Before Improvement

After Improvement

No space to put toes

Space is created

One operator was putting parts through a "go-no go" gauge all day long, a very monotonous job.

It may help us to imagine a conversation at the dinner table between this operator and his son, who asks, "Hey, Dad, what did you do today at work?" If we were this operator, how would we respond to that question?

When I mentioned these points to the newly assigned vice president of manufacturing, a good friend of mine, he told me that he felt embarrassed to take anyone, including his friends, family members, and customers, onto the shop floor. As in this case, we do not need any sophisticated concepts to figure out whether we have problems. We simply need to open our eyes to see if we have these symptoms in our workplace. These symptoms are the result of everybody's behavior, nothing but a reflection of our thinking.

Just as we hear or see disorder, crime, or drugs in our cities, we can see similar symptoms in our workplace. Issues such as safety, ease of work, and creation of a self-managing environment are often neglected. Also, people's desire to control their destinies, to use their creativity, and their desire for self-expression are constrained.

To begin to deal with these issues, I propose we get down to genba (the shop floor) where the action is. Instead of scientifically disecting problems into pieces, analyzing them, and obtaining the solution from experts, we need another approach. As long as we keep following Tayloristic thinking, we will never comprehend the approaches we are talking about. It is almost like looking for lost objects only in the lighted areas, i.e., away from the shop floor. A common Zen expression here is, "Not knowing how near the truth is, we seek it far away" (*Nine Hundred Dragon River* by Hakuin, p. 42).

USING EVERYBODY'S CREATIVE POWER

In my previous book, *The New Manufacturing Challenge,* I said that the worst kind of waste is the waste of not utilizing people's talent. In this sense, even the people at the top of the organization should be considered useless if they do not contribute ideas to move the organization forward. And it is even worse if they do not support and/or provide opportunities for others to utilize their creativity.

In order to address these problems and reach our vision of excellence, we need to be creative. The persons at the top need to be even more creative so that others can utilize their creativity, too. We should also understand that superficial vision leads to superficial results. The use of computers or new management techniques is not an end by itself; we do not need to have experts tell us how bad the situation is; we do not need to think about the problems in the office when there are untapped resources out there on the shop floor.

Again, a critical element of shop floor management is an idea of self-management—each individual contributing to the whole, yet each being self-sufficient. Even though the problems on the shop floor seem big, especially when managers try to solve them by themselves, by using everybody's creativity, we can do it. We can make it happen. After all, since these problems were created by ourselves, we should be able to address them if we put our minds to it.

Of course, people on the shop floor need to play a much bigger role. Even though each situation may be different and people's minds may not change overnight, we need a vision that everyone can digest and buy into at any time. If we can develop such a universal vision, we should be able to find our way to our future.

> If you want to build a ship, don't gather your people and ask them to provide wood, prepare tools, assign tasks, . . . Just call them together and raise in their minds the longing for the endless sea.
> —Antoine de Saint-Exupery

In preparing for the journey through this book, an overview of shop floor management is presented in Exhibit 8.

Exhibit 8. An Overview of Shop Floor Management

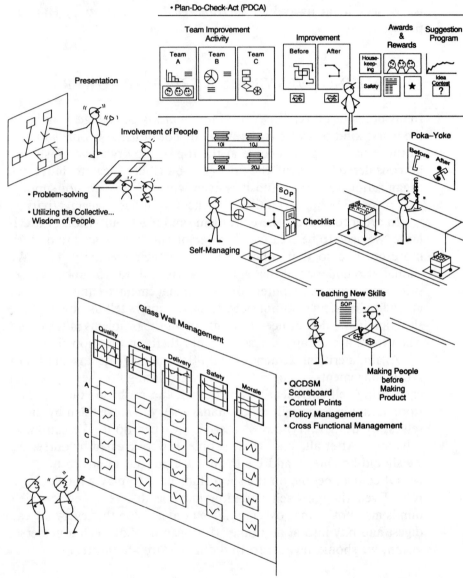

Exhibit 8. Continued

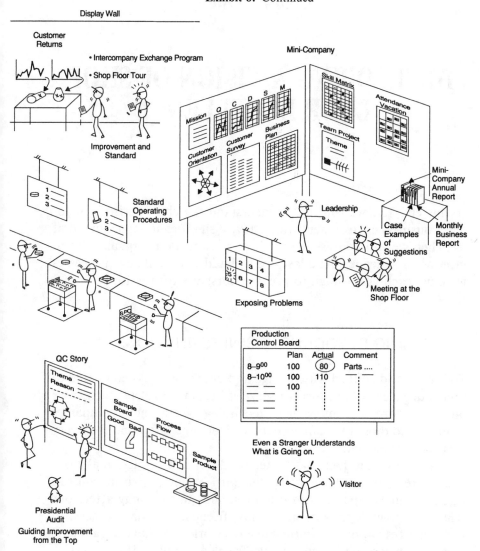

Display Wall

Customer Returns

• Intercompany Exchange Program

• Shop Floor Tour

Improvement and Standard

Mini-Company

Skill Matrix

Mission Q C D S M

Customer Orientation

Customer Survey

Business Plan

Attendance Vacation

Team Project Theme

Standard Operating Procedures

Leadership

Mini-Company Annual Report

Case Examples of Suggestions

Monthly Business Report

Meeting at the Shop Floor

Exposing Problems

QC Story

Theme Reason

Sample Board

Good Bad

Process Flow

Sample Product

Production Control Board

	Plan	Actual	Comment
8–9⁰⁰	100	(80)	Parts ....
8–10⁰⁰	100	110	
— —	100		

Even a Stranger Understands What is Going on.

Visitor

Presidential Audit

Guiding Improvement from the Top

Chapter One

DEVELOPING A VISION OF SHOP FLOOR EXCELLENCE

In this chapter, we will try to understand the characteristics of today's business environment which have a significant impact on all of us. Then we will address the need to transform our organization to meet new challenges. And last, we will address the change processes we must each go through to prepare ourselves for the future.

SAILING IN TODAY'S BUSINESS ENVIRONMENT

Today's world is filled with change and uncertainty. As compared to even a decade ago, products or services become obsolete much more quickly. More and more new technologies and new companies emerge, and those that cannot cope with change often find their very existence threatened.

In spite of the fact that better products and services make our lives more convenient, a quickly changing business environment can threaten our companies and our jobs. This in turn may affect our relationships with co-workers, family, friends, and many others. In fact, changes happening in the business world may have a traumatic impact if they result in sudden layoffs or bankruptcy. If we are foresighted and prepared, however, these changes can provide increased opportunities for utilizing our potential. Instead of riding in stormy seas, we can alter our course and find a clear path through them.

To this point, someone once said, "Even if we cannot change the direction of wind, we can trim our sails to get where we want to go." In keeping with this idea, the purpose of this book is to prepare ourselves for such turbulent times by developing skills to manage the situation better and explore a better work life.

Exhibit 1.1. "We cannot direct the wind . . . but we can adjust the sails"

CHANGING ENVIRONMENT—PAST VS. FUTURE

To begin with, let us study the environment in which we live. Exhibit 1.2 summarizes our changing environment, comparing the past to the future and listing major reasons for such changes. Of course, specific situations may differ from this table. Yet, if we look around us, we may find some interesting trends. Turning our eyes to the international scene, for example, as more countries join the Western world from the old Eastern bloc and developing nations, more and more people will participate in the free market, free trade, and free information exchange of our society. These people then become new members of our global society as suppliers of labor and brainpower as well as beneficiaries of goods, services, and knowledge.

Opening this gate is similar to conducting a brainstorming exercise on a global scale, with more people exchanging their ideas and values, and utilizing their collective wisdom. We may at times find this situation chaotic because of its massive impact on our political, social, and economic systems. As more people travel, watch TV, read, and exchange ideas, the process of change seems to take its own course.

So, even if the environment we live in seems chaotic, if we find more people contributing their talent as well as gaining benefits, such

Exhibit 1.2. Changes in Our Environment

	Past	Future	Reason for Change
Predictability in business	Predictable	Unpredictable	Fast rate of innovation
Stability in people's values	Stable	Changing	Fast pace of modern lives
Profile of customers	Mass	Diversified	Diversified individual tastes
Importance of employee skills	Low	High	More complex jobs
Pace of progress	Periodic	Continuous	Contributions from more people
Profile of managers	Directive	Leading	Higher dependence on people
Management system	Results-oriented	Process- and results-oriented	Assurance is gained from managing the process well

an environment is in fact, desirable. We should also note that this globalization of business activities follows the free market system of using everybody's ideas and values.

If we understand this point, the strains caused by these changes may be better understood. Yet, as democracy requires everyone to contribute ideas and values to the whole, as opposed to blindly following someone who happens to be in a position of leadership, each of us should seek the answer for ourselves. In other words, collectively, we are the reason for the change. And at the same time, therefore, it is up to us to become either a beneficiary or a victim of such changes.

OUR VISION

History has shown us that many factors influence progress. Clearly, creativity in overcoming hurdles seems to be one major factor. Further, when creativity is tied with survival or prosperity, we find ourselves even more driven.

Now, if we look back on our personal experiences, we may find that our vision and actions have changed over time as well. By assessing these changes further, we may see if we are deepening our understanding as to what is important in our (work)life and how creative we have been to grow continuously. The organization as a whole may also go through a similar process. So, we might ask: (1) Is our organization growing to meet new challenges? and (2) Are we moving forward to create our own future?

In order to respond to these questions, we need to consider many factors, such as intensified competition, changes in management or unions, shifts in customers' taste, changes in working relationships with peers, guidance from leaders, level of accomplishments, or new insights gained from newspapers, TV, and the like. Since vision is something individuals or groups of people within the organization create, each of us should examine how these factors might impact our collective vision.

Then we may further ask ourselves: (1) Is our vision changing in a positive direction or negative direction?, and (2) What can we do about it?

CREATING AN ORGANIZATION
WITH SELF-MANAGED PEOPLE

Of course, if we move to a remote mountaintop and live as hermits, we might find a different solution to our question. Yet, most of us find ourselves in an environment where change is the norm. Therefore, we need to develop self-management skills so that we can sit in the driver's seat and chart our own course into the future.

To do this, however, each of us needs to:

• Understand our business environment better
• Be more alert to forthcoming changes
• Share and utilize information effectively
• Take initiative to continuously improve our skills and position

If we use sailing as an analogy again, this situation is similar to sailing in a stormy sea (Exhibit 1.3). Unpredictable waves, wind, and rain may make it most difficult to steer the boat and get to where we want to go. We must have good knowledge of our environment, read the forthcoming changes, share information well among our

Exhibit 1.3. Sailing in a Stormy Sea

To avoid hazards, we need a clearly established position, a competent crew, a shared vision, teamwork, and sound strategy.

crew members, and continuously upgrade the skills of the crew. Like today's business environment, there is not much room for misjudgment.

If we consider that this sea of change in our society is the result of good intentions, such as a free exchange of information, a free market economy, better utilization of people's talent, and so on, and we see that we ourselves are the cause of the changes as well as the ones impacted, then we should be able to find ways to steer the boat to get where we want to go, by practicing the same principles.

To do this well, however, we need to be self-motivated, self-thinking, and self-controlled. In other words, we need to be self-managed. Whether we work in an organization or not, and regardless of our title or rank, each of us should accomplish a certain mission as a part of our job.

OWNERSHIP AT THE SOURCE

In contrast to a military- or power-based society, what we see now when we look around is that people's individual abilities are becoming the major driving force of these mass changes in society. As more information is made available, more people's talents are utilized, and the free market economy provides greater opportunity for more people. This allows more people to excel than before. Within this self-induced chaos, we find an opportunity-filled world for those willing to test their potential.

While increased self-management skills will give individuals closer control over their destiny, they also provide major benefits for the company and the society, as summarized below:

Addressing problems at the source. Even if there are capable people who can solve our problems at the top of the organization, there would certainly be limits as to how much information could be absorbed by them as well as how fast it could be converted to action. If instead people can solve problems at the source, additional resources, such as support staff or extra layers of management will be unnecessary. Also, addressing problems at the source saves a precious resource—time.

Serving the customer better. As we solve problems, we can better control the process so that we can continuously serve our customers better. Here, the customer is the person in the next process, not only the end user of the product or service. Since each person on the shop floor is adding value to the process, total customer satisfaction, or total quality control of all company processes is only achieved when everyone in the organization is involved in addressing the problems at the source and maintaining good standards.

Developing highly motivated people. Self-management puts people's destiny more in their own hands. It will give them increased responsibility and allow them to utilize higher-level skills. By applying creativity to solving problems, people will develop greater pride and confidence in their abilities. In other words, companies can prosper by unleashing the potential of highly motivated people as they grow with the company.

LOOKING OURSELVES STRAIGHT IN THE MIRROR

We know that without ownership of what we do, it is hard to accomplish things and have pride in ourselves. Also, without ownership, we may simply find ourselves drifting as the business situation changes. However, as we also know, looking at ourselves in the mirror and reviewing our progress is not easy when we are too busy with day-to-day activities, or even consciously trying to avoid facing the issues. We may be living in the past and trying to ignore new competitive threats.

Similarly, because of the way things have been done, it may be difficult for people at the shop floor to speak up with a new improvement idea to the boss. Also, cleaning up our own area may not seem worthwhile if nobody else practices it. Yet if we are to be honest with ourselves, we may have to act upon our belief. An organization without people's ownership is similar to a nation without true democracy. We must be convinced that by practicing what we believe in, we can accomplish our vision.

As we look at ourselves in the mirror periodically, we should review our organization's progress or lack of progress objectively. For example, we may ask if the people on the shop floor are gaining more ownership in running the business, or if the gap between management and workers is narrowing.

ACHIEVING EXCELLENCE IN SHOP FLOOR MANAGEMENT (SFM)

To answer these questions, we need to look at a business with the idea that the shop floor is the most crucial point of conducting business, where the tire hits the road. It is where values are added, goods are produced, and services are provided to satisfy our customers. We need to address problems and explore opportunities at the source, rather than looking at the company, say, strictly from a financial point of view. Even though numbers are important in developing a perspective of the total situation, the company cannot function without addressing reality on the shop floor. From this perspective, each customer and each employee are respected for their values.

Instead of finding better ways to do things right and control the process at the point where value is added, we see that the traditional way of conducting business has created an environment which encourages just the opposite. Exhibit 1.4 lists some of the problems that we find at the shop floor, and shows that we need to look at our work in more detail.

Exhibit 1.4. Problems Generated from Lack of Proper Shop Floor Management

Key Concerns	Problems
Basic skills are missing, e.g., reading, math	Someone else has to do the work and rectify the problems. (This may happen if management does not pay any attention to the growth of people and treats people simply as extensions of machines.)
No clear definition of requirements, e.g., inspection standards	Supervisor must be called every time something comes up that is unclear. Time is wasted, and often poor decisions may be made, creating even more problems.
Lack of discipline to follow standards, e.g., housekeeping, workplace organization, work standards	Extra work is created—e.g., rework, janitorial work, unnecessary fire fighting, problem-solving work to identify and correct the situation. Also, the same or similar problems may be repeated over and over again.
Lack of problem-solving skills	Staff, engineers, or managers need to be involved to solve the problem. People's creative talent is not utilized, overhead cost will be increased, and support staff's time will be taken away from more important jobs.
Inflexibility in meeting customers' demands	People cannot cope with changing demands. Self-control ability is missing. This may generate waste in more fire fighting, additional people, machines, computers, etc.
Inability to cope with frequent introduction of new models	As model change occurs frequently, most of the work has to be done by engineers rather than having detailed work done by people on the shop floor.

Whatever we do, any company's operations may be broken down to a chain of processes as shown in Exhibit 1.5. Here, the higher the effectiveness we can achieve at each process, the better the end result as measured by defect rate, performance against a standard, or on-time delivery.

If we measure defect rates, Company A's rate is 23%, while Company B's is 5%. So, if Company A is competing with Company B, it requires more than four times the resources of B to fix the problems. If we also consider all the fire fighting Company A needs to do as well as the impact of these on customer relationships, we can easily see the advantage Company B enjoys over Company A.

Exhibit 1.5. Impact of SFM on Effectiveness of Company's Operation

Company A

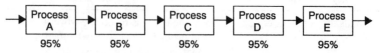

Total Effectiveness = (95%) x (95%) x (95%) x (95%) x (95%) = 77%

Company B

Total Effectiveness = (99%) x (99%) x (99%) x (99%) x (99%) = 95%

Here, we should note that the process may represent (1) a manufacturing process to make goods, (2) a service process dealing with people, (3) an information process dealing with paper or computers, or (4) a management process to share information, get things done, and lead people effectively.

The point is, if we cannot control the process or ignore the basics of SFM, chaos will be created. Exhibit 1.6 describes the typical impact of lack of SFM on a company's key performance. As shown in Exhibit 1.5, even though the impact of each process across the system seems small, when compounded, the total impact can be enormous. Furthermore, increased product diversity and introduction of more new products will magnify the situation. In order to improve customer satisfaction while minimizing waste, therefore, we should find ways to control each of these individual processes better.

Exhibit 1.6. Impact of Lack of Shop Floor Management on Company's Business

Quality:	We need to add additional resources for inspection so that defects are not handed on to customers.
Cost:	Additional resources include not only inspectors, but also expediters, managers to put out fires, etc.
Delivery:	It takes a longer time to get things done. Also, scheduled ship dates may be missed, with the risk of adding more inventory.
Safety:	People's safety and environmental concerns may not be addressed adequately because of the fire-fighting nature of the operation.
Morale:	Morale goes down as more fire fighting is necessary.

CONTROLLING THE PROCESS

As we try to control a process, then, we need to develop some kind of feedback system, as shown in Exhibit 1.7. The premise here is that proper feedback of information allows us to take corrective action and thus control the input or process itself better.

If we measure productivity as representing performance of the process, it may look like this:

$$\text{Productivity} = \frac{\text{Output}}{\text{Input}} = \frac{\text{Output}}{\text{Minimum Input + Waste}}$$

or

$$\text{Productivity} = \frac{\text{Value Created}}{\text{Values Invested}} = \frac{\text{Performance in QCDSM (Quality, Cost, Delivery, Safety, Morale)}}{\text{Man + Machine + Material + Method + Measurement}}$$

In other words, we need to control these 5Ms to eliminate waste and provide high-quality products on time to our customers at low cost while providing a safe environment and high morale for people in the organization. An important question that we will address throughout this book, therefore, is how to provide adequate feedback and control the process most effectively and efficiently.

Exhibit 1.7. Feedback System to Control the Process

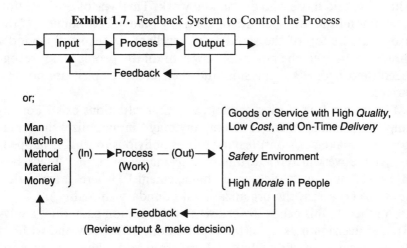

(Review output & make decision)

Reflecting on Exhibit 1.5, we should recognize that even 99 percent effectiveness is still unsatisfactory. If we put ourselves in the shoes of the customer who receives that remaining 1 percent, this should be quite obvious. We need to remember that one defect represents a total failure on the part of the organization that provided the good or service to the recipient.

TRADITIONAL AND PROGRESSIVE ORGANIZATIONS

If we are to control the process at the source and have the whole organization prosper, we cannot depend solely on certain people who are "responsible" for doing this. Rather, we should seek to involve everybody in the organization, utilizing their talent so that the whole organization and everybody in it performs better and benefits.

Of course, many hurdles must be overcome if everyone is to be involved in this process. Oddly, however, a very common hurdle is the idea that improving their own work is still foreign to many people. This is especially true when it comes to solving problems as a group. Without encouragement from their managers or peers to make improvements, this hurdle may seem higher than it really is.

To better understand the benefits of a progressive organization, two models of organizations are compared in Exhibit 1.8. The spindle-shaped model on the left represents the traditional organization where skill and knowledge are concentrated in a small number of management or staff people. There is division of labor between those who think and those who do manual work. This type of organization is common in feudal societies or centrally planned economies. If the people at the top of the spindle are excellent, in theory this model should work. Yet, the potential power of all the people is not recognized, and people's ownership and their creative spirit are not apparent.

Even in a free market economy, similar situations exist. For example, top management of a company may "monopolize" information, and make decisions, leaving others oblivious to what is happening. (Here we will refer to this type of management as "black box management" or "brick wall management," where information does not go across the organizational boundary smoothly.)

In theory, this can still work when information gathering, analysis, and decision making at the top are done effectively and without delay. But in today's turbulent business world where the pace of

Exhibit 1.8. Traditional and Progressive Organizations

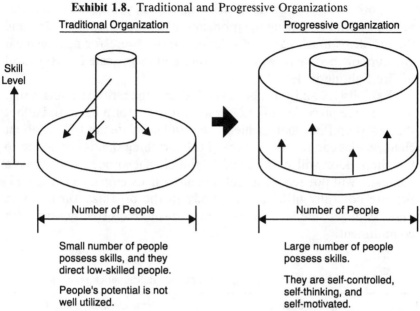

Traditional Organization   Progressive Organization

Skill
Level

Number of People   Number of People

Small number of people
possess skills, and they
direct low-skilled people.

People's potential is not
well utilized.

Large number of people
possess skills.

They are self-controlled,
self-thinking, and
self-motivated.

change is rapid and new technologies and products pop up frequently, the chance of black box management being effective becomes slim.

Information overload or a traffic jam of miscellaneous information at the top is symptomatic of black box management. Since the contribution of people on the shop floor is limited to manual skills, more and more fire fighting has to be done at the higher levels of management, robbing managers of precious time needed to steer the organization in the right direction. As the late Konosuke Matsushita pointed out, we should realize that "only the intellects of all employees can permit a company to live with the ups and downs of and requirements of its new environment."

Reflecting such a notion, the thicker cylinder on the right in Exhibit 1.8 represents a more progressive organization where a much larger pool of organizational talent is utilized. Here, people may contribute suggestions for improvements, participate in problem-solving activities, and work as a team rather than merely focusing on individual concerns. Also, as their skill base broadens, they may clean up and organize their own work areas, conduct basic maintenance jobs, and become so flexible in doing multiple jobs that the group may become self-sufficient, functioning as a mini-company, or an autonomous organizational unit.

In other words, instead of being managed, people manage themselves. Instead of solving the problems at the top, they are addressing the problems much earlier on, leaving more room for management and support people to work on future and large-scale issues instead of fire fighting issues.

Exhibits 1.9 and 1.10, however, indicate the attitude changes that need to take place for an organization to transform itself and adopt the new shop floor management. Naturally, we are not talking about changes that can be made overnight. Everything that is connected to the shop floor will be affected in the change process. Yet since a company will not realize its full potential if its employees' capabilities are not fully utilized, everybody in the organization needs to make changes one at a time—continuously, consistently, and with commitment.

Exhibit 1.9. Typical Thinking of People in Traditional Organizations

Exhibit 1.10. Attitudinal Differences of People in Traditional vs. Progressive Organizations

Level	Traditional Organization	Progressive Organization
Top Management	Lack of knowledge on shop floor activities: "Let me focus on my stuff."	Can feel the pulse of the shop floor. "How can people on the shop floor be more involved?"
Manager	Simply gives orders: "Do as I say."	Guides people to develop ownership: "How can I help you?"
Support Group	Focus on their own jobs: "I can solve that problem."	Shift to focus on Improvement. "How can I delegate my job?"
Operators	Leave brains at the time clock: "I gave up speaking to my boss."	Respect boss as teacher, coach, or facilitator. "Here are suggestions."

The change process will require many people's involvement. Every attempt to hit singles and bunts counts, as opposed to everybody waiting to see a few star players hit home runs. To accomplish this change in attitude we need a good leader—a catalyst—and individuals with self-improving initiative; not a dictator and a passive audience.

DEVELOPING A PROGRESSIVE ORGANIZATION

Of course, some may still prefer the traditional type of organization, especially because of the efficiencies created by the division of labor. Certainly someone who is used to doing something over and over may be better equipped than others to do that job. Yet, if we push such an idea to the point of dividing those who use their brains from those who use their hands, we may not only be underutilizing the talents of people but we are lacking respect for the individual.

To understand this point better, let us look at a specific example. I find it very strange, but in many traditional organizations the supervisor on the shop floor does not conduct even a five- to ten-minute daily meeting with his or her people at the beginning or end of the shift. Yet, this type of meeting should be compared to a quarterback's huddle in football. By analyzing the situation, the team can confirm a strategy to perform better. Without this huddle, how can the team deploy strategies to perform well?

Still, some may think it is more efficient for a supervisor to communicate one to one with each employee rather than stop the line to meet with everyone. While this argument may sound reasonable, there is a potential of not utilizing people's talents. For example, not everyone will understand the concerns of the organization about meeting the targets on key items. Or people may not be informed about new products, new processes, or engineering changes, so that they can be better prepared or contribute their ideas (see Exhibit 1.11).

From the people's viewpoint, if communication with supervisors is limited, then when a machine starts to make noise, vibrate, or consume more oil than normal, if defects start to show up, or if an interesting idea comes to mind, there may be no opportunity for discussion or brainstorming.

Another common characteristic of traditional organizations is that people on the shop floor are called "direct or hourly labor." Again, this is a notion that people on the shop floor should be involved only in *doing* jobs, as opposed to *managing* their jobs. In the worst case, problems may be characterized as a dichotomy between brain and muscle, creating a gap wide enough to cut off crucial communication, coordination, and cooperation. Because of this, people on the shop floor may even develop hostile attitudes, or become withdrawn or indifferent.

Exhibit 1.11. Developing Better Communication (Floor Meeting)

Supervisor

Team Members

"Can we rotate our jobs?"

"What about this idea?"

"Yesterday's production was... We will have new products coming... Anyone have any questions? Let's be careful on safety... Have a good day."

"So, we did better..."

Just as in the case of the economic failure of communism in the Eastern bloc, if we alienate people by concentrating power, skills, or information at the top, such a rigid hierarchy will not allow people's creativity to flourish. Instead of constraining them within rigid boundaries, we need to find ways to address people's concerns and unleash their creative power.

In contrast, if we can come up with approaches where everybody participates in improvement activities, they may encourage people to upgrade their skills, utilize their creativity, and develop pride and higher self-esteem in their jobs—and most likely in their personal lives as well. For this very reason, we should try to transform our organization at all possible levels, creating a harmonious blend of guidance from management and self-management on the part of shop floor people.

In summary, the transformation of a traditional type of organization to a progressive one will generate huge benefits:

- More people's creativity will be utilized. Since creativity is one of the fundamental characteristics of human beings, it is more humanistic to involve everyone.
- We can tap into the unknown potential of people. If we provide opportunities for people in the organization to contribute their talents, the growth potential will be unlimited, as history has proven.
- Since skills will not be monopolized by a few individuals, the higher overall skill level of people will make it easier to coordinate activities and get the necessary work done smoothly.
- As the capabilities of people are realized and better utilized, the organization as a whole will become more competitive. The difference in mass between the two organizations in Exhibit 1.8 reflects the difference in their competitiveness.

A note of caution here is that letting people utilize the potential of their creativity does not necessarily mean a "free hands" situation where they can do anything to explore their potential at their whim. Business is an ongoing concern, and resources such as time or money are always limited. Thus, we need to figure out ways to allocate resources intelligently and have people prove their contribution to the company's progress.

WHAT WE SHOULD WORK ON

In order for us to develop a progressive organization, however, we need to work on several areas:

- *Develop clarity in vision.* As shop floor activities and individuals' roles and responsibilities change, people may become uncomfortable. We need to confirm our vision and core values if we are to establish excellence in our work.
- *Develop customer orientation.* By viewing the next process as a customer, every person in the organization needs to grasp the importance of customer orientation and find ways to ensure customer satisfaction.
- *Promote involvement of everybody.* In order to address customer orientation, we need to tap into people's creativity and emphasize customer satisfaction, which may require the roles and responsibilities of people to change.
- *Increase problem-solving capability.* As more responsibility is borne by each individual, in order for the organization to be more responsive to customer demand, each individual's problem-solving skill base needs to be upgraded.
- *Provide adequate leadership.* Instead of "managing" the situation, more leadership qualities will be required of managers. More and more of the traditional managing functions will be taken care of by people's increased self-managing capabilities.
- *Clarify the management support system.* The management process needs to be redefined and clarified to accommodate the new thinking and values as well as individuals' new roles and responsibilities.

The subjects listed here are broad in scope, but they must be addressed if we are to accomplish our vision. A critical point here is that it is the people at the shop floor who need to understand these subjects and execute them. In other words, this is the ultimate competitive edge of the organization which is based on the total value-added work of everybody in the organization.

As we address each of these subjects more fully in the following chapters it is important to remember that they are also closely linked to each other. As the shop floor is the place where all of the different disciplines meet, instead of narrowly focusing on one subject at a time, we need to find an integrated approach.

In order to do this, instead of treating each of these subjects individually, we will study each subject's linkage with other subjects as much as possible. This approach will seem repetitious in some cases, but I believe it is necessary in order to deepen our holistic understanding of shop floor management.

This subject of SFM requires a different kind of learning. Simply accumulating knowledge does not add value by itself when it comes to the practice of SFM. Just like talking about swimming in the classroom can do little to build up muscles or improve skills, our orientation should be effective execution rather than intellectualization. Learning the essence of shop floor management, therefore, requires returning to the material over and over as we move on; it takes years of actual practice.

The numerous appendices and exhibits in this book are included for the purpose of providing tools, reference points, and checklists to aid readers in retaining the key points and to make it easier to reflect upon them later.

WHERE DO WE STAND NOW?

As we develop an understanding of SFM, we need to assess where we stand in relation to some of its key elements. To do this, we might rate the organization, either the company or department, in each category discussed above. (Use Exhibit 1.12 for a self-assessment.):

After we assess where we stand now, we need to ask ourselves if we are committed to transforming the organization from a tradi-

Exhibit 1.12. Assessing the Level of Shop Floor Management

Category	Rating (0 = poor; 10 = excellent) and Comments
Clarity of vision (Core Value)	
Customer orientation	
Involvement of everybody	
Problem-solving capability	
Leadership	
Management support system	

Note: While the assessment may be quick and brief now, we will study these elements in detail in subsequent chapters. (As a part of the assessment, we may refer to a sample of people's perceptions regarding their work at the shop floor, as shown in Appendix 1.1.)

tional one to a more progressive one—whether the organization itself is a unit, a department, or a whole company.

As illustrated in Exhibit 1.8, gaining ownership at each individual's level and being able to involve everyone in the practice of shop floor management takes a tremendous effort. There will be changes in the roles and responsibilities of people, people's problem-solving capabilities, leadership skills, and the management system. In other words, as problems are addressed at the source, more managers and staff people will spend their time on future-oriented issues while assuring the coordination, cooperation, and communication among people. Top management also will assure that all of these happen and will think about future business directions.

Whether we are at the front line, top management, middle management, or support staff, everybody will be affected by such changes, and everyone will need to find meaning in what he or she does differently. Thus, we also need to ask: Is there a shared understanding, and commitment? Are people willing to try?

THE CHANGE PROCESS

As we can imagine, changes of this magnitude do not happen automatically or overnight. In a sense, this is a cultural change process for the whole organization. It may even be compared to the development of children into adults. In order to understand the organization's change process and prepare ourselves better, let us think back on our own experiences.

Since our behavior results from our way of thinking, unless our thoughts are on point, we will not have the right behavior. As a result, the outcome may not be satisfactory. In that sense, what we think or how we think is often more important than any specific action.

Exhibit 1.13 shows changes in the thinking process as applied to children and to adults who are learning a new sport or new skills.

As you can see, all three cases follow similar steps, even though the objectives are different in nature. Also, we may realize that often stimuli do not trigger reactions to the point of changing habits, and the process may stop at step 2 or 3. An individual's upbringing, concerns at a given time, and other factors, naturally, can affect behavior even if the stimulus or training process is the same.

However, the nature of the change process still seems to be con-

Exhibit 1.13. Learning from Different Change Processes

Steps	Learning as a Child	Learning Tennis	Changing One's Lifestyle
1. Stimulus from outside	Touched a hot pan, and burned fingers.	Saw a tennis player with a good ground stroke.	Found some beautiful scenery.
2. Impact on our mind	Big surprise; don't like that hot thing at all.	Every movement made sense, and it was strong and beautiful.	Triggers a memory of happy days of childhood.
3. Change in attitude	In the kitchen, there is a dangerous thing.	I have a strong desire to break the old habit.	I want to regain those good old days.
4. Change in behavior	Don't reach for things that look like pans.	I'm trying to hit differently, like the player I saw.	I'll try to renew relationships with friends.
5. Change in habit	Life is more in my control if I am more attentive to my surroundings.	As I experience success, I realize that if I want to improve, I can learn from good examples.	I'll find more frequent happy moments with friends.

sistent. And since organizations are collections of individuals, we may be able to apply the same process to the organization. That is, if change is necessary, then the organization may need to go through steps similar to those described here. Again, however, we need to realize that the same stimuli may not affect every individual in the same way.

Since we live in a complex world, full of new information or stimuli, moving through these steps requires an increasing level of effort before any new behavior becomes a new culture within the organization. This means that if we do not clarify each step and sort out the relevant information, we may be disturbed by new stimuli and get lost in the process before we accomplish anything. As with successfully accomplishing a new year's resolution, therefore, sorting out the stimuli (i.e., distinguishing important information and noises), developing a clear vision, and having a strong desire to accomplish the objective should be the first key steps in the growth of our organization and ourselves.

Exhibit 1.14 shows how the change process can be applied to an organization. Again, the first key steps are to sort out the stimuli, develop a clear vision, and have a strong desire to realize that vision. That is to say, for an organization to achieve coherent behavior, first, it needs to establish shared values and vision. Then, this becomes a foundation to accomplish the organization's mission as a group.

Even if this is understood in concept, we still need to realize that there is a difference between knowing what we do and doing what we know. Therefore, we need to make practicing our new thinking a habit. Once internalized, however, we may find such process is the equivalent of "making people," or making a whole new person in the organization as Matsushita pointed out.

CHANGING OUR DESTINY

If we look back, our society has advanced from animalistic ways of communication in the prehistoric era, through sign language, spoken language, and written words, to the use of television and computers—even to the point of sending messages over satellite networks or fiber optics. As a result, we are able to respond to new information very quickly. And this new information triggers new insight as more and more people are involved in the process of sharing information, thus causing chain reactions.

Naturally, this process has had a significant impact on our society. As we find ourselves in the middle of mass-scale information

Exhibit 1.14. Change Process Applied to an Organization's Culture

Steps	Change in Organization
1. Stimulus from outside	Competitive threat is here; more new products and ideas are introduced.
2. Impact on our mind	Remember days when we all worked hard.
3. Change in attitude	It is really becoming necessary to work as a team.
4. Change in behavior	We'll try to solve problems as a group because they are everybody's problem.
5. Change in habit	When we find signs of improvement, we'll share them more often, and gain confidence.

exchange, therefore, we should realize that our responses to information (stimuli) can change each of our lives significantly. To summarize, Exhibit 1.15 describes the nature of the change process that an individual or organization may go through, even leading to changes in our destiny. For the sake of discussion in this book, we will call this the *behavioral change model.*

The point here is that, depending on how we respond to outside stimuli, our individual or the organization's destiny will be determined accordingly. Of course, we need to be skilled at sorting out the stimuli and deciding whether or not they are meaningful. Yet, if we seek out good ideas, maintain a positive attitude, practice good behavior or habits, and take each step one at a time, I am optimistic that we can change our destiny accordingly. As Walt Disney said, "If we can dream it, we can make it."

As we face our challenges in business and the need to continuously improve our organization's performance, it becomes very important to progress through these steps in such a manner that both the individual and the organization as a whole can find meaning in it.

CLARIFYING OUR VISION AND MISSION

While our day-to-day focus may change depending on the stimuli we receive from outside, our fundamental values do not change so

Exhibit 1.15. Changing Our Destiny (Behavioral Change Model)

Steps	Description
1. Stimulus from outside	Information gained from outside
2. Impact on our minds	
• Generate idea	• Find something new compared to previous knowledge base
• Clarify idea	• Check with frame of reference, e.g., priorities that have been known to be effective
• Experiment with idea	• Try different things with this idea in mind to see if it is meaningful
3. Change in attitude	Change the frame of reference, or priorities
4. Change in behavior	Adopt new framework or new paradigm into our behavioral patterns
5. Change in habit	New behavioral patterns become way of life
6. Change in destiny	Development of new state of mind brings a new potential in our lives

Exhibit 1.16. Vision of Shop Floor Excellence

• Shop is core of activity	• Open/transparent organization
• Mutual trust	• Involvement of people
• Belief in the change	• Housekeeping
• Positive morale	• Care for product
• Working together	• Achieving total quality
• Homogeneous group	• Ease of communication
• Understanding internal customers	• Learning
• Love of product	• Everything in its place
• Exposing problems	• Discipline in complying with procedure
• Motivated people	• Responsible for own area

radically. To illustrate, Exhibit 1.16 summarizes the vision of shop floor excellence as viewed by the people who attended a shop floor management workshop I gave in Spain. As we review these comments, we find that even if our backgrounds may differ, our fundamental beliefs are similar. Also we may realize that if we are to change our behavior with regard to the way we manage the shop floor, we need to find ways to clarify these values and use them as our yardstick to measure our day-to-day behavior.

As an organization needs to renew itself and thrive until it accomplishes its mission, it needs to go through the change processes described in Exhibit 1.13 over and over again. Just as a person without core beliefs can easily lose sight of the vision in the midst of turbulence, the same is true for any organization. (See Exhibits 1.17 and 1.18.)

Ultimately, we need a vision for the future that everyone can digest and buy into at any time. If we can develop such a universal vision, beyond time and national boundaries, both our companies and the society at large will benefit. As we move forward in this book and as we go through our own change process, we should be able to develop our own vision of excellence and get ready for it.

SUMMARY

- In order to prosper in today's turbulent business environment, each of us needs to prepare and internalize skills for responding to change.
- When everyone addresses problems at the front line (i.e., shop

Exhibit 1.17. Daily Shop Floor Meeting at Matsushita. Here, a supervisor conducts meetings at the beginning and at the end of the shift to share important information to run his "mini-company." As much as creating the vision and changing our behavior is important to grow as a person, or as a team, it may be important to remember that there is a big difference between getting the idea and practicing it.

Matsushita

Exhibit 1.18. Information Retention. Here, results of a study verify the importance of practicing the idea and hence developing a good habit to internalize the idea.

Method	Recall After 72 Hours (up to)
Hear only	10%
See only	20%
Hear and see	50%
Verbal participation	70%
Physical participation	80%
Hear, see, and practice	90%

floor), all of us become problem solvers, reducing the need for additional resources such as extra support staff or layers of managers.

- Self-management puts people's destiny in their own hands. People will have greater pride, self-esteem, increased responsibilities, and contribute more to the company and society.
- In achieving excellence in shop floor management, traditional problems such as the dichotomy between manager and subordinates and a lack of coordination between functions need to be resolved.
- Even though the effectiveness of each process may look small, when compounded throughout the whole organization the total impact can be enormous. If we can manage each of these processes better, we can significantly improve customer satisfaction while reducing waste.
- For shop floor management to be successful, the impact on the organizational structure, the management system, people skills, and attitude issues also need to be addressed.
- The first major steps of change are sorting out the stimuli we receive as an organization, developing a clear vision, and having a strong desire to accomplish that vision. As we move down these steps, we may find that even our destiny is changing.
- The vision of shop floor excellence is something everyone of us needs to seek as opposed to being given to us by someone else. As we train our own minds, we should be able to hold a vision of excellence in our own hands.

Chapter Two

DEVELOPING A CUSTOMER-ORIENTED ORGANIZATION

One of the most important points to realize our vision of excellence is our attitude toward customers. When we are busy in day-to-day work, however, we tend to forget them and become occupied with our own concerns.

In order to better orient ourselves, we will first look at customer-supplier relationships in our society at large to get a broad picture. Then, we will apply the idea of customer satisfaction in our own organization. We will, then, study how each unit of the organization can address the needs of customers to develop a total customer-oriented organization.

THE CUSTOMER-SUPPLIER RELATIONSHIP IN OUR SOCIETY

In our daily lives, we buy things without thinking about how many people are involved in producing them. In fact not only are manufacturers involved, but, beginning with the mining of raw materials, suppliers, and transporters, many more persons are involved. Those who have contributed to getting these products into our homes or workplace may be from many countries. In some cases, they may have traveled the oceans several times before reaching us.

If this is the case for products, what about information? Surrounded by a multitude of information sources such as radios, TVs, videos, computers, fax machines, phones, books, and movies, we once again find ourselves in the middle of a tremendously complex customer-supplier linkage. Furthermore, each generation passes on thoughts to the next generation, parents to children or teachers to pupils. Without the coordinated activities of a great many people, we could not have achieved our current standard of living, nor could we sustain it today.

LISTENING TO THE VOICE OF CUSTOMERS

Through the news media, we see massive changes taking place internationally. In our immediate surroundings, we see more business competition stimulating the introduction of new products and services, and the pace of this change seems to be accelerating. If we think carefully, these trends have something in common. The power base is becoming more and more decentralized, and people are sharing information more freely. As information becomes more accessible and people acquire more knowledge, more people are participating in various new activities.

The change process has something in common with these trends, too. That is, a groundswell of change is taking place, as people take more ownership. Often, old barriers are being broken down—as symbolized by the fall of the Berlin Wall in November 1989—not by the use of power in the traditional sense but rather by people's will to change. Similar processes are taking place in various parts of the world.

Massive changes are taking place in the corporate world as well. Not just emerging companies but also those with a long tradition are seeking ways to meet customers' needs better than their competitors. As a result, corporate restructuring is becoming commonplace, resulting in changing roles and responsibilities for many of us.

Almost no change, however, takes place without pain. In fact, pain is almost expected since, by definition, change requires energy. Following the law of physics, the bigger the mass (or number of people, in the case of organizations) and the larger the rate of the change, the greater the required energy to accomplish change. The amount of energy a tanker needs to change its course, is far greater than that needed to navigate a canoe. In order to make these changes smoothly, however, the energy should be generated from within, taking the form of its people's own initiative.

Still, we may wonder why we need to change. One way to think about this is that change is taking place because, more and more, we are listening to the voices of our people, our customers, and trying to address their needs. Of course, there are problems in our society, but it seems that we share a dream for a better future.

WHAT IS A CUSTOMER-ORIENTED ORGANIZATION?

One way to see how change in our society relates to shop floor management is to look at a company's focus on satisfying its customers' needs. Whoever provides better products or services to customers wins the competition. Of course, this is a tough goal for producers of services or products, but it is certainly best for customers. Looking inside the company, we find customer-supplier relationships as shown in the following exhibits.

First, as you see in Exhibit 2.1, there are external customers and internal customers. The customer-supplier relationship forms a closed loop. That is, as customers' needs are identified (marketing), products designed (design) and manufactured (supplier–fabrication–assembly), and they are sold to customers for their use (shipping–customer). Furthermore, unsatisfied customer needs from current products are identified by the marketing function in order to come up with better products. Accordingly, everybody in the loop is continuously aiming to better satisfy his or her customers.

Here we should note that the customer-supplier relationship applies not just to the flow of material, but also to the flow of information, as well as to such industries as service or construction. In these industries, the manufacturing process is represented by such value-adding processes as answering phones, delivering food, providing banking, transportation, or building houses. Whatever the activity, the term "manufacturing" may be simply interpreted as "producing value" for the customer, since, after all, every business function should be value producing.

Another very important point is that the loop in Exhibit 2.1 also represents a continuous improvement cycle. If each and everybody in this loop satisfies the next process better, then everybody can pros-

Exhibit 2.1. Customer-Supplier Relationship Across Different Company Functions

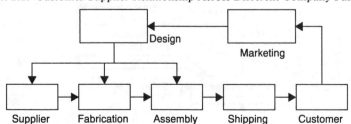

Note: Each arrow indicates a customer-supplier relationship.

per. Even if the market is saturated, if we keep identifying unsatisfied needs of customers, and designing and manufacturing products (or services) to meet those needs, our company should succeed. When this happens, we can say that the people in such a company are sitting in the driver's seat, charting a course toward the future.

UNDERSTANDING THE CUSTOMER-SUPPLIER RELATIONSHIP

Let us further look at an organization's internal and external customers and suppliers. Exhibit 2.2 shows a manufacturing organization in the automotive industry. Here, putting the emphasis on developing a broader picture and sharing it with co-workers allows them to better steer the company. Drawing this type of chart also aids in developing a clear understanding of the important role each process plays in getting the job done and meeting customer expectations. Again, in order to provide total customer satisfaction throughout the customer-supplier linkages, all processes must be well under control; no single process should be out of tune.

Let us look at our organization in even more detail. This time, we look at the customer-supplier relationship in one organizational unit. Typically, there are multiple customers and suppliers. For example, Exhibit 2.3 was developed by a maintenance/engineering unit within a manufacturing organization.

Exhibit 2.2. Customer-Supplier Relationship Chart for a Manufacturing Organization

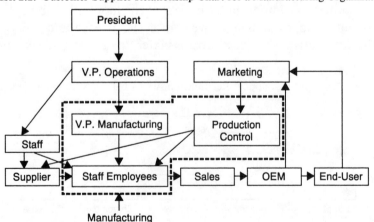

Courtesy Borg-Warner

Exhibit 2.3. Customer-Supplier Relationship Chart for a Maintenance/Engineering Organization

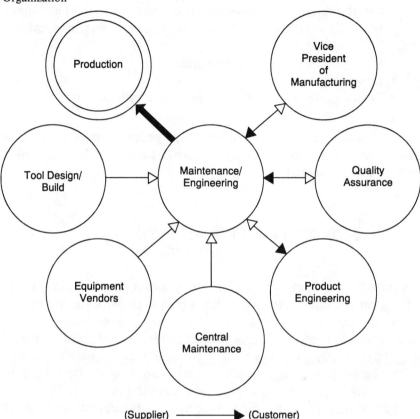

(Supplier) ⟶ (Customer)

Note: The arrows may point in both directions, indicating that depending on the situation one may be a customer or a supplier. For example, one may provide material to another whereas the other party may provide information as feedback.

Courtesy Borg-Warner

As shown in the exhibit, the big arrow pointing to Production indicates that it is the maintenance/engineering unit's major customer. Some of the arrows point in both directions, because depending on the situation the same customer is also a supplier. For example, one group may provide materials to another, while the second party provides information as feedback.

If people in each unit of the organization draw customer-supplier relationship charts, as shown in these examples, and compare the charts among different groups, several benefits will be derived:

- Developing a broader picture of one's job
- Identifying key customers
- Clarifying the interrelationships of organizations that cannot be easily conveyed by traditional pyramid-shaped organizational charts
- Clarifying roles and responsibilities
- Educating new employees
- Focusing people's efforts on customer satisfaction

In other words, such an exercise will help people to develop a better understanding of the company's internal functions through which business is conducted.

MOVING FROM LOCAL OPTIMIZATION TO TOTAL OPTIMIZATION

As the customer-supplier relationship becomes clear, collectively focusing on customer satisfaction leads people to work on continuous improvement. As history has shown us, there is no end to customer's demands nor to improvements to meet those demands. Improvement is, by definition, going beyond the constraints and gaining solutions with new insights. Regardless of whether constraints are related to man, machine, material, method, or measurement it is important that all of us see the broader picture of our organization and clearly understand our mission, role, and responsibilities. And, as everyone in the organization understands the importance of satisfying customers better, we can develop a totally customer-oriented company.

While the concept may be understandable, the actual practice may still not be so easy since most of us have a tendency to "optimize" our area of interest. In the case of production, for example, operators may prefer long production runs with fewer setups if they are focusing only on their own efficiency. Material handlers may like large batches because they require fewer delivery trips. Yet this focus tends to build up inventory, increase total cost, and increase the customer response time because of the lack of flexibility.

The models shown in Exhibit 2.4 illustrate this point. The model on the left shows three different groups within a company, each focusing on its own area of interest. They might represent fabrication, subassembly, and assembly, or operations A, B, and C. Or they

Exhibit 2.4. A Comparison of Total and Local Optimization

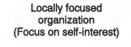

Locally focused
organization
(Focus on self-interest)

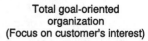

Total goal-oriented
organization
(Focus on customer's interest)

Skill,
knowledge
level

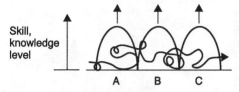

A   B   C

Each organization is focusing
on its own interest. Skills are
possessed in a narrowly
defined area of responsibility.
Materials and information flow
is disrupted because of people's
extreme self-interest.

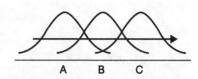

A   B   C

Different organizations are sharing
information. More understanding
and coordination develop among the
people as a whole. Materials and
information flow is smooth because
of people's customer-oriented
approach.

could be marketing, engineering, and manufacturing; or suppliers, manufacturer, and sales dealerships.

Here, we can see that each group's narrow focus results in a lack of communication, a lack of shared goals, and a lack of cooperation. People speak different languages as well. For example, marketing people speak a language that design or manufacturing people do not understand, and assembly people do not communicate well with fabrication people or outside suppliers.

As you can imagine, if we focus only on our self-interest we will create problems at the organizational boundaries, blocking people's view of the larger picture or inhibiting understanding of the customer's language. The result will be high inventory of material or information, long processing time, and often high reject rates due to the lack of adequate feedback.

This situation is compared to the organizational model shown on the right where there is more communication, coordination, and cooperation. Here, we should recognize that techniques such as kanban, job rotation, and visual control are developed to satisfy customers better and reduce the boundary problems that are apparent in the model on the left. (See my book, *The New Manufacturing Challenge,* for detailed explanations of these techniques.)

With the help of these simple tools, people can communicate better across organizational boundaries without much difficulty and without taking the time of higher level management. As a result, things get done much more smoothly, as indicated by the straight arrow in Exhibit 2.4. (Also, see Exhibit 2.5 for examples.)

Exhibit 2.5. Breaking the Walls Down. An open office is created at Borg-Warner (left picture). Motorola's Ted Woods, Vice President of Operations, is breaking the wall down to improve communication (right picture). Putting up walls is a sign of Tayloristic thinking and results in a customer-unfriendly organization. It makes communication more difficult and creates "black boxes."

Courtesy Borg-Warner   Courtesy Motorola

WORKING ON OUR MINDSET

Even though the ideas suggested here sound simple, they also have a deeper significance in collectively working on our mindset. That is, customer orientation relates to selflessness, openness, humbleness, and our faith to practice these techniques to make them work. If we do not practice these principles on our own initiative, by definition, we still have walls within our own minds.

Instead of self-centered thinking, we need to practice selflessness. Instead of hiding things and feeling insecure, we need to be open. Instead of ignoring customers, we need to be humble and to appreciate them. Instead of using experts to solve problems, we need to have faith in involving everybody in addressing problems for customers and to believe that it will eventually work.

The point is, customer orientation should be practiced with as many people as possible to develop an organization that itself will evolve towards total optimization, that is, total customer satisfaction. And for this to happen, we need to work on our mindset. Also, in order to get everyone's cooperation, we need to emphasize simplicity and clarity.

Still, old-style organizations as represented in the model on the left in Exhibit 2.4 do not facilitate sharing skills or knowledge while maintaining an expert mentality. Instead of encouraging a broader viewpoint, people tend to maintain a narrower one; instead of being customer oriented, people tend to remain self-centered.

The following are a few examples of such thinking:

CASE 1: We think that our skills and knowledge will protect our jobs if we do not share them with others.

CASE 2: We are more defensive and suspicious of change or new ideas which may threaten the way things have worked for so long. For example, we may say to new ideas: "We have tried that before," "Why do we need to change?" etc.

CASE 3: Instead of conducting meetings to share ideas, we prefer one-to-one communication because it seems more efficient. There is no benefit in sharing ideas or recognizing someone's good work in the meeting.

CASE 4: Even when we spot obvious problems, if they are not in our area, we will not try to help.

With these attitudes, individually each of us may succeed in protecting our job in the short run, but we will not grow in the long run. Since customer orientation is not a high priority in such thinking, we may even be surprised one day to find that the company is going out of business. Again, we need to understand the broader picture and to orient our thinking towards customers. Furthermore, we need to identify ourselves with customers and obtain their satisfaction in order to assure our future.

DEVELOPING THE NERVOUS SYSTEM IN OUR ORGANIZATION

Our work typically consists of satisfying several different customers as described in Exhibit 2.3. When put together, then, we see our organization consists of different units that are linked often in an intricate network, similar to our brain's nervous system. (In fact, as our brain recognizes different patterns through our neural network, our organization creates certain value through our intricate communication network.)

If we use a model to compare this type of customer-supplier relationship to the traditional view of organizational structure, it may look like that in Exhibit 2.6. Here, in the more traditional organization, information needs to flow through a preestablished chain of command, making the organization very rigid—and often causing a traffic jam of information. For example, as was true in old Egyptian kingdoms, in large armies or large traditionally run companies, a mission or strategy is developed at the top without involving people.

Exhibit 2.6. Comparison of Conventional and Biological Organizations

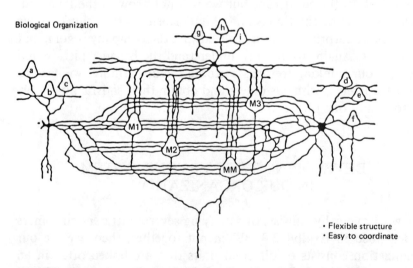

Note: This comparison was developed to illustrate the point on organizational development by Jean Bounine and Kiyoshi Suzaki in *Produire-Juste à Temps* (Paris: Masson, 1986). The concept of biological organization was originally developed by Stafford Beer in *The Brain of the Firm* (London: Allen Lane, 1972)

Then, people are "used" to following commands from the top without being asked to think for themselves.

When people's talents are very limited, such an approach may be a practical option. But when proper guidance and education are provided, many organizations find that more delegation of authority and self-management becomes possible with minimum guidance from the top. In a customer-oriented organization, (i.e., an organic or biologic type organization) information can flow as required by the customer-supplier relationships. And as such organization develops a broadly shared view by closely knit people, it becomes flexible in meeting the customers' needs much more quickly. (In a way, the shift from the traditional organization—which tends to prefer its scale economy—to a more customer-oriented organization represents the growth of our own society, enabling it to meet the specific needs of individuals.)

In developing a customer-oriented organization, it should be noted that even if there is no linkage established to satisfy customers, the empowered people will, by themselves, initiate the development of a new channel or new nerves to break the barrier—similar to the development of the brain's nervous system. Thus job titles and job descriptions mean less in a customer-oriented organization. Each job is critical; the most important job is to satisfy customers, internal or external.

CLARIFYING THE FLOW OF WORK

As we develop a close communication linkage of customer-supplier relationships on a company-wide scale, we find that it forms a network of flow of information and goods as symbolized by the biological organization in Exhibit 2.6. At the shop floor, these may be represented as a flow of work as shown in Exhibit 2.7. In the exhibit, along with a description of the processes, key features of the line and products are described. Also, samples of products are displayed for people to get an idea of how parts fit together.

We may also establish standard operating procedures at each work station representing the relationships of processing parts or services from one step of the operation to another step, consecutively. In Exhibit 2.8, basic tasks for press brake operators are posted. The items here include procedures for housekeeping, setup of dies, ma-

Exhibit 2.7. Description of Process Displayed in a Japanese Company

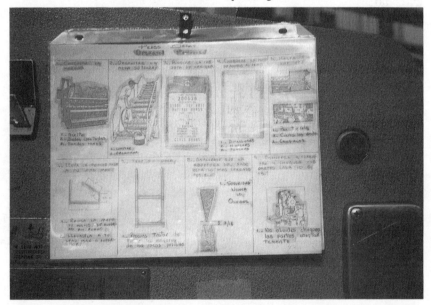

Courtesy Matsushita

Exhibit 2.8. Standard Operating Procedure

Courtesy Fireplace Manufacturers, Inc.

chine maintenance, key steps of operation, how to read drawings, and rules of kanban. What is surprising about these procedures is that a teenage supervisor who was an immigrant developed them on his own without much formal training.

As described here, the flow of work may represent each specific step of the operation, description of processes, or quality control procedures. Also, since most companies thrive on developing new products and continuously improving and delivering them to customers, we need to come up with a solid system for doing this. Exhibit 2.9 shows a network of customer-supplier relationships across different organizations within a company.

Even though the company depicted in Exhibit 2.9 is still young in its approach to building quality at the source, understanding its customer-supplier relationships has helped its people to build the teamwork necessary for continuous improvement.

Exhibit 2.10 shows another company's flow of work with more detailed processes. Here again the arrows indicate customer-supplier relationships. Feedback loops and decision points are indicated by dotted lines and diamond shaped figures, respectively. Please note that the company that devised this chart made it a basis of their quality assurance system, building in quality at each step of the process.

Exhibit 2.9. An Example of Company-Wide Customer-Supplier Relationship

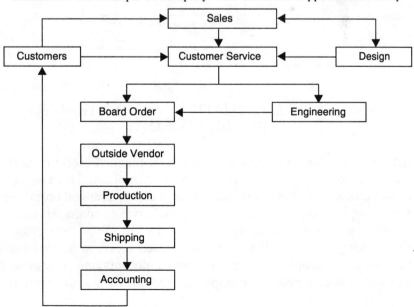

Exhibit 2.10. New Product Development Process Flow Chart

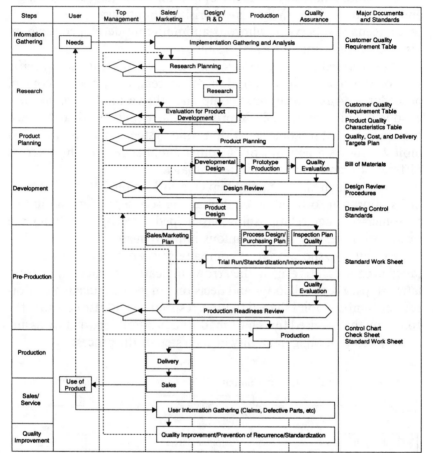

CUSTOMER ORIENTATION IN A CENTRALLY PLANNED ECONOMY

Let us for a moment compare the centrally planned economy and a market economy in relation to customer orientation. There seem to be similarities between the people under centrally planned economies and those in companies with a traditional style of management. In contrast, with a market economy and a democratic process of decision making, people in the West have gained access to many amenities that many people in other countries cannot imagine. Things such as many TV channels, thousands of supermarket goods, cars, stereos, videos, and credit cards cannot be easily imagined by those who have to wait in long lines for small amounts of food.

Even though a central authority may have the power to deal with external threats and make decisions for its people, such authority- or power-oriented minds may not be concerned with the specific needs of the people internal to the organization. We have seen this result in bureaucratic nightmares.

The lesson for us to learn here is that if we see our companies functioning as centralized governments in making decisions and getting things done, our managers may easily fall into the same bureaucratic nightmare as found in a centrally controlled economy.

Of course, some may argue that because of threats from outside or because people lack the ability to address issues themselves, someone has to be in a position of making decisions for them. Even though this may be the case at times, it is also important to note that this is the very reason we develop a specialist or expert mentality that excludes consideration of people. Consequently, the following important points must be made:

- When people are able to acquire skills, they become capable of self-management, as shown in the historical development of market economies.
- If people cannot exercise self-control or self-management, it may be because managers have not provided adequate tools or the proper environment.
- We need to make our system simple and comprehensible by everybody and provide adequate tools or means to encourage people's self-management skills.

Since we, the people, represent both customers and suppliers, ultimately, all of us should address each of our customers' needs, solve problems, and continuously improve. With such thinking, everybody should be able to grow and take their destiny in their hands.

UNDERSTANDING CUSTOMERS' MINDS—PUTTING OURSELVES IN THEIR SHOES

In order to satisfy customers, however, all of us need to extend our thoughts to understand customers' minds. Whether customers buy goods or services, we are dealing with *people*. Unless we are able to understand these people as individuals—their feelings of joy, sorrow, frustration, anger, happiness, and their desires—we will not be able to produce goods or provide services to our customers' satisfaction. In other words, we, as suppliers, need to be able to put ourselves in our customers' shoes to do our work properly.

Realizing such a need, the production department of an aerospace and defense contractor developed the customer survey form shown in Exhibit 2.11. After the form was developed, internal customers were asked for comments. As more customer feedback was gained,and as a sharing relationship was developed between customers and suppliers, the people from the production department could focus their efforts to better meet customers' expectation.

Another example—from Toledo Scale—is found in Appendix 2.1. It should be noted that the form is standardized for all units of the organization and is distributed as a part of an employee handbook to familiarize everybody with the importance of customer satisfaction. This form is used as a part of a quarterly rating system— even rating the support staff for their contribution.

In order to listen to customers' voices and summarize them in an organized fashion, a table called Customer Quality Requirements Table may be used (see Exhibit 2.12). As you can see, customers' requirements are tabulated to categorize their needs clearly for a par-

---

Exhibit 2.11. Customer Satisfaction Survey

Dear Customer:

How are we doing? Please fill out this card and return it to your supervisor. Thank you.

	(circle one or more)		
Service:	Good	Fair	Poor
Kit complete?	Yes	No	
If not, what is missing?	Fixture	Cutters	Inserts
	Planning	Routing	Gauges

Part No: _____

Operation: _____

Thank you for your cooperation.

Courtesy BFM Aerospace

Exhibit 2.12. Customer Quality Requirements Table

LEVEL 1	LEVEL 2	LEVEL 3	PRIORITY	(RELATED PARTS NUMBER)
(1) NO MACHINE/ FAILURE	(110) DOES NOT BREAK FROM MECHANICAL STRESS	(111) MACHINE IS USED BEYOND THE LIMIT	9	EL-98, EL-104
	(120) DOES NOT WEAR		7	FB-102, 111
	(130) DOES NOT CORRODE		6	SA-101
(2) EASY TO OPERATE	(210) SIMPLE TO OPERATE	(211) GOOD OPERATOR'S MANUAL (212) EASY TO READ DISPLAY	9	
	(220) GOOD MANEU-VERABILITY	(221) SMOOTH GEAR SHIFT (222) EASY TO TURN	8	
	(230) EASY TO FIX PROBLEM WHEN NECESSARY	(231) GOOD OPERATOR'S MANUAL (222) EASY TO EXCHANGE PARTS	8	
(3) MINIMUM IMPACT TO OUTSIDE ENVIRONMENT	(310) SMALL NOISE		6	
	(320) LITTLE SMELL		5	
	(330) SMALL VIBRATION		6	
	(340) NO POLLUTION	(341) NO WASTE (342) NO OIL LEAKAGE	8	
(4) ENERGY EFFICIENT	(410) ...	...	...	

ticular type of industrial equipment. Also, reflecting the voice of the customers, these items are prioritized to describe the profile of customers objectively. As obvious as it may sound, if we do not listen attentively to our customers' voice and meet their needs, we will not survive in our business.

CRITERIA FOR CUSTOMER SATISFACTION

What this means for us is that we need to define clearly the key items in satisfying customers so that everyone can effectively work together to address them. To simplify this point, Exhibit 2.13 summarizes the key customer needs in a tree form. Here, all specific items may be covered under three broad headings. In other words, if we can satisfy our customers continuously with high-quality (Q) products or services, at less cost (C), and with shorter and more timely delivery (D) than competitors, we should do well. For simplicity's sake, let us call these the QCD criteria for customer satisfaction.

Also, since all employees in the organization may be viewed as customers from the total company's point of view, their needs must also be satisfied. Therefore, if we add safety (S) and morale (M) to address employee concerns, QCDSM become the major criteria for an organization's success. In other words, if we focus on these five items, we should be able to cover most of the major concerns of the organization. (Note that environmental issues may be included under S.)

Naturally, however, improvement in QCD or QCDSM does not happen automatically. It takes everybody's willingness and dedicated effort. Also, no single improvement can guarantee success forever. Like it or not, we need to keep moving ahead. As someone once said, "Even if we are on the right track, we will get run over if we just sit there."

Exhibit 2.13. Needs Tree for Customer Satisfaction

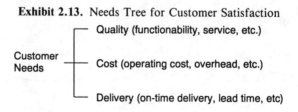

ADDRESSING CUSTOMERS' NEEDS

What it means is that, if we are not addressing any of these indices on customers' needs, we should seriously reconsider the way we spend time at work. Later in this book, we will review different ways to accomplish this, such as upgrading our skills, working on problem solving, providing leadership, and developing management systems to support these activities. Since addressing customers' needs is a foundation of business, we should make sure that a linkage develops between these subjects as shown in the relationship matrix in Exhibit 2.14. Since this matrix can also serve as a self-evaluation checklist of our shop floor management, all squares should be assessed regarding the organization's activities and effectiveness of such activities.

Of course, the impact on QCDSM may vary depending on the specific approach we take. But, first, we need to make sure that these approaches address customers' needs. Then, we need to find ways to

Exhibit 2.14. Addressing Customer Needs Through Our Work

		Approaches to Address the Customers' Needs			
		Upgrade Skills (e.g, Follow SOP)	*Problem Solving (e.g., Make Suggestions)*	*Leadership (e.g., Provide Recognition)*	*Management System (e.g., Goal Setting, Follow-through of Plans)*
Customers' Needs	Quality				
	Cost				
	Delivery				
	Safety				
	Morale				
Chapters Referenced		Chapters 4 & 5	Chapters 6 & 7	Chapter 8	Chapters 9 & 10

Note: As we check each square in the matrix, for example, we need to ask: (1) How do we learn and then practice new skills so that certain customers' needs are addressed? (2) When we make suggestions, which customer needs are satisfied? (3) Do we recognize people's efforts in addressing certain customers' needs? or (4) Do we have a management system to measure the progress in meeting key customers' needs?

Chapters 2 and 3 deal with customer orientation, and Chapters 11 and 12 address integration and implementation. The organization's mission and vision should be reflected in all squares of the matrix.

coordinate these activities well so that we can become good at what we do.

DEVELOPING CUSTOMER ORIENTATION THROUGHOUT THE COMPANY

Many people think they know how the company operates based on their own point of view. Yet a clear and comprehensive understanding rarely exists. For this reason, it is indeed important to clarify the customers' needs and for everybody to develop a customer orientation. Only when each unit of the organization understands who the customers are and what their needs are will we develop a basis for doing business and moving forward.

And once the importance of customer orientation is understood by all units of our organization, we can begin to understand the needs of the end user and deploy them throughout the organization, from marketing to design to manufacturing, and so on as shown in Exhibit 2.1, thus developing a customer orientation throughout all of our business activities.

If customers' concerns relate to quality, then our quality assurance system should play a role to help in assuring customer satisfaction. If cost is the concern, then our cost control system may help address that need. And if delivery is the concern, our production planning and control system may assist us. Overall, these systems should function as a network so that people on the shop floor can be involved as much as possible, in contrast to the way traditional companies handle the situation (see Exhibit 2.15).

To recapitulate the points mentioned above:

- We need to break down organizational barriers by practicing customer orientation; that is, form should follow the needs of customers.
- We need to address problems at the source; for example, inspectors, expeditors, and specialists may not be able to provide solutions on time.
- We need to utilize customer-friendly approaches, for example, utilization of customer surveys, poka-yoke (a fail-safe mechanism), and kanban (a production control mechanism).

Above all, addressing the problems and customer requirements at the source is the key to our progress.

Exhibit 2.15. Comparison of Customer Orientation Between Traditional and Progressive Companies

	Traditional Company	Progressive Company
Structure	- Form comes first	- Need comes first
	- Central control	- Decentralized control
Organizational Responsibility	- Top/staff provides order	- Top/staff assists the rest
	- Top/staff is responsible	- Everybody shares responsibility
Customer Orientation	- Crude	- More refined
	- At the top/specialist	- By everybody
Key Player		
- Quality	- Inspector, quality staff	Everybody, including shop floor people, is involved
- Cost	- Industrial engineer	
- Delivery	- Expeditor, scheduler	

EXPANDING THE CONCEPT OF THE CUSTOMER-SUPPLIER RELATIONSHIP

Before we end this chapter, let us look at the customer-supplier relationship from yet another angle. As international competition becomes fierce, often trade barriers are erected and protectionist movements arise. While customers may benefit, unfavorable situations, such as the loss of jobs, may also occur. If a company's mission is to satisfy its customers, it must contribute not only to its immediate customers, but to its country as well, since one is a part of the other. Therefore, a company's value may be related to how much a company is in turn valued by the citizens of the country. Since every company's activities should be related to the benefit of all human beings, we can say that the public is always the best judge of the company's conduct.

Next, let us think of ourselves. If we think of ourselves as customers, then who are our suppliers? Can we think of our parents as suppliers, providing love and raising us to become who we are now? Neighbors, friends, and teachers have also had an impact on us. Even people who have written books and manufactured clothes, TVs, and bicycles have had an impact on us, in terms of building our knowledge and creativity, as well as increasing our experience base. Our ancestors can even be seen as our genetic suppliers—without them we would not be who we are. We are the result of all the processes that these suppliers of ours have gone through. That is,

Exhibit 2.16. Communicating the Message to the People

Note: At Grand Rapids Spring & Wire, the warehouse is used for all employee meetings, and the basement for classroom training. Identifying the employees as important customers from the company's point of view, people at this company create time and space to share ideas and get the message across.

Courtesy Grand Rapids Spring & Wire

what happened in the past has a cause-and-effect relationship on who we are at this moment.

And finally, if we think of all of the customers that we may influence, we may focus on what we can contribute, instead of thinking only about personal gain and losing the broader perspective. This little exercise in customer–supplier relationships should make us think about each one of us in relation to our world at large.

SUMMARY

- While we tend to be engrossed in our own thinking, it is important not to lose perspective on how we receive goods and services as customers and how we also provide these as suppliers. Our society is composed of networks of customer-supplier relationships.
- The recent trends both in international events and the business environment indicate a shift in the power base from the traditional one to that based on people taking more ownership.
- Customer-supplier relationships exist in our own organization as well. Whether it is processing information or materials, as in the case of processing end users' voices to design to manufacturing, etc., or processing parts from operation A to B to C, etc., every person in the organization needs to satisfy his or her customer(s) to make the system work.
- To share this point, it is advisable to develop a customer-supplier relationship chart for each unit of the organization.
- If everybody is customer-oriented, we can develop a total goal-oriented organization as opposed to locally focused (i.e., self-centered) organization.
- Centralized control may be ineffective in decision making and in utilizing people's capabilities today, especially when people's abilities have increased.
- As we develop a customer-oriented approach, we will find a more developed and refined flow of work in addressing the needs of customers, but not necessarily with the lines of authority found in traditional organizations.
- Understanding the customers' minds, clarifying their needs, establishing the flow of work accordingly, and doing these better

continuously, we can break the cumbersome organizational barriers and shift towards a more progressive organization.

- For this to happen, every person in the organization needs to focus on satisfying his or her customers, internal and external. As everybody does this, they also benefit since the customer-supplier relationship is a closed loop system.

Chapter Three

ESTABLISHING A COMPANY WITHIN A COMPANY

In order to apply customer orientation in our job, we need to ask how we can satisfy customers from the shop floor up throughout the entire organization. Naturally, we want to eliminate any barriers impeding communication and take actions necessary to accomplish this. Further, we want each and every person within the organization to fully explore his or her abilities.

Utilizing the idea of "making people before making products," this chapter illustrates a way to practice customer orientation by involving everyone. First, we emphasize the idea that "Everybody is the president of his or her area of responsibility." This means that each unit of organization is equivalent to a "mini-company" where people are the owners and run such a mini-company to accomplish its mission. We will also compare a traditional organization—we will call it "black box management"—and a progressive organization that we call "glass wall management," and find ways to make necessary changes.

THE CUSTOMER-SUPPLIER RELATIONSHIP BETWEEN BOSS AND SUBORDINATES

If we expand the idea of customer-supplier relationships, we can see such relationships represented in a company's hierarchical structure as well. (See Exhibit 3.1.) Here, managers may see people at the shop floor as their customers, in conveying the idea to get things done. Also, people at the shop floor may view managers as customers, in proposing improvement ideas and getting resources for implementation.

In a traditionally run organization, however, the boss is always

Exhibit 3.1. Customer-Supplier Relationships Across Organizational Hierarchies

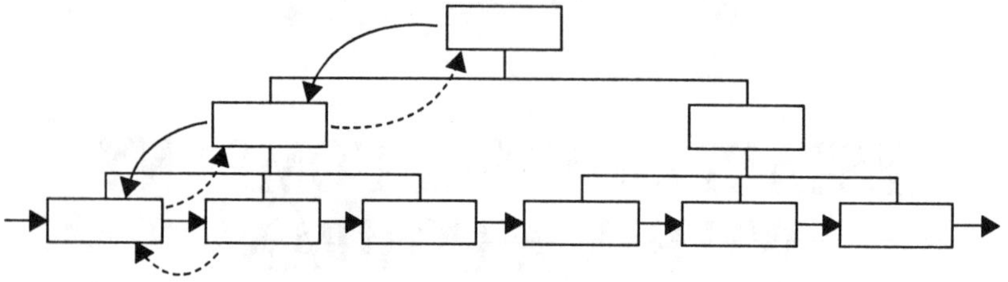

Note: Each arrow in the exhibit indicates a customer-supplier relationship.

considered to be right, and people simply follow what the manager tells them. Thus, people develop a "just-tell-me-what-to-do" attitude, while the manager takes on one of "just-do-what-I-say." People's potential for growth, therefore, is severely limited.

In a progressive organization, on the other hand, managers understand that performance depends on how effectively people's talents are utilized. Since just telling people what to do does not help in exploring people's potential, managers need to find ways to allow personal growth. In other words, instead of stating, "Just do what I say," the manager may ask: "What do you think?" And instead of utilizing their own wisdom or creativity to solve problems, managers need to use their wisdom to enable others to utilize theirs.

THE PEOPLE-ORIENTED ORGANIZATION: MAKING PEOPLE BEFORE MAKING PRODUCTS

Providing people with the information they need, problem-solving tools, and an educational environment allows them to grow—just as children grow under their parents' care. If managers recognize that they are powerless when their people do not get the work done, they will be more likely to view their employees as their customers.

To illustrate this point, think of a case where an operator ignores a work procedure, causing a machine breakdown or a large number of defects. In a traditionally run company the operator may be fired, but such action will never guarantee better performance in the future. If people have pride and a feeling of ownership in their jobs, however, they will be eager to prevent problems from happening.

Again, we need to address the problem at the source. Instead of giving up, if managers think hard about "making people before making products," as Konosuke Matsushita pointed out, we may then develop an organization that can address problems at the source. In other words, a customer-oriented organization should be a people-oriented organization.

Accordingly, a major role of managers in a people-oriented organization is to develop people's capabilities. That's why we say in quality jargon, "Quality control starts with education and ends with education." If a manager simply fires people and hires new ones when things are not working, no value is added to the organization because there is no opportunity for people to grow within it.

THE MINI-COMPANY CONCEPT

In the business world, we know that for a president to run a company successfully, he or she should be able to perform key managerial jobs effectively. The more successful the company is, the more confidence investors will have in it. In turn, that track record will help the president and his or her colleagues to explore further opportunities, thereby paving a way to the future.

If we think about it, the same situation applies *within* each company as well. If we view the next process as the customer and the previous process as the supplier, then every individual in the organization can in fact be viewed as the president of his or her area of responsibility, providing products or services to satisfy customers. Let us call each of these settings a "mini-company." In a way, then, everybody is running a company within a company (see Exhibit 3.2).

Exhibit 3.2. Everybody is President of His or Her Own Mini-Company

Or we can think of every unit or every department of a company running as a company.

In one sense, it may appear as though every unit of the organization is operating independently rather than as a team. Yet the customer-supplier relationship among units of organization will provide a vital check-and-balance mechanism to assure customer orientation while promoting self-management.

As an example, let us see how the stockroom staff for a high-tech product manufacturer practiced this idea. First, people in the stockroom developed a customer-supplier relationship chart (similar to the one in Exhibit 2.3) depicting the stockroom as a mini-company (Exhibit 3.3). They named their mini-company "Material Movers

Exhibit 3.3. Customer-Supplier Relationship Chart for a Stockroom

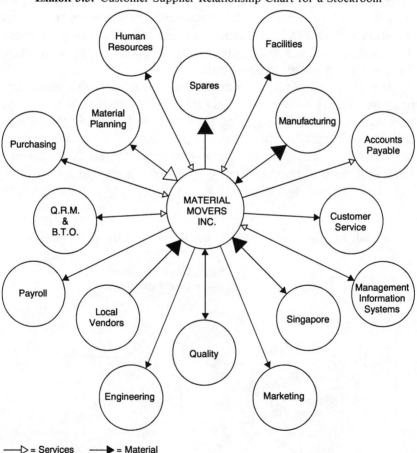

Inc.,'' illustrating the importance of moving materials in and out of the stockroom, as opposed to the no-value added process of simply stocking materials.

As before, the arrows in the exhibit indicate the customer-supplier relationships, which are often reciprocal, indicating various material and information flows in and out of the stockroom. The width of the arrows indicates that certain customer-supplier relationships are stronger or weaker than others, while the flows of services and materials are distinguished by the white and black arrowheads.

Going through this type of exercise, we should remind ourselves that keeping busy and blindly conducting the work does not necessarily result in satisfying customers. So, looking at the customer-supplier relationship chart, the people from this stockroom asked themselves the following questions:

1. For each major customer in the chart, how carefully and how often have we listened to their voice?
2. Have these customers been satisfied with the service the stockroom has provided?
3. Are these customers' requirements clear to the people in the stockroom?

Then, the people from the stockroom decided to meet with their major customers, face to face. Even though some of the complaints from customers were found to be either out of their control or caused by other departments, these customers appreciated the concern of the stockroom people, and everybody found the meeting to be very productive.

RUNNING YOUR OWN MINI-COMPANY

Following such a way of thinking, every unit of the company should be able to set up and run a mini-company that involves everybody (see Exhibit 3.4).

Here, steps 1 through 6 represent the mini-company's business plan, whereas steps 7 and 8 represent the mini-company's monthly, quarterly, semi-annual, or annual report. Also note that it is crucial to exchange the mini-company business plan and its reports with colleagues. In this way, key concerns can be effectively shared through-

Exhibit 3.4. Steps in Running a Mini-Company

Step 1. Name the mini-company.

Step 2. Write a mission statement for the mini-company.

Step 3. Make up a company profile by listing its people and describing its machines, etc.

Step 4. Develop a customer-supplier relationship chart for the mini-company and discuss the meaning of the arrows.

Step 5. Clarify the objectives of the mini-company.

Step 6. Develop plans of action to achieve objectives, then execute plans.

Step 7. Monitor the progress, and celebrate the accomplishment as appropriate.

Step 8. Repeat this cycle at regular intervals.

out the process of plan development as well as plan execution. (Details of these processes will be discussed in Chapter 10.)

Conducting this type of exercise will help define the business environment in which the mini-company functions. As a matter of fact, not only do mini-companies have customers and suppliers, but there are the equivalent of bankers and employees involved as well. For example, managers may be seen as the bankers, shareholders, or venture capitalists who provide the mini-company with resources (people, equipment, time, money) to get the job done and to satisfy customers.

THE FRONT LINE SUPERVISOR AS PRESIDENT OF A MINI-COMPANY

Since presidents have an obligation to those who provide resources, they must be able to (1) describe the way their companies are run, (2) gain concurrence in the use of resources to get the job done, (3) execute plans as agreed, and (4) summarize progress and report to the "bankers."

To illustrate this point more specifically, Exhibit 3.5 shows an example of a mini-company structure for a front line supervisor. This supervisor's roles and responsibilities in relation to other groups are summarized in Exhibit 3.6.

Here, support people are seen as suppliers. Also note that there may be reciprocal relationships, that is, materials or information may travel in both directions. Furthermore, in order to run a mini-

Exhibit 3.5. Front Line Supervisor's Role and Responsibilities in Relation to Other Groups

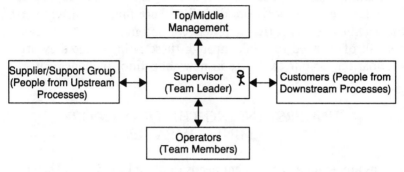

Exhibit 3.6. Roles and Responsibilities of Supervisor as President of Mini-Company

1. Working with top/middle management (bankers or venture capitalists)
   - Developing goals and approaches to achieving them.
   - Assuring that these goals and approaches are in harmony with the direction of the total organization.
   - Executing plans, checking the progress, and reporting results with adequate explanation. Periodic summary of progress may be called an annual report or semi-annual report of mini-company.
2. Working with operators (team members)
   - Sharing of goals and approaches to achieving goals; utilizing operators' ideas to accomplish them.
   - Executing plans, attaining goals and approaches for achieving goals as a group.
   - Providing necessary education and training as well as appropriate feedback as to how things are going.
3. Working with people from downstream processes (customers)
   - Practicing the idea of "next process is your customer."
   - Understanding the customer's requirement clearly.
   - Controlling the process to assure customer satisfaction.
4. Working with people from upstream processes (suppliers)
   - Providing feedback as a customer of their service.
   - Obtaining support in accomplishing goals in areas where certain skills are missing.
   - Receiving education and training to upgrade the level of shop floor control.

Note: For more detailed roles and responsibilities of supervisors, please refer to Appendix 3.1 for a self-evaluation checklist. This type of checklist should be followed up not because the boss says to, but rather because it helps us to develop self-esteem in our own jobs.

company well, it is important to develop effective reporting and information sharing processes with both customers and suppliers.

The roles of supervisors described here may be different from the way business is currently practiced, and may seem too idealistic. Yet, all of us need to think through these points since they are the foundation for our challenge in new shop floor management.

UNDERSTANDING THE FRAMEWORK OF MINI-COMPANIES

Just as any company president needs to obtain funds and keep investors informed about the company's operation by presenting appropriate business plans, every one of us, as president of our particular area of responsibility, needs to do the same. In other words, accountability comes with our responsibility.

Therefore, regardless of rank in the organization, every person should understand what he or she is accountable for and how performance of his or her operation is reported. Furthermore, an effective reporting mechanism should allow us to see the relationship between the mini-company's contribution and the overall performance of the division, or company.

Exhibit 3.7 describes examples of mini-company structure for various functions, from line operator to president of the company.

Ultimately, since each individual is a president of his or her area of responsibility, he or she, with respective employees, should manage his or her mini-company. What this means is that each mini-company should self-check or self-inspect its own work. Of course, improvement is a part of each mini-company's responsibility as well.

In addition to customers, suppliers, employees, and investors, there are other stakeholders in our mini-companies, for example, community members and family members of employees. In these cases too, we should clarify how we share progress with these stakeholders, as well as how their voices and concerns are reflected in running the mini-company.

THE MEANING OF MISSION

As we view our organization as a collection of mini-companies—all of them networked by customer-supplier relationships—each mini-

Exhibit 3.7. Structure of Mini-Companies as Viewed from Different Job Responsibilities

	Customer	Supplier	Banker	Employee
Line Operator	Operator down-stream	Operator upstream	Supervisor	Machine
Supervisor	Supervisor down-stream	Supervisor upstream	Production manager	Operators
Production Manager	Shipping dept.	Receiving dept.	V.P. Mfg	Production employees
V.P. of Man-ufacturing	Distributors, end users	Engineering, sales	President	All report-ing to him
President	Users, com-munity	Suppliers	Bankers, share-holders	All em-ployees

company should have its own mission or value statement. (See steps 1 and 2 in Exhibit 3.4.) The idea may be unfamiliar to many, but if people are to have ownership in what they do and identify with their group, developing such a statement will help them work as a team and share understanding of the company's situation, values, responsibilities, and vision.

What is the meaning of the mission? Is it simply a collection of words? Or, does it carry some weight? To me, it represents the will-power and creativity of people—the very core of the organization. Machines and materials do not have willpower by themselves. But we are different from machines or materials: we have a desire for self-expression that cannot be ignored. So, when we prepare our organization's mission statement, it should be something that we can identify with.

As much as we have an appreciation for life, a company's life should be identified with its mission. Rather than viewing a mission statement as a collection of words that are interpreted only at face value, therefore, I feel we need to respect the values behind the statement as something more valuable—as the equivalent of the organization's life. And if we think like that, whatever we do in our organization should become an expression of our mission. In other words, if we see our mission as reflecting the intrinsic values of the organization, our current situation or orientation should be contrasted to our guiding principle, or mission. Then, the difference between the two represents the problems needing resolution. Or, to express this as a formula:

Organization's Problems = Mission (vision to be accomplished)
                                        − Current Situation

So, in order for our organization to prosper in harmony with its environment, we need to develop capabilities to adjust our course according to the intrinsic value that we call our mission.

DEVELOPING A MISSION FOR MINI-COMPANIES

As much as each individual in the organization is respected for his or her creativity and self-expression, we propose here that each mini-company develop its own mission statement. Even if some may worry about discrepancies with the over-all mission of the organization, if people express their creativity and maintain customer orientation, I am certain that each mini-company's mission will be closely linked to the overall mission. At the very least, it will provide a basis of discussion for working out any discrepancies.

Exhibit 3.8 gives examples of mission statements and mini-company names developed by groups of people from different companies. As you may notice, these mission statements are presented in different ways. The first statement by the production department turned out to be a long sentence that its supervisors required many hours to develop. It also reflects the difficult process of integrating many people's opinions. However, when finished, the department members all signed their names and hurried out to the shop floor to explain their thoughts and ask for the operators' comments. (The total number of people in this department was almost a thousand).

The accounting department came up with a mini-company name, Baxter Accounting Service, that people could relate to—perhaps reflecting the intention of providing a personalized service. The quality assurance department made their point with humor: "Quality Makes Cents, Inc." In the case of the warehouse operation, the name "Material Movers, Inc." symbolizes people's intention to practice just-in-time production, instead of being tied to the typical notion of warehouses as storage facilities. As indicated by these examples, creating a company name often gives people a sense of identity,

Exhibit 3.8. Examples of Mini-Companies' Mission Statements

Establish and support a managerial process that will lend itself to ongoing improvement in our ability to make a profit by:

(1) increasing our knowledge and skill level, along with our understanding of the business, as it exists in today's global market, to

(2) bring about committed and involved employees that will appreciate being armed with tools and skills necessary to reduce variation, solve and exterminate problems, and overcome obstacles as they arise, while

(3) always holding at the very core of their "decision-making process" our operational expense, inventory, and throughput, and

(4) being equally concerned in meeting every need of our customer, especially in the area of Quality, Cost, and Delivery, which

(5) will result in the proper allocation of our resources and our enjoyment from long-term viability.

> —"G.B. Company"
> (Production department
> of a Midwestern automobile supplier)

Establish sound accounting control over the activities of the operation while providing strong financial leadership/guidance to the operating management team.

> —Baxter Accounting Service
> (Accounting department
> of a Midwestern automobile supplier)

Implement total quality improvement program.

> —Quality Makes Cents, Inc.
> (Quality assurance department
> of an aerospace and defense
> contractor)

Continually enhance the process of receiving, stocking, and issuing material in a timely manner and improve inventory accuracy.

> —Material Movers, Inc.
> (Warehouse operation of a hi-tech
> electronics company)

We at the Shipping Company, Inc. are committed to high quality shipment with no product damage or shipping errors for our customer satisfaction.

> —Shipping Company, Inc.
> (Shipping department
> of a household appliance company)

makes everyone in the mini-company more goal oriented, and allows them to develop greater ownership and pride in what they do.

The case of the small appliance manufacturer's shipping department warrants special recognition. We should note that this succinct statement was developed by immigrants who had limited formal education or knowledge of the English language.

As for specific approaches to developing a mission statement and assuring that it is carried out please see Appendix 3.2, which explains some techniques used to collect people's opinions and how the mission is developed and shared with people. While the case example is for a medium-sized plant in the United Kingdom, we should be able to apply a similar process to any mini-company situation as well.

Even though coming up with a mission statement and a mini-company name may take some time, these exercises should be meaningful for the people in the organization, in creating an opportunity to relate to each other while expressing their shared vision. Especially when very little teamwork is yet developed in the group, these exercises can help break the ice so that people will communicate better and accomplish tasks as a team.

BENEFITS OF MINI-COMPANIES

If we understand the mission, what we are to do and why, and if we try to live with the mission in mind, our behavior should change accordingly. In some factories, there are still people who stop work immediately when the bell rings even if they are in the middle of screwing a bolt on a car. What may happen is that the next shift will start their work without completing work on the bolt.

Of course, such behavior is very questionable. Yet it is understandable when industrial engineers design jobs or supervisors demand that people simply follow instructions without explaining the reasons why. Subsequently, people develop the attitude of "This is my work and that is your work" without thinking about *why* they are doing their work. Then, people's creativity suffers and their care for the customers is lost.

But if people learn the reason for tightening the bolt, they can begin to explore their unrealized potential. They may learn why such bolts are so important when they study their function, and they may even come up with better ways of tightening bolts or may even eliminate the need for bolts by new tightening methods or new designs.

As shown here, if every person develops the self-expression necessary to accomplish our mission, we may be able to tap the unknown potential of people.

While implementing the mini-company concept is something every person should be doing as a part of his or her job responsibility anyway, if we can go through this exercise with the majority of the people in the organization, then many benefits will be realized. (See Exhibit 3.9.)

It may be noted here that often young minds or individuals with

Exhibit 3.9 Benefits of Running a Mini-Company

- People develop a *sense of ownership.*
- By focusing on certain subjects as a group, people learn to *work as a team* effectively.
- Developing a mission, customer-supplier relationship chart, etc. will help people to *focus on clear objectives.*
- By practicing customer orientation and sharing the process of developing a business plan and progress report, *barriers will be reduced* between units of organizations.
- Business plan and progress report exercises will help *clarify the management process* for everybody.
- By sharing these processes as a group, people can *check and balance* the process easily.
- By putting things on paper, more things will be clarified to *develop enhanced commitment* from everybody.
- By having the mini-company focus on customer orientation, *cross-functional linkages* will be enhanced.
- As more checks and balances are done, there will be *less redundant effort.*
- By having many people go through this process, more weaknesses will be exposed, thereby *identifying areas for improvement.*
- As the steps are simple and easy to understand, most people will be able to *participate* with little difficulty.
- As each mini-company's plans and progress are shared, the total organization can more easily develop *goal congruence.*
- As this exercise can be done without anyone imposing it, it helps to *reduce fear.*
- As the mini-company framework is the same at all levels, a comprehensive management framework is developed *tying the lowest level of the organization to the highest level.*
- As the business plan and annual report represent each mini-company president's efforts, these documents describe the essence of how things are managed.
- Consequently, these documents will be used for *career appraisal* or for further advancement.

entrepreneurial spirit who have engaged in these mini-company exercises can bring fresh insights and offer tremendous potential to the company.

To see how we practice such an idea as we proceed, let us ask ourselves the following questions:

1. How often do we meet to share the progress of the operation with the investors/bankers?
2. What is the mechanism for developing a business plan and approving the funds to run the mini-company?
3. Do we have the equivalent of an annual report to summarize the performance of our operation?
4. Is the management system clear to everyone, allowing everyone to participate?

Since people may be interested in promotions or in starting their own businesses at some time in the future, we should remind ourselves that understanding and practicing the mini-company concept should give us a head start in becoming good managers, presidents, or community leaders.

GLASS WALL MANAGEMENT

Even if the idea is understood, running mini-companies in an isolated setting is not good enough. The company needs to find ways to further tie people's creative resources together. One approach Konosuke Matsushita proposed is the idea of glass wall management. (Note: The literal translation is glass window management.) Here, "glass wall" indicates open communication throughout the company. His belief is that if pertinent information is shared with everybody, all people in the company can participate in managing the company collectively. (See Exhibit 3.10.)

The key characteristics of Glass Wall Management include:

• It is consciousness-driven.

• Everything is aboveboard.

• Progress is shared.

• A free market system is practiced within the company.

Exhibit 3.10. Making the Management Process Visible to Everybody (Glass Wall Management)

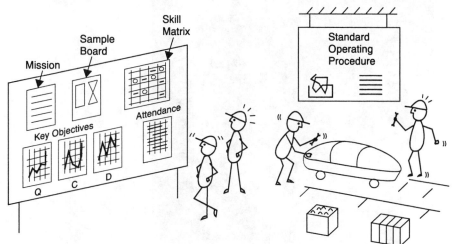

This idea sounds simple, yet Matsushita's genius was founded on practicing the idea to the fullest potential in his company. From sharing key management information to displaying the process sheets, or from posting sample products to showing recent customer returns at the shop floor—good or bad, all relevant information was shared so that everybody understood the situation.

In Exhibit 3.11 information on quality, cost, and delivery are posted on the shop floor with their breakdowns by department and project. Furthermore, once a month the plant manager conducts a meeting with all employees in front of this display to share the state of business, key concerns, and future prospects.

In order to clarify the point, let us next compare glass wall management, a progressive management style, to what I call a black box (or brick wall) management—the traditional style (see Exhibit 3.12). Please note, however, that the exhibit may exaggerate differences between the two styles of management in order to distinguish between the two.

As shown in the exhibit, there are fundamental differences between these two management styles. One is very power and hierarchy oriented, while the other is more democratic. If we were to make our organization more people-oriented, however, we should clarify what we do, better organize our work area, and make the management process visible. For this to happen, our shop floor should be self-

Exhibit 3.11. Key Management Information Shared in the Factory

Courtesy Matsushita

explanatory so that people can be involved and their self-managing skills promoted.

EVEN A STRANGER SHOULD UNDERSTAND
OUR SHOP FLOOR ACTIVITIES: A STRANGER THEORY

To evaluate how we practice glass wall management, one criterion I recommend is to check if our shop floor can answer all key questions in such a way that even a stranger unfamiliar with the organization can understand the nature of shop floor activities as well as their relationship to the total business. There should be a place for every-

Exhibit 3.12. Comparison between Black Box Management
and Glass Wall Management

	Black Box Management (traditional companies)	**Glass Wall Management** (progressive companies)
Top Management	• Work hard to manage • Tough evaluation from investors but usually paid well • Try to outsmart competitors by ability at the top • Results oriented • Short-term oriented • Use people as extensions of machines; layoffs are common	• Work hard to lead, guide, and coordinate • Share destiny with investors, suppliers, and people • Try to win competition by using the creativity of everybody in the company • Results- and process-oriented • Long-term oriented • View people as sources of creativity, share burden in hard times
Middle Management/ Staff	• Specialize in certain field, tend to have narrower view • Do not share knowledge • Do not help others; do not get help from others • Direct people to get things done • Enjoy solving problems without interacting with others • Protect the current job from others	• Experienced in various fields, tend to have broader view • Share knowledge, ideas, experience • Help others; get help from others • Lead, guide, empower people to get things done • Enjoy solving problems through interaction with others • Try to eliminate the current job in order to do more important job
People at the Shop Floor	• Not asked to use brains • Not encouraged to upgrade skills • No ownership of what they do • Do not control their destinies • Creativity is hidden • Small share of contribution to the success of the company	• Encouraged to use brains • Need to continuously learn more advanced skills • Have ownership of what they do • Try to control their destiny • Creativity is exposed • Large share of contribution to the success of the company

(continued)

Exhibit 3.12. Continued

	Black Box Management (traditional companies)	Glass Wall Management (progressive companies)
Investors	• Making money and growing the company do not have to be correlated • Push top management • No moral responsibility to people • Have a short-term view of making money	• Large shareholders want to grow with the company • Work with top management where meaningful • Moral responsibility to people by large share-holders • Large shareholders have a long-term view of making money through building business
Mentality Common to All Stake-holders	• Unique/special skills are the way to survive; sharing of skills is not a high priority • Results oriented • Short-term oriented (making money is an end unto itself) • Pay counts as a large part of job satisfaction • People need to take care of their own future by themselves • More materialistic	• Unique skills are the way to survive, but sharing of skills among people is crucial • Results and process oriented • Long-term oriented (make people before making products; make right products before making money) • Pay is a part of job satisfaction • People need to take care of their own future by themselves, but collectively they can help each other • More humanistic
Use of Management Tools	• Most techniques, such as just-in-time or total quality management, are for specialists to practice • People are not integrated as key contributors in the use of these tools • There is little effort to involve shop floor people, e.g. sharing of management information • All activities are hidden, not easy to tell what is going on especially at the shop floor	• Techniques such as just-in-time and total quality management are internalized by people • People are integrated as key contributors in using these tools • There is a great effort to involve shop floor people, e.g. different avenues for people to participate • Goals and approaches to accomplish goals are openly shared, easy to tell what is going on

thing with everything in its place—marked, labeled, and organized. Not just materials, machines, parts, and the like, but also information should be organized, including such items as work procedures, customer-supplier relationships, and key management indices.

Often, visitors may ask "Where does this part go next?" "Are these defects?" "Are you ahead of schedule or behind schedule?" "What are examples of improvement?" "How many suggestions have been generated this month?" or "What are the quality control procedures?" Or others may ask, "Is key information always attached to the materials or machines" or "Do people understand why they are doing this work?"

The point is, rather than finding someone to answer each question as it is raised, the answer should be self-explanatory even to strangers by good organization of workplace or through effective display of information. And if we practice this idea, our shop floor will be much more people friendly, enabling us to utilize the talents of people at the shop floor to address these key concerns right then and there.

In other words, if we can practice good glass wall management, we will utilize the collective wisdom of people better, and vice versa. If we are too busy taking care of our own urgent tasks, however, we may not think like this. But we should make an extra effort to address these concerns because practicing these ideas should reflect our concern for customers and our own people.

CHANGING ROLES AND RESPONSIBILITIES

The mini-company idea relates to self-management in that it views every person as the president of his or her area of responsibility. Instead of being managed, we want everyone to manage to the best of his or her ability. Instead of not being informed, everyone of us should be able to respond to such questions as (1) What is the mission? (2) What are the problems? and (3) What are the processes of addressing the problem?

Yet some of us may still say "Just tell me what to do," as opposed to taking initiative. Some bosses may still take the attitude "Just do what I say," as opposed to seeking the potential in subordinates. The question is, if we continue such attitudes, how can we create our future?

As in Exhibit 2.4, which compared local and total optimization for different job functions, we can develop a similar idea in a model representing a vertical view of the organization (Exhibit 3.13). Here, levels A, B, and C represent top management, middle management, and employees. The linkage mechanism in the model on the right represents glass wall management in action. Also, we should recognize that holding daily meetings at the floor, posting a clear standard operating procedure, sharing key management information by the use of what I call "scoreboard," or using management techniques called policy management (see Chapter 10) are important in reducing the boundary problems that are apparent in the model on the left. Furthermore, the mini-company concept will play a major role in clarifying the management reporting mechanism to help move the organization from the left to the right. (Also, see Exhibit 3.14.)

While we may understand this in concept, changing our mental attitude to practice these ideas is not necessarily easy, especially when we have habits that have developed over time. Yet, there is a saying: "If we do what we've always done, we will get what we've always

Exhibit 3.13. A Comparison of Local to Total Optimization (Vertical View)

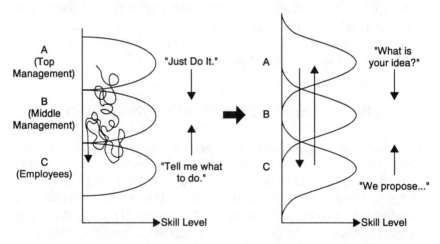

Each level of the organization is focused on its own interest. Skills are possessed in a narrowly defined area of responsibility. Flow of information is not streamlined.

Different levels of the organization share information. More understanding and coordination develops among people. Flow of information is streamlined.

Note: Goal–oriented organization requires both linkage mechanisms and people's initiative to participate.

Exhibit 3.14. Mini-Company President and His Scoreboard. The supervisor's smile in the picture indicates his confidence in managing his mini-company. His scoreboard must be showing good progress while his people are working together to accomplish the mission of this mini-company.

Courtesy Aisin Seiki

gotten.'' Where possible, we need to start to practice even one small step at a time. As in learning a team sport, the more we exercise, the better we will become.

The business situation may change. Management may change. New formidable competitors may emerge. Yet, people's mindsets often do not change as easily. Such are the barriers to overcome. The important question, therefore, is, "What can we do to control our destiny?" In order for us to develop the capability to adjust the sails to get where we want to go, even if we cannot change the direction of the wind, let us continue to explore what we *can* do in the remaining part of this book.

SUMMARY

- Because people within the organization are viewed as customers from management's viewpoint, a customer-oriented organization should be people-oriented.

- We need to address problems at the source in order to move forward. Managers need to subscribe to the idea of "making people before making products" for an organization to grow.
- Every person in the organization may be viewed as the president of his or her area of responsibility, and must deal with customers, suppliers, employees, and bankers in running his or her mini-company.
- Reflecting changes in business, the traditional view of roles and responsibilities needs to be changed drastically in order to transform the organization into one that better fits today's business needs.
- To develop ownership in people and for them to be more customer-oriented, every unit of the company should practice the mini-company idea. People can develop their own business plan, execute that plan, and report to their boss (banker) with annual reports, etc.
- Mini-companies may be established at all levels of the organization as everybody has customers, suppliers, bankers, and employees. For operators, their employees may be their tools, machines, systems, etc.
- The mission of an organization represents life, willpower, or creativity. We need to respect and use such intrinsic values as the basis of running our company.
- Starting with the development of a mission statement and a mini-company name, setting up a mini-company will not only help individuals to have more self-esteem, but also will help companies address the problems at the source with highly motivated people.
- There is a greater need for people to coordinate their work among themselves. Our traditional chain of command may need to be modified to allow a smoother flow of information.
- By practicing "glass wall management" and sharing key management activities with people, we can clarify many things. This enables organizations to better utilize the collective wisdom of people.
- Activity on the shop floor should be self-explanatory even for visitors who are unfamiliar with the situation. This is a good indicator to assess the level of people's involvement in any organization.

Chapter Four

INVOLVING EVERYBODY IN THE PROCESS OF CONTINUOUS IMPROVEMENT

Having studied shop floor management in relation to customer orientation and the mini-company concept, in this chapter we will look more specifically at how an organization can continuously improve its performance with everybody involved.

First, we will see how an organization can advance itself by addressing its needs continuously. Then, we will discuss ways to accomplish our mission by defining the game we play at the shop floor. Next, we will study the process of continuous improvement, emphasizing setting and practicing standards.

SURVIVAL OF THE FITTEST

Our business world is similar to the natural world in that survival of the fittest is the name of the game. When we study the evolutionary process of different species, we find that certain species have adapted to environmental changes better than others. Interestingly, for example, cockroaches have adapted to changes continuously over millions of years, surviving not only climatic changes but also the introduction of modern insecticides. In contrast, the dinosaurs could not cope with sudden climatic changes.

In the business world, too, a company needs to adapt to changes in order to survive. Governed by the law of survival of the fittest as practiced in our free market system, the bottom line is that everybody needs to be involved in serving the customer better with minimum waste.

As soon as we are born into this world, each of us brings a fundamental desire to survive. Yet, that is not the whole purpose of our lives as human-beings. According to A. H. Maslow, there exists a hierarchy of needs as shown in Exhibit 4.1. He postulated that if the needs at one level are satisfied, needs at the next level will emerge and the individual will attempt to satisfy the higher level of needs, thus continuously climbing up the ladder of needs hierarchy. Even though there may be differences because of people's personalities, this model at least, gives us an idea as to how we may behave in our daily lives.

ADDRESSING THE ORGANIZATION'S NEEDS

If individuals have such a hierarchy of needs, then what about organizations? Since an organization is a collection of individuals, it would seem to behave in a similar manner, trying to satisfy ever higher levels of needs. In other words, an organization may desire to survive, or to make money, or to try to improve and to contribute to our society. Although individuals are physically separated from each other within the organization, they do communicate among themselves verbally or visually.

If this is the case, how do we compare people in traditional and progressive organizations. If we use the brain as an analogy for the

Exhibit 4.1. Hierarchy of Needs

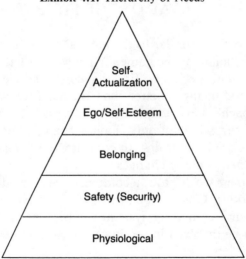

organization, the question is whether or not each brain cell is well utilized. For example, if too much energy is consumed at the top of the organization, say on external or political matters, and no attention is paid to developing the organization internally, people on the shop floor will wither away.

In contrast, if we practice glass wall management well, it is similar to developing a well-formed nervous system or neuro-network in our brain where our brain cells are actively functioning. So, if we believe in self-managed people who address problems at the source, our organization itself may be able to achieve its self-actualization by achieving its mission.

KEY POINTS FOR ORGANIZATIONAL INNOVATION

Reflecting the point above, for an organization to be innovative, we need to work on the following key points:

- Top management should clear their own minds in order to identify ways to explore the potential of people.
- There must be a change from power-oriented thinking to people- and customer-oriented thinking.
- The power base must shift from the top of the organization to a lower level (the mini-company concept), so that each decision can be made at the lowest possible level.
- Top management should help coordinate these activities and provide the necessary support.
- As each person in the organization can be considered the president of a mini-company, everybody should go through the points mentioned above by themselves as well.
- As we execute these ideas, everybody needs to try to eliminate his or her own job to create more room for growth for everybody else.

If top management fails to do this, the problems developed inside the organization may be compared to a cancer or heart defect. In other words, if the balance within the body is upset and one cannot detect the signs of disease, even nature's own defense system may not be enough to save it.

SETTING UP A SCOREBOARD:
DEFINING THE GAMES WE PLAY

If we accept the premise that everyone's involvement is essential to survive and prosper, then we need to know what role each of us must play in this game, and how to play as a team. We may also need a scoreboard to see how we are doing. In other words, if we have consolidated everybody's ideas to come up with a mission statement for our mini-company, then we should have defined the goals of the game, and hence, the scoreboard.

In fact, since we now know that customer orientation is the key to business success, and that QCDSM (quality, cost, delivery, safety, and morale) are the criteria for customer satisfaction, each mini-company should have a scoreboard to measure its progress in relation to these objectives. As much as everyone watching a sport can tell the status of the game with the aid of a scoreboard, everyone in the organization can understand the performance of his or her team by monitoring the mini-company scoreboard.

While some people would prefer not to see the scoreboard when the score is bad, their discomfort may provide the stimulation necessary for improvement. Also, a little pain early on is far preferable to a sudden big pain such as a layoff later on. Simply stated, we need to be attentive, flexible, and able to change our strategies just as members of a sports team will do to win their game.

In order to use the scoreboard effectively, however, let us remember: (1) objectives should be measurable and largely controllable by the group, (2) the number of key objectives should be manageable, e.g. five or so, (3) these specific objectives should be tied to the company's overall objectives, and (4) people should acquire tools and appropriate support to work on these objectives.

Exhibit 4.3 shows examples of QCDSM measurement as candidates for the scoreboard. Exhibits 4.4 and 4.5 show scoreboards developed by Leegin Creative Leather Products for their overall manufacturing organization and for one department within it. By clarifying these objectives, people in this company could share progress much better than before. Reflecting on the changes, a stockroom supervisor, Victor Paredes, commented,

"Before, we were like horses. We were just walking a path. We did not know if we were ahead, if we were behind, if the company was

Exhibit 4.2. Management Scoreboard on the Shop Floor

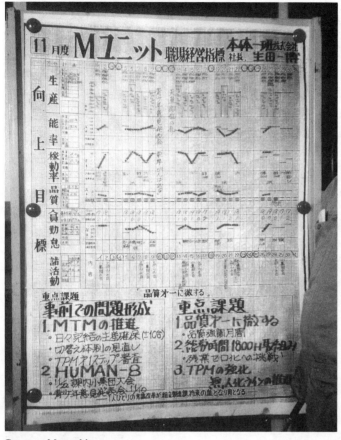

Courtesy Matsushita

Exhibit 4.3. Examples of QCDSM Measurement

Q (Quality)	Quality acceptance level, rework, number of customer complaints, defects
C (Cost)	Productivity, overtime, expenses, floor space
D (Delivery)	Conformance to schedule, lead time, volume of production, sales volume
S (Safety)	Number of accidents, number of safety related suggestions
M (Morale)	Absentee/tardy rate, turnover rate, number of suggestions

Exhibit 4.4. Scoreboard for a Manufacturing Organization

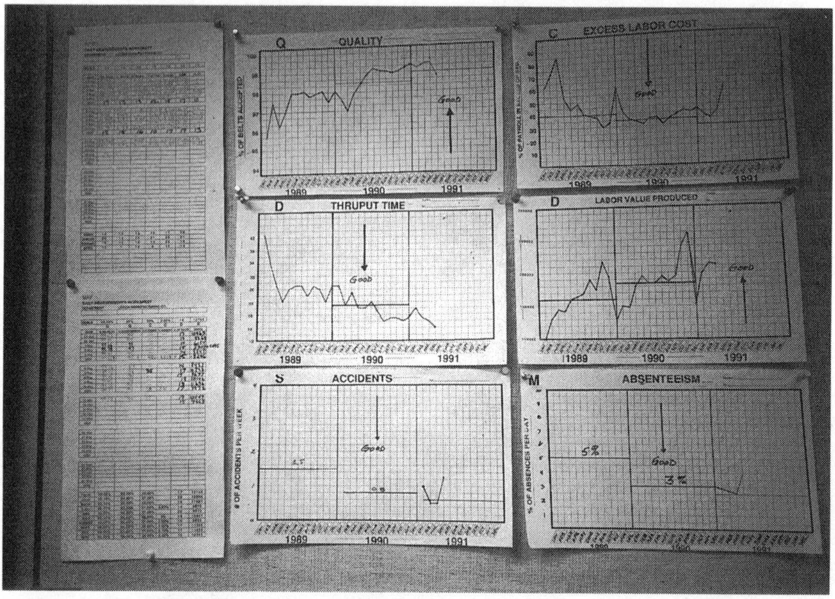

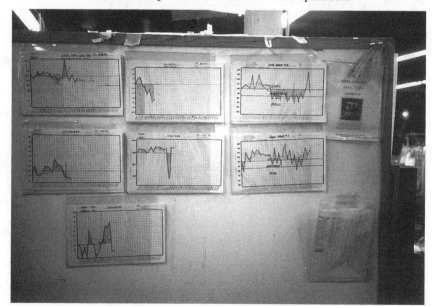

Courtesy Leegin Creative Leather Products

Exhibit 4.5. QCDSM Scoreboard for a Department

Courtesy Leegin Creative Leather Products

making money or not. We did not know anything. We just came here, we worked eight hours, and that was it.

We did not know what our goals were, what our mission was, what our objectives were. We did not know which direction we were going. Then, we started this program [Shop Floor Management], and everything has come to the surface. The top management started sharing more information with us. They got us involved. There has been a very dramatic change. Now we know where we are going, what our goals and objectives are, and what the company goals are.

—From *The New Shop Floor Management*
video education course by Kiyoshi Suzaki,
SME, 1992

Furthermore, the daily, weekly, and monthly meetings became more focused while a monthly department award based on QCDSM criteria became an important event for everybody.

DIAGNOSTIC TOOLS FOR MONITORING THE ORGANIZATION'S HEALTH

While QCDSM measurement may clarify the status of the organization, we need to further involve people and think of ways to improve. For this to happen, we also need to acquire good diagnostic tools and establish many checkpoints throughout the organization so that each of us can readily address the organization's needs.

If we pursue the idea of self-management here, rather than having someone else responsible for checking, everybody should be responsible for examining the health of his or her organization. Even though some may think there are still too many checkpoints to handle, as may be found from the many exhibits and appendices included in this book, the challenge here is to think of ways to involve many people in using these tools.

Again, since no one person can do the job by himself, we need to figure out ways to involve people to do the job, to diagnose the health of the mini-companies, and to take corrective action. To illustrate, Appendix 4.1 shows a checklist used as a diagnostic tool by Toyota to assure the basics of its Production System. We should find here that follow-up of the basics is strongly enforced by using this detailed checklist.

As we learn more about new shop floor management, we should not forget that utilizing such checklists and diligently following up the basic practices are often much more important than theoretical or abstract knowledge.

SIGNS OF SHOP FLOOR EXCELLENCE

If we envision progressive organizations having such characteristics as respect for the individual and utilization of collective wisdom what specific characteristics can we find on the shop floor? The items in Exhibit 4.6 summarize the signs of shop floor excellence:

Exhibit 4.6. Signs of Shop Floor Excellence

- *QCDSM scoreboard.*
  Whether for a whole company, a division, or a unit of an organization, we need an appropriate scoreboard to record our progress. Whether or not such a scoreboard exists or is effectively used will tell the level of people's participation in management of the shop floor.
- *Number of suggestions.*
  The number of suggestions indicates the morale of people in general, and is a measure of the total creativity of the organization. A high number typically indicates good quality, cost, delivery, and safety performance as well.
- *Absenteeism, claims, and grievances.*
  These also indicate the level of people's morale, and people's interest in their work.
- *Housekeeping and organization.*
  A disorganized workplace implies a lack of attention to the most basic point of business. How can we expect people to practice more complex tasks amidst general disorder? (Often, I explain in my talks that if we cannot accomplish this basic task it is a waste of time to talk further about more advanced techniques.)
- *Use of charts, graphs, and pictures on the shop floor.*
  Whether they are effectively displayed or not and whether they are updated or not will indicate the level of improvement orientation. (This can also be considered a part of workplace organization.)
- *Sharing information by visual aids, company newsletter, etc.*
  People's growth within the company relates to the level of stimulation they get from different means. Visual display of a colleague's accomplishment and seeing his or her name in print in newsletters or on bulletin boards may influence people's attitude and behavior about their own growth with the company. (In some cases, people may shy away from such publicity. Yet, I think these people may not be having enough success to be appreciative of such efforts. As they begin to feel more successful, and become conditioned to it, such shy feelings should fade. I encourage going over such psychological hurdles as early as possible.)
- *Meetings on the shop floor:*
  Daily, weekly, or monthly meetings will provide a setting to establish critical

Exhibit 4.6. Continued

interface with management. Furthermore, it is important to confirm strategy
as the quarterback huddles with his team during a football game. (Suprisingly,
however, I find there are still many companies all over the world that do not
have regular shop floor meetings. Many managers assume this is a waste of time.
But meetings are a means to involve people and share ideas about continuous
improvement. Even if people are unaccustomed to such practices, with proper
guidance from managers, they should learn to utilize their hidden talents better.)

- *Top management's participation in improvement sharing events.*
  Their presence and supportive comments in people's improvement-sharing
  events will send a message of orientation toward continuous improvement
  with everybody involved. If top management is concerned about the growth of
  their people, how can they not be interested in attending these events?

- *Visibility of top management on the shop floor.*
  Top management's presence on the shop floor conveys a message that the shop
  floor is the engine of the company. When people can share some of their recent
  improvements with top management, it indicates that there is a very small gap
  between top management and the shop floor. When this does not happen,
  managers may be managing the shop floor without feeling its pulse.

- *Effectiveness of education and training.*
  Instead of what some people call "The Program of the Month," where management's orientation shifts quickly from one program to another, progressive
  companies tend to have organized education and training programs that are
  closely tied with employees' growth.

- *Clarity of the management process.*
  As in the case of the glass wall management principle discussed earlier, unless
  the management process is clear to people, there is little chance for everyone
  to be involved. A good criterion again is to see if even a stranger can understand
  what is going on.

- *Use of standardized procedures.*
  The level of shop floor management is also measured by effective use of standardized procedures. Standardized procedures are appropriate not only for
  particular jobs, but also for housekeeping, organization, visual aids, meetings
  on the floor, etc.

- *Mechanism to expose problems.*
  The more advanced a company is, the more mechanisms it will have for exposing problems early. As in the case of using standards, if everybody can see
  problems at the source and has the ability to address them, then and there, the
  better the situation will be. Rather than depending on reams of computer output, and professionals or specialists, progressive companies tend to develop in-
  genious ways for exposing problems so that they can be taken care of by the
  people.

A small footnote to the points above about manual charting: Instead of having someone else
do the plotting on the chart or having a computer to do it, progressive companies tend to have
operators manually plot the data. By doing this, people "own" the information on the chart
and are able to think about it, as opposed to blindly believing the computer-generated numbers.

While we will come back and study these further, it may be meaningful to evaluate the level of our organization—our mini-company—with regard to each of the above items. Then we will see which items our organization needs to work on.

The task may seem big, but like tearing down the Berlin Wall, with adequate support from the top and people's dedication and perseverance, we can move forward one step at a time. The good news here is that we do not have to do this as individuals; we can tackle the task as a group.

PROCESS OF CONTINUOUS IMPROVEMENT

If we consider that the overall improvement activities of a company represent its total creativity, then what is the process of continuous improvement, and how can we effectively involve everyone in this process? One basic concept is the cycle described in Exhibit 4.7.

The steps are summarized as follows:

1. Study the current operation and standardize the work procedure.
2. Find the problem areas.
3. Solve the problems and develop improved methods.
4. Implement the new methods.
5. If the new methods are satisfactory, develop new work standards. Then go back to item 2 and continue the cycle.

As we find here, standardization and improvement are both critical elements for continuous improvement. Like two sides of a coin, both are needed to make continuous improvement possible.

Exhibit 4.7. Cycle of Continuous Improvement

Standardize

Implement
New Methods

Expose
Problems

Solve
Problems

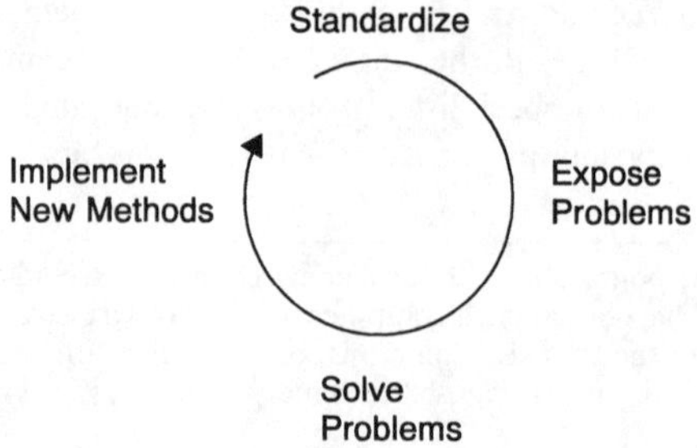

IMPROVEMENT AND STANDARDIZATION

Improvement is an activity that enhances quality, cost, delivery, safety, or morale (QCDSM). Standardization and maintenance of standards are activities to maintain the current condition, following predetermined procedures. Even though improvement may look more appealing because of its eye-catching nature, both are equally important.

As Exhibit 4.8 indicates, without maintaining standards there will be no effective improvement. In the "good" case in the exhibit, standards help to anchor or secure the position every time improvement is made so that we can move forward without regressing. The "bad" case, however, shows that if we do not have the ability to maintain standards, our time will be consumed by fire fighting or reinventing the wheel. Thus, only limited progress will be made.

Typically, companies with a long track record of improvement involve everyone in diligently maintaining standards. In fact, these companies tend to emphasize the importance of standards, update them frequently, and share good practices among all parts of the organization. Accordingly, the effectiveness of the whole organization goes up.

Let us think, for example, of a car production line where safety is of utmost concern. Now, if an operator does the job differently each time, then the cars this company makes will have different safety characteristics, most likely leading to a hazardous situation. Even when the work does not directly relate to safety or product liability, the inability to practice standardized operating procedures

Exhibit 4.8. Improvement and Standardization

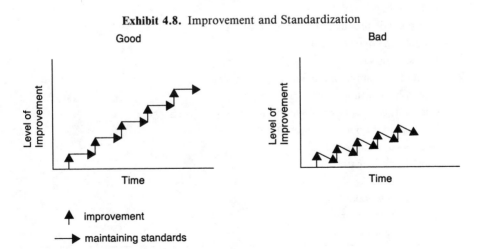

Exhibit 4.9. Objectives in Setting Standards

- Reduce variability, increase predictability
- Enhance repeatability, confidence, consistency
- Clarify procedures
- Ease of communication
- Ease of troubleshooting
- Set good discipline
- Develop awareness
- Provide basis for improvement
- Provide mechanism to expose problems
- Provide base for education and training
- Measure baseline
- Eliminate rework, rejects, safety, product liability problems, etc.

(SOP) may result in inconsistent projects, rejects, or rework. Summarizing these points, Exhibit 4.9 shows the major reasons why standards are important.

If the standards described above are so important, how can we involve everybody in practicing them? Before answering this question, we will first study some examples which fall into the broad definition of standards (Exhibit 4.10).

As these examples indicate, setting standard behavior gives

Exhibit 4.10. Examples of Standards

- Yellow lines on the floor
- Color coding
- Last piece of production left on top of die
- Production control board
- Line stop procedure
- Level of minimum and maximum inventory
- Andon light with displayed explanation
- Checklist, e.g., machine maintenance, safety, shift change, etc.
- SOP (standard operating procedure)
- Quality control process table
- Cross-training matrix
- Sample board
- QCDSM scoreboard
- Education procedure
- Improvement board

Exhibit 4.10a. Yellow Line for Better Organization

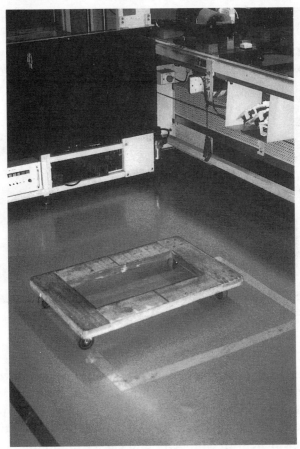

Courtesy Matsushita

Exhibit 4.10b. Use of Standard Operating Procedure (SOP)

Courtesy Matsushita

Exhibit 4.10c. First and Last Piece Inspection

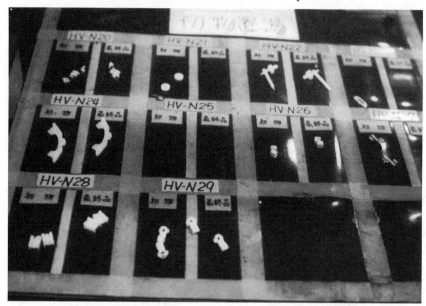

Courtesy Tokai Rika

everybody an opportunity to follow and to do the job well. In that sense, even issuing company newsletters on time should be a standard practice so that all articles are delivered on time for editing and publishing. Since complex or unclear standards tend to confuse people, we should again recognize the importance of practicing glass wall management with simplicity and clarity in mind.

PRACTICING STANDARDS

Practicing standards at work is similar to learning the basic strokes of tennis before moving to more difficult ones. Just as repetitive training is necessary to play good tennis, the same is true for practicing standards. Further, both a good coach and a player with strong initiative are prerequisites for progress.

Another analogy may also prove useful. Exhibit 4.11 compares a company's operation to a symphony orchestra. As shown in the exhibit, we may find that standards are like a musical score, helping all players to operate in harmony. In the case of the orchestra, trained ears may perceive problems immediately, such as out-of-tune

Exhibit 4.11. Comparison of Company's Operation and Orchestra

Orchestra	Company's Operation
Musician	Operator
Instruments	Machines, tools
Conductor	Leader
Scores	Standards

instruments or players who are not following the rhythm or melody as prescribed by the score. Just as musicians use their auditory impulses to help the orchestra's performance, we need to think of ways to develop a similar nervous system for our company so that problems are exposed and dealt with quickly.

While we will address ways to effectively expose problems later in Chapter 6, various approaches to practicing and reviewing standards are listed in Exhibit 4.12. Of course we need to teach people not just by visual means, but whenever there are points requiring special attention. A manager of Komatsu, Ltd. in Japan, Megumu Kubo, comments, "'If this isn't done, it creates these specific problems. In such a way, we give people immediate examples of potential

Exhibit 4.12. Practicing and Reviewing Standards

- *Visual Displays.*
  Showing good and bad practices by pictures or actual samples tends to appeal to people's conscience.
- *Education and Training.*
  Teaching people so that they understand the consequences of not following procedures. Illustrating good and bad examples is often found to be most effective.
- *Meetings.*
  Direct communication between supervisors and people on the shop floor is critical to point out the importance of following standards. Supervisors should make their points clear by using immediate examples and sound logic.
- *Slogans.*
  Putting a slogan on the wall may raise people's awareness. Better yet, these slogans may be generated from employee suggestions.
- *Awards.*
  Aiming for awards will help to focus people's efforts. Awards may range from a plant award to a presidential award, or from a supplier qualification award to a national quality award.

Exhibit 4.13. Use of Caption to Convey the Point.

The caption next to the description of the critical process reads: "This process plays a major role in assuring the safety of the product."

The caption on the standard operating procedure reads: "key points of my work."

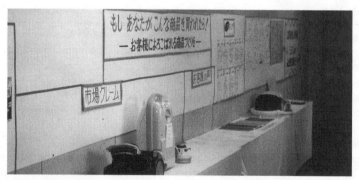

The caption next to the customer return reads: "What if you buy such a product?"

Courtesy Matsushita

defects. Upholding the standards and providing necessary guidance
. . . This is extremely important.''

Our instruction should be positive. Instead of depending on disciplinary actions to correct people's bad habits, appealing to their conscience is a healthier and often more effective way to focus people's attention on practicing standards.

As we encounter any specific learning at work, or meaningful ideas gained through books, seminars, and the like, we might remember and communicate them to others so that they can also benefit. By doing so, the organization as a whole may modify its behavior and achieve good discipline. Also, the more we talk and confirm the meaning of these experiences, the more likely the organization will be to incorporate them into its fundamental values.

As discussed in our behavioral change model in Chapter 1, we can then develop good habits as an organization even to the point that the organization's destiny may change. In other words, by sharing these stories and having people identify with the situations, these experiences are internalized as important lessons for everyone in the organization. And as the organization as a whole accumulates such learning experiences over time, its values will be strengthened.

STANDARDS REPRESENT AN ORGANIZATION'S CAPABILITIES

While we found similarities between an orchestra and our shop floor activities, there are some differences, too. For example, in the case of the orchestra, it may take time for a musician to learn to follow the score. In the case of shop floor activities, however, we should develop a standard so simple that everybody can learn it in a few days. The basic ideas are: "If it is too complex, then something is wrong (and needs improvement)," and "What students have not learned, we have not taught yet."

For an orchestra, the standards (scores) are created by the composer. In our case, however, standards are developed and then improved continuously by the operators and support staff. Of course, in traditionally run companies, standards may be developed only by engineers. In progressive companies, however, much more responsibility is given to operators to contribute their talent in developing and practicing standards as well as teaching standards to others.

Ultimately, therefore, the level of standards represents the organization's capability. While we will discuss the concept of control points in Chapter 9 in detail, here it is important to realize that control points are key parameters of a company's operations, and the total number controlled by the people in the company indicates how well the company is run. So, just as airplane pilots check gauges that indicate critical parameters of flight, control points are indicators of the health of the organization, representing the level of standards.

So the more capability people develop, the more standards and control points they will be in charge of. Therefore, the number of control points should be represented in a similar profile to the skills profile for traditional and progressive organizations shown in Exhibit 1.8.

What this means then is that standards, control points, objectives, and the mission of the organization are all interrelated (see Exhibit 4.14a and 4.14b). As shown in Exhibit 4.14a, shop floor standards must be maintained and upgraded to achieve the desired level of control points. Then, control points are closely related to objectives, and objectives are tied to achieving the organization's mission. Also, striving to accomplish the mission, business plans are developed and executed accordingly. Thus, these represent a cause-and-effect relationship in managing the company to accomplish its mission.

Investigating this relationship more closely, if we incorporate the mini-company, improvement projects, and the job of each operator into this picture, their interrelationship may be represented as shown in Exhibit 4.14b. Here, we see the company's management framework from a hierarchical point of view—i.e., company, mini-company, project, work station—as well as from the management process's point of view—i.e., mission, control points, and business plan. Arrows indicate interrelationships among them. Of course, a mission will give us a direction, objectives, and control points; standards will give us specific focus and measurements; and business plans will give us strategies to achieve objectives. The point here is that all of these need to be linked together to produce a maximum result. Without enhancing the level of standards at the shop floor, the potential to accomplish the mission will be limited.

Since management of the continuous improvement processes relates to going through the plan-do-check-act cycle (planning, executing the plan, checking its effectiveness, and acting upon the result to standardize and/or further improve the process), we need to go through this cycle at each level shown in Exhibit 4.14a and 4.14b. In other words, we need to go through the cycle for reviewing mission,

Exhibit 4.14a. Relationship Among Standards, Control Points, Objectives, and Mission of Organization

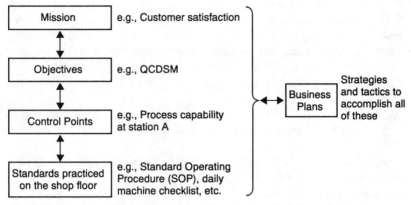

Exhibit 4.14b. Relationship Among Standards, Conrol Points, Objectives, and Mission Across the Company

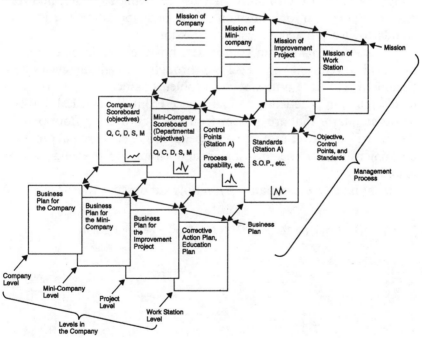

Exhibit 4.15. Practicing Standards in the Traditional Organization

- There are no clear standards.
- Even if there are standards, the description of standards is not clear to everybody.
- There is no clear relationship between operating procedures and their impact on quality, cost, delivery, safety and morale.
- The standards have too many parameters, i.e., key parameters are not clearly defined.
- Standards that describe the steps of operation are meaningful only for operators who are new to the process, but are not used as a base for continuous improvement.
- Standards are tied to performance incentives, yet since they are narrowly defined, people tend to manipulate the system.
- There are general standards but it is not clear who does what.

objectives, control points, and standards at each level of the company. We should then realize that by clarifying such a framework and involving everyone in maintaining and upgrading the level of standards, we can accomplish our mission.

Compared to well-run companies, however, traditional companies tend to reinvent the wheel, go through fire-fighting cycles continuously, and have a number of problems associated with the lack of discipline in practicing standards (see Exhibit 4.15). Exhibit 4.16 shows standards that are unclear from the view of shop floor people. As shown here, after realizing that people were confused about critical dimensions of the drawing, a new simplified drawing was released.

In a Japanese company, by simply addressing the problem of

Exhibit 4.16. Standards Need to Be People Friendly

Before   After

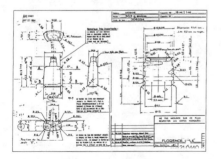
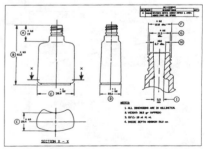

unclear standards and involving operators, the defect rate of fine chemical products went down from about 10 percent to 1 percent in a matter of several months. In a Midwestern medical equipment company, as people began to develop specific standard operating procedures for running machines, they found that capacity of an expensive machine tripled.

Of course, we may have developed a habit of trying to solve problems from the office. But, as these examples indicate, those who have focused on working on specific problems and facing reality (genjitsu) at the shop floor have benefited tremendously.

USE OF STANDARD OPERATING PROCEDURE TO CONTROL THE POINT OF ACTION

The point is, if everybody is trained to look closely at the critical point of action where ultimate value is added, we may realize huge benefits. In order to understand this better, let us see in detail how standard operating procedures (SOP) may be used to achieve such gains.

The purpose of using SOP is to achieve the highest value-adding work by combining man, machine, and material in the most effective method so that we can make quality products, at low cost, on time, safely, and without overburdening the operator. Or, SOP should aim for eliminating waste, reducing fluctuation, and eliminating overburden. Accordingly, SOP should represent a basic rule that everybody has to follow in making a product or providing a service.

In order for each individual to utilize SOP well, however, several key criteria must be met:

- SOP focuses on operator's movement.
- SOP applies to repetitive operation (whether once a minute or once a month).
- SOP is created on the shop floor.
- SOP is developed by operators where possible.
- SOP is to be improved/modified continuously.

As an example, Exhibit 4.17 illustrates SOP as practiced at Mazda. Here, the major features of this SOP are that it includes information such as:

- Cycle time (time between completion of the last product and completion of the next product)

Exhibit 4.17. Example of Standard Operating Procedure

PROGRAMMED OPERATION CHART	Process	*Interior Sealing*	Model Type	*P045 4Dr*	Standard Stock in Process	●	Protector		Mo. XXX Date		P.I.C.		Chart No.	
	Station	*8st.*	Cycle Time	*0.94*		*1 unit*							Date Issued	
			Operation Time	*0.93*									Leader	

Operation Content	Operation Content	Operation Content	Operation Content
1	**2**	**3**	**4**
Take Hole-Covers.	*Confirm the Broad-Cast table.*	*Set Hole-Cover.*	*Apply sealer.*
Mark	Time *0.02*	Mark	Time *0.02*	Mark	Time *0.03*	Mark	Time *0.07*
5	**6**	**7**	**8**
Apply sealer.	*Apply sealer.*	*Open the Rear Door.*	*Apply sealer.*
Mark	Time *0.09*	Mark	Time *0.08*	Mark ✚	Time *0.04*	Mark	Time *0.17*
9	**10**	**11**	**12**
Apply sealer.		*Apply sealer.*	*Go back to the start.*
Mark	Time *0.06*	Mark	Time *0.02*	Mark ◇	Time *0.31*	Mark	Time *0.02*
13	**14**	**Regular Operation**	**Motion Chart**
		Mark of Key Operation	Quality ◇	Safety ✚	
Mark	Time	Mark	Time		Mark	Time

Courtesy Mazda

108

- Net working time
- Number of in-process inventory
- Protection devices, e.g., helmet, gloves, eyeglasses, earplugs
- Date issued, date revised
- Content of operation
    - Description of operation (one motion, one step), e.g., apply sealer
    - Time required to finish each operation
    - Cartoon describing the nature of job
- Motion chart to describe the sequence of motion with brief layout
- Key quality and safety areas marked

By using cartoons, the instruction aims to achieve QCDSM goals in a people-friendly manner.

DEVELOPING STANDARD OPERATING PROCEDURES

In order to describe an operation in a concise manner, the following basic rules should be followed:

Exhibit 4.18. SOP at Glass Master Control

PAGE NO.: 1.
PART NAME: 3A4534 Lever Line
OPERATION NAME: Spotweld Pin to Bracket
WRITTEN BY: Mary Key Ganger

Note: 15 minutes before beginning process, put knobs in knob heater and turn on the heat stamper.

NO.	OPERATIONS ANALYSIS	NO.	MAIN STEP	QTY.	SFTY	EASE	KEY POINT	ILLUSTRATIVE DESCRIPTION (REASON FOR VITAL POINT PREP & CHANGE OF JIG & TOOL, COMB OF PROC., DIMENSION, ETC.)
	Work Station Set Up: -Brackets to the right in box. -Pins to the right in bread pan.		Work Station Set Up				-brackets right -pins to the right	
1.	Pick up bracket out of the box using right hand. Use left hand to help unhook the other brackets if necessary. Position bracket so ridge is protruding from the flat plate on the top. Bent edge should be bent downward. Grasp the top and bottom edges of the protruding wings with left and right hands. This will position bracket correctly for inserting into press. (the large flat portion in horizontal plane with bend facing toward your body) Place bracket on the bottom die of the press. Hooks on the left side of bracket will fit into openings of the die and front bend will be flush with front of die. Make sure holes are lined up to correspond with those in the die.	1.	Get brackte with left hand and position in die.					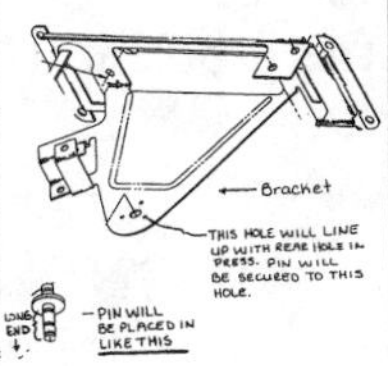
2.	With right thumb and forefinger grab the edges of the collar pin and place into the hole in the top of the bracket. The long end of the pin must point downward.	2.	Place collar pin in the bracket.					
3.	At the same time reach up with your left hand and grasp the guard. As soon as the pin is in place and right hand is out of the way, pull guard down over the bracket. This will automatically trip the spotwelder & seed the collar pin into place.	3.	Pull guard over bracket with left hand to activate spotwelder.				3. This is an automatic trip device and should be used wiht caution.	
4.	Remove bracket from the welder by grasping left hand and place to the left on cardboard to cool. Pick up 8 more out of box to get ready for welding	4.	Remove bracket from the welder by grasping left hand and place to the left on cardboard to cool.				4. This will leave right hand open for grasping new bracket.	
5.	When cardboard piece is full, gently place the welded bracktes into the large box to the left. Allow for all parts to cool 5 minutes before proceeding. Do several of these as needed for complete job. Wheel cart around to left side of lever & spring clip assy. area.	5.	Place brackets in pan and allow to cool for 5 minutes before using.	X			5. Box to the left.	

Courtesy Glass Master Control

- One motion, one step
- Start the sentence with verb, e.g., "locate a hole cover"
- Write detailed descriptions for critical areas of operation, e.g., "locate a cover, take cover, confirm label, set cover, apply sealer," etc.
- After a detailed description is completed, summarize into key points of operation as appropriate

In order to practice SOP effectively, the following considerations should be made:

- SOP should be displayed where the action is, not in the drawer of the engineer's desk
- By comparing prescribed work to actual work, we can expose problems to be resolved. Differences indicate that there are problems such as waste, unevenness, or overburden of work. Another way to state this is:

Problem = Planned Performance − Actual Performance

- SOP is like a mirror in which we see ourselves. If there are no changes in SOP for a long time, then, it means no improvement has been made.
- SOP should be used to train employees.
- When there are problems in the areas of QCDSM, SOP may be reviewed to address the real cause of the problem.

In other words, after checking the difference between target and actual performance in QCDSM, we should go back to SOP to correct the problem. (For more details of SOP, see Appendix 4.2.)

MAINTAINING STANDARDS WITH EVERYBODY INVOLVED: A WOODEN PAIL THEORY

To show that no major improvement can be accomplished without maintaining proper standards, Exhibit 4.19 illustrates the wooden pail theory. As much as finding a leak in the pail is important to keep from losing water, we need to figure out a good mechanism to

Exhibit 4.19. Wooden Pail Theory

Bad
Wooden Pail

Good
Wooden Pail

Just as most water runs out of
the pail, if certain standards are
not practiced, the linkages that
are necessary to tie operations
together will be broken.

As most water is retained in the
pail, good maintenance of
standards further builds people's
capability to help the organization
move forward.

maintain standards and build upon it. Again, we should find that standardization and improvement are inseparable.

Furthermore, just as housekeeping in our workplace or maintaining city streets requires everybody's cooperation to practice the basic standards, whether or not one can practice certain standards ultimately reflects the value of each person, which in turn reflects the values of the organization. Only when these standards, mechanisms to practice and upgrade standards, and people's skills are integrated can we progress further.

GUIDING IMPROVEMENT ACTIVITY FROM THE TOP

Using standards and involving everybody as a base, top management may establish the cycle shown in Exhibit 4.20 to develop company-wide improvement activities.

The shop floor is where theories and reality collide. No matter how much knowledge we may have acquired, without proper discipline, nothing can get done in reality. In order to promote the cycle of continuous improvement, therefore, managers need to have hands-on experience to understand the minds of people.

Exhibit 4.20. Guiding the Cycle of Continuous Improvement

Providing Tools
for Improvement

Providing
Adequate
Feedback

Providing an
Atmosphere
that Fosters
Improvement

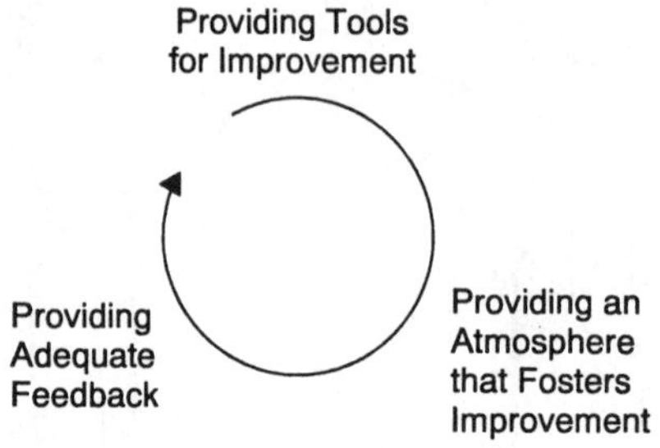

As improvements are made and appropriate feedback given, we can start to involve more people and provide more tools for making further improvement. In this process, however, some people see middle management as a wall or barrier to improvement. Yet if managers see themselves as presidents of their own mini-companies, they should guide the cycle of continuous improvement in their own areas of responsibility.

As these mini-company presidents succeed in running their businesses, they should try to eliminate their jobs, standardize and delegate jobs to subordinates, and open up the time to explore more important responsibilities as opposed to trying to hang on to their current positions indefinitely. Isn't this essentially what happens to all companies that prosper?

If we subscribe to the mini-company concept, the idea applies to everybody. So, following this self-managing idea, we must find the answers by ourselves, as opposed to waiting for (unfavorable) answers from someone else.

COMMUNICATING THE BASICS
OF THE MINI-COMPANY

As we realize the importance of shop floor management, we find that summarizing the essence of information and sharing it effectively with people are important jobs especially for those in management positions. In order to convey the basics of the mini-company to promote continuous improvement with everybody involved, a one-page display such as that shown in Exhibit 4.21 may be posted on the shop floor and explained to people.

Exhibit 4.21. Basics of Mini-Company

In conducting our jobs, we understand that each of us has customers, suppliers, bankers, and employees to work with. So, each of us may be considered as the president of our company.

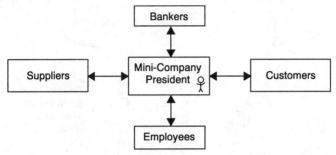

If we think of our supervisor as the president of our mini-company, we will work on the following basic points collectively:

- We have a mission for our mini-company.
- We have specific objectives (QCDSM) in order to accomplish our mission.
- We monitor progress of our performance on our scoreboard.
- We conduct regular meetings at work to share the progress.
- We develop a plan of action to achieve our objectives.
- We share our accomplishments in the workplace.
- We make presentations or report progress to bankers or peers as appropriate.
- We upgrade our skills and work together, collecting wisdom from everybody.
- We share progress in the annual report of our mini-company.
- We practice the PDCA cycle of continuous improvement to move forward.

SUMMARY

- Our business world is similar to the natural world in that survival of the fittest is the name of the game. The bottom line is, we need to involve everyone to serve the customer better with minimum waste.
- In order to prosper in today's business environment, we need to transform our organization from a traditional to a more progressive one. As much as individuals seek to satisfy their needs from a lower level (i.e., physiological needs), to a higher level (i.e., self-actualization), the organization as a whole may accomplish the same, thereby reflecting people's values.
- As we encourage everyone to be involved in the process of continuous improvement, each employee should take initiative without waiting for someone to do the work for him.
- If we define the work clearly and set up a scoreboard to moni-

Exhibit 4.22. Involving Everybody in the Process of Continuous Improvement

tor how well we are doing in such measures as QCDSM (quality, cost, delivery, safety, and morale), this will help people to focus their efforts as a team.

- This transformation process may be management driven as well as employee driven. However, in order to make the transition smooth, self-managed approaches should become the cornerstone.
- From the individual's point of view, the process of continuous improvement may follow the cycle: (1) standardize, (2) expose problems, (3) solve problems, and (4) implement new method.
- The importance of standardization cannot be stressed enough. Especially when people are more interested in overnight success, yet fire fighting is common and morale is low, addressing the basics with everyone involved is critical.
- Even if we have sophisticated equipment and innovative ideas, if the basics are not covered, the organization's potential may be limited. So, let us pursue the potentials by addressing each key element of operation: man, machine, method, and material.

- Progressive companies tend to practice good discipline in following standards. Also, standards are practical, to the point, and revised frequently to reflect improvement. Without standards as a basis, improvement is difficult to make, hence, the company's mission is hard to accomplish.
- From the company's point of view, the process of company-wide improvement activities may follow the cycle: (1) providing tools for improvement, (2) providing the atmosphere to foster improvement, and (3) as improvement takes place, providing feedback so that more individuals will want to be involved.

Chapter Five

UPGRADING EVERYBODY'S SKILLS

As we pursue our vision of shop floor excellence with customer orientation while involving people, we realize that shop floor management works only when people's skills can be upgraded. Ultimately, all of us should be self-managed to get the job done. So, in this chapter, we will study how to upgrade skills, and develop a positive attitude toward continuous improvement.

MATCHING SKILLS TO THE NEEDS OF THE ORGANIZATION

Doing our work effectively and efficiently requires many different skills. Some are improvement-related or specific job-related skills, others are interpersonal or managerial skills. For us to manage ourselves better and to address problems or opportunities as they arise, we must first clarify the needs. Then, we need to strive to overcome the hurdles by educating ourselves and upgrading our skills so that we can eventually sit in the driver's seat of our destiny.

Since our performance will be considerably different depending on how much we enjoy our work, the organization's skill needs should match individual interests if at all possible. Also, following the free market system, the supply and demand of certain skills match at certain price points, hence, driving people to acquire more valuable skills. Ultimately, therefore, it is everybody's responsibility to learn more meaningful skills over time and apply them effectively.

From the organization's point of view, whether or not its people are learning new skills effectively will impact its course in business. We can hire people with needed skills from outside. Yet because our competitor can do the same, there is no competitive advantage we can create. An important question, then, is how can an organization develop skills that its competitors cannot easily match?

SKILLS FOR SELF-MANAGEMENT

In order to upgrade our self-managing skills and address problems at the source so that both individuals and the whole organization can benefit, we need to work on several different types of skills. They include:

- *Skills related to maintenance.* These are the skills to maintain standards, follow procedures correctly, and to complete the job on time without accident or defects.
- *Skills related to improvement.* These are the skills to identify problems and follow through to solve them, either individually or with a group of people.
- *Skills related to individuals.* These are analytical and workmanship skills for individuals, propelling them toward self-improvement even under difficult situations.
- *Skills related to teamwork.* These are communication and leadership skills needed to become effective team members, to contribute ideas, and to work toward accomplishing the team's mission.
- *Skills related to specific tasks.* These are technical skills requiring understanding of the specific knowledge of the job, e.g., proprietary technology, know-how, etc., required to get the job done.
- *Skills related to management.* These are managerial skills to coordinate, communicate, and cooperate with others to get the job done. Mastery of all the above skills may be needed to be truly effective.

As we see here, we need to acquire several different skills to be fully effective at work.

UPGRADING OUR SKILLS

Instead of having people with little hope for personal growth, a company needs to create its competitive advantage by practicing the idea of "making people before making products." And once people share the belief that "our potential is unlimited," such an organization can bring many challenges and growth opportunities to its people. When facing the difficulties surrounding us, however, such belief may not be easily obtained.

One experiment with fleas in a glass conveys this point. When a cover was put on top of the glass, the fleas eventually stopped jumping after hitting their heads many times. Even when the cover was taken off later, the fleas did not escape, thinking that it was useless to try any more. Contrasting this, with some experience—even if it is limited—we may be convinced that our potential is in fact great—much more than we had imagined. As obvious as it may sound, it is important to provide a supportive environment and encourage people to adopt a positive attitude, even to get out of our comfort zone. People say, "Where there's a will, there's a way." In our case, the individual's will is the driving force to accomplish our mission. Despite a lack of resources, if we are determined, we can often invent ways to overcome hurdles.

If we look back on our experiences, each of us may find certain memories supporting this point. For example, wasn't there a time when we were amazed at ourselves for accomplishing some task that seemed impossible? Maybe it was getting a job done on time, or it was even a moment of fine play in sports, or music. Or it may have been an instance of good teamwork. Whether at work or elsewhere, or whether by an individual or by a team, it is rare to find a person who has not experienced this feeling of accomplishment.

Looking back on these experiences, it seems that a key to our progress is to condition ourselves with successes and accomplishments. No matter how small they may be at the beginning, the confidence that we gain will encourage us to challenge the more difficult tasks one step at a time, just as our children do as they grow up.

Exhibit 5.1 illustrates different examples of advancing our skills. A natural way to change our behavior in a positive direction (and move on up the ladder of change described in Exhibit 1.15) is to condition ourselves to establish a basic pattern of building up our confidence so that we can further explore our potential. In a similar sense, sharing ideas and developing an open atmosphere in the group will help internalize the success of other people so that individuals as well as the organization as a whole may gain confidence and accept more challenges for further progress.

Exhibit 5.1. Building Successes

Level of Difficulty	Movement	Mathematics	Shop Floor Management
Elementary	Move body	1 and many	Housekeeping
	Crawl	1,2,3 . . .	Organization
	Walk	$1 + 1$ . . .	Follow standards
	Run	2×4 . . .	Identify problems
Intermediate	Ride a tricycle	3.141592 . . .	Practice SPC
	Drive a car	$3(X + 5Y)$	Use problem-solving
		. . .	tools with team
	Fly airplane	dx/dt . . .	Run mini-company
Advanced	Fly to the moon	$\Sigma f(\partial\mu/\partial t +$	Run company
		. . .	

GROWING WITH THE ORGANIZATION

As human beings, we bring to life our will to live and our creativity. We learned new skills in childhood as we explored numerous things. We also learned tremendously from our parents, neighbors, teachers, and playmates. Still, it seems that the core of our growth is our will and creativity. In this sense, if we truly believe our will to live is tied to our creativity, we should then realize that it is very inhuman to take the opportunity to utilize creativity away from people.

Provided with the proper environment, therefore, all of us should be able to continuously grow and upgrade our skills. After all, this transfer of skills from one generation to the next is how we have progressed as human beings.

If we agree on the need to transform the organization from a traditional one to a more progressive one, let us next understand an organization's skill requirements. Here, as Exhibit 5.2 demonstrates, the higher the skill level, the more time we typically spend in improvement or innovation-related jobs, such as development of strategy, new products, new manufacturing processes, new markets, new management processes, or upgrading organizational capabilities. Producing more and satisfying customers with fewer people will, in turn, enable more people to use their creativity and increase their abilities. If we do this well, the organization itself will become more creative and capable as a whole (see Exhibit 5.3).

Yet, to accomplish this, each of us in the organization needs to think of ways to simplify our job, or develop machines or tools to

Exhibit 5.2. Profile of Skills Used in Organization's Hierarchy

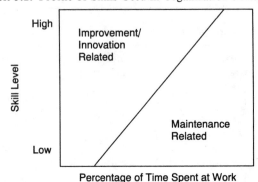

do the job. At the same time, we should be able to develop new skills that will enable us to perform more important jobs. Also as beneficiaries of those who have already contributed to the progress of our society, we need to understand that it is our responsibility to upgrade our skills and contribute to others.

PUTTING INTELLIGENCE ON THE SHOP FLOOR

What, then, can we do? As a first step, we need to clear our minds and assess the situation objectively. Even if we are in a fire-fighting mode, we still need to find time to cover the basics, organize ourselves better, and equip ourselves with fundamental skills. Whatever job we do, we need to be able to do the basics right. Starting to work on time, reading, writing, listening, speaking, and knowing arithme-

Exhibit 5.3. Upgrading Our Jobs at All Levels of the Organization

	Eliminate the Current Job by:	Create the New Job by:
Top Management	Delegation to people	Searching for new business opportunities
Middle Management	Delegation to employees	Broader responsibilities
Employees	Delegation to tools, machines, systems	Broader responsibilities
Tools, Machines, Systems, etc.	Simplification; use of new ideas, new technologies	Broader responsibilities

tic are some of the basics. Practicing workplace organization, taking care of machines and tools, and following work procedures may be the next level of prerequisite skills.

Since each individual is to do things right then and there and to self-manage, a lesson many progressive companies have learned is that their ultimate sustainable competitive advantage is their people. Machines, equipment, computers, and systems may be duplicated, but people with shared values, who work well as a team, and who are equipped with collectively upgraded skills cannot be easily duplicated or challenged by competitors.

Further, if all of the company's management is working with the idea of "making people before making products," it may even be feasible to reduce some of the problems of our society such as crime and drug abuse. After all, most people work in some type of organization. So, if their creativity is better utilized, it should be possible for people at large to benefit both as creators of products and services and as beneficiaries.

In striving to prosper in today's business, therefore, practicing self-improvement at each individual's level and managing each and every process is essential. All standards need to be followed, all checkpoints need to be verified, all processes must be under control even to the degree of retightening the bolts of machines, caring for each individual's morale, and fine-tuning the management processes.

In order to gain insight in practicing the idea of putting the intelligence where the action is, let us next closely study an example in Exhibit 5.4. The picture may not look like anything extraordinary on the surface. Yet, it illustrates several important elements of SFM.

The elements in the photograph that merit attention are numbered to correspond to the numbers below:

1. *Production control board.* Every hour, planned and actual production volumes are compared. When scheduled goals are not met, operators mark the actual number in red and write their comments in the remarks column. This helps supervisors and operators to work together in taking corrective action as needed. Though this manual method puts ownership with operators, it may also provide information that is more meaningful for supervisors than a week-old computer report. Also, this key information is posted near where the action is. (Again, the fact that the operators put the numbers, comments, or dots on the chart will make them *own*

Exhibit 5.4. Putting People's Intelligence at the Point of Action

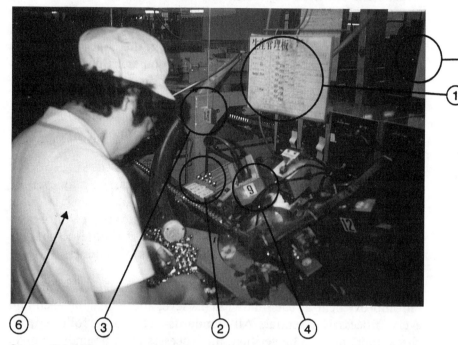

Courtesy Tokai-Rika

the process, as opposed to blindly believing the output from the computer.)

2. *Rack of defects.* As defects are found, they are categorized and put into the designated rows on the rack. This rack, then, displays the pareto chart of problems. According to the nature of defects, corrective action can be taken. This was a suggestion from an operator. (It makes sense to have a person closest to the situation make such a suggestion.)

3. *Yellow tag.* The tag that hangs down is linked with the andon (trouble light) to expose problems and to get supervisors' attention on problems. Whether the problem is related to quality, production schedule, machine, etc., the operator can pull this tag and ask for the supervisor's help by lighting up the trouble light. Of course, as more problems arise, the supervisor will be called more frequently, thus stimulating him to solve the problems. (This practice exemplifies the importance of the shop floor from the support people's viewpoint.)

4. *Maintenance checkpoint.* The numbers on the machine indi-

cate the checkpoint of machine maintenance. By clearly indicating the checkpoint, even a new employee can understand how to do the necessary maintenance, e.g., cleaning, oil lubrication. (The point is to make everything self-explanatory, practicing glass wall management.)

5. *Standard operating procedure (SOP)*. SOP is posted at each workstation. Operators are instructed to suggest ways to upgrade the SOP. The date of revision on the SOP indicates how long it has been since the last improvement was made. (Again, SOP is near where the action is.)

6. *Operating in standing position*. Before, the operator worked sitting down. Now, by changing the layout and combining the work with previous workstations, the operator is multiskilled. As a result, production is smoother and more flexible in meeting the customers' demand changes while the operator does not have much back pain, inventory is lower, and space is better utilized. (Progress depends on how much cooperation we can get from the people at the shop floor.)

Exhibit 5.5 is yet another example from a medium-sized leather belt company in the United States. Here, people from the shop floor

Exhibit 5.5. Making a Presentation on the Shop Floor

Courtesy Leegin Creative Leather Products

are making a presentation to management and their peers about their improvement. To make it interesting and easy for the audience to understand, presenters are using pictures of improved areas. After the presentation, these displays are posted in the cafeteria and hallways for everybody to see.

The first photograph was taken in 1985; the second is from 1991. Even if the time and place are different, the message is the same—if we address the problem where the action is, we are better off. The company in the first example is expanding overseas rapidly, and the second company has achieved an annual sales growth of more than 30 percent over the last four years.

While there may be no easy win in this challenge, just like trying to keep our house in order, every one of us needs to work one step at a time. Today should be better than yesterday, and tomorrow better than today. The process reminds me of learning to play baseball. First, we need to do basic exercise such as batting practice. Then we should try to hit bunts and singles in our baseball games rather than trying to hit a home run right at the beginning.

While top management may be busy in focusing their attention on corporate strategy, the skills of everyone in the organization need to be upgraded as a part of such strategy to raise the overall capability of the organization. They will then generate more strategic options for the company to choose from.

THE ROLE OF MANAGERS AND SUPPORT PEOPLE

To do this, an important role of managers and support people is to upgrade the skills of their people. Unfortunately, however, many of us do not practice or do not know how to practice this well. Some of the problems encountered by managers and staff people are listed in Exhibit 5.6.

As a result, we may not take responsibility and allocate sufficient

Exhibit 5.6. Typical Management Problems in Upgrading People's Skills

- Do not realize the importance of upgrading skills.
- Insecure about teaching new skills.
- Assume that many people are not capable of learning.
- Focus on upgrading their own skills first.
- Have not gained skills required to teach or lead people.

time for education, leaving people behind. It is understandable that we may have been influenced by traditional or autocratic bosses in the past, thereby maintaining distance in relationships with people. Yet, if we understand the need to accomplish our vision, we will be able to subscribe to the ideas presented in Exhibit 5.7.

WORKING ON IMPORTANT JOBS ONE STEP AT A TIME

Thinking of the time we spend at work, we need to remember that there are urgent jobs and important jobs. Even though urgent jobs need to be done quickly, if we work only on them, we may be near-sighted and continue to fight fires for the rest of our lives without making any fundamental improvement. In other words, if we spend time chasing fires and not upgrading our skills, our future will be quite limited.

So, we need to remember that those who are busy in firefighting will be easily lost in the turbulence. Furthermore, not just as individuals, we need to think of ways to work on the important jobs as a group as well. For example:

- We may categorize our tasks into urgent and important job categories. Then, we may check that the amount of time we spend is well balanced.
- When we think we need more time, money, staff, or tools, ask if we have learned to address the one factor that is under our control, i.e., upgrading our own ability? How have we been

Exhibit 5.7. Ideas for Managers and Staff in Upgrading People's Skills

- Think of people as customers whose skill development needs are to be satisfied. Only through them, can managers and support people get the job done.
- Develop faith that people can do a better job if they are given proper opportunities.
- Be open and friendly with people, even listening to their personal problems.
- Find good qualities in people, do not dwell on their weaknesses.
- Provide instruction with sincerity and empathy, do not just tell people what to do.
- When subordinates make mistakes, instruct them with reason. If instruction is not clear, remember "What the operators have not learned, we have not taught yet."

improving our own skills to prioritize, communicate, allocate time, and execute our job better?

- Do we experiment and try to explore our potential? If we are insecure in doing so, aren't we limiting our own potential?
- Do we see failures as setbacks or as important investments for the future? We may list a few examples of major and minor improvements, study how they happened, and learn from these experiences.

INSTRUCTING PEOPLE TO CONDUCT THE JOB—JOB TRAINING

Recognizing the importance of upgrading our skills, let us next study how we learn new skills. Here, the customer is a trainee learning new skills, the supplier is a trainer, and the process we are studying is a teaching process (see Exhibit 5.8). In effect, we go through a cycle:

1. Plan to provide training (*plan*)
2. Execute training (*do*)
3. Review how the idea is digested and practiced (*check*)
4. Share the applications of skills, and provide feedback to improve the training process and standardize it (*act*)
5. Go back to item 1 and continue the cycle. Refine the training programs.

Since this process is universal to any teaching process, the same principles apply whether we are learning jobs on the line, learning how to read, or learning problem-solving skills.

So, the principle is simple. Yet, it is execution that makes the difference. For example, if in Company A teaching a particular job or a particular problem-solving skill to a person takes three days and

Exhibit 5.8. Teaching New Skills to a Trainee

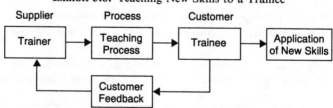

in Company B it takes three months or more, the overall difference in the organization's performance in today's fast-paced business environment can be quite enormous.

For this reason, we need to find ways to train people with less involvement of outside specialists or centralized training organizations. Rather, the training process should be simplified and done right on the shop floor.

Appendix 5.1 details the four basic steps of job training: (1) preparation, (2) explanation and demonstration, (3) execution, and (4) follow-up. Even though the instruction may seem too structured, in order to control the work at the shop floor, we need to master such training processes.

In other words, managers and support staff should go to the shop floor and practice the method of instruction as described in this Appendix by picking a process. Also, the operators in one area can practice teaching their jobs to someone from another area. Afterward, discuss what went right and wrong, and what was learned from this exercise among trainers and trainees.

ENCOURAGING PEOPLE TO UPGRADE THEIR SKILLS

As people upgrade their skills, they may find this an interesting challenge and realize that by doing so, both individuals and the whole company can progress.

While we will study how leadership and management support systems influence this process in chapters 8, 9, and 10, let us share in Exhibit 5.9 a few approaches to encourage people to upgrade their skills. (See pages 128 through 131.)

KEEPING OUR MINDS OPEN

Realizing the need for upgrading our skills continuously, let us next think about our attitude toward this challenge. As we do our jobs and gain experience over time, we tend to develop habits. This has its merits, but if we always depend on our old habits, we may not meet the stringent requirements of today's business.

We need to *see, listen,* and *learn* without prejudice. We need to be able to ask others without being embarrassed when there is something we don't know. If we are humble and open, we may even learn

Exhibit 5.9. Encouraging People to Upgrade their Skills

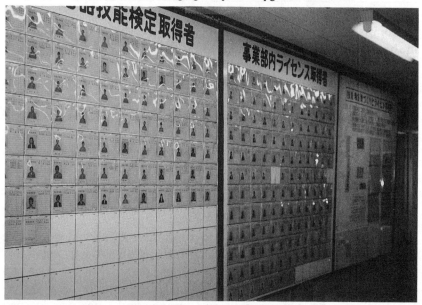

a. Skills matrix: Everybody's skill levels are posted with skills they have mastered, date mastered, and date of employment. This encourages further skill upgrade.

b. Operator's license: Each operator has a license card to conduct certain jobs. In this case, where an important product liability process needs special attention, the card is posted at the work station indicating that only the qualified operators can do this job.

Exhibit 5.9. Continued

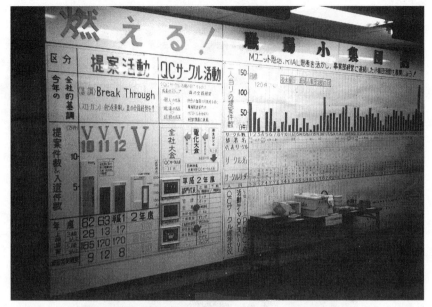

c. Suggestion board: Numbers of suggestions are posted by groups. The goal of this factory is 120 suggestions per year per person. The emphasis is on ideas that people can implement by themselves.

from three-year-old kids. Also, people may offer their ideas much more willingly.

Of course, to evaluate the situation and make a sound analysis, we still need to have knowledge as a base. But if our knowledge is superficial, then our judgment will be skewed, making it difficult to assess things properly. Therefore, it is often much better to start out with no knowledge, to look at the situation afresh and learn to use our own wisdom to the maximum.

In other words, if we face the problem squarely and if we are surrounded by people who can help us assess the situation without bias from titles or background, then we can say that we have the right open-minded posture, or genba-oriented mind, to address the problem. As a result, not only will our own lives be enriched, but the company will also benefit.

Especially because we are busy in our everyday work, we need to be careful to recognize the importance of having clear minds. Instead of being driven by momentum, we need to be able to stop and think about our work every now and then. Not only does each individual

Exhibit 5.9. Continued

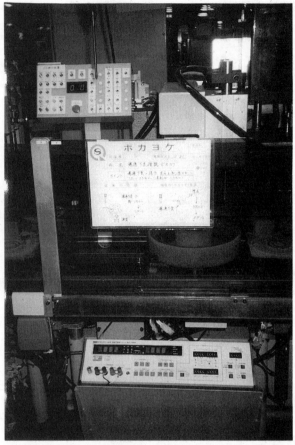

d. Posting ideas: As ideas are implemented, some are posted near the point of implementation with brief descriptions of the before and after situations so that other people can learn from them. Posting the name of the person who made the improvement gives him or her recognition.

need to practice this, but the organization as a whole needs to provide a setting to promote such behavior. (See Exhibit 5.10.)

MENTAL ATTITUDE TOWARD
CONTINUOUS IMPROVEMENT

In the process of conducting our jobs and upgrading skills, we have learned to distinguish between urgent jobs and important jobs. If we

Exhibit 5.9. Continued

e. Quality circle award: As teams make presentations and win awards, their pictures are posted on the information board in recognition of their efforts.
Courtesy Matsushita

are not careful, however, we may think that fire-fighting jobs are more important than basic improvement and maintenance activities. Even though "urgent" jobs may catch people's attention, we need to come up with a good balance. Otherwise, we may end up working on urgent jobs for the rest of our lives without making headway in any fundamental way.

Similarly, certain individuals have a tendency to look for breakthroughs while others may focus on the small steps of continuous improvement, as shown in Exhibit 5.11. Yet what we need is a good balance between breakthroughs and continuous improvement. Of course, most of us want to hit home runs when we play baseball. Or we may want to win a million dollar jackpot instead of working hard. But we should be careful not to lose our perspective as to which is the more prudent course.

To extend the analogy of practicing bunts and singles into busi-

Exhibit 5.10. Developing an Open Mind

As Individuals

- *Base our judgment on facts.* It is not necessarily bad to follow habitual ways of doing things, or proven theories and principles. But if we depend on these too much, we may not see subtle differences taking place or we may elect to ignore the facts that do not match our thinking. We should not jump to conclusions hastily.

- *Develop customer orientation.* This is easy to say but difficult to practice. For example, if we are too self-centered, we may not hear our customer's voice clearly. Thus, we need to have faith that customer orientation will work out best for us. Humbleness and selflessness will make us listen to customers without bias.

- *Use problem-solving tools.* If we are open-minded and customer oriented, we can identify problems much more readily. To solve them, we should be able to use our creativity and newly acquired skills. This is not so much a function of degrees or titles as a willingness to expand our own potential.

- *Practice the plan-do-check-act cycle.* Since we need to solve problems in order to make improvements, an important process is the plan-do-check-act cycle. We are often busy in fire fighting, but we need to learn to plan well, and conduct work as planned. Then, we need to follow through by checking results and taking proper action accordingly, e.g., standardize when things work well, or analyze problems further to correct the situation.

- *Utilize collective wisdom of people.* To achieve anything as an organization, teamwork is essential. Instead of depending on others, or focusing on self-interest, each of us needs to contribute whatever we can, and participate in management of the total organization.

As an Organization

- *Share a vision.* If a company wants to accomplish anything, it needs to share its vision with people in a way that makes it clear and understandable to everyone.

- *Deploy the vision.* Because vision by itself may not stimulate people to act, there should be a mechanism for sharing the vision in specific terms with people while reflecting the real needs of the business.

- *Develop comprehensive management systems.* As people are the most valuable resource of the company, there should be a management system that promotes utilizing people's collective wisdom. In order to have people participate and contribute their ideas, however, the system needs to be easy for everyone to follow.

- *Educate and train.* It is critical to understand the potential of people and develop career plans for them. Since the company needs certain skills from its people, it should point them toward acquiring those skills.

- *Celebrate success.* Enjoying shared successes feeds energy back into the system and promotes good discipline. Even if progress is limited and problems are abundant, by sharing the success with people and confirming the commitment to improve, people will develop a broader viewpoint toward their work and the spirit to explore their potential.

Exhibit 5.11. Comparison of Breakthroughs and Continuous Improvement

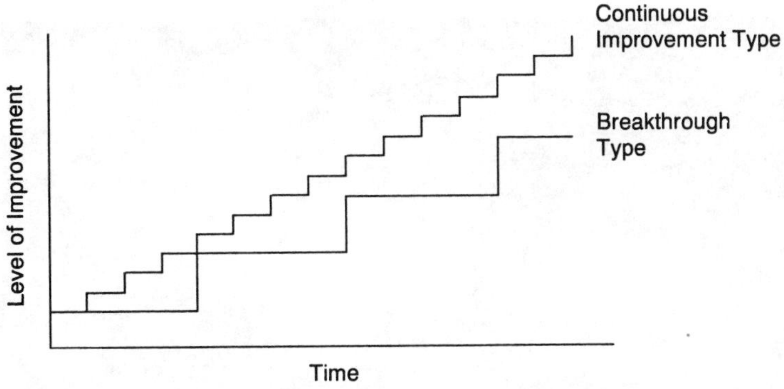

Note: Continuous improvement involves everybody, whereas breakthroughs tend to depend on fewer people.

ness, let us briefly review how companies deal with people's suggestions. An employee of one large company who was laid off commented that he had never been asked for a single suggestion during his last sixteen years of service. On the other hand, at another foreign company that is steadily increasing its market share in the same industry, the average suggestion rate is more than thirty per employee per year, and more than 96% of these suggestions are implemented. Clearly, the first company has not found ways to realize the potential of its people yet.

If these suggestions indicate the creative talent of people, then what is the nature of these suggestions? The answer is that some are as simple as drawing a yellow line on the floor to designate an area to put a trash can, labeling or color coding tools, or providing a tray to put a workpiece on. (See Exhibit 5.12, pages 134 through 139, for examples.) While we will touch on suggestion programs in detail in Chapter 7, we should recognize that money is not the only driver for people to be creative and contribute their ideas. Rather, an environment in which people's creativity is appreciated and utilized can result in easier, safer, more convenient, and less wasteful jobs—for people's own benefit.

A CASE OF AN OPERATOR'S IDEA

To understand how important it is to explore people's creative talent and build up the organization's capability, let us look at a case of an

Exhibit 5.12. Examples of Suggestions

a. An operator made a box out of scrap metal.

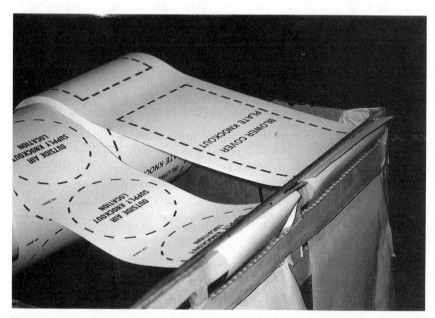

b. The picture above shows a mechanism that makes it easier to peel off labels, especially when operators are wearing gloves.

Exhibit 5.12. Continued

c. Color coding helps identify priorities of jobs.

d. Adjusting angle of the table makes the job easier.

Exhibit 5.12. Continued

e. Guide collates sheared sheets automatically.

f. Roller helps to move heavy door easily; a line drawn on the floor by roller keeps people from putting things in the area.

Exhibit 5.12. Continued

g. By having conveyor kicking up, two operators can do the job from both sides with easy access.

h. Two models with different hole configurations have been combined to one part number by putting extra holes in each.

Exhibit 5.12. Continued

i. Labeled area designates location for next die to run.

j. By attaching conveyor to press, die changeover is made much easier.

Exhibit 5.12. Continued

k. Sweepers are hung up in a small open space where they do not impede people's movement.

l. To encourage suggestions, people's names are posted along with the number of suggestions made.

Courtesy Fireplace Manufacturers, Inc.

139

operator's suggestion. In a semiconductor factory, a young operator was concerned about improving the yield of the process. Her supervisors and managers were also concerned, because when compared with other plants, it was clear that this plant's performance left much room for improvement. No matter how hard everyone tried, however, they always fell short of their goal.

One day on her way to work, as she waited at the railroad crossing for a train to pass, she felt the ground shake under her. She wondered if this vibration might be causing problems for the machine she worked on. Later, at work, she tried to ascertain whether the factory floor shook when trains passed by, but she couldn't feel anything.

Still she wondered, and told her supervisor about her idea. Her supervisor then shared this idea with the plant manager. Even if the machine this operator worked on was far enough away from the railroad, other fine machinery might be affected.

"That's it!" the plant manager exclaimed when he heard the idea. A long deep trench was dug between the factory and the railroad, and the trench was filled with water. Lo and behold, the yield went up.

While this story comes from a semiconductor factory in Japan, the moral of the story may well be applied to our individual situation as well. How can more people become involved in improvement activities? How can we encourage more people to be interested in their work? There may be no simple answers. Yet, by continuing to ask these questions, we may develop our own answer as to how things can be done differently. The process may take time. Yet if we are to accomplish our mission, we need to deal with our problems just as this young operator did on the southern island of Japan. In reference to this example, therefore, we might ask the following questions:

What led the operator to think of improvement? It appears that people in this semiconductor factory shared the concerns of the factory, perhaps in their daily, weekly, or monthly meetings or through displaying charts with targets. Also, exchanges of various improvement activities may have encouraged people to talk about improvement ideas among themselves. Stimulation generated from such an atmosphere must have triggered this operator's thought even while she was waiting for the train to pass by.

Why did this operator share her idea with her supervisor? As opposed to a traditional work environment where there is a fear of crossing the boundary and sharing ideas, this factory's work environment must have been oriented toward achieving prosperity through teamwork on everyone's part. The supervisor had broader knowledge and was able to make judgments about complex problems for the operators. Therefore, the operator discussed her idea with her supervisor, and the supervisor shared it with the plant manager. It appears that communication was open without many hurdles.

How important is it to have these ideas come from the shop floor? To utilize the collective wisdom of people is more important than ever before in today's competitive world. The company that practices this will be much better off than those that do not. The same may be true for individuals within the organization as well. Still, people with traditional management style may ask "What can we do if there are so many suggestions?" Yet, that is the wrong question in this setting. The real question is, "If there are under-utilized talents at the shop floor, what can we do?"

How can we process these ideas effectively? A successful system will not only generate many ideas but also find ways to implement them effectively. One without the other will limit the potential. However, only people can improve the system or make it work.

CHALLENGING PEOPLE TO OVERCOME HURDLES

Thinking about the huge tasks ahead of us, we may be discouraged by time constraints, budget limitations, or contractual constraints from unions. Or we may say that things cannot be improved because of the president, or that person, or the mindset of our managers, or this machine, or that tool. But instead of counting the reasons why it cannot be done, each of us should do our best within our span of control. Such is the spirit of self-management.

But some may still ask, "What's in it for me?" Again, the point is that if we ask others to come up with solutions for us, or if we ask others to do their part before we do anything, we may not gain much ground. In team sports as in business, if that is our attitude, the game may be already lost before we start to play. We need to ask "what in me can I contribute and explore for the betterment of the company?"

For any organization, there are constant challenges to overcoming hurdles. Some of the most difficult ones are its internal constraints such as people feeling insecure about giving away their knowledge to others. Yet, by teaching skills to others and learning new skills along the way, everyone in the organization can move forward.

Instead of focusing only on our own individual interests, there should be a sharing of missions, values, and common interests as members of the organization. Management's role then is to share this idea so that people can grow with the organization. On the other hand, the people's role is to express a drive for self-improvement by contributing ideas starting from their own areas. It will take some time. Yet just as parents enjoy the growth of their children, and children enjoy finding room for their self-expression, the process of change may bring something unforgettable.

SUMMARY

- In order to gain self-managing abilities, we need to acquire skills that match the needs of the organization and marketplace. Reflecting the diversified needs of society, we need to obtain various kinds of skills to respond to the needs.
- One way to improve skills is to find ways to simplify one's job or make a machine do it. By delegating the work to machines, tools, or subordinates, we can make time for expanding our skills or tackling more important or difficult tasks.
- The more we simplify our jobs, the more we can prepare to take on more for the future. The more we can put intelligence into the way we do things at the shop floor, the more we will have time to expand.
- Instead of fighting fires or dreaming of instant breakthroughs, we need to pay more attention to doing the basics right. This includes such things as teaching new skills to trainees.
- We need to differentiate important jobs and urgent jobs, and learn to work on more important jobs. We should realize that

fire-fighting jobs may not go away unless we work on important jobs.
- We should recognize that our mental attitude is often a barrier to making improvement. We need to have open minds and be able to use our judgment on facts.
- As opposed to trying to hit home runs, we may actually gain more ground by making continuous improvement one step at a time with everyone involved.
- In order to develop self-managing skills, a critical factor is everybody's desire for self-improvement.

Chapter Six

ACQUIRING PROBLEM-SOLVING SKILLS

In order to sit in the driver's seat of our destiny, we need to be equipped with skills to overcome the difficulties we encounter. In this chapter, therefore, we will study the nature of these skills and learn how to acquire them.

First, we will discuss the importance of acquiring willpower for self-improvement. Then, we will see how everybody can utilize his or her creativity to overcome the difficulties we face in our work. Next, we will learn many tools for problem solving. And finally, we will study ways to expose problems in order to facilitate the problem solving activities.

ACQUIRING WILLPOWER FOR SELF-IMPROVEMENT

Without a desire for self-improvement, there is no self-management. As discussed previously, instead of merely doing what the boss tells us to do or being constrained by manpower, machines, money, or material, we should be able to use our own resources—that is, our brainpower—and to challenge ourselves to go beyond these constraints.

On the shop floor, problems are everywhere, ranging from housekeeping to machine maintenance, from improving the quality to increasing productivity, from developing effective communication to fostering teamwork to accomplish the mission. In effect, these are problems with quality, cost, delivery, safety, and morale (QCDSM) that we have to solve in order to accomplish our mission and satisfy our customers with minimum waste.

If we were all equipped with problem-solving skills and practiced these skills whenever we could, and in whatever situation we found ourselves in, wouldn't that be better than waiting for someone else to do the job for us? The late Konosuke Matsushita commented:

> What we are facing today is a very difficult era. It is difficult to forecast what may happen. It is difficult to know what to depend on or what guidance to seek in managing the company. Naturally, one consequence is that we are forced to be in the position of conducting business and managing the company in the dark.
>
> Yet if we say that this is due to the environment in which we live, this situation may never change. This is when our thinking needs to change. What I mean is that while it is true that we may not know what may happen in the future, what will happen in the future is a result of what we do today. Therefore, I think it is important for every one of us to wish and try to accomplish something with conviction, and to develop a positive stance and viewpoint to create our own era.
>
> Even in a very difficult business situation, if the responsible person has a strong will to overcome the difficulty, the necessary wisdom will always be gained. We are not amateurs just starting in our work, we have experience and wisdom with us. So if we have the will to accomplish something even under very difficult circumstances, which is based on our way of life and philosophy, I believe they will support us in finding the way.
>
> —From the introduction to
> *The Sayings of Konosuke Matsushita*

Konosuke Matsushita spoke from his lifelong experience. In fact, he did not even finish elementary school, and he went through severe difficulties before he created Matsushita Electric Industries, which today has a total sales volume of $60 billion. Thus those who wish to overcome personal obstacles may find his words especially encouraging. He says, in effect, that constraints are constraints only because we think of them as such. Therefore, the only true constraints are our own constrained minds.

There are many programs and seminars that offer new cutting-edge technology or management concepts to help us go beyond our constraints. Each addresses some subject from a different angle and promises some gain. But because some companies try one new program after another in hopes of a quick fix, their bewildered employees refer to them as the "program of the month."

Since our business situation is already turbulent, the impact of these programs may add even more confusion on the shop floor. When the world begins to look complex, then going back to basic disciplines often helps us maintain our perspective. We are sur-rounded by problems waiting to be resolved. Yet, Konosuke Matsu-shita says, in essence, that where there is a will, there is a way. It sounds simple, yet especially in these fast-changing times, we may need such solid beliefs as our foundation.

Matsushita also made the point that collecting people's wisdom is the key to an organization's success. In fact, the history of man-kind tells us that as we encounter inconveniences, we often find ways to overcome them. Despite failure after failure, somehow we have managed to improve.

As we witness our standard of living improving over centuries, therefore, we should appreciate the works of those in past genera-tions and then find ways for us to add value for our society. Being overly dissatisfied or worried about problems means being waste-ful—as opposed to utilizing the creative power that is our gift as human beings.

USING EVERYBODY'S CREATIVITY

Understanding the importance of our willpower, let us next take a look at the problem-solving activities on our shop floor. Even though each of us may manage a household budget and address many prob-lems at home, when it comes to work, there are some who think that problem-solving activities are for certain people with special skills or advanced educational backgrounds.

Yet given the opportunity, most people can solve problems at work as well. When we look at improvements people implemented on the shop floor, for example, many of them seem so simple after the fact that it seems surprising that nobody implemented them be-fore. (Remember Exhibit 5.12.) In most cases, ideas that come from people's common sense are much more effectively implemented than complex solutions.

This is evidenced by the millions of suggestions generated in companies like Toyota, Matsushita, and Toshiba—often more than fifty suggestions per employee per year, with a participation rate of more than 90 percent, and an adoption rate of more than 80 percent. Many of these companies are so advanced that their statistics include only suggestions already implemented—that is, the adoption rate is 100 percent.

A point to remember here is that none of these ideas is meant to generate millions of dollars of savings or even hundreds of dollars. Rather, each one aims to make an operator's job easier, faster, safer, less tiring, more accurate, or more convenient.

If some people still feel that each of these suggestions is insignificant and will not impact the bottom line of the company, they should realize that when many people contribute their ideas, these suggestions or team improvement projects will not only solve individual problems, but will also contribute to enforce standards as people pay attention to more details. Therefore, when the number of suggestions goes up, typically all of the QCDSM indices go up, too.

Since the number of suggestions represents the total creativity of the organization, if top management considers a suggestion program important, they should be actively involved so that the program itself will not fail. If presidents of mini-companies realize that it is important, they should lead or guide people to generate ideas for everybody's own benefit. If individuals believe it is important to explore their creativity and reach their potential, they should be interested in making suggestions until they succeed.

Thus a large number of suggestions should indicate:

- People's brains are active and their creativity is being utilized.
- Performance is better in terms of QCDSM.
- Management is paying attention to helping people to explore their potential.
- There is a lot of coaching, guiding, and sharing of ideas.
- There is coherence in management thinking toward continuous improvement with everybody involved.

Why, then, do these programs often fail? Whether the failure is total, or because certain departments are inactive in an otherwise successful program, typical examples of reasons for failure include too much emphasis on reward, too long a feedback cycle, too great an emphasis on large improvements, lack of patience to make suggestions work, and too much reliance on someone else to implement ideas. In such situations, therefore, people are not finding fun in making improvements and using their creativity.

HAVING FUN WITH "SHOW AND TELL"

Rather than thinking about difficult theories, let us see how some people engage in "show and tell" type activities to enjoy the fun of making improvements. One example is an all-employee event called an "idea contest" that is now popular in Japan. Started at Honda, the idea contest encourages employees to use their imagination and creativity in coming up with something extraordinary, something that goes beyond their daily jobs. In Honda's case, the "All Honda Idea Contest" is held once a year and exhibits are displayed in a large field for everybody to take a look at.

Exhibit 6.1 shows examples of such ideas. As you see here, people's creativity is stretched, providing fun for people.

Another example is Teamwork Day at Xerox. In order to promote employee involvement and recognize teams who were successfully using the problem-solving process, the first Teamwork Day was organized in 1983 in a plant cafeteria with thirty teams displaying their projects and six teams making presentations. As interest grew, more plants, including those overseas, participated, and in 1991, there were simultaneous Teamwork Days held with satellite connections and with a combined attendance of more than 10,000 people. (See Exhibit 6.2 where thousands of people are viewing exhibits for learning and celebration.)

Exhibit 6.1. Idea Contest

a. Bicycle: We can eliminate unused portion of wheels.

Exhibit 6.1. Continued

b. 3-D swing: This swing can move in three dimensions.

c. Survival car: This car can climb up stairs.

Courtesy Honda Motor Co.

Exhibit 6.2. Teamwork Day

Courtesy Xerox

NECESSARY MENTAL ATTITUDES
FOR ACTIVE PROBLEM SOLVING

As seen in these cases, given the appropriate environment, people can be very creative. Yet there are a number of reasons why we do not get over the hurdle and start to enjoy making improvements. Interestingly, the majority of the reasons (summarized in Exhibit 6.3) are due to people's traditional mindsets and attitudes.

On the other hand, people who have crossed the hurdle and acquired the habit of continuous improvement have a different mindset and attitudinal posture (see Exhibit 6.4). Relating these to the Idea Contest or Teamwork Day, it should not be surprising to find that people who participated in such contests have a positive attitude toward making improvements. Also, contest visitors may have found that using creativity and coming up with ideas is fun and that everybody can do it.

Exhibit 6.3. Mental Attitudes that Block Improvement

Mindset Issues

- "I know everything is moving fine. There is no problem."
- "We have tried everything. I have all the reasons why things will not work."
- "This is how we have done it for many years. This is the best method for us."
- "It's not my responsibility to make improvements."
- "Improvements cost money. Give me ten thousand dollars, then I can fix it."
- "I'm too busy to do anything."

Attitudinal Issues

- Not studying in spite of a lack of knowledge.
- Not trying. Easily giving up. Not experimenting.
- Complaining to managers, staff people, others.
- Not asking for comments or suggestions from others.
- Taking a "what's in it for me?" attitude.
- Assuming that making improvement is not fun.

Exhibit 6.4. Mental Attitudes that Promote Improvement

Mindset Issues

- "There is no end for improvement."
- "Don't think of excuses for why it will not work. Think positively."
- "Always consider the current situation as imperfect."
- "Do away with a fixed mindset."
- "Let's think from a broader perspective."
- "Keep working on improvement so that fire-fighting will eventually go away."

Attitudinal Issues

- Unless we force ourselves to the corner, no ideas will be generated.
- Ask "why" repeatedly to get to the root cause and fix it, permanently.
- Collect people's wisdom, as opposed to depending on one's own wisdom.
- Implement good ideas immediately; stop bad habits immediately.
- Even if it isn't perfect, let us go ahead one step at a time.
- Work can be fun. Coming up with ideas and implementing them is a satisfying experience.

In meeting people from different companies, I have noticed that people with positive attitudes usually have a sense of purpose and feel good about contributing by whatever means it takes. Furthermore, I have found that whether it is in Japan, the United States, Europe, or elsewhere, the creative power of people does not differ by country at all. People generally share a common belief that they can make their lives better.

IDENTIFYING PROBLEMS

To utilize our creativity, let us next see how we identify problems i.e., opportunities for improvement. Of course, problems may be pointed out by someone else, such as our managers. But we should also develop a habit of identifying problems and coming up with solutions by ourselves. Such is the attitude of self-management. (See Exhibit 6.5.) Most importantly, if we aren't able to identify problems

Exhibit 6.5. Mental Attitude Toward Identifying Problems

Consciousness	• Maintain awareness that problems exist everywhere.
Self-Esteem	• Develop self-esteem as opposed to only following someone else's instructions.
	• Think of improving our workplace by ourselves.
Challenging Spirit	• Always assume that there must be a better way.
	• Don't think something is impossible.
Common Sense	• If we feel overburdened, wasteful, or inconsistent in QCDSM—think of ways to fix it.
	• Feel right about what's happening? If not, ask why.
Customer Orientation	• Ask customers about their problems, listen to them attentively.
Shop Floor Orientation	• Search for problems on the shop floor.
	• Ask people about their concerns.
	• Use tools to expose problems effectively.
Objectivity	• Observe the situation objectively, without prejudice.
	• Don't jump to conclusions.
Analysis	• Ask "why" repeatedly when troubled to reach the root cause of a problem.
	• Utilize measurement systems and statistical methods.
Teamwork	• Utilize other people's skills, knowledge, and experience.
	• "None of us is as smart as all of us."

clearly, that is in itself a problem. This may sound funny. Yet it indicates the lack of vision or mission. We need to remember that the difference between our vision as defined by our mission and the reality we face defines the problems we need to address. A manager at NUMMI, a Toyota-General Motors joint venture in California, commented on his learning experience:

> "When I was asked to attend the general manager's meeting the first time, I was happy to attend because I thought I could say that there were no problems in my department. And I said so when it was my turn to report. Then, this General Manager from Toyota looked straight into my eyes and said, 'Steve, when you say you do not have a problem, that is the problem.'"
>
> At this moment, I realized that in order to succeed in this business, I have to change my way of thinking totally.
> —From *JIT Kakumei no Shogeki* by Kiyoshi Suzaki, p. 14.

TOOLS OF PROBLEM SOLVING

Even if we have a positive attitude and challenging spirit about solving problems, without tools and organized steps to do so we may end up spinning our wheels. For example, if we try to tackle a very complex problem from the beginning, we may be exhausted before long. Or if we need to gather people from many different functions to conduct a meeting, even establishing communication among them may take a long time.

To illustrate this point, I would like to share a visit I made to a well-known furniture company in the United States. There, a staff person mentioned to me that one team project had been going on for more than a year and a half without producing any results. The indication was that they still met occasionally, but it was not clear if they got any help from others or if there was any target date set to complete the project. Clearly, such team problem-solving activities were quite new to them, and they were lacking experience.

One top manager did tell me proudly, however, that they had done more training in the last year alone than in the previous twenty-five years combined. Yet, when I found a very professionally developed eighty-page Employee Involvement Team Manual in a binder with thick glossy paper, and remembered the ineffective team project mentioned above, I detected a very troublesome sign. The thinking at the top was not reflected adequately in action even though their intentions were good.

A few years later, I learned that this company was laying off many people. Here again, we should realize that there is a big difference between theory and practice, that is, a difference between knowing what to do and doing what we know.

So, knowledge itself is not enough, we need to execute. Yet, execution is not enough; we need to be effective in execution. And to be effective, we need to develop customer (i.e., people) friendly approaches (see Exhibit 6.6).

To be effective, it is also good to start with small projects so that we can get used to accomplishing something with the basic tools of problem solving. In other words, we have to crawl before we can walk. In the process, managers or facilitators need to be as attentive as parents so that the team (baby) does not try to climb straight up the wall to no avail.

The problem-solving tools we may use range from common sense and our inherent creativity to more advanced ones which may require a strong analytical mind. To familiarize ourselves, Exhibit 6.7 shows

Exhibit 6.6. Problem-Solving Tools Can Be Customer-Friendly. Here cartoons are used to teach people how to solve production problems. Even though there are more than a dozen nationalities represented among this company's employees, this easy-to-read material could convey a message quite effectively.

Courtesy Alps Manufacturing (USA)

Exhibit 6.7. Various Problem-Solving Tools

Basic Problem Areas (QCDSM)

- Quality
- Cost
- Delivery
- Safety
- Morale

Basic Problem-Solving Concepts and Techniques

- Using common sense, creativity, intuition
- Simplify, combine, and eliminate
- Elimination of seven wastes (from overproduction, waiting time, transportation, processing, inventory, motion, and product defects)
- Elimination of eighth waste (not utilizing people's talent)
- Asking "why," five times
- 4-M checklist (man, machine, method, and material)
- 5M1E checklist (4-M plus measurement and environment)
- 6M1E checklist (5M1E plus management information)
- Practicing the "three reals," i.e., real scene (genba), real thing (genbutsu), and real fact (genjitsu)
- Attacking the key area first (i.e., use pareto principle)
- Controlling the scatter/uncertainty
- Practicing glass wall management
- PDCA (plan-do-check-act) cycle
- Looking at the picture from shop floor point of view
- Using QC story, or other organized problem-solving steps (see Chapter 7 and Appendix 7.3)
- Brainstorming/group meeting
- Memos to record new thoughts or problems identified during work

Specific Tools

1. Industrial engineering (IE)

  - Man-machine chart
  - Work combination chart
  - Process analysis
  - Material flow analysis
  - Setup time reduction
  - Product-oriented layout
  - One-piece flow production
  - Cross-training and multiprocess handling
  - Cycle time analysis

2. Quality control (QC)

  - Seven tools of QC—histogram, cause-and-effect diagram, check sheet, pareto diagram, graph, control chart, and scatter diagram

(*continued*)

Exhibit 6.7. Continued

---

2. Quality control (QC) (continued)

- Seven new tools—relations diagram, affinity diagram, tree diagram, matrix, matrix data-analysis diagram, PDPC (process decision program chart), arrow diagram
- Others—fail-safe mechanisms (poka-yoke; for details see Appendix 6.1), flow chart, run chart, Taguchi method

3. Value engineering (VE):

- Value = Function/Cost
- Parts commonality, variety reduction

4. Reliability

- Fault tree analysis (FTA)
- Failure mode and effect analysis (FMEA)

5. Production and inventory control

- Workplace organization
- Lot size reduction
- Leveled production
- Pull vs. push system (kanban vs. MRP)

6. New product development

- Inventory list of technology
- Quality function deployment (QFD)
- Design for manufacturability

7. Management

- Organization—leadership, communication, teamwork, motivation
- Marketing—market segmentation, attribute analysis, sampling
- Economics—pricing, supply and demand, net present value
- Decision science—operations research, linear programming
- Finance/accounting—financial analysis, cash flow analysis
- Time management
- Project management—Pert chart, Gantt chart, flow chart
- Competitive strategy—benchmarking, etc.
- Others

Note: Because of the space limitation in this book, we will not explain these tools in detail. However, we should note that depending on the person's area of responsibility and the nature of the work, certain tools may be more effectively used than others. Tools may also be used in combination. (See Appendixes 6.1 and 6.2 for descriptions of examples of problem-solving tools.)

various tools. Most people will not need to know all of these tools in conducting their work. Yet, where possible, we should develop the ability to pick and choose them as needed. Just as we need to build up our muscles and learn specific techniques to play tennis, golf, or baseball, we need to do the same if we want to play the game at work effectively.

LEARNING SKILLS TO ENRICH OUR CAREER

Since the tools to solve problems will vary depending on the nature of the problems we deal with, let us establish some general guidelines for using such tools.

To start with, we need to realize that as much as our organization is to perform better with renewed targets every year, individually we should do the same for our own growth. To do this effectively, we should set our skill enhancement targets somewhat higher than what we can easily achieve. Also, learning a few skills is not good enough today.

As illustrated in Exhibit 6.8, a narrow skill base will be vulnerable in a changing business environment compared to a broad skill base where a person's primary skill is complemented by several peripheral skills. As more new responsibilities are expected from every one of us, we need to learn more managerial skills, technical skills, interpersonal skills, and the like. Rather than taking the traditional approach of looking for someone with special skills to match specific

Exhibit 6.8. Improving Our Skill Profile

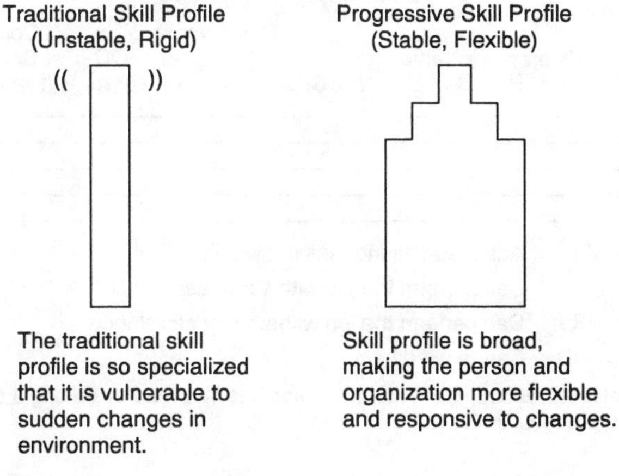

Traditional Skill Profile
(Unstable, Rigid)

Progressive Skill Profile
(Stable, Flexible)

The traditional skill profile is so specialized that it is vulnerable to sudden changes in environment.

Skill profile is broad, making the person and organization more flexible and responsive to changes.

job requirements like plugging pegs into a hole, therefore, we need to think of making ourselves flexible so we can adapt to a changing business environment. The traditional apprentice-type of training needs much improvement.

If we look back at the list in Exhibit 6.7, we will find tools we are skilled at using and other tools we are unfamiliar with—both individually and as a whole organization. Specifically, we can determine which tools we are familiar with, which tools we use frequently, and which tools we can teach others. Then we can develop a skill matrix to monitor the level of individual skill profiles and plan for improvement. Exhibit 6.9 shows such a matrix, where skills for doing the specific jobs (operations) and skills for problem solving (tools) are combined in one table. Exhibit 6.10a shows a similar matrix, used by a Japanese manufacturer, that is posted with people's pictures. Exhibit 6.10b shows another similar application for a small manufacturer in California.

A skill matrix, or cross-training chart, as it may also be called, can be used to assess a person's respective skills and try to match them to the needs of the business. Naturally, if a person or an organization has a unique skill profile, it may create a unique potential. On the other hand, personal interest may drive a person or organization in a direction that does not meet the needs of the business.

Unless coordinated well, a gap may be created between the skills and the needs of the business. Therefore, mini-company presidents need frequent coaching and guidance in developing their people through career education and proper job assignments so that training

Exhibit 6.9. Skill Matrix

Operator's Name	Operation's Name					Tool's Name			Comments & Schedule for Training Needs
	A	B	C	D	.....	SPC	Kanban	7QC Tools..	

Note: Level I: Attended training, has knowledge

Level L: Can perform the job with some assistance

Level U: Can perform the job without any assistance

Level O: Can teach others

As skill level is advanced, the level in the matrix is changed by adding a stroke to the letter from I to L to U to O.

Exhibit 6.10a. Skill Matrix Posted in Japanese Automotive Parts Manufacturer

資格取得一覧表

Courtesy Tokai Rika

Exhibit 6.10b. Skill Matrix Posted at a Small Manufacturer in California

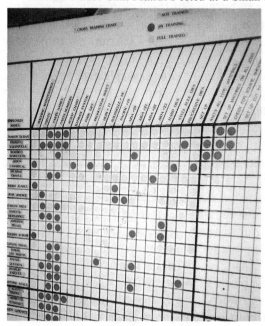

Courtesy Fireplace Manufacturers, Inc.

is focused on the skills needed to accomplish the mission of the organization. To do this, we may develop a special focus first, then continue with job rotation and skill enhancement so that we can develop broader views and a deeper skill base.

DEVELOPING THE HABIT OF MUTUAL LEARNING

In order to acquire problem-solving skills, we may conduct classroom education and training, on-the-job training, read books, watch videotapes, attend seminars, visit other departments or companies. Yet, if we do these only as an individual, our growth will be limited. For example, we can read books or attend seminars on our own, but we may not share our new knowledge with anybody else. Instead of simply going through education and hoping that it will work, we need to develop a good follow-up mechanism.

In other words, if we are individually focused or fearful of sharing ideas with others, we go back to our three-hump model in Exhibit 3.13 where every function (or person) is focusing on self-interest—that is, local optimization as opposed to total optimization. As a result, the whole organization may suffer. Most likely, individuals will also suffer in the long run because of the lack of mutual learning and stimulation from others.

To overcome this problem, let us think how we may promote mutual learning. An example may be to share the key points of a book or seminar by writing a one-page summary where people may be assigned chapters of a book and report back to the group every week. Or they may actually implement ideas gained from the chapter as their assignment and share the results with the group in the meeting.

At Tokyo Electric Company, a Japanese electric appliance manufacturer, the company often buys pertinent books for managers to read. Managers are asked to write one-page book reports, with the idea that when someone writes a summary, he or she will digest the contents better than when just reading it. In UBISA, a Spanish cable manufacturer, managers read my previous book chapter by chapter with their employees and applied ideas gained from the book in their work setting. Each accomplishment was summarized on one page and was shared with all employees. After a few years of progress, they not only translated my book into Spanish but also started a consulting and education company to share their knowledge with other organizations.

At Matsushita's Vacuum Cleaner Division, newly released books are displayed in the hallway, and employees can check them out of the company library later. Many companies use newsletters, improvement display boards, or a case book of improvements made by people to share accomplishments as well. In any of these examples, however, the key is for people to use their own initiative for continuous learning. These mechanisms for sharing knowledge have to go hand in hand with each individual's self-improving initiative. Exhibit 6.11 summarizes various means of sharing knowledge and experiences. Glancing through this list, we may ask how well our (mini-) company is practicing these ideas.

If we can share ideas, knowledge, or experiences among ourselves and have fun, work becomes more enjoyable, especially when these activities relate to improving our workplace and accomplishing our vision. While we will come back to the subject of sharing in Chapter 8, for now we should remember that sharing with others or teaching others is a very good way for individuals to internalize their own skills.

Simply giving employees manuals or books, showing them videos, or sending them to seminars does not guarantee progress for them or for the organization. We need to provide an atmosphere conducive to improvement and provide feedback to or receive feedback from the people. Then we need to find ways to keep improving the process to accomplish our mission.

TOOLS TO EXPOSE PROBLEMS

While tools for solving problems are critical, it is equally important to be able to expose problems *effectively* so that appropriate tools

Exhibit 6.11. Mechanisms for Sharing of Knowledge and Experiences

- Self-study group to read books, and apply techniques
- Display of newly released books to lend to people
- Company newsletter, plant newsletter, describing improvements
- Display of improvements to show what people have accomplished
- Sharing of experiences in memos and meetings, e.g., trip report
- Summary of case examples of improvement to be shared in education
- Sharing rally where people share cases of their improvement
- Company-wide idea contest, and teamwork day

Exhibit 6.12. Cycle of Continuous Improvement

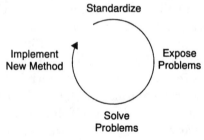

for solving them can be used. Exhibit 6.12 shows a cycle of continuous improvement. In order to manage our shop floor better, we need a good balanced capability to practice each of these steps well.

Here, we should know that effectively exposing problems will not only help in maintaining the standards but will help to guide us better and to involve everybody in improvement activities. To say it differently, we need an organization-wide "pain-inducing mechanism" so that problems are exposed to get people's attention when we are off the course. For an organization to function as a team, pain—or problems—should not only be dealt with in specific areas but should be shared throughout the company as appropriate.

Since any organization should have its mission, specific objectives and plan of action to accomplish these, and standards to maintain the gain already achieved, the problems of the organization need to be exposed in each of these areas so that problem-solving process takes place throughout the company. To illustrate this, Exhibit 6.13

Exhibit 6.13. Nature of Problems Found in the Company

Problem (Defined Here as the Gap Between What is Ideal and What is Reality)	Key Factors to Effectively Expose Problem
• Mission vs. Current Orientation	Clarity and ownership of mission, and people's level of conviction and conscience
• Objective vs. Current Status	Validity of objectives, ownership by people, and means to achieve objectives
• Plans of Action vs. Reality of Action	Validity of plans, ownership by people, and means to practice plans of action
• SOP vs. practice of SOP	Ease of following standard operating procedure without generating waste, or causing customer dissatisfaction

Exhibit 6.14. Inventory Covers Problems

Raw Material

Finished Product to Customers

Sea of Inventory

Poor Scheduling

Line Imbalance

Lack of House-keeping

Machine Breakdown

Quality Problems

Long Set-Up Time

Communication Problem

Vendor Delivery

Long Transportation

Absenteeism

summarizes the ways we should look at problems in a company or mini-company. (Needless to say, the pain level needs to be carefully monitored; not too big, nor too little.)

With regard to problems or pains, just-in-time production or the lean manufacturing concept emphasizes that inventory is the root of all evil, covering problems and preventing us from making continuous improvement (see Exhibit 6.14). So, as we try to reduce inventory by reducing the lot size or by other means, we can uncover and address problems accordingly. Then, we keep reducing the inventory, uncovering problems, and addressing problems until we eliminate waste from the shop floor. While this process may be somewhat painful, it will help the company to focus its efforts in a pragmatic fashion and develop a streamlined operation.

Exhibit 6.15 conveys a similar message, except that in this case we are talking about the management of our resources in general. So,

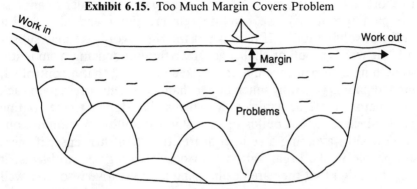

Exhibit 6.15. Too Much Margin Covers Problem

Work in

Work out

Margin

Problems

Note: Margin includes too much manpower, machine capacity, space, material, etc.

in addition to inventory, we look at such extra or wasted resources as manpower, machine capability, space, and material above what we need to attain the expected level of performance. Thus, as we take away these wasted or underutilized resources, we can utilize our resources better and focus our efforts to attain our goals.

In other words, if we use extra manpower, as an example, the symptom is more than enough time to do the work. While inventory represents the time that material sits as work-in-process, underutilized time of people is time-in-process. One refers to processing the workpiece, the other to processing the time of people.

The faster material moves, the easier it is to discover and address problems. The busier we get, the more apparent the need to make improvements. So, as we try to reduce extra resources, we should be able to make improvements, as opposed to tying up resources and not adding value. While such an approach may sound hectic, if we are not paying attention to the wasted resources, we may find people spending time pondering without adding value. Even though some open time for creative thinking or rest may be necessary, we still need to be careful so that it is not out of reason.

So in summary, key reasons for reducing inventory or taking away people's extra resources are:

- Exposing problems rather than covering them up
- Prioritizing problems by applying the idea of "management by exception"
- Focusing attention on problems
- Providing impetus to use creativity
- Utilizing our resources constructively

In short, the idea is simple, "No pain, no gain." In order to address the pain (problems), we can use our creativity and all relevant problem-solving tools. If pain is not the right word, we may substitute the word stimuli or challenge. If we think practicing them is still something of a pain, we might also keep in mind that a controlled, limited pain is generally much better than a sudden, severe pain such as a major layoff or bankruptcy. This is also similar to the routine physical exercise that builds up our physical ability to maintain our good health, avoiding a sudden heart attack. In this sense, if there are people in the organization who do not recognize problems, it may be a sign that they are not utilizing their creative resources well to make continuous improvement. Hence, this way of facilitating the

Exhibit 6.16. Basic Tools for Enforced Problem Solving

- *Agreement on the target, and discipline to follow up.* Goals without specific target dates are goals without meaning. If we are to move forward, we need to set deadlines for accomplishing certain tasks. In some cases, we may have to set targets even if detailed steps for reaching them are still unclear. Then, we need to have the discipline to follow up by using the PDCA cycle.

- *Reduction of inventory, lot size.* By reducing inventory, we can expose problems such as setup time, quality problems, layout problems, housekeeping and organization, or absenteeism.

- *Andon (trouble light).* If there is a problem identified by operators that needs immediate attention, a light will be turned on automatically or manually by the operator, so that necessary action may be taken by supervisors and/or support people.

- *Jidoka (line stop).* This mechanism stops the line (or machine, etc.) when there is a problem, inducing people to take action. If the line never stops at all, that may be considered wasteful since problems remain hidden.

- *Discipline in workplace organization.* As we organize our workplace, many problems will surface for people to work on. Pictures of good and bad examples of organization may be posted with some comments.

- *Reduction of distribution of reports.* Just as inventory hides problems, paper inventory behaves the same way. By reducing the distribution, we can see whether or not recipients find certain reports absolutely necessary.

- *Limitations on meeting time, presentation time, etc.* This will force people to focus on priority items.

- *Reduction of manpower.* This will force people to generate ideas to improve productivity. (Typically, it is recommended that the most skillful person in the group should be moved to another area so that others can grow without feeling that their jobs are threatened.)

- *Cross-training/job rotation.* This will allow expansion of people's skills and at the same time enable them to look at their work areas with a fresh view. Displaying the dates of employment and of qualifications for certain jobs should show each individual's growth.

- *Use of checklists.* Routine use of appropriate checklists will help identify problems. A checklist may be posted to indicate the levels of machine maintenance, attendance, compliance to certain work procedures, inspection, or housekeeping and organization.

- *Use of control charts, production control board.* Any abnormalities will be identified to initiate corrective aciton.

- *Display of mini-company (QCDSM) scoreboard.* "What gets measured, gets done." The target will indicate what game we are playing, and how well— naturally, this should not be used to punish a lack of performance.

- *Sample board.* The sample board will catch people's attention to enforce quality criteria.

- *Display of problem or defective parts.* These will draw attention to performing a quality job.

(continued)

Exhibit 6.16. Continued

- *Display of standard operating procedure at each work station.* Discrepancies between actual work and work procedures will indicate need for training or for improving the work procedure. If SOP is not updated, it means that no improvement is being made.
- *Display the names of the ten worst suppliers.* Problems need to be exposed in order for people to fix them.
- *Display the number of days before new product introduction, number of days without accident, number of days without any defect, etc.* These displays will help everybody work as a team. When there is a problem, everybody will recognize it.
- *Newsletter.* Preparation and discussion of department news may trigger thoughts for improvement. If an article is not received from a particular department by the deadline, the newsletter may be published on time but with a blank area for that department.
- *Other tools.*

  Display of new products with request for everybody's suggestions, e.g., people may place stickers with their comments on the product to indicate the nature of the suggestion.

  Award program, e.g., for housekeeping, department of the month, safety, etc. with evaluation results posted.

  Written annual or semi-annual report of mini-company to share progress and identify existing problems.

  Use of top management, staff, or consultant as a stimulator and periodic auditor.

  Application for awards such as Malcolm Baldrige National Quality Award.

  Presidential audit, quality audit, etc. (see Chapter 11 for details).

  Invitation to customers to exchange ideas.

  Visits to other parts of the plant, other factories.

  Visits to customers and customer surveys.

  Use of memos or flipcharts on the shop floor, serving as reminders when problems are found so they will be dealt with later.

---

process of problem solving may be called "enforced problem-solving activity."

Exhibit 6.16, pages 165 through 172, describes the basic tools for enforced problem-solving and examples of their applications that we should be familiar with. (Please also refer to my book, *The New Manufacturing Challenge,* Chapter 7, "Strengthening Our Nerves and Muscles," for more information.)

These techniques are all oriented toward the people at the shop floor so that we can address the problems then and there. As men-

Exhibit 6.16a. Clock to Monitor the Line Stop. When the operator stops the assembly line because of parts shortage or some other problem, the total elapsed line stop time each day is monitored by this clock with green, yellow, and red zones.

Exhibit 6.16b. Various Approaches Used for Emphasizing Housekeeping and Organization. After several years of effort to take 100 or so pictures of the shop floor organiation every month, not only did this company grow significantly, they found dozen of "family" albums to record its history.

Pictures displayed to generate pride in people.

Courtesy Fireplace Manufacturers, Inc.

Exhibit 6.16b. Continued

Numerous albums indicating the progress.

Awards for recognition.
Courtesy Fireplace Manufacturers, Inc.

Exhibit 6.16c. Display of Checklist. The workplace should be comprehensible to new employees or even strangers. This picture shows a machine checklist posted at the machine along with SOP, etc. While this checklist has a place provided for it, other documents may still be better organized for ease of use. Even though this may sound like a small point, those experienced in shop improvement activity will agree about the need to pay attention to detail and letting people know that there is no end to improvement.

Courtesy Grand Rapids Spring & Wire

Exhibit 6.16d. Use of Production Control Board

Courtesy Fireplace Manufacturers, Inc.

Exhibit 6.16e. Use of Statistical Process Control and Skill Matrix Chart

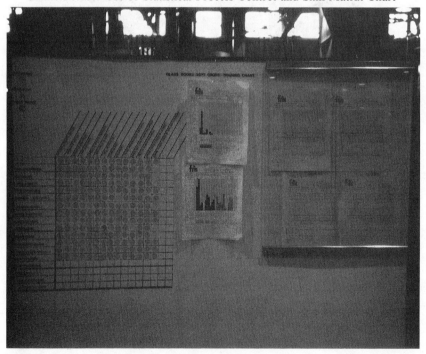

Courtesy Fireplace Manufacturers, Inc.

Exhibit 6.16f. Display of Mini-Company Scoreboard. In order to deal with limited space, people came up with the idea of hanging the board with rope and pulley so that the board can be raised when not in use.

Board is up when not in use.   Board is down when in use.

Courtesy Grand Rapids Spring & Wire

Exhibit 6.16g. Display of Quality Problems. This display indicates the importance of addressing the source of problems by displaying the quality information in a cause-and-effect format.

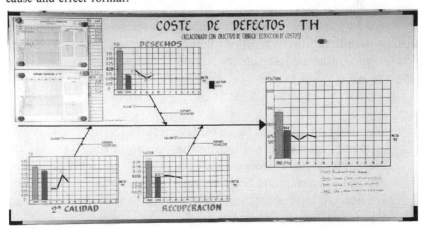

Courtesy UBISA

Exhibit 6.16h. Newsletters for Employees

tioned earlier, if something is not right, we should be prepared to monitor the symptom at the shop floor for thirty minutes—or even a full day if necessary—until we can identify the root of the problem. In other words, what we need are approaches or tools that help us to identify problems and better utilize everybody's creativity. The point is, as people are accustomed to sharing problems, people will contribute more ideas.

Instead of solving problems themselves, therefore, managers and support people should think of implementing these approaches effectively so that more people can contribute their talents. However, just as too much sudden exercise can be harmful to our bodies, we need to pay attention to certain aspects of these activities:

- We need to introduce these tools carefully so that the exposed problems are addressed before they get too excessive.
- We need to have problem-solving skills to go with problem-exposing systems and tools.
- We need to have a mechanism to monitor the whole process so that it remains under control.
- We need to address the problems both as individuals and as a team.

- As progress is made, we should celebrate with everybody and build confidence to further move forward.

In other words, if these tools are introduced haphazardly, they may hurt the organization and demoralize people. Management may lose credibility and solidifying people's efforts may become difficult. Therefore, coordination of planning, support and feedback from management, and education becomes very important.

To conclude this chapter, let us review a checklist from Toyota to identify problems (Exhibit 6.17). As shown here, the points are

Exhibit 6.17. Checklist to Identify Problem Areas

Improvement of Methods of Operation and Machine Tools

- Are materials, tools, products placed in an appropriate fashion?
- Can machine operation and processing methods be improved so that operation becomes easier?
- Can machine layout and transportation devices be improved so that operation can be made easier or more efficient?

Savings of Materials and Consumable Items

- Are oils and other consumables used in the most effective fashion?
- Are there ways to prevent steam, air, etc, from leaking?
- Can we improve materials, processing methods or tools and jigs so that materials yield can be improved?

Improvement of Efficiency for Office Work, Establishment of Control Methods

- Is redundant work done at multiple locations?
- Can any work be eliminated?
- Are there ways to improve the paper processing work?
- Are there ways to proceduralize work methods?

Improvement of Work Environment and Prevention of Safety Hazards

- Are lighting, air, and temperature controlled appropriately?
- Are dust, gas, and bad odors removed efficiently?
- Is safety equipment installed appropriately? Is it functioning well?

Improvement of Performance and Improvement of Accuracy

- Can design, or processing methods be changed to improve performance?
- Are there ways to achieve better consistency of products?

Note: Also see Appendix 6.3 for idea generation checklists.

Exhibit 6.18. When Solving a Problem, Ask "Why" Repeatedly

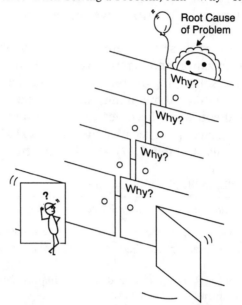

pragmatic, but not too conceptual. The audience is the people at the shop floor, not the specialists. The keys to success are discipline, involvement, and commitment.

As we explore new territory with self-managing people, "customer friendliness" remains as a key phrase to remember. Whether it is a new tool or new program that we want to introduce, we need to put ourselves in our customers' shoes and develop an ability to think about a situation from their point of view.

So, let us ask:

- Do we agree with the notion that necessity is the mother of invention/improvement?
- What tools or approaches should we use to expose problems so that more people are induced to utilize their creative power in solving them?
- What success stories can we share to indicate the effectiveness of enforced problem solving?

SUMMARY

- Improvement skills are not owned by certain people. Everybody can contribute ideas.

- Most improvement ideas come from our common sense. Also, common sense ideas are typically much easier to implement and keep up with as compared to complex solutions.
- With regard to an organization's total creativity, a good measure is the number of suggestions generated by its people. Also, the number of suggestions reflects many things, e.g., levels of quality, cost, delivery performance, safety, and morale of people.
- Before many people are involved in improvement activities, we need to clear typical mental roadblocks, e.g., "we have tried everything," "what is in it for me," etc. Instead, some of the important thoughts are: "There is no end for improvement." "Think positively." "Be flexible." "Be persistent." "Think as a group." "Go one step at a time." "Work can be fun."
- There are many different ways to solve problems, but one of the key points to remember is "Don't think too big from the beginning. Practice a few ideas at a time. Then see how things go and explore and challenge more difficult ones." Continuous improvement is a journey, not a trip.
- Problem-solving tools are like carpenter's tools. We need to be able to make good use of them.
- We need to realize the importance of broadening skills as a part of career planning. Also, mutual learning becomes an important process to be practiced in today's rapidly changing environment.
- If the needs of satisfying customers with minimum waste and survival of the fittest are understood by everybody, the notion of enforced problem solving will be grasped fairly easily.
- In order to promote improvement activities, we need to be able to expose problems effectively so that people can focus on addressing them as opposed to not knowing which one to focus on. Especially when our ability is underutilized, we should be willing to induce certain stimuli or challenges so that we can move forward.
- Exposing problems (by enforced problem solving), supporting problem-solving activities, implementing solutions and practicing standardization should go hand in hand. An important role of managers is to coordinate all these activities on an ongoing basis.

Chapter Seven

PRACTICING PROBLEM-SOLVING SKILLS

So far, we have learned that in order to achieve shop floor excellence we need to satisfy our customers, involve everybody, upgrade skills, and acquire problem-solving skills. Yet, since acquiring skills does not produce any value by itself, we will learn effective ways to practice those skills in this chapter.

First, we will study various activities for problem solving. By going through a few examples, we should be able to understand the nature of a typical problem-solving process. Then, we will learn more about suggestion programs and team improvement activities. Furthermore, to better coordinate these activities, we will study basic management concepts for continuous improvement.

RELENTLESS PURSUIT OF IMPROVEMENT

As business competition becomes fierce, striving to achieve the highest performance in order to meet the competition can mean something more than what many of us are accustomed to. For example, even after high process capability is established to produce quality goods, this should not stop our pursuit of improvement. The next challenge may be to deliberately reduce the grade of raw material, or increase the production rate and still find ways to meet the customer's needs at lower cost and higher quality.

In a sense, this is an application of the jidoka or line stop concept, or it may be compared to the reduction of water level shown in Exhibits 6.14 and 6.15. As mentioned in the previous chapter, we may also take deliberate measures to expose problems and then apply our creativity to solve them. The point is to question the status quo, and to go beyond conventional thinking by fully utilizing our creativity.

Three examples from Japanese manufacturers of consumer electronics illustrate these points:

Example 1. During an economic slowdown in the 1970s, an electronics company was asked by a major automobile manufacturer in Japan to reduce the price of their car radio significantly. Instead of rejecting the request as unreasonable, people responded to this challenge. After deliberate efforts to cut cost, they met the goal—at an even larger margin than had been requested.

Example 2. During a recession in 1930, when most companies were laying off people, the inspiration came to one company president to retrain factory workers to sell unsold stock. After six months, the company not only sold out the stock but they were also back in full gear—ahead of their competitors.

Example 3. When a major electric appliance company started to supply motors to a company in the 1980s, they were instructed to use a lower grade of steel in order to reduce cost. Even though this supplier was proud of its product's high quality and had enjoyed high growth in its business, this was an important learning experience for their management.

The first two examples indicate that even in very difficult situations, people can often find a way to solve problems if they are forced to. Naturally, people do not want to be under pressure to come up with answers. One response may be to avoid the pressure. The other is to take these problems as a challenge and strive to achieve something. In fact, those who can come up with ideas under pressure often develop confidence in themselves to keep them growing much further.

Once people experience success, just like a winning sports team, the organization may register it in its memory and exhibit it in high spirit and perseverance. And as these experiences accumulate, they provide added stimulation for solving new problems and moving forward. People start to see the light at the end of the tunnel or start to believe in becoming the number one manufacturer in the world. So, success breeds success.

The third example indicates that a challenging spirit can extend to suppliers through coaching, guidance, or persuasion by manufacturers. In effect, today's companies compete to see who can develop a better capability in terms of establishing a total chain of value-added networks. So, going beyond the arm's length relationship and developing shared values can become the important tie among these companies.

CLARIFYING APPROACHES FOR PROBLEM-SOLVING ACTIVITIES

As you see from these cases, just as the nature of problems varies, so does the problem-solving process. A simple problem may require one person or a small group of people and may take a short time to solve; more complex problems may require several people and take much longer. Whether it is our work or baseball, therefore, the more we train and acquire diversified skills, the better we can deal with different situations.

Accordingly, if a company or mini-company wishes to perform well, it needs to develop a range of approaches (activities) for people to fully practice their problem-solving skills. In fact, a comprehensive and easily accessible approach is as important as the problem-solving skills themselves. So, the key question is, "Is a range of approaches offered to people? And are they customer friendly?"

If tools for problem solving are not utilized or certain approaches to problem solving are not bearing fruit, then managers are the ones who need to resolve this problem. Remember, it is estimated that more than 80 percent of a company's problems are related to management.

In order to address the needs of the organization, Exhibit 7.1 summarizes a range of typical approaches to problem solving which are practiced by many progressive companies:

Exhibit 7.1. Approaches for Problem Solving

Approach	Participants and Nature of Activities	Measure of Effectiveness
Suggestion Program	Individuals or groups; problems tend to be immediate problems. Focus is first on involvement of people and then on effectiveness of program.	Number of suggestions as key index; then, content of suggestion

Exhibit 7.1. Continued

Approach	Participants and Nature of Activities	Measure of Effectiveness
Self-Managing Team, Quality Circle, Team Improvement Activities	Groups of people mainly from the same work area; support and guidance may be given from management and support staff. Focus is on self-management.	Number of completed projects; content of improvements
Management Driven Task Force, Project Team, Self-Study Group	Group of people; members may be determined according to the nature of problem. Often a multifunctional approach is taken.	Timing, and results
Improvement Based on Organization's Functional Responsibilities	Everyone in the same organizational unit performs its routine functional responsibilities. Also, improving the performance of organization as set by annual or semi-annual business plan.	Approaches and results with emphasis on consistency
Strategic Planning, Policy Management	Management and staff, addressing the strategic direction of company. Typically, long-term oriented. As appropriate, strategy or corporate policy is deployed throughout the organization using other approaches described here.	Clarity in overall approaches and results accomplished
Cross-Functional Management	Cross-functional teams, addressing the key cross-functional issues of the company. Typically committee structure, addressing such company-wide issues as quality, cost, and delivery.	Identification of key problems and monitoring progress

BASIC STEPS OF PROBLEM SOLVING

As we gain experience in using problem-solving tools over time and share our experience with others, we may find that there are certain steps we commonly take when making improvements. As we use these common steps company-wide, the organization as a whole may find it easier to communicate the process of improvement among its people.

For us to become familiar with such a process, let us first study an example of problem solving (Exhibit 7.2). Even if this example seems simplistic, if we want to practice problem-solving activities

Exhibit 7.2. Steps of Problem Solving

Step	Example of Thought Process	Comments
1. Recognition of Problem	I often spend time in looking for things.	• Level of awareness should be high to be able to think of problems at work. • This may be attributed to supervisor's proper guidance and support, or to colleagues' influence.
2. Idea Generation	What if I organize things by color?	• May ask why the problem exists, and what to do to help. • Idea may come from exposure to others practicing similar ideas, or from prior training and education.
3. Experimentation with Idea	I'll categorize things and choose colors by category.	• Energy level should be high enough to take action on own. • Previous experience, and colleagues' or supervisor's influence may contribute to action orientation.
4. Check Effectiveness	It looks nice, clean, and easy to maintain for me. But other people are not cooperating by practicing the discipline.	• After implementing idea, checks to see if the end result is as expected.

Exhibit 7.2. Continued

Step	Example of Thought Process	Comments
5. More Idea Generation	What if I post signs so that everyone understands which color corresponds to what item?	• If expected result was not obtained, analyzes and asks why again. • It takes additional energy and perseverance to be able to think further. Clues may come from anywhere, including supervisors, colleagues, books, etc.
6. Experimentation of Idea	I'll make and post signs so that everyone understands the meaning of color coding.	• Giving up is easy, but if the problem can be solved, it will help self-esteem.
7. Check Effectiveness	Now, things are organized at all times.	• Check if end result is satisfactory. • Check if new method is easy to maintain.
8. When Effective, Standardize	I will maintain this system. As new things are to be stored here, I will categorize, assign color, and update signs as needed.	• If the end result is satisfactory, standardize the procedure so that the status can be maintained without much trouble.

company-wide, then understanding people's thinking processes becomes a key prerequisite for managers.

If we understand how people behave better at work, we may eliminate confusion by setting criteria that everyone understands. For example, operators need to ask an inspector or supervisor whether the product they are working on meets quality standards. Over time, this results in people wasting a significant amount of time looking for someone else. Alternately, if operators make their own judgments without a clear understanding of standards, numerous rejects may be found later.

Such wasteful practices may be minimized by putting up a display of good and bad products in the form of a sample board at the point of action (see Exhibit 7.3). Then, educating people to follow the standard may enable them to adhere to guidelines without wasting time or material.

Exhibit 7.3. Example of a Sample Board for a Leather Belt

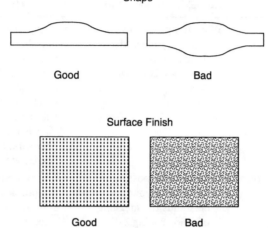

Shape

Good   Bad

Surface Finish

Good   Bad

Note: A picture or a real sample may be posted to make it easy to differentiate good from bad.

A CASE OF CONTINUOUS IMPROVEMENT— "MY FINGERS HURT"

The next example comes from a Sony's operator's experience in Japan. A new employee was assigned to a final inspection where video tape recorders were tested. To do her job, she had to connect and disconnect a plug hundreds of times a day, causing her fingers and hand to hurt (see Exhibit 7.4a, Case 1).

In such situations, we may either complain or simply get used to it. She did complain about this job. If she had been left alone, she might have gotten used to it eventually. In this case, however, her supervisor brought her a rake-like jig and asked if she would try it. (see Exhibit 7.4a, Case 2).

The operator was very surprised by this. Instead of accepting the status quo, people there seemed to be trying to find better ways of doing the job. Even though the jig was not made in any fancy way, it worked and did not cause any pain in her fingers.

One week passed and she came to her supervisor, saying, "Thank you so much for the jig. My work is much easier than before. And while I was using it, I also came up with an idea." She then showed her new jig, saying, "Since there are four plugs, I put four openings in the jig. Also, I added some rubber so that products won't get

Exhibit 7.4. Improvement of Unplugging Plugs at Sony

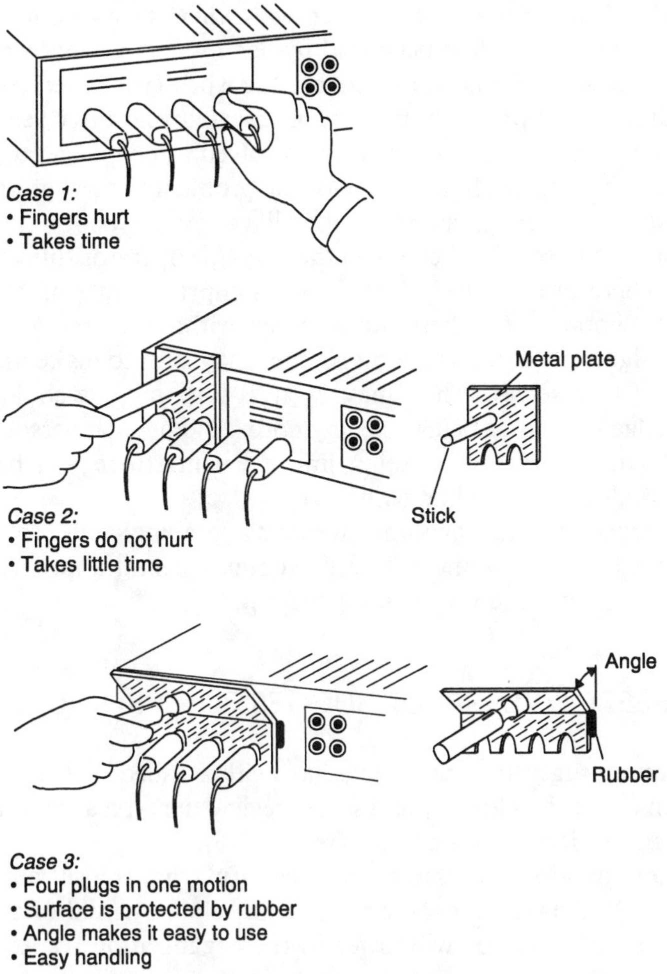

Case 1:
• Fingers hurt
• Takes time

Metal plate

Case 2:
• Fingers do not hurt
• Takes little time

Stick

Angle

Rubber

Case 3:
• Four plugs in one motion
• Surface is protected by rubber
• Angle makes it easy to use
• Easy handling

scratched. Furthermore, as plugs are taken out when the jig is pushed forward, I changed the angle. . . . And, I modified the wooden stick, so that it is easy to hold.'' (See Exhibit 7.4a, Case 3.)

This time, it was the supervisor who was surprised. Only one week after joining the company, a new employee had started to make improvements that improved productivity and quality. The supervisor suggested she apply for a suggestion award. Later, she received not only a monetary award, but the ''Rookie of the Year'' award, as well.*

*Based on a conversation with Bunji Tozawa, Japan HR association.

We might ask, "What caused her to be interested in utilizing her creativity?" In this case, the moment was when she murmured, "My fingers hurt." If she had been told by her co-workers that whenever new people start, it takes time before the work gets easier, the same procedure would probably have been repeated year after year. Even though a problem may appear to be resolved as people get used to a situation, in fact, the hidden root of the problem has not gone away.

Instead of being patient, words like, "What about this?" or "What if you use this?" changed the way this operator thinks of her work. Therefore, not only was there an improved rate of progress, but more importantly, there was a change within the person. As such words trigger people to think more, they may start to make improvement by themselves. They may even absorb more techniques or knowledge instead of being idle anymore. And as such person grows after having a taste of making improvement, there will be more people following a similar path.

In order to encourage improvements company-wide, therefore, let us next look into one of the most fundamental approaches for problem solving, the suggestion program.

EFFECTIVE USE OF SUGGESTION PROGRAMS

Since many suggestion programs have either failed or became dormant in the United States, let us first review the typical reasons why many suggestion programs fail (Exhibit 7.5).

If a suggestion program is not successful, that is itself an indication of (1) management taking too lightly the potential of people's talent, and (2) lack of willpower in the organization, especially in management, to make improvements in the program and make it work. For these reasons, if a program fails, I would suggest management is 99.9 percent responsible. (By the way, when a program becomes successful, it should be acknowledged that everybody has contributed, instead of management getting all the credit.)

In spite of difficulties, however, there are many successful suggestion programs where people have contributed their ideas to make their programs work. Exhibit 7.6 gives such examples.

In any case, monetary incentives should be limited if we are to focus on involving the total work force. Some other activities to stimulate ideas are sharing examples in meetings, or posting pictures on display boards. Awarding special points for suggestions relating

Exhibit 7.5. Why Suggestion Programs Fail

- People jump into the program without much preparation, or commitment
- The program is developed more as an independent entity than as part of a total approach toward continuous improvement
- Most people do not share the understanding that the higher the number of suggestions, the higher the morale of the people, and the better the performance in quality, cost, delivery, and safety.
- Getting more people involved in even a small improvement is not considered important.
- The people who make suggestions are different from those who implement them, i.e., people are not responsible as project leaders for implementing ideas.
- The evaluation process is too complex; it takes too much time and effort. By trying to be fair and accurate, it ends up creating a bureaucratic nightmare.
- There is no strong initiative to learn from successful companies to promote the program
- The accomplishments are not shared with people. As a result, people do not get feedback or stimulation.
- The lack of feedback to people regarding their progress, either good or bad, makes them think that the program is not important to management.
- The feedback to a person making a suggestion is taken lightly. There is not enough coaching and guidance given for the person to grow.
- The reward may be too high, leading people to think their small idea does not count.

Exhibit 7.6. Examples of Suggestion Programs

Type	Description of Program	Comments
Informal	No awards are given. Suggestions are considered as a part of job.	Consciousness-driven, easy to administer
Donut/Lunch	Free donuts or lunch are given to the team when a certain number of suggestions are made	Emphasis is on teamwork
Potluck	Everybody gets a ticket for each suggestion for a draw every month to win an award.	Emphasis on having fun.
Formal	Awards vary from entry award to profit sharing contributions. Jackets, hats, etc. may be given, too.	More formal type program.
After-the-Fact	Only ideas that have been implemented qualify. Especially suited for those who have experience.	Easy to administer; emphasis on people's ownership to implement ideas.

to a focus subject such as safety or housekeeping for a month may accentuate the program. Also, department awards may be given in addition to individual awards.

In order to gain everyone's participation, suggestions can be shared in a meeting, before-and-after pictures can be prominently displayed, or interesting examples may be featured in a newsletter together with the number of suggestions submitted by each department. Exhibit 7.7 shows before and after pictures of improvements that have been posted for everybody to see. As pictures are turned in every month, supervisors get together and vote for the gold, silver, and bronze prizes. Monetary rewards are then given, but they are to be spent as a group to promote teamwork.

A general recommendation is to focus first on small improvements emphasizing people involvement and then, as the number of suggestions increases, to work on improving the quality of sugges-

Exhibit 7.7. People's Suggestions Displayed

Courtesy Fireplace Manufacturers, Inc.

tions. Typically, suggestion programs have four phases of development as described in Exhibit 7.8.

Exhibit 7.9 shows good examples of suggestions summarized in a brochure form so that people can get the idea of a suggestion program. Also, it gives recognition to those who contributed. Each page corresponds to one suggestion, and covers (1) title of suggestion, (2) name of the person who made suggestion, (3) description of problem, (4) how the idea was generated, (5) implementation of idea with exhibit (cartoon), and (6) effect. Of course, cartoons make the expla-

Exhibit 7.8. Implementing an Effective Suggestion Program

1. *Preparation Phase.* Managers explore starting a new program or revamping a dormant one. Without their full support, though, the program may be initiated with high expectations—much like shooting fireworks—that it may not be possible to sustain. To avoid this, proper preparation is a must. There must be a commitment at the top to make it work. The objective is a successful, long-lasting program. If expectations are unrealistically high, people will lose confidence and the program will be short-lived. One effective exercise to increase understanding of the program is to list ideas that have already been implemented at the shop floor. Doing so will give people an idea of what can be done on their own initiative.

2. *Startup Phase.* Getting the taste of success is the key here. When the number of suggestions starts to slow down, as typically happens, it is time for managers (and employees) to come up with ideas to improve the situation. Perhaps people's suggestions have not been focused on what they can do on their own. Managers' impatience, failure to follow up suggestions, or lack of understanding and leadership in the program may be the problem. Unless these problems are resolved, the future of the improvement program will be in jeopardy.

3. *Expansion Phase.* Once the number of suggestions increases and then stabilizes, people will have established a much stronger experience base. There may be both interesting and mundane ideas. Since the participation of people is typically more important than the content in this phase, the quality of suggestions may vary. On the management side, there may still be problems such as a lack of sharing of improvement ideas among people, lack of recognition (awards, articles in plant newsletters, etc.), and insufficient guidance. These problems need to be addressed before the program can be declared a success.

4. *Further Improvement Phase.* The content of suggestions improves in this phase and many ideas are implemented throughout the company. People have developed pride in their ability to make improvements. Higher morale results in more interest in learning problem-solving techniques. Also, there is a good linkage with team improvement activities. In many ways, people perceive that making suggestions is a part of their job.

Note: After putting more emphasis on implementation, many Japanese companies simply report the implemented ideas as suggestions after the fact.

Exhibit 7.9. Sharing Suggestions with Brochure

Courtesy Japan Railway—West Japan

nation interesting and easy to follow. In a sense, this fifty-page book-let represents the annual report of the suggestion program, sharing the small improvements of the shop floor with everyone.

While some people may want to share or implement ideas without going through a suggestion program, the clear benefits of a formal program are listed in Exhibit 7.10. To get a flavor for what people think of suggestion programs, Appendix 7.1 describes practitioner's comments about the suggestion program at Matsushita Electric Industries' vacuum cleaner division in Japan. For Matsushita as a whole, the total number of suggestions is over four million; the average number of suggestions per employee is forty-five annually. The highest number of suggestions by a single employee in the division was more than two thousand in one year.

Exhibit 7.11 shows one of the regular Wednesday meetings at Matsushita's Vacuum Cleaner Division, where people come to see managers and support people to discuss their ideas. Though completely voluntary, the meetings are considered an important opportunity for managers to provide proper guidance and coaching. Without proper guidance, people will not come back, so this provides a good educational setting as well as a critical testing ground for managers and support people's leadership abilities.

Exhibit 7.10. Benefits of a Formal Suggestion Program

- Making suggestions and sharing the progress of the program helps to orient our unconscious minds to conscious improvement-oriented minds. (This may help change people's behavior, habits, and even their destiny.)
- The simple act of writing down a suggestion clarifies our thought process.
- By keeping individual records, each person can see his or her progress.
- It helps the boss and co-workers learn about the progress. The number of suggestions represents the creativity or health of the organization.
- It makes it easy to communicate with others, e.g., to share ideas with people in other departments, new employees, etc.
- It will expose areas where support is needed. (If people are reluctant or embarrassed to write, naturally, they should be offered help to overcome such problems.)
- Reviewing the suggestions will help people think of more suggestions in the future. It will also reveal the patterns of suggestions.
- By monitoring the number of suggestions by each person, managers can provide support where needed. There may be healthy competition among people, too.
- The program will provide an important interface between the individual employee and his or her boss for proper support, guidance, and feedback.

Exhibit 7.11. Weekly Suggestion Counseling Day

Courtesy Matsushita

EFFECTIVE USE OF TEAM IMPROVEMENT ACTIVITIES

While suggestion programs focus mainly on individuals, team-oriented improvement activity is another important problem-solving activities for groups of people. Whether you call them self-managing teams, quality circles, or small group improvement activities, the emphasis is on a group of people developing their own initiative to address problems found in their own area. The major features of these team improvement activities are summarized in Exhibit 7.12.

As with suggestion programs, the practice of team improvement activities follows a similar process of preparation, startup, and expansion to further improvement. The difference, however, is that these are *team*-oriented activities aimed at elevating people's skills for self-management. Ultimately, therefore, these teams should be able to run as mini-companies, while maintaining proper linkages to the total company operation. (See Exhibit 7.13.)

DEVELOPING A TEAM-ORIENTED ENVIRONMENT

Since a mini-company is a unit of an organization made up of people working together to achieve common objectives, teamwork is necessary to accomplish anything. Moreover, if teams are run well, their accomplishments should be more than the sum of its individual members' accomplishments.

This is contrasted to specialists and managers who often think that just by collecting people and giving them simple tasks, things

Exhibit 7.12. Major Features of Team Improvement Activities.

- The team is composed of people mainly from the same work area.
- The focus is on improving problems on the shop floor, e.g., QCDSM.
- The emphasis is on self-management and the use of the team's collective wisdom.
- Support and guidance may be given by management.
- The team contributes to achieve company's mission as well as their own.
- The team explores everyone's creativity and self-esteem.
- The team makes use of problem-solving tools, such as the seven QC tools.
- The team addresses improvement as well as maintenance activities.
- The team functions continuously, aiming for continuous improvement while involving everyone.
- The team values respect for the individual, i.e., people's creativity.

Exhibit 7.13. People Using a Display Board to Describe the Problem-Solving Process. A big story board helps to show the progress of team improvement activities. The information is developed in a team meeting and posted at the shop floor.

Courtesy Borg-Warner

will work. However, we should realize the importance of good teamwork where individuals support and work with each other effectively. Exhibit 7.14 shows key characteristics of an effective team. Also, Appendix 7.2 gives more details of the characteristics of the team and a checklist to evaluate team's effectiveness.

As teams share concerns, focus their efforts, and collectively utilize the abilities of all members, they begin to function like a well-developed sports team. That is, just as the game strategy will vary depending on the skills of each player, the behavior of a team will also reflect the talents of its members.

If a team cannot gain cooperative spirit from its members, naturally, it will not be able to achieve its goals. For example, if we imagine a baseball team where each fielder is trying to become a star player at the expense of others, or day dreaming in the middle of the game, the team will not have much of a chance to win. If the shortstop and third baseman argue about who is supposed to catch the ball coming their way, it may go through the gap and into left field

Exhibit 7.14. Key Characteristics of an Effective Team.

- Has a clear team mission and objectives.
- Exhibits strong leadership.
- Synergy of team members is apparent.
- Exhibits a good combination of skills and knowledge.
- Shares information well, i.e., glass wall management.
- Members support each other.
- Works hard and has fun together.
- Keeps learning as it moves forward.
- Individuals feel that they have grown as individuals with team.
- Has a good track record of progress.

before they settle their argument. As unlikely as it may sound, we may fall into this type of trap very easily.

With regard to personality issues among team members, we may think that differences in personalities among us can make our lives more interesting. We may find that there are no people who are not needed. On a team composed of people with diverse characteristics, one may be slow, another may be too rigid, and so on. Yet each may contribute his or her own talent. The slow person may come closer to the core of issues than other people. The rigid person may make sure certain steps are followed, assuring higher quality. In fact, a team consisting entirely of very "smart" people often stalls in the middle of the project.

Today's workplace reflects the turbulent nature of our marketplace. As our work becomes more complex and requires a quicker response, we find it getting harder for any one person to accomplish anything. More participation from everyone is needed; no one person should take lightly his or her contribution to the team.

In order to break down communication barriers and to work as a team, many Japanese companies favor an open office arrangement. Honda even developed their own term, *wai-gaya,* which represents the sound of people brainstorming in different areas of the office of shop floor. Furthermore, all top management share a big open room so they can practice wai-gaya at the top management level as well.

As obvious as it may be, if everybody's focus is on individual goals the end result will not be a team's success. Just as both a good coach and a willing athlete are necessary for success in team sports, we need the same at work.

PRACTICING PROBLEM SOLVING AS A TEAM

Yet, team-based problem solving may not be easy, especially when a team is new. If the team is inexperienced, developing trust and honesty is important. As we socialize, share joys and sorrows together, and review what went well or poorly after the day is over, we will gain a better understanding of teamwork and get to know each other as individuals. All of us being human, we need to satisfy such needs in our work as well as outside of it.

In practicing problem-solving activities as a team, one tool commonly used in Japan is the QC story, describing the typical steps in solving a problem for better quality control. Some also call this the CI (continuous improvement) story. As shown in Exhibit 7.15, this format helps us to think through and practice the improvement process step by step as well as to communicate the process of improvement to others in a straightforward, easy-to-understand fashion. (Although there are different problem-solving steps which are known by other names, the basic idea is the same as that described here.)

As an example, Exhibit 7.16a indicates how teams monitor their progress at Juki, a Japanese sewing machine manufacturer. Here, each step represents one hole on a golf course. As the team moves forward following the steps of the QC story, the magnet also moves one step at a time until the nine holes (nine steps) are completed. Exhibit 7.16b shows how people in a Continuous Improvement Users Group use the QC story for a team presentation. This large board makes the presentation easy to deliver for presenters as well as easy to digest for audiences. (In order to evaluate team improvement projects, Appendix 7.3 shows detailed key checkpoints for teams to successfully execute the project.)

Exhibit 7.15. The QC Story

1. Identify problem
2. Describe situation
3. Set goals
4. Analyze root causes
5. Develop countermeasure
6. Execute countermeasure
7. Evaluate accomplishments
8. Standardize
9. Discuss lessons learned and future plans

Exhibit 7.16a. Display of Teams' Progress Using QC Story

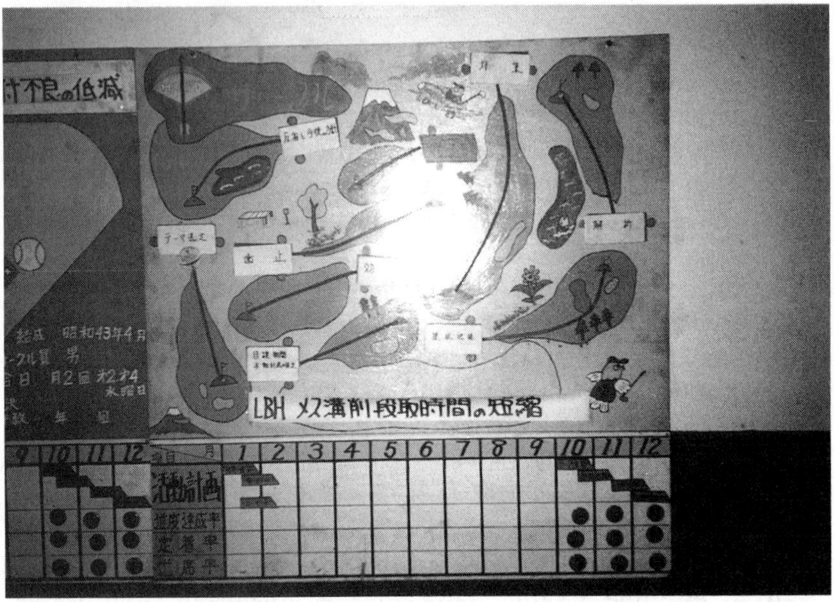

Courtesy Juki

Exhibit 7.16b. Use of Story Board for a Team Presentation

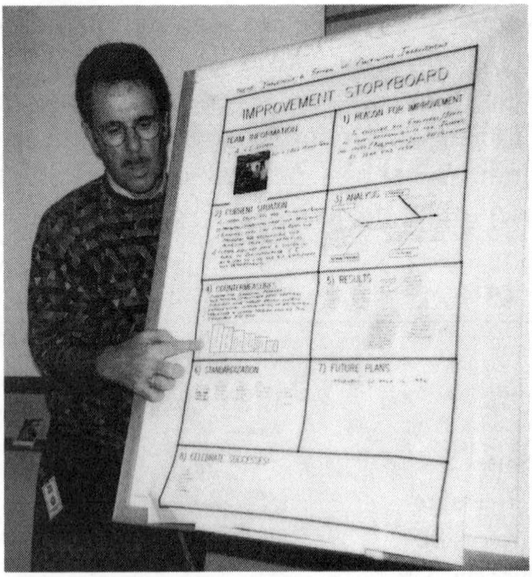

Courtesy Clipper Belt Lacer/Continuous
Improvement Users Group

As mentioned before, our orientation on the shop floor is self-management. If people are given proper opportunities, they can often accomplish much more than traditional managers assume—even though it may present many hurdles along the way.

To help facilitate the process of learning, therefore, managers and staff people need to coach people and let them experiment—even let them make a few mistakes from which to learn. At the same time, people need to take the initiative to explore their potential.

Since the upgrading of people's self-management skills should translate to the company's growth, we should consider this the natural way of conducting business. Also, as much as the desire for self-expression is a cornerstone of a child's development, this process represents the people's growth process in our organization.

INTERCOMPANY EXCHANGE PROGRAM

If we share the dream of continuous improvement that involves everybody, we may expand the definition of team to include those outside of the company as well. For example, manufacturers and suppliers may cooperate, and even companies from unrelated industries may share the process of continuous improvement. Here, this activity is referred to as intercompany exchange.

At Toyota for example, Toyota Production System Study Groups are jointly formed with suppliers to share the idea of continuous improvement with an emphasis on mastering Toyota's production system. Similarly, a group of individuals from the Young Presidents' Organization (YPO) and The Executive Committee (TEC) in Southern California started their own self-study group activities on continuous improvement. Furthermore, with seven or eight companies in a group, groups of companies formed Continuous Improvement Users' Groups (CIUG) in the Midwest to promote the idea of continuous improvement. (For details of these activities, see Appendix 7.4.)

As another example of such sharing, teams from such companies as Northern Telecom, Digital Equipment, and Kodak have visited the teams at Motorola to exchange ideas and experiences for mutual learning. Randy Bauder, a trainer at Motorola's Government Electronics Group, comments, "We have had teams . . . visit us, talk to our teams face to face, and share their experiences, and it's been an extremely positive event. The energy, the creativity, the excitement, the spontaneity, the sincerity of these other organizations has really helped to spark our people.'' (From *The New Shop Floor Management* video course by Kiyoshi Suzaki, SME, 1992)

As noted here, with a shared vision of continuous improvement, we can develop such a program on our own or join an intercompany exchange program as a means to continue our self-improvement process.

MANAGING THE IMPROVEMENT PROCESS WITH PDCA

As we use problem-solving tools and implement suggestion programs, team problem-solving, or intercompany exchange programs, our organization as a whole will internalize the necessary skills and start to find its path to the future. Again, as in any competitive sport, the essential requirements are a desire for self-improvement, discipline, and hard work.

In order to manage this process company-wide, one very useful concept is the plan-do-check-act (PDCA) cycle (see Exhibit 7.17). We might also remember that this cycle applies in different subjects, as we discussed in relation to achieving mission, objectives, control points, and standards (see comments on Exhibit 4.14), or in training (see comments on Exhibit 5.8).

Since the concept of PDCA is easy for everyone to remember, this simple principle can be used to guide the process of continuous improvement company-wide. Please note, however, that to start this cycle in practice, the steps ''check'' and ''act'' should be taken before ''plan.'' This is because proper checking and action are pre-

Exhibit 7.17. Basics of Management Concept for Continuous Improvement: PDCA

Plan	Clarify objectives, mission.
	Decide means to achieve objectives (develop plans).
Do	Execute plans.
Check	Verify that plans were executed as expected.
	See if objectives were achieved as planned.
Act	If objectives were not met, analyze and develop countermeasures.
	As appropriate, develop standards and carry over the learning to the next ''plan.''

Exhibit 7.18. Cycle of PDCA

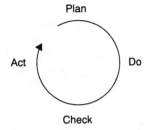

requisite for good planning. Nevertheless, we typically refer to this cycle as PDCA, and since it is an ongoing process for moving the organization forward, it is shown as a continuous cycle in Exhibit 7.18.

Pictorially, the process of improvement may be illustrated as if we were rolling the PDCA wheel up a hill (Exhibit 7.19). As you see, each problem-solving cycle corresponds to a PDCA cycle. Also, since different levels of the organization will be going through this cycle, if we look at the whole organization, the management cycle of PDCA may be illustrated as in Exhibit 7.20 where each unit of the organization is practicing the cycle of PDCA, solving one problem after another.

Practicing the PDCA cycle, however, requires a certain discipline. If we do not practice this discipline but continue the practice of fire fighting—that is, plan-do-plan-do—there will not be much progress. Plans will be tried out without coordination as if people

Exhibit 7.19. Rolling the PDCA Wheel for Continuous Improvement

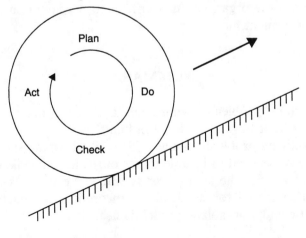

Ehxibit 7.20. Practicing the Cycle of PDCA Throughout the Organization

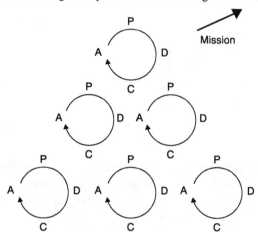

were blindfolded. As obvious as it may be, whether or not the whole organization practices the PDCA cycle will make a big difference for its performance.

Of course, analytical skills are very important. For example, in the fire-fighting mode, people often overlook the importance of checking what has already happened and analyzing why it happened. For this reason, we should carefully examine how the PDCA cycle is practiced logically—step by step.

Ideally, PDCA cycles should be harmoniously established at all levels, like the heartbeat of the organization. Even though we will not discuss this coordination in detail until Chapters 9 and 10, we should remember that developing a mechanism to assure total team effort within the organization is critical to developing a company-wide improvement movement.

SUMMARY

- Learning problem-solving tools and practicing them at the shop floor have to go hand in hand.
- Practicing problem-solving skills is like learning sports. As in sports, we need to be able to use our skills immediately as the need arises. The shop floor is where the tire hits the road. Rather than a too academic or theoretical approach, a pragmatic and workable approach is needed.

- The organization needs to provide different approaches for people to contribute their problem-solving skills. These include suggestion programs and small group improvement activities.
- For any approach to be meaningful, managers need to make the process customer-friendly (people-friendly) while people need to have a desire for self-improvement.
- Some common steps have been found effective in solving problems, such as the QC story format. Everyone benefits if we can use such methods without reinventing the wheel. Also, with such steps, we can communicate the improvement process with others in a straightforward, easy-to-understand fashion.
- In order to practice problem solving organization-wide, the organization as a whole needs to practice such people-friendly concepts as the QC story and PDCA.
- Practicing problem solving as a team requires the initiative of people, effective guidance and facilitation, and a supportive environment. A team should behave like a mini-company to accomplish its mission.

Chapter Eight

LEADING PEOPLE FOR CONTINUOUS IMPROVEMENT

In previous chapters, we have studied the vision of shop floor excellence, customer orientation, people involvement, and problem solving for continuous improvement. Now we will turn to the role of leadership in promoting all of these subjects.

First, we will review the new role of leaders in today's business by emphasizing the point that leadership is situational rather than dependent on titles or responsibilities. Then, we will study various situations to learn how to guide people in improvement activities in instilling the idea of ownership and self-improvement. Next, we will study ways to share success and improve communication at the shop floor, both verbally and visually so that a sense of camaraderie can be created. And finally, we will discuss positive reinforcement in changing our behavior or habits to better control our own destiny.

MANAGERS AS LEADERS: EMPLOYEES AS CUSTOMERS

Someone once said, "Managers are people who do things right . . . leaders are people who do the right things." In other words, while doing things right (efficiency) is important, it does not count unless you are doing the right things (effectiveness). Instead of narrowly focusing their efforts, therefore, managers today need to develop a broad understanding of business and a high level of leadership skills in order to be effective.

What this means is that the potential of the organization is often determined by how much the manager can envision people managing their own work. Instead of trying to do it all him- or herself, the manager needs to challenge people to stretch their potential. The more he or she teaches and the more people internalize skills and gain confidence, the more the manager can delegate responsibility and prepare better for the future.

While eliminating our current jobs may still sound counterintuitive, recent events in the Eastern bloc countries should remind us that monopolizing power or skills does not pay off in the long run. Similarly, for those who live in a free market system, the prudent strategy is to keep moving ahead courageously while acquiring more skills and insight to open up our future. In that sense, glass wall management should not be limited to sharing information; it should promote the sharing of skills, insight, and management philosophy as well.

In doing this, managers should overcome the fear of losing control. Since they set the examples for others to follow, they should think of people as their customers and give away skills to the people, and encourage others to do the same. To clarify these points, Exhibit 8.1 compares the characteristics of a traditional manager with those of a progressive manager. Of course, our upbringing from childhood has had so much influence on us that we cannot change our attitude, behavior, or habits easily. Yet just as people in the Eastern bloc have had to struggle for betterment, each of us needs to work for the changes constructively rather than become a roadblock to progress.

In a sense employees are the manager's customers. Whether or not the manager can lead them effectively depends on the ability to put himself or herself in their shoes. By doing so, the manager can make judgments considering the benefits to the overall organization.

Exhibit 8.1. Characteristics of Traditional and Progressive Managers

	Traditional Manager	**Progressive Manager**
Attitude Toward Skills	Monopolizes skills	Lets go of own skills by teaching others
Attitude Toward Information	Monopolizes information	Shares information
Attitude Toward Power	Prefers centralized power structure	Favors decentralized power structure
Attitude Toward People	Closed, insecure	Open, trusting
Management Style	Supervises people, enforces rules	Leads people effectively, encourages self-management

Also, this idea should apply not only to managers but to everybody. By taking a customer-oriented or selfless viewpoint, we can all develop the ability to see and respect different opinions.

To summarize, a good leader will be able to do the following:

- Carefully listen to people (customers), and learn from them in order to identify the needs of the organization.
- Find out people's problems, and help to solve them.
- Teach people, and provide them with skills, ideas, and suggestions.
- Respect people, and set an example for them to practice what everybody believes in.
- Involve people in the process of assessing both problems and opportunities, and come up with new directions for the organization.

Practicing these points will not only help people and the organization as a whole, but it will help the leader's personal development and enrich his or her life as well.

LEADERSHIP IS SITUATIONAL

Whether at work or at home, whether with friends or with business associates, there are moments for everyone to take initiative. In fact, our free market system and our orientation toward freedom of information are good representations of this belief. Instead of others telling us what we should do, we should be able to express our own beliefs and create our own destiny within a given set of circumstances.

For example, whether it is picking up trash from the floor without anybody asking or speaking up in front of people to make a point, if we are truly and genuinely acting upon our own feelings and behavioral standards, other people will be attracted and even enlightened by our behavior.

So, in my view, this leadership is not the type found in traditional organizations where only someone with power can influence the rest of the organization. Instead leadership is situational, depending on the time, place, and occasion. There are times when managers must lead, and times individuals must lead. Managers may, however, provide opportunities for people to take more initiative as the situation allows. Pete Machuga, a plant manager at General Electric's Ohio Lamp Plant, comments:

> I think leadership is sort of a nebulous thing. It's knowing when to lead, knowing when to direct, knowing when to listen, when to talk, and those aren't things somebody can say here's the rules on. You know it in your gut.
>
> —From *The New Shop Floor Management* video course by Kiyoshi Suzaki, SME, 1992

Of course, from a business point of view, if we wait for others in the power position to make decisions on a day-to-day basis, our organization will fall behind more progressive companies that promote self-management and utilizing people's creativity effectively.

A DESIRE FOR SELF-IMPROVEMENT MAKES THINGS HAPPEN

Soichiro Honda, the founder of Honda Motor Company, illustrates leadership qualities in his own way.

> If we are determined to make things happen, I believe that human beings can do most things. In the early days when Honda was founded, we bought half-burned machines and restored them. When we manufactured piston rings, we made inspection jigs by ourselves because we could not afford to buy them. When we did not have money, it simply meant that we had to do things ourselves. So we did.
>
> When we built the factory I mixed concrete myself. When the factory was built, we had no windows. So we gathered broken glass, melted it in a melting pot, and made glass—which was not necessarily smooth at all. When we do not have money, we simply need to use our wisdom and muscles.
>
> —From *One Day, One Story* by Soichiro Honda, p. 29

When more wealth is created in our society, we tend to take things for granted, and we may not use our wisdom as much. Many companies as well as individuals have fallen into this trap. To lead a group of people toward achieving any mission, we should not forget this basic point. Accordingly, we should ask ourselves the next fundamental question: "Without our will and creativity, what can we accomplish?"

Whether running a company or leading a team in an improve-ment project, all leaders should have a strong desire to accomplish the mission—more than anyone else in the group. Otherwise, they should not be leaders. This differs from the traditional view that "managing" is more important than "leading." So, let us answer the following questions:

- In today's business environment, why do leadership qualities seem to be more in demand than before?
- If achieving the mission is of primary importance for the orga-nization, then titles, corner office suites, etc. become second-ary. Yet, some of us are hung up on these. What does this imply? Are we placing "form" ahead of "substance"? If so, why?

GUIDING IMPROVEMENT ACTIVITIES

As people learn and start to practice problem-solving skills, provid-ing proper guidance is critical to success. Even though managers may generally feel themselves under the pressure of time, if properly han-dled, a little time invested to help guide people in improvement activ-ities will bring a sizable return, both in economic and personal terms.

Let us, then, first look at the coaching process in making im-provements. By putting ourselves in the coach's position, we will figure out what can be done at different stages of improvement activ-ities. If leaders are to lead, they must understand the improvement process at the shop floor and be able to provide guidance whatever the situation is.

1. When people first start to think about improvement, often no ideas come to mind. In such instances, the coach may offer advice:

- "Think of small improvements first, not big ones. "
- "Often a good starting point is in workplace organization (cleaning, organizing, and arranging). Then, think of things we don't like to do, things that are dangerous, inconvenient, redundant, or troubling."

2. To trigger someone's thinking about improvement, when a manager sees someone working with some difficulty:

- "Don't you think this step is somewhat inconvenient? I wonder if we can do something about it."
- "I heard that Mr. X came up with an interesting idea. So, why don't we visit him and check on it?"

3. To set an example as a manager for everyone to think about improvements. In addition to simply participating in suggestion programs, award programs, and the like, managers also need to practice what they preach:

- "Her idea is such a great one. Why didn't I think of it?"
- "Here is my idea. What do you guys think about it?"
- "This is an important problem for our organization. Could anyone come up with any suggestions?"

4. To guide people to think of what they can do to improve the situation as opposed to pointing a finger at someone else:

- "Let's ask what we can do for our organization. Aren't there many things that we can improve before making others be responsible for improvement?"
- "Frustration is OK. After all, if we didn't get frustrated, we human beings could not have advanced this far. As I understand it, our brain power is only three percent utilized."

5. To encourage people to write down suggestions on paper, especially those who don't feel comfortable with writing:

- "Let me show you how you might write down such an idea and apply it to the suggestion program."
- "What is important is not how you write, but the essence of your idea."
- "A little drawing may be just fine to get the message across."
- "Look at the example of Mr. So-and-so. Notice how he uses the sketch effectively for others to understand."

6. To find ways to support and implement ideas someone else came up with:

- "What can I do to help you?"
- "As much as possible, I encourage you to implement ideas by yourself. The person making a suggestion should become the project leader of that suggestion."
- "If an idea is difficult to implement, let us think of something much easier that you can do."

7. To follow up the implementation:

- "Now I see how things can be different because of your idea. You should be proud of yourself!"
- "Even if some people may think this is a small improvement, I think it's a great idea. From my experience, I can tell you that every small step counts for us to get better!"
- "This is a great idea! We should share this in our supervisor's meeting and display it with before and after pictures so others can benefit. Perhaps we should make this an article in our newsletter, too."
- (Introducing Mr. X to Mr. Big-Wig.) "Mr. X has been making

Exhibit 8.2. Leading People by Example

a great contribution to improve his workplace. Why don't you explain your recent idea to Mr. Big-Wig?''

8. To further encourage and stimulate people, a presentation to peers and management may be appropriate. The following is a comment from someone who heard his school classmate's presentation on the employee suggestion program at his company's convention.

> When I saw it was his turn to make a presentation, I realized my heart was beating faster. Then I was even more surprised when he started to make his presentation. He explained his subject well. He used graphs and charts to make points clearly. He seemed to be quite confident. Then I realized that I was naive to simply come to work. I felt somewhat embarrassed and could not even speak to him after the convention.
>
> —Memo statements of an employee who later turned out to be a major contributor to Toyota's suggestion program. From *Toyota's Suggestion Program* by Yuzo Yasuda, p. 129.

When coming up with ideas or making contributions, our titles in the company should not constrain us. What is important is which ideas or decisions contribute the most, not whose idea or decision it is. In that sense, someone's value as a person should have nothing to do with his or her title or background. In fact, in relation to the subject of improvement, whether a person is great or not should be judged by his or her contribution to the society. Touching on this point, Soichiro Honda said, "Great people are not at the top of the organization. They tend to be hidden but doing the very important jobs to contribute to our society" (From *One Day, One Story* by Soichiro Honda).

HAVING PRIDE IN OUR WORK

"Empowering people," "instilling pride in people," or "guiding people for improvement"—we say these are important. But being busy in fighting fires, we may get confused or lose perspective about addressing these important issues. In order for us to keep on track, how can we confirm our beliefs and find enjoyment in what we do?

Illustrating this point, one person may be busy "making money" by constructing a building; another may be "building a church" where people can gather to share their beliefs. Even though the work is the same, there is a clear difference in perception between these two people. The one who is busy making money almost has the answer in his hand (i.e., the joy of accomplishing the mission to build the church) but is unable to see it because his mind is busy thinking about something else.

Similar situations exist on the shop floor, too. One may work for money; another may constantly look for ways to improve products and satisfy customers or to make the job easier or safer. The work may be the same, but the level of pride and satisfaction that goes with it may be quite different.

We may then wonder why people's perceptions are so different? Is one materialistic and the other spiritual? Who is right? Who is happier? What is the impact on us as individuals? Soichiro Honda gives us a hint:

> Our work has to be new at all times. Also, we can tackle any work with a new set of eyes. It is my pleasure to visit Honda factories since every time I visit, there are always changes and new things happening.
>
> When I walk the line side, young employees stop me, saying, "We made the changes this way. It made our work easier and more productive," etc. Their faces are lively, not the faces of persons who are used by machines. This may be because they are tackling their work, pursuing the future—making it better today, and an even better future tomorrow.
>
> —From *One Day, One Story*
> by Soichiro Honda, p. 23.

A supervisor who was promoting a suggestion program at Toyota shared his thoughts in his way:

> A leader does not have monetary reward. People may think I am a fool to take care of others. But rather than struggling to earn more money or a better title, I am finding something special. The people's minds touch each other, and that encourages me to go on. Looking in the eyes of people, and listening to their simple "Thank you," I find something wonderful.
>
> —Adapted from *"Toyota Suggestion Program,"*
> by Yuzo Yasuda, pp. 61 and 62.

Even though the answer may have to be found by each individual, let us ask: Isn't it important especially for leaders to share the vision and mission of the organization with their people so that they can participate in the joy and sorrow of making headway into the future? Also, isn't it important for each of us to find meaning in what we do? If we have pride and conviction in what we do, what can we accomplish? Or what can't we accomplish?

On a recent visit to a renowned European company, I asked an operator, "Do you know whether you are ahead or behind schedule?" The operator could not answer. I was shocked, and I told the management as much. In my view, managers should not let such situations happen. Even though there has been noticeable improvement in this company, this incident raised the concern that people's talents were not being utilized. To me, it is almost a crime when people lose the desire for self-improvement, or are not given the opportunity to express their potential.

SHARING SUCCESSES

While effective leaders may pick a moment in the course of their work to listen to or encourage people, a more formal way to generate interest in improvement may be to share the achievements at periodic conventions or meetings. Some companies call such an occasion a "sharing rally" or "show and tell" to reflect their purpose of spreading the good news throughout the company. As indicated by the comments from the Toyota employee described above, when we are exposed to a stimulating environment, we often find an unrealized potential in ourselves.

The benefits of a well-executed sharing rally are numerous. Exhibit 8.3 summarizes the major points. In addition to the points made in Exhibit 8.3, when a certain format, such as the QC story, is used in making the presentation, there are additional benefits. Not only is it easy to follow the steps of the presentation, but also the QC story will help others to learn the steps of problem solving with actual examples. As experience accumulates and the steps of problem-solving become second nature, they may be modified or made much more free form.

After attending an event such as a sharing rally, show and tell, or an all-employee meeting, people will develop a sense that everybody is working together to accomplish the mission of the com-

Exhibit 8.3. Benefits of Sharing Rallies

For Presenters

- Preparation helps to organize thoughts. The process will provide a good training ground for becoming a good communicator, planner, and manager.

- Following the PDCA cycle and going to regularly held sharing rallies helps to develop a rhythm of continuous improvement. The process will help develop a habit of "completing" the project, provide an opportunity to review how much has been accomplished, and clarify what is still missing.

- Speaking to an audience will build confidence. Making a presentation is like competing in sports. Just as scoring runs in baseball makes you feel good, making a presentation about improving your work should also make you feel good about yourself.

- Getting comments and questions is a stimulating learning experience. The audience's interest in your work as described in your presentation will refresh your own view of your work. You may be surprised how well you can answer people's questions. This will help build your confidence. Also, people's comments may give you new insights.

- Recognition feeds more energy in continuous improvement. Well orchestrated, awards, rewards, and words of recognition may make the efforts a long-lasting memory for the presenter. Also, sharing this experience with friends, spouses, and others may make the workplace more humane and not just a place to earn money.

For Leaders (as Organizer, Facilitator, Judge, or Referee of a Sharing Rally):

- Through guiding people before and after the presentation, leaders can learn more about their people's skills and plan accordingly to help them. This exchange of ideas with presenters will also provide an opportunity to share knowledge and educate people in the audience at the same time. Leaders may be surprised at the hidden abilities of people that are exposed in this process.

- Leaders can use such gatherings as opportunities to report on the status of the company, and reaffirm the company's values on continuous improvement and customer satisfaction.

- Leaders can use this as their own learning experience. Teaching, coaching, guiding, communicating, or empowering people are all necessary skills for today's business leaders. By interacting with their groups, effective leaders will be able to maximize the total creativity of the organization. Whether or not the gathering is a success often depends on the leader's skills in orchestrating the activities in the preparation phase. This setting may turn out to be a place for leaders to learn how much they did not know regarding the potential talent of their people. Be humble and learn from everyone! It will not hurt; it will enrich the lives of all of us.

Exhibit 8.3. Continued

For the Audience:

• By listening to the presentations and questions and answers, the audience will learn presentation skills as well as how to use different tools of problem solving. Even though it is the presenters and leaders who convey the process of making improvement, it is up to the audience to get the most out of it.

• Audience members may be stimulated by seeing people doing a good job for the organization. People want to be a part of a successful team. Such an event will also help condition people to success, proving that the organization is on its way to accomplishing its mission. As successes build up, people may even develop a mentality that nothing is impossible.

• The audience may develop a feeling of togetherness and camaraderie as a team. As interaction takes place and successes are shared, people may confirm the vision of their work and enjoy the fact that everybody is working together to build the future.

pany. Thus, confirming progress with these types of gatherings at regular intervals will be an important step in moving the company forward.

IMPROVING COMMUNICATION AT THE SHOP FLOOR

Odd, but one practice that still seems to be lacking in many companies is to have supervisors conduct regular meetings on the shop floor. The absence of such daily or weekly meetings indicates that no close linkage has been established between management and people on the shop floor.

Some supervisors may say "We don't need such meetings because we have enough one-to-one communication. Meetings are a waste of time." However, without meetings how can everyone together share the concerns of the organization, share successes and failures of improvement ideas, review performance as a group, and agree on improvement ideas?

If we put ourselves in their shoes, it should be obvious how shop floor personnel might feel. Exhibit 8.4 shows some of the comments typically heard from people on the shop floor in traditionally managed companies:

Exhibit 8.4. Comments Heard at the Shop Floor in Traditionally
Managed Companies

- All the discussions management people do in the office have nothing to do with what we, on the shop floor, should be concerned about.
- There is no setting where we are encouraged to voice our opinions, either small or large.
- Management says we should voice our opinions anytime, but there is no channel of communication that we feel comfortable using. There is too much distance between us to share our thoughts with them.
- Management says that they have an open door policy. But only a few people go and talk one to one with our manager.
- Since managers don't listen to us, we don't feel like sharing things with them. Even if we have great ideas that could save the company money, why should we bother to tell them?
- It's not just communication between management and us, we also have serious problems among ourselves. Since there is no setting for us to share concerns, small or large, we tend to get frustrated. Even if some problems can be resolved by exchanging ideas, we tend not to do it. We hesitate to make waves.
- Since there is almost nothing shared between us and management, we have no basis to respect them. It is like a business deal. We just come to work, get paid, and go home. There might be something more in our work, especially since we spend so much time there, but since we do not talk about it we don't know what that may be.

To improve the company's competitiveness, there have been many programs introduced in the shop floor. Some people talk about statistical process control, total quality management, just-in-time production, lean production, total productive maintenance, and on and on, yet whatever these programs are named, if the opinions expressed in Exhibit 8.4 represent a majority of the people's attitudes, then it is my opinion that nothing will work. Perhaps some programs may seem to work on the surface, but not in reality with people from the floor fully involved.

If Exhibit 8.4 represents the current situation of the company, each leader or supervisor should think what can be done differently—as the president of a mini-company, just like an entrepreneur starting up a business. He or she should share the vision, missions, objectives, and problem-solving process. Each meeting on the shop floor, then, becomes a board meeting of the mini-company.

Of course, a meeting area should be created to do this. Even though "meeting skills" may be initially lacking, requiring a man-

Exhibit 8.5. A Daily Shop Floor Meeting. A supervisor conducts a daily meeting with his people. Most of these employees had limited education when they joined the company. Yet as they learned problem-solving tools on the job, they became important assets for the company. Here, a teenage supervisor is using a Pareto chart to communicate the key concerns of his mini-company.

Courtesy Fireplace Manufacturers, Inc.

ager to prepare an agenda and assist in running the meeting, over time people should develop skills to conduct an efficient meeting.

COMMUNICATION WITH VISUAL AIDS

In order to assure communication with people on the shop floor, the use of visual aids may be found very effective (see Exhibit 8.6).

To enhance communication and stimulation on the shop floor, displays may be posted in meeting rooms, conference rooms, the cafeteria, or in hallways. I found companies that do not conduct shop floor meetings also do not utilize big empty wall spaces, reflecting a lack of people involvement. Please note, however, that if the charts are not updated, they will send the wrong message as well. When this happens, I often call these "death certificates"—instead of "living documents".

Exhibit 8.6. Visual Aids for Enhanced Communication

Displays

- Operating performance scoreboard of QCDSM:
  These may be considered just like a baseball scoreboard
- Awards:
  These represent the memory of hard work, or milestones of progress
- Banners with important messages or slogans:
  Reminder of people's shared belief
- Improvement board:
  Descriptions of improvements shown by pictures and exhibits with comments
- QC story board:
  Summary of material as it may be presented at the sharing meeting
- Pictures:
  Showing workplace organization, before and after pictures of improvement,
  reminding people to work on the important jobs
- Cross-training charts, skill matrix:
  Showing the skill base of each team member
- Charts on attendance and number of suggestions:
  Indicating the health of the organization

Company Newsletter Articles

- Topic of the month
- Department news written by department heads
- Announcement of awards
- Number of suggestions by departments
- Examples of suggestions
- Success stories
- New employee introductions
- Quizzes, anniversaries, "employees' corner," etc.

As for newsletters, it is not the thickness or professional style of the newsletter that we are concerned about, but the ability to convey the sense of fun, recognition, teamwork, and sharing that is going on in the company. In that sense, people should be sharing the efforts of writing articles rather than having a staff person do the job for them.

Also, remember that a picture may be worth a thousand words. To inform people about upcoming events taking place in and around the factory, for example, a one-page daily newsletter named "Early

Bird," is published for the eight hundred employees at Matsushita's Vacuum Cleaner Plant. Instead of thinking that this takes time and effort, we need to believe that if it is important, we will make it work anyway. (When I mentioned this, a department of Robert Bosch in Germany started their own bi-weekly newsletter. Even though 75 percent of the 100 or so employees there are foreign workers, this type of initiative is propelling this group forward.)

Exhibits 8.7a and 8.7b display samples of customer returns and in-process rejects so that everybody can clearly see the impact of their work on the customers. The comments above these displays read: "How would you feel if you bought such a product?" and "Making quality products, you are the key individual."

In Exhibit 8.8, after improvements are made, the displays used for presentation are posted on the wall to remind people of the good habits of continuous improvement.

To benefit from today's high-tech environment, at Rapid-Line of Grand Rapids videotape is used to share people's accomplishments. People responsible for improvements in a given area speak into the home video camera about the progress they have made.

As you can see, there are many different ways to share progress with each other. Used effectively, these will help develop a stimulating environment where people enjoy working, feeding the energy back into the system. Therefore, even when we are busy, we should not forget to share progress with people and provide appropriate feedback. (For more information on the use of visual aids, see Appendix 8.1.)

Looking around however, I still find many companies where people get very little feedback about their performance. Positive or negative, we need to develop ways to communicate this information so that people know where they stand as well as where they should be in relation to their goals. So, let us ask:

1. What means do we have for providing feedback to people and sharing their progress? How effective are they?
2. What other means can we think of to share progress?

While there are many different ways to share successes such as a newsletter, improvement board, picture board, story board, shop floor meeting, or award program, consistency and perseverance are key prerequisites for success.

Exhibit 8.7. Display of Samples of Defects

a. Display of Customer Returns.

b. Display of In-Process Rejects.
Courtesy Matsushita

Exhibit 8.8. Display of Improvements Posted on the Wall

Courtesy Leegin Creative Leather Products

RECOGNITION AND REWARDS

Since positive reinforcement can motivate everybody to learn and grow, effective leaders are typically good at finding opportunities to recognize and reward people. The key attitude here is "Work can be fun." An important role of the coach, then, is to identify or develop a setting where people can find interest in their work. This may require some innovative thinking. But, if we are not careful, we may develop a program that ends up in confusion, creating discord among people.

One form of recognition that often results in discord is monetary payment. While the program needs to be fair, leaders should stress the fundamental reason behind the program, that is to recognize people's good work. Accordingly, a company that requires the equivalent of lawyers and accountants to evaluate an accomplishment or assess the benefit of a suggestion in order to calculate the amount of the award is totally missing the point. On the other hand, successful recognition and reward programs seem to have several key features in common (see Exhibit 8.9).

People should feel that it is part of their job to contribute to satisfying their customers, eliminating waste, making their own job easier, and working as a team. At the same time, leaders should feel that an important part of their job is to provide opportunities to

Exhibit 8.9. Key Features of Successful Recognition and Reward Programs

- Simple to administer, not bureaucratic
- Quick to respond and evaluate
- Modest monetary reward
- Personal recognition
- Emphasis on fun and enjoyment
- Top management's interest and commitment

celebrate success and encourage everybody to move forward. Considering the diverse backgrounds of people in today's work force, however, programs need to offer a good balance of monetary incentive and recognition under proper guidance from management. Also, it is advisable to review recognition/reward programs for their effectiveness from time to time. And finally, thinking of people's growth with the company, these rewards and recognition may be tied to career planning.

LETTING PEOPLE GROW WITH THE COMPANY

In order for organizations to continuously improve, managers need to realize that how people generate ideas for improvement and implement them is ultimately what counts, regardless of their titles or background. Practicing such an idea, Soichiro Honda never claimed ownership of the company he founded. He always thought that exercising his power and authority to force his ideas on the employees would have a destructive impact.

As an example, except in the early days of Honda Motor Company, he did not get involved in hiring or even attending the company's board of directors' meetings. He says, "If you hire only those people whom you understand, the company will never get better people than you are. . . . Always remember that you often find outstanding people among those whom you don't particularly like" (From *Honda Motor—The Men, the Management, the Machine* by Tetsuo Sekiya, p. 161).

Regarding exercising power as a founder of the company, Soichiro Honda said, "We had much greater power than those who joined us later. Imagine what would have happened if we attended a board meeting with such great power. Such a meeting would have been like a meeting with predetermined conclusions. If they were left alone, on the other hand, they would do their best'' (ibid., p. 185). He even resigned as the president of Honda Motor Company at a relatively young age, thus "eliminating his own job" so that the organization could move forward.

Honda believed in young people because they are without a past, yet they have creativity. If we are confined by the past, we cannot be creative or learn new ideas easily. So all of us should learn to unlearn the old events and knowledge that do not add value to what we do. Instead of hanging on to the past, we need to encourage people to grow.

In terms of what we may be able to do at different levels of the organization, Exhibit 8.10 summarizes ways to eliminate our current jobs and use our creativity to gain future jobs.

If we compare this exhibit to Exhibit 5.3, which dealt with up-grading our jobs, we should realize that they are the opposite sides of the same coin. By coaching and guiding others, we should try to

Exhibit 8.10. Eliminating Our Current Jobs

Level of Organization	Means	Results
Top Management	Coach, guidance and delegation	Empowered people with improved self-managing skills. More time and resources become available to address more important issues
Middle Management	Coach, guidance and delegation with enhanced self-management skills	Empowered people with improved self-managing skills. More time and resources become available to address important issues, e.g., new processes, new products, etc.
Employees	Idea generation with ownership and pride, i.e., self-management	Improved machines, tools, systems, operations. More time and resources become available to address important issues, e.g., more skills
Tools, Machines, Systems, etc.	Improved machines, tools, systems	Better use of people's talent and available resources to satisfy customers, which reduces the burden on people

eliminate our own jobs. And as we try to do so, we can encourage others to grow as well as for us to move forward. As counterintuitive as it may sound, we have to digest this process and collectively find a way to practice this. We should also remember that our own competitive environment will not allow us to behave in any other way.

As our business strives for better performance amidst fierce competition, all of us will be affected by such things as reducing the layers of organization to make decisions more quickly, cutting out the middle man in order to be more efficient, or eliminating certain steps of an operation to become more productive. Painful as it may be at times, such is the process in which many of us are engaged to move our companies—and society—forward. The point here is that we are to eliminate the "waste" but not the "person." The basis of our effort should be to add value to society in whatever we do.

A remarkable example of this thinking is the story of Dr. Jonas Salk. As a medical scientist in 1955, he developed the vaccine that wiped out polio, the paralyzing childhood disease. When numerous parents offered him their heartfelt thanks, he insisted it was not *his* vaccine. He never patented it, never received royalties from its sale, and made sure that all qualified laboratories would always enjoy equal access to the formula.

In a recent magazine article Dr. Salk said, "My job at the moment is to help people to see what I see. If it's of value, fine. And if it's not of value, then at least I've done what I can do," (From *Vis a Vis,* a United Airlines monthly magazine, January 1992).

Contrasting this, if managers put a strong emphasis on monetary reward, it may skew our balance to short-term interest or promoting materialistic needs, as opposed to addressing higher needs in our needs hierarchy, such as self-actualization. Similarly, if the company's focus is on developing people's capability and achieving its mission in the long run, the recognition or reward program needs to be tied with people's career planning, base and bonus pay, job security, and the like.

At Honda of America Manufacturing, the Voluntary Involvement Program (VIP) combines team-based improvement activity, a suggestion program, and quality award and safety award programs under one overall rubric. Points are given for each accomplishment, and these points will continue to accumulate throughout the employee's (or as Honda calls them, associate's) career. The highest award, the Honda Award, is Honda's Accord automobile and a special vacation for two people anywhere in the world.

As this case indicates, a company may provide several different ways of recognizing people's efforts, reflecting the difference in people's values and skills. Managers then need to understand both the people's needs and the mission of the company to figure out the best possible combination so that both the people and the company will grow. (Exhibit 8.11 summarizes different kinds of rewards and awards.)

Also, reward and recognition may be tied with accomplishments and contribution to the organization, but not limited by one's educational background. In the case of Honda, most employees believe that anyone can become the president of Honda regardless of his or her academic background. Soichiro Honda even said that a movie theater ticket is better than a diploma, because you can't get into a movie with a diploma. Practicing his words, an assistant plant manager I met at Honda of America did not have a college degree and started as an operator.

PHRASES MANAGERS SHOULD NOT USE

Up to this point, we have reviewed different ways for leaders to function effectively on the shop floor. Whether in a short conversation in the hallway or in a meeting, if managers are to gain people's trust there are certain phrases managers should avoid. Exhibit 8.12 shows examples of such phrases compiled by Toyota.

The key phrase here, once again, is "customer orientation."

Exhibit 8.11. Ways to Recognize People's Efforts

- Pat on the shoulder
- Memo of recognition
- Pay, e.g., regular and overtime pay
- Profit sharing, bonus pay
- Awards, e.g., quality, safety, team, suggestion, attendance
- Skill upgrading, e.g., certification
- Career planning, counseling
- Promotion
- Benefits, e.g., health insurance, deferred compensation, etc.
- Vacation days
- Job security
- Fun at work

Exhibit 8.12. Managers' Words That Block People's Participation

- That much, everybody should understand . . .
- Since we haven't tried it before, it probably won't work.
- It didn't work when I tried before, it clearly is not going to work now.
- This is out of date.
- It won't work as smoothly in reality as calculations may indicate on paper.
- Since we have many plans now, I will study your idea later, when I have time.
- Let us discuss this some other day.
- Let us see how it goes for a while.
- Why do we need to change? It is working fine.
- We have rules on this that we cannot violate.
- I think engineers would say that it is impossible.
- The idea is off the wall. Managers won't buy such an idea.
- It does not work in our company.
- They can do it in the United States. But it is not possible in Japan.
- The world is more complex.
- I don't think you would understand this.
- The idea is good, but we don't have the budget.
- It may create something troublesome later.
- It is no use talking to me.
- Don't bother me, I'm working.
- What kind of idea is this? Can't you do something about it?

Courtesy Toyota; from Toyota's education material for managers/supervisors

Managers need to be sensitive and be able to think from their customers' point of view. In other words, instead of machines or systems, people must be considered to be at the center of the shop floor.

Also, the more positively we talk with each other, the more collective wisdom we can bring into play. The more people are involved, the more power we can generate among ourselves, helping all of us to accomplish our goals. In order to realize such power, Exhibit 8.13 summarizes a few key reminders for supervisors and managers in their interactions with people.

Another point: Don't be right all the time. If you are, people will be afraid to share their ideas with you. If you find that you are wrong in front of subordinates, be humble enough to admit it. Then, people may gain confidence and be willing to participate much more. Also, because people often think managers are busy chasing fires, it is difficult for them to initiate a conversation unless there are signs of interest on the manager's part. Yet managers often wish that people

Exhibit 8.13. Reminders for Managers

- Indicate that you are willing to listen
  - Observe people, their attitude, and their work area to see if there are any changes
  - Show interest in the person
  - Show a stable, calm, and self-composed posture, not a restless, nervous, and unstable one
  - Look the other person in the eyes
- Indicate that you are listening attentively
  - Nod as appropriate to indicate that you are listening
  - Confirm the key points of the talk
  - Ask constructive questions, expand the discussion, and relate it to issues that are important for the organization
  - Offer your own opinion, but not as a conclusive statement, and ask for comments

---

would talk to them as friends. I still remember the voice of one manager at Komatsu in Japan, saying to me that the best part of his job was to be stopped by the operators for a conversation.

Even though recognition, rewards, or career planning programs may help in developing a positive work atmosphere, if managers use certain phrases such as those in Exhibit 8.12, a negative atmosphere can easily develop. In this sense, we should take a few minutes to really listen to ourselves and see if we fall into the trap of using those phrases.

Lastly, let us think about the time we gave or received applause, and how we felt at the time. Remembering how we felt then, can we find the opportunity to do this more often? Can we do this as a company, a division, or at the mini-company level?

QUALIFICATION OF LEADERS

Recently, I was surprised by a comment from the vice president of operations of a medium-sized company. In relation to difficulties encountered in introducing new products with a shorter lead time, he commented at a top management meeting, "If we were like Honda, we could develop a new model in three years because they have many engineers and lots of money to spend."

As I knew how hard Mr. Honda and his colleagues had worked when the company was small and how diligently they developed their capability, this comment saddened me. Of course, this vice president may have come from a much larger company with a big enough budget to hire engineers to do the job. Yet, I believe those words are not the words of a leader.

If a person in a position of leadership is making excuses as to why things cannot be done, there will certainly be limits to what the whole organization can accomplish. I believe qualified leaders should convey encouraging messages to people, share a positive yet prudent vision even under difficult circumstances, and involve others in coming up with ways to move forward.

On this topic of leadership and taking a positive attitude to encourage people to reach their dreams, I want to share one more story of Soichiro Honda. When the company was very young, making small engines and selling them to be attached to bicycles, he one day gathered his employees, stood on an orange crate and announced to all of thirty or so employees that this company would someday become the number one manufacturer in the world.

Not many people are bold enough to speak those words. But is this not the mark of a leader who can convince people to move ahead even under difficulties? Anyone who is to achieve something must have a challenging spirit. He or she has to be creative and have faith in his or her own abilities and those of colleagues. Being creative means going beyond conventional ways of thinking. He or she needs to share beliefs, lead people, challenge them, and prove that these beliefs will bear fruit. This is not an easy task. Yet those traits are what qualify people to be leaders.

PROVIDING POSITIVE REINFORCEMENT TO CHANGE OUR BEHAVIOR

As illustrated in this chapter, whether it is by means of presentations, display boards, newsletters, or reward or recognition programs, people who share their success will help to build their own confidence while stimulating others. Also, managers who practice managing by wandering around (MBWA) and those who exchange ideas, or formulate career planning can influence people's attitude toward continuous improvement.

Thus, seeking growth for their people and the organization, effective leaders will use any opportunity to provide adequate feedback and guide people's growth. And as we go through these experiences together, and move up the ladder of our behavioral change model, we will gradually define our own destiny (see Exhibit 8.14).

In other words, as we move forward with each step, we get closer to changing our destiny, or we are blocked at certain steps—unable to overcome the hurdle(s) to move forward. For example, certain "stimuli" or information may change our minds, or it may not affect them at all. Or, even if our *minds* are affected, we may or may not change out *attitude,* and so on.

A case in point: During my visit to one company, I recommended to management that they might provide a display board for each mini-company to post improvements made. Since there had been many improvements made that had not yet been shared well among people, taking pictures and providing comments with the pictures on a board would not only recognize those involved in the improvement, but also would develop an atmosphere for sharing successes throughout the company. Then, awards could be given according to the levels of improvement or people's extra efforts. Furthermore, if the company did this every six months, such practice would encourage people to develop the habit of practicing PDCA, linking it to the semi-annual report for mini-companies.

I further explained the model in Exhibit 8.14, indicating the importance of changing our behavior to meet the needs of business. Managers and supervisors in the meeting room then discussed my recommendation to see if it was feasible to implement the idea in the next three months. About ten minutes later, they concluded that it was a good idea, but it would be difficult to implement.

Exhibit 8.14. Impact of Providing Feedback on Our Behavior

Get Stimuli	Change our destiny by providing stimulation in such form as:
↓	• Floor Meeting • Sharing Rally
Change Mind	• Award Program • Pictures on the Wall
↓	• MBWA • Newsletter
Change Attitude	• People's exchange visits to customers, etc.
↓	• Displays of improvement, etc.
Change Behavior	• Use of Glass Wall Management Principle
↓	• Career planning
Change Habit	and finding people growing . . .
↓	
Change Destiny	

I asked why, and listed the "hurdles" on the flipchart as they commented. They included: time, lack of people, people's mindset, and the like. Then I asked what the ingredients were to overcome the hurdle, and again listed their responses. They included: more time, more people, faith, and so on.

Certainly, adapting new ideas often takes time and effort. Even though the people in the room understood the model illustrated in Exhibit 8.14 in concept, in reality it is not reflected in our behavior so easily. Also, I noticed here that the "hurdle" was not so much the people's mindset. Rather, it was the mindset of *management* that prevented things from happening. Konosuke Matsushita said, "First, you need to think that you will succeed. That is the key for success. And if you think you will, I am sure you will succeed." As simple as it sounds, I believe that those who take a leadership role need to digest his words fully. What I found amazing is that I heard such comments commonly used in Matsushita.

Exhibit 8.15. Publication of Team Improvements. As improvements are made by various Quality Circles in this 1,000-employee company in Japan, selected ones are compiled in a book once a year as a reference to employees. Also, there is an annual quality circle convention during which selected teams compete for various awards. One full day is dedicated to presentations made by these teams. Practically every team uses QC Story format.

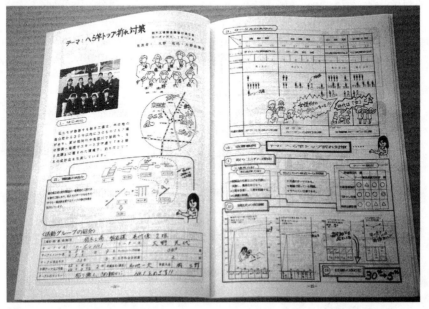

Courtesy Daiwa Seiko

To lead or to empower people, we need to develop a belief in what we do. And as we look ourselves in the mirror, every now and then, let us remember to ask ourselves:

- How often do we hear people applauding a job well done?
- How often do we see displays of recent improvements updated?
- How often do we see people's names in the company or plant newsletter?
- Do we have regular shop floor meetings where we share improvement ideas?
- How effective are reward or recognition programs?
- How effective is the career planning?
- How do these reflect the value of the company?
- What can we do to improve even further?

SUMMARY

- Today's managers need to develop stronger leadership skills. Effective leadership will make people's skill upgrading possible. Also, as people's skills increase, the leading, guiding, and coaching roles of managers become more important than before.
- Leadership is situational. Position or title should not equate with the leadership role in progressive companies. Leadership tied with self-improvement is a reflection of our self-managing drive.
- The role of managers is to eliminate their jobs and create more important jobs for themselves so that the organization can continuously grow as a whole. People should do the same and acquire more skills to move forward.
- Even though traditional managers tend to monopolize skills, a progressive manager/leader will share skills by teaching others to accomplish the mission. Strong dedication to the mission, as opposed to reliance on power and authority, will attract others to follow. In other words, a manager needs to see his or her people as customers to communicate ideas.
- In guiding people through improvement activities, a manager needs to function as a coach, providing guidance whenever the opportunity arises.

- In order for this to happen, managers may exercise their coaching abilities by practicing management by wandering around (MBWA), encouraging people from the inception of idea generation to the follow-up of implementation.
- Holding regular meetings with operators on the shop floor and providing an area for them to meet will promote people's ownership. Also, using visual means of communication such as displays is an effective way to develop an atmosphere for continuous improvement.
- Managers need to have consistency and perseverance in pursuing their vision. If this is not done, management will lose credibility. Once lost, it is difficult to regain.
- Accomplishments of people need not be strictly tied to large monetary awards, but may be tied to recognition, career planning, base and bonus pay, and job security.
- Leading people is not an easy process. It ties to how well one can adhere to the mission. Gaining leadership ability often requires a combination of challenging spirit, creativity, perseverance, communication skills, and trust. It should require life-long practice. Yet, it is more a process of training our mind rather than acquiring specific techniques.
- As we provide adequate feedback or stimuli to people by such means as displays, newsletters, meetings, presentations, MBWA, career planning and counseling, etc., the people's attitude, behavior, and habits may change, leading to defining a new destiny for the organization and each individual within it.

Chapter Nine

MANAGING SHOP FLOOR IMPROVEMENT ACTIVITIES

As we develop a vision, identify customers, involve people, practice problem solving, and find ways to lead people, we still need good management discipline to coordinate these activities. In this chapter we will study how we set goals, and practice PDCA cycles for continuous improvement. We will also examine how we may better manage time on the shop floor using supervisors as an example. Further, we will introduce the subjects of control points, documentation, and presentations as ways to clarify our management processes.

GOAL SETTING

Even though the span of control will vary according to the person's responsibility, every individual in an organization should have some goals to shoot for—whether they are individual goals or team goals—just as a baseball team shares the goal of scoring more runs than the competitor to win the game. If we clearly understand the rules of the game we play, we will have a much better chance of performing better and enjoying the process.

Traditionally, however, the goals were set at the top of the organization without involving those lower down. Often, these goals were not clearly explained to the people, or even worse, the goals, as the people understood them, were conflicting. As a result, people had to manipulate the system in order to achieve their prescribed individual goals, instead of contributing toward achieving the total goals of the organization. But if we can develop a broader understanding of the business, and define more appropriate measures for people's performance, we may be able to link the individual's goals to the total goals of the organization. To examine this further, let us look at the role of the front-line supervisor.

While we studied quality, cost, delivery, safety, and morale (QCDSM) as major goals in the previous chapters, some supervisors may have focused only on delivery goals, such as schedule compliance, while others may have pursued multiple goals, such as QCD or QCDSM. Naturally, we want to be able to address the diversified needs of customers. The more supervisors develop their skills to handle multiple functions and goals, the better the whole organization can function.

In order for us to incorporate such thinking in our work, Exhibit 9.1 summarizes the nature of goal setting at different stages of prog-

Exhibit 9.1. Goals of Supervisors at Different Stages of Shop Floor Management

Level 1 (lowest):	Schedule compliance is the major goal. Quality is checked by another department. Cost reduction is a goal but will be handled mainly by manufacturing engineers. Minimum planning for achieving goals is done.
Level 2:	Quality and delivery (QD), or cost and delivery (CD) are considered the major goals. Other goals may also exist, but the main effort is spent on managing individuals as opposed to working on processes. Planning to achieve goals is done on an ad hoc basis.
Level 3:	Quality, cost and delivery (QCD) are major goals. Morale and safety are also considered important but no goals are set. Communication with employees is becoming more frequent, discussion with employees becomes more two-way. Some problem-solving tools are used in planning.
Level 4:	QCDSM are major goals. Supervisors realize the importance of people's involvement. As people take more responsibility, supervisors can spend more time on important, long-term, or chronic problems. Also, as goals are developed, approaches for achieving goals are evaluated, reflecting people's problem-solving abilities. More sharing of progress with people becomes apparent.
Level 5 (highest):	There are multiple goals with different priorities. Design changes and new product development as well as supplier issues may be discussed, involving other departments. Supervisors' goals parallel much more closely the company's overall goals. Goals become more realistic as people upgrade their skills. Working with customers and suppliers becomes an integrated part of planning. At this stage, people will be able to describe the concerns of their organization, how those may influence the performance of the company, and how they are addressing the problems.

ress in shop floor management. As people's skills are upgraded, the goal-setting process will also be upgraded. However, we need to pay attention to a number of key points (Exhibit 9.2).

BENCHMARKING

One way to come up with goals is to learn from the practices of other companies or departments. Especially when we are busy fighting fires or concerned about internal affairs, we may forget to notice how others are doing until they have outstripped us. To illustrate benchmarking, Exhibit 9.3 shows the results of a semiconductor test done by Hewlett-Packard. Exhibit 9.4 is another study by International Motor Vehicle Program (IMVP) comparing car assembly plants.

The data in these exhibits speaks for itself about the need for significant improvement for those who are behind. Also, as compared to measuring the company's competitiveness by sales volume, profitability, or market share, this type of study result can address more specific issues for the people at the shop floor—failure rate, inventory level, space, and so on. If our company is rated low in this type of study, we may have to accept that the approaches taken in

Exhibit 9.2. Key Points of Goal Setting

- Goals should offer a challenge to people, rather than an estimate of what may happen.
- Goals need to be persuasive for people to buy in and have ownership.
- Goals should be measurable, i.e., what gets measured gets done.
- Goals may be set by comparing performance to other organizations or companies, i.e., benchmarking.
- Goals may be set according to the necessities of the business.
- Goals may be suggested by people and then discussed with their managers.
- Goals may be slightly above the ability of people to make them challenging.
- Goals should reflect the analysis of past performance.
- Along with goals, certain tools such as problem-solving techniques should be provided to people.
- Respect people's feeling of ownership and provide necessary support for them to use their creativity to achieve goals.
- Achieving goals should help achieve the mission.

Exhibit 9.3. Comparative Study of Semiconductor Quality (1980)

Company	Receiving Inspection	Failure Rate per 1000 Hours	Quality Rating
J1	0.00	0.010	89.9
J2	0.00	0.019	87.2
J3	0.00	0.012	87.2
A1	0.19	0.090	86.1
A2	0.11	0.059	63.3
A3	0.19	0.267	48.1

the past may not be good enough. A major rethinking of approaches will be needed before it is too late.

At Xerox, people conducted their first benchmark study in 1982 to assess the viability of the Wire Harness Service Center within Xerox. Its quality, cost, and delivery performance was compared with that of outside suppliers, to see if it made more sense to use a low-cost outside supplier than to build the harnesses internally. Since hundreds of jobs were at stake in this operation, union people were involved in the study. The results showed a large cost differential between Xerox's internal wire harness operation and its suppliers, that is, Xerox was 25 percent more expensive than other domestic suppliers.

With benchmark data that nobody could dispute, Xerox formed a task force of three managers and three union people to figure out

Exhibit 9.4. Comparison of Car Assembly Plants (1987)

	GM Framingham	NUMMI Fremont	Toyota Takaoka
Assembly Hours/Car	31	19	16
Assembly Defects/Car	135	45	45
Assembly Square feet/car-year	8.1	7.0	4.8
Inventories of Parts	2 weeks	2 days	2 hours

Note: NUMMI (New United Motor Manufacturing Inc.) is a joint venture between Toyota and GM in Fremont, California.

From *The Machine That Changed the World* by J. Womack, et al., p. 83.

a strategy to become competitive. After six months of hard work, the task force came up with ideas that eventually resulted in improving performance and saving three hundred jobs. Since then, Xerox has used such benchmarking as a normal procedure in running their business.

Testing competitors' products, collecting information from suppliers, and using public information will help in developing benchmarks to set performance targets. Benchmark studies may also be practiced to assess the company's work methods and find ways to make improvements by involving people on the shop floor. For example, we may find new insights about better ways to process paper, respond to customer complaints, reduce delivery time, or handle customers.

Here are a few more examples. (1) When Xerox conducted a benchmark study of copy machine servicing, they studied how competitors responded to service requests, from phone call to completion of repair, to discover what they could learn from others. (2) When Soichiro Honda, the founder of Honda Motor, visited overseas for the first time, he saw Phillips screws for the first time in his life. When he introduced their use at home, assembly jobs became much easier. (3) An operator at Matsushita says that when he had some spare time, he visited do-it-yourself shops to pick up new ideas from the products displayed there.

As these examples indicate, we can stimulate ourselves to continuously improve by benchmarking others. Also, if we are curious and interested in doing things better, even if it is difficult to obtain direct information about competitors, we can visit other departments or noncompetitors to pick up ideas. By taking these opportunities and getting help or guidance from management, challenging goals may be set to shoot for.

Goals may be related to QCDSM, and specific benchmarks may even be to emulate a recognized leader like McDonald's in terms of quick delivery, Nordstrom's in terms of customer service, Toyota in terms of quality level, or a do-it-yourself shop in terms of suggestion ideas. Even if the gap between the present level of operations and the benchmark is wide, we may focus people's efforts by using such information as a yardstick and aim to fill the gap one step at a time.

As goals are set, managers should help their people to think in broader terms, not just focusing on quantity of production, for example. This will shift the planning from something of a ritual to a much more meaningful process with specific plans of action. Then, the progress should be monitored and necessary support provided accordingly.

Benchmarking may be conducted for wages as well. On one hand, we may want to increase wages as people acquire more skills. Yet, the reality is that if competitors are fighting hard and profit margins are squeezed, even if everybody's skill levels are higher than before, wages may not be increased accordingly. Benchmarking of this kind may bring a sober reality in front of our eyes. Yet, in order to thrive in today's competitive environment, we cannot close our eyes and be internally focused. We need to set a goal and utilize everybody's creativity to accomplish that goal.

MANAGEMENT CYCLE

As goals are set, we need to figure out how to achieve them. Here, we can use the PDCA (plan-do-check-act) cycle of continuous improvement as a basic management discipline. This is similar to sailing a boat and reaching a destination by monitoring progress (Exhibit 9.5).

Exhibit 9.5. PDCA Cycle Practiced in Sailing

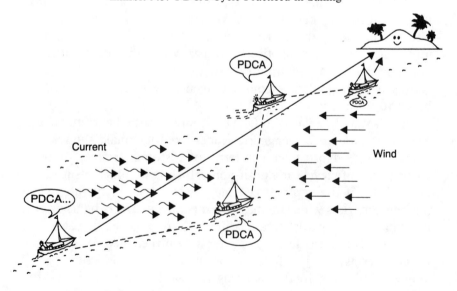

For example, we may set a course by considering wind direction, current, weather forecast, and the like (plan). Then, we sail according to the plan by aiming at a certain point on the compass (do). Later, we will review our progress by comparing our location to the original plan (check). By figuring out the reasons for deviation (act), we can recalculate the course (plan) and redirect the course of our ship (do), and repeat this process until we get to our destination.

The time it takes to go through the cycle will differ depending on the nature of the work and the needs. In our shop floor activities, the PDCA cycle may involve an hourly review of production goals, or there may be quarterly reviews of operations. In fact, the cycle may be daily, weekly, monthly, semiannual, or annual. As we become more organized, we will have these established in such a manner that everyone knows what needs to be done without even thinking about it—much like our biological rhythm.

In reality, however, there may be different stages of progress to fully digest this management cycle, as shown in Exhibit 9.6, where the shop supervisor and his or her people's activities are used as examples. Here, the effectiveness of PDCA is reflected in the way meetings are run. As more checking and acting take place, the planning step should become much easier.

DEVELOPING THE RHYTHM OF PDCA

Developing the PDCA cycle is like exercising regularly to develop muscles. The more you go through the cycle, the better shape you will be in. First, move slowly and tackle easy problems. Then, gradually increase the speed and tackle more difficult problems until, ideally, the whole organization has developed strong muscles to tackle substantial tasks and move forward with consistent rhythm (see Exhibit 9.7). In many ways, therefore, the PDCA rhythm may be compared to the human heartbeat, that is, the stronger and steadier the heartbeat, the faster and smoother we can move. (And, of course, if we have no heartbeat, we need CPR to restore it.)

Looking around us, this biologic rhythm also seems to apply to a group of people. For example, people on a sidewalk, even if they are strangers, tend to form groupings and often end up walking in

Exhibit 9.6. PDCA Cycle of Supervision at Different Stages

Level 1 (lowest):	There is no planning. Everything is decided on an ad hoc basis. This is a fire-fighting mode of operation. The process is PD-PD-PD . . . (plan-do-plan-do) without much review, analysis, or standardization. As a result, the same problems may keep resurfacing.
Level 2:	There is minimal planning, e.g., a daily or weekly review of operations. This typically takes the form of reporting numbers. There is no medium- or long-term thinking horizon. Everybody thinks they are doing their best. There is little "check" in the PDCA cycle. People tend to think there is no time to analyze problems. If they analyze, they try to do it by expressing opinions in meetings and trying to come up with a solution based on recollection rather than facts or data. As a result, it ends up taking a lot of time to reach any meaningful conclusions.
Level 3:	There are regular meetings on a daily, weekly, or monthly basis to review performance indicators. There is still fire fighting, but because people are now diligent in following the PDCA cycle, examples of success start to appear. Charts may be displayed on the shop floor to record the progress. However, it typically requires more than three cycles of PDCA before the cycle becomes internalized by everyone. This demands strong leadership, and everyone must work together to follow up plans and keep from falling back into old habits.
Level 4:	Meetings are held to discuss a number of different subjects, including quality, cost, delivery, new product introduction, design change, etc. There are multiple projects underway at different levels, often on a cross-functional basis, and several major projects may have been completed successfully. People can see the big picture more clearly after going through several PDCA cycles. Good habits and confidence are being developed, and communication among people is much smoother than before.
Level 5 (highest):	Meetings are more efficient, perhaps with committees to plan and review performance. There are closer links to the higher level PDCA cycles in the organization, i.e., strategy development and execution. People have gained confidence in practicing PDCA and improvement activities are obvious to everybody. There are many events to share successes and recognize improvement. From these and even from conversations on the floor, it becomes very noticeable that people's skills are vastly upgraded.

Exhibit 9.7. Developing the Rhythm of PDCA Is Similar to Developing Muscles Through Regular Exercises

step. The same kind of biological rhythm is observed in nature. For example, in the mountains of Asia, one variety of fireflies produces a random pattern of light flashes when they first appear on a summer evening. But as the night progresses, the flashes become more and more synchronized, until the whole mountain seems to light up at regular intervals.

In business, every revolution of the PDCA cycle propels the organization forward just as our heartbeat pushes blood to circulate throughout the body. When the cycling stops, however, the progress stops and the organization loses its momentum.

Looking closely within an organization, however, we can find different levels of PDCA cycles. A daily performance review on the shop floor may be one, while there may be weekly, monthly, and yearly PDCA cycles at other levels of the organization as well. The point here is that only when these are well orchestrated and coordinated, will they compound the power of people working together just as a well trained body functions.

It may take time, but once such a rhythm is established, it will become the autonomous heartbeat of an organization. In other words, the PDCA cycle will provide a solid managerial process with clarity and simplicity and drive the organization forward. When everybody's cooperation and dedication are gained in this process, the organization will become a tightly knit, totally integrated entity. (See Exhibit 9.8 for an illustration of different levels of PDCA cycle practiced in the organization.)

Often, however, people mistakenly think that they are practicing PDCA even though they haven't been calling it by that name. In reality, this is rarely the case. For example, the discipline to follow through is often missing, there may be no analysis, and there is no learning reflected in future plans. Furthermore, no data is collected, no standards established, and no documents prepared to prove that there is any "follow through" of plans. As a result, people cannot share ideas easily and similar mistakes may happen repeatedly.

Another typical problem is that there is no common ground to share the progress. So though each unit of the organization may be going through its own PDCA cycle, there is no clear mechanism to tie these together. In other words, when each PDCA cycle is established and treated independently from the rest, it is very difficult to gain the integrated power of different operations. Instead, there may be a lack of clarity, confusion, and a lack of discipline.

Therefore, we should ask ourselves:

- Are our organization's PDCA cycles clear to everybody?
- What are these PDCA cycles?

Exhibit 9.8. Organization and PDCA Cycle

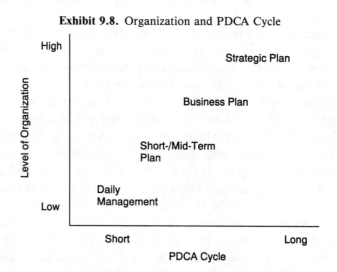

- Is everybody in our organization practicing the discipline of "following through" in the PDCA cycle?
- How are these PDCA cycles tied together?

MANAGING TIME
ON THE SHOP FLOOR

The power of the PDCA cycle lies in its consistency and in people's discipline in practicing it. It is similar to practicing standards, where repetition builds a solid foundation for the organization's progress. In contrast, the lack of standards hides the problem and makes it difficult for people to take corrective action.

Although each individual should practice PDCA even if others do not, when groups of people practice the PDCA cycle and use the standardized procedures effectively, their compounded power is enormous. In order to achieve this from the shop floor up, let us study PDCA cycles in relation to the supervisor's job. By reviewing how supervisors spend their time on the shop floor, we should be able to find out how well the company's managerial system is functioning. (See Appendix 9.1 for an example of supervisor's daily, weekly, monthly, and yearly activities.)

As you see in the Appendix, there are many activities to be covered by supervisors during the course of the day, week, month, or year. It is for this reason I call the supervisor a "general manager" or "president" of his or her shop and find the supervisor's job so critical in practicing SFM. (Problems often arise because many managers and support people do not realize the importance of these supervisors' and hence the shop floor people's work.)

By comparing our own situation to this Appendix, however, we should ask ourselves (1) Are supervisors of these activities effectively controlling the situation on the shop floor? and (2) Have they developed a certain rhythm so that things are clicking with little interruption from fire fighting?

In other words, even though each company's structure and its people's roles and responsibilities differ, if we study Appendix 9.1 carefully, it should help us to appreciate the importance of effectively practicing PDCA in the work area. No matter what title we may carry, we should not forget to look at the business from the point of view of the shop floor and find ways to address the problems right then and there as much as possible.

MANAGING IMPROVEMENT ACTIVITIES WITH CONTROL POINTS

Just as we may frequently check car speed, our location on the map, or fuel level during a trip, we should practice a similar concept when running a company or mini-company. Whether the journey we take is in a car, sailboat, or business enterprise, even if we know the destination and the charted course, without an adequate monitoring and feedback system we may lose our way. Here again, we see the PDCA cycle as a necessary feedback system for keeping us on track.

This means that the goals, approaches, and PDCA cycles discussed above should be well orchestrated so that the organization will move to the right place at the right time, heading to accomplish our mission. In order to establish clear checkpoints for management activities and establish a network of control within the organization, let us next look at the concept of control points, or as some call them, management points—parameters that we need to check frequently in running our company. Exhibit 9.9 shows examples of control points for a manufacturing plant.

Whether it is a car journey, a production process, or the process of management itself, in order to control the process, we need to check not only the output but the root causes as well. Depending on their characteristics, therefore, control points are divided into *control items* at the outcome of the process, and *check items* at the root cause of the process. (Note: Control items may also be called *baseline measurements* and check items may be called *root-cause measurements*.)

In the case of a journey by car, for example, the control item may be car speed. We want to control this within a certain range, say between fifty and sixty miles per hour, so that we will arrive at the destination on time, and safely. There may be several check items, as shown in Exhibit 9.10. Examples of control items and check items in the company setting are shown in Exhibit 9.11.

The importance of these ideas relates to an often-used phase, "What gets measured gets done." In other words, these measurements are important in defining the name of the game we play. In

Exhibit 9.9. Examples of Control Points

Category	Examples
Sales and Marketing	
Quality	Number of customer claims, customer satisfaction survey results
Cost	Marketing, sales support, and service expenses
Delivery	Sales volume, market share, response time to service, forecasting accuracy
Safety	Number of accidents, number of safety suggestions
Morale	Attendance, number of suggestions, number of presentations
Research and Development	
Quality	Product reliability, manufacturability, serviceability, return factor, number of engineering changes
Cost	Service effectiveness, expenses
Delivery	Number of new products, patents, cycle time, forecasting accuracy
Safety	Number of accidents, number of safety suggestions
Morale	Attendance, number of suggestions, number of presentations
Manufacturing	
Quality	Number of customer claims, defect rate, rejects of operation
Cost	Production per man-hour, expenses, overtime, yield
Delivery	Number of missed deliveries, production lead time, inventory level
Safety	Number of accidents, number of safety suggestions
Morale	Attendance, number of suggestions, number of presentations
Finance and Management Information System	
Quality	Number of errors in billing, accuracy of financial report, level of internal audit
Cost	Programmer productivity, computer system utilization effectiveness
Delivery	Report timeliness, payroll timeliness, days of accounts payable and receivable
Safety	Number of accidents, number of safety suggestions
Morale	Attendance, number of suggestions, number of presentations

Exhibit 9.10. Examples of Control Points for a Car Journey

Control Item: Control point at the outcome of process
- Car speed
- Direction

Check Item: Control point at the root cause of process
- Man (driver):   Tired, bored, sleepy, etc.
- Machine (car): Engine temperature, oil pressure, etc.
- Method: Steering, gear selection, etc.
- Material: Fuel level, oil level, etc.

---

selecting and practicing control points at work, however, a few points need our attention (see Exhibit 9.12).

Exhibits 9.13 and 9.14 show examples of control points practiced in a manufacturing company. The table in Exhibit 9.13 represents the key control points in relation to the flow of material (or information) in a cross-functional (horizontal) direction.

The table in Exhibit 9.14 represents the key managerial indices in relation to the hierarchical (vertical) direction. Together with the QC process table, these may be compared to a cloth which needs both horizontal and vertical threads to make a whole.

Note that even though the subject matter is different, the same concept can be used for either a manufacturing or a management process. Also, these tables clarify the control points and control methods, making it easy for everyone to find critical information related to the process, i.e., who, what, when, where, why, how, and how much (5W2H). Exhibit 9.15 indicates how important it is that the information be in a form usable by people at the shop floor. Filing these documents away in an engineer's office is not the way SFM should be conducted. To convey the importance of controlling the process where the action is, the message above the QC Process

Exhibit 9.11. Examples of Control Points in Business

Control Item: Control point at the outcome of process
- Production volume, as applied to production
- Sales volume by sales person, as applied to sales

Check Item: Control point at the root cause of process
- Production capacity, machine breakdowns, attendance of operators, etc., as applied to production
- Skill level, number of sales calls, product knowledge, etc., as applied to sales people

---

Exhibit 9.12. Key Considerations for Applying Control Points

Control Items

- Control items are selected from the results of our work, e.g., QCDSM.
- The number of control items may vary depending on function and responsibility. Higher responsibility typically means more items to deal with, reflecting the person's span of control.
- To ensure quick response time, control items need to be chosen from representative measurements that can be collected easily.
- Display of charts covering an appropriate time period is recommended for ease of review.
- In order to act quickly when abnormal indications are identified, the following considerations should be established beforehand as much as possible:
  - Clear criteria to indicate abnormalities in the process
  - Analysis of potential root causes and development of procedures to take action
  - Definitions of people's roles and responsibilities for reporting and taking action

Check Items

- Check items are selected from the items that influence the outcome.
- Analytical capability is required to choose the items best suited to the situation.
- The number of check items may depend on the potential causes that are to be controlled. Typically, the lower the risk, the fewer there are.
- Judgment or a trial-and-error process may need to be used in selecting the important check items.
- In order to respond quickly, check items need to be chosen from representative measures that can be collected easily.
- Use of check sheets, control charts, and other means of visual display is recommended for ease of review.

Exhibit 9.13. Control Points for Manufacturing a Product (A Portion of a QC Process Table)

Process	Control Point	Cycle	Specification	Graph #	Respon-sibility	Reporter	Standards
Receiving	Visual Inspection	1 per lot	No rust	ins-11	supervisor	inspector	FS-0103
Lathe-2	Outer Dia.	2 after setup	100±.1	ch-21	supervisor	supervisor	FS-1123
...	...	...	...	...	...	...	...
...	...	...	...	...	...	...	...

Exhibit 9.14. Control Points for Managers (A Portion of a Management Process Table for Production)

Objectives	Control Point	Cycle	Control Level	Graph #	Respon-sibility	Report (day of month)
Production	% Compliance to Schedule	Mo.	100% ±5	GK-21	Pres.	Admin. Dept (5)
	% Compliance for Product X	Mo.	100% ±5	GK-23	Mgr.	Production (5)
	Average Response Time	Mo.	30 Day ±2	GK-24	Pres.	Production (5)
. . .	. . .	. . .	. . .	. . .	. . .	. . .

Note: This table is called a Management Process Control Table, as opposed to a QC Process Table since control points are more for management use.

Exhibit 9.15. QC Process Table Displayed at Matsushita

Courtesy Matsushita

Sheet reads: "We are conducting our work by following the Process Sheet."

In other words, the ideas of goal setting, PDCA cycles, and control points are all summarized in these tables together with such things as location, people's responsibilities, measurement methods, frequency of measurement, and so on. Whenever abnormalities are observed, in order to gain control over the situation, problem solving should take place following the PDCA cycle (see Exhibit 9.16). Here, the cause-and-effect diagram indicates the relationship between check items (causes) and control item (effect).

Using the car journey as an example again, the driver may become aware that the car is slowing down. In that case, he will go through the check items to see if there is anything abnormal. By quickly reviewing such items as shown in Exhibit 9.10, he may find that he is too tired to keep his foot on the accelerator. So, the solution may be to change drivers or to stop for a cup of coffee.

The specific situation in our business setting will be different and more complex compared to this example. Yet the idea is the same. One caveat, however, is that we need to clarify these items as much as possible so that not just one person is familiar with the situation, but other people can follow the steps without difficulty. Again, that is the reason standardization is so important.

Preparing tables such as those shown in Exhibits 9.13 and 9.14, therefore, allows us to clarify procedures and share this information readily even with new employees. A good network of control points throughout a company can act as the nervous system of the organiza-

Exhibit 9.16. PDCA Cycle Practiced to Control the Process

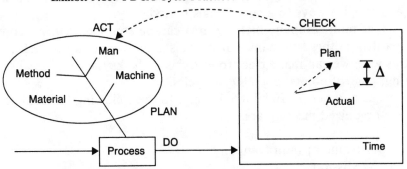

Note: The control chart on the right represents the control item. The items on the left— e.g., man, machine, method, and material— indicate check items.

tion. Thus by monitoring these control points—more like monitoring gauges of a modern airplane to accomplish a safe, comfortable, fuel-efficient, on-schedule flight—we should be able to tell whether or not we are on the right track to accomplish our mission.

Furthermore, if we can combine the nervous system (intelligent network of control points), with muscles (problem-solving and execution capability), and with a strong heartbeat (rhythm of the PDCA cycle), we should have developed a fairly well-balanced body (organization).

ORGANIZING OUR MINI-COMPANY MEETING AREA

Like the sailor, the driver, and the airplane pilot who all use some means of goal setting, control points, and PDCA cycles to get to where they want to go, we need to steer our organization so that we can accomplish our vision. But what specific tools can we use on the shop floor? How can we practice the idea of the QC process table and the management process table in an effective manner, say, from a supervisor's viewpoint?

One pragmatic approach is to use a visual display board to post key management indices (control points). This serves as a scoreboard because the setting we are in is similar to a game, like baseball, where a group of people are playing together to achieve a common goal. And depending on the needs of the "mini-company," we can (1) develop a set of key indices (as in Exhibit 9.9) to monitor the direction of the organization, (2) share these among the group, (3) update the progress towards goals of the organization in floor meetings, and (4) strategize ways to achieve goals periodically.

Our mini-company meeting area can be equipped with a scoreboard and other key management tools as shown in Exhibit 9.17. In this way, we can make clear to everybody the key ideas of goal setting, control points, and PDCA cycles.

The numbers in Exhibit 9.17 refer to the following features of a well-organized meeting area:

1. Name of mini-company
2. Mission
3. Names and pictures of people
4. Customer–supplier relationship chart

Exhibit 9.17. Organizing Our Mini-Company Meeting Area

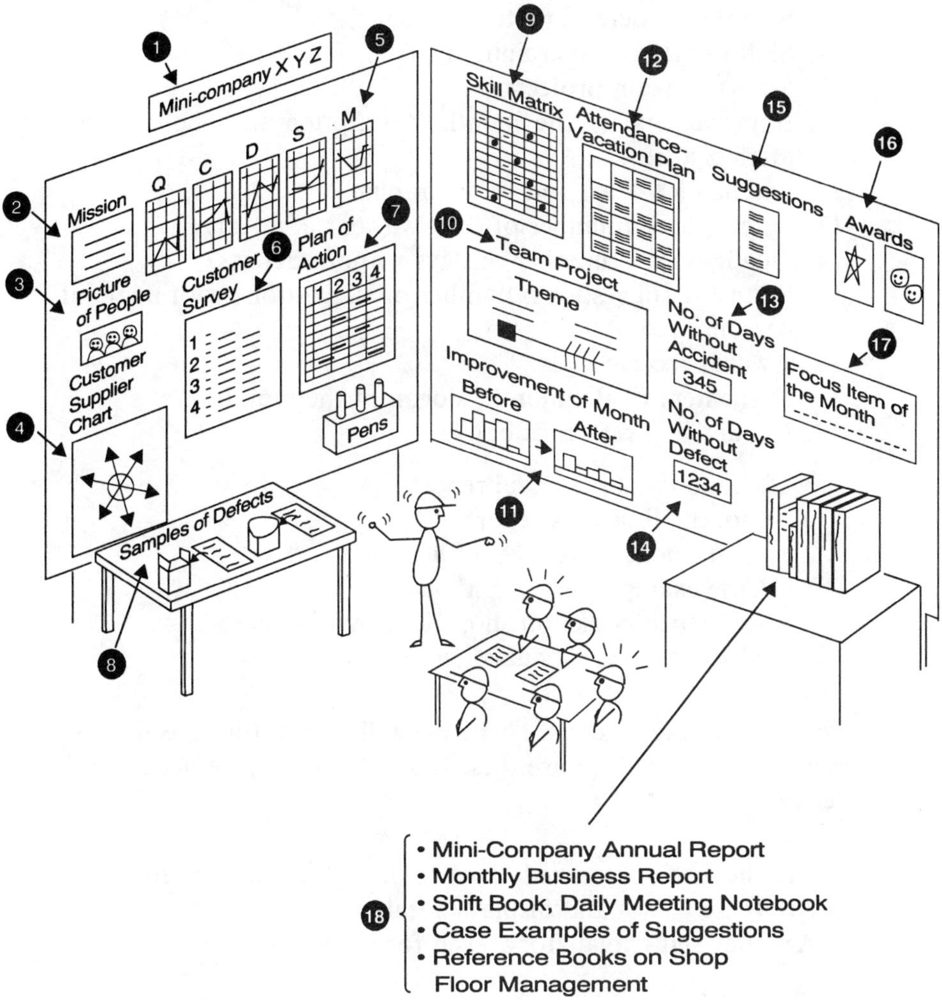

5. QCDSM Measurements (example)

Q : Defect rate (%)
C : Productivity (unit/hr)
D : On-time shipment (%)
S : Days without accident
M: Number of suggestions

6. Customer survey results (e.g., weekly from internal customers)

7. Plans of action (summary of business plan)
8. Samples of defects (with comments)
9. Skill matrix (cross-training matrix)
10. Status of team projects
11. Improvement of the month (description with before-and-after pictures)
12. Attendance chart and vacation plan
13. Safety clock (number of days without accident)
14. Quality clock (number of days without defects)
15. Status of suggestions; number of suggestions with name of person
16. Awards received
17. Focus item of the month; slogan of the month
18. Documents, reference books

  • Mini-company annual report
  • Monthly business report
  • Shift book, daily meeting notebook
  • Case example of suggestions
  • Reference books on shop floor management
  • Miscellaneous manuals, etc.

As described in Appendix 8.1 where we discussed the effective use of visual aids, in order to use these tools effectively, we need to ask ourselves:

  • Are they well organized, e.g., color coded, labeled, etc.?
  • Are these charts and displays speaking to us?
  • Are they self-explanatory, even for strangers?

In other words, items in this exhibit should indicate the level of control by themselves, making it easy for everyone to find critical information related to the mini-company's operation—who is to do what, when, where, why, how, and how much (5W2H) (see Exhibit 9.18).

Every day, people meet at this mini-company meeting area to review key points of operation (QCDSM). As people's comments are transmitted upward in the organization, management concerns are shared in the meeting as well, assuring two-way communication.

Of course, a complex operation will have a scoreboard with many control points. At the top management level, such a scoreboard may include sales volume, profitability, return on investment,

Exhibit 9.18. A Mini-Company Meeting Area with Scoreboard

Courtesy Glass Master Control

customer complaints, on-time-delivery performance, and so on (see Exhibit 9.19).

ORGANIZING THE WORK STATION

As much as we need to share key management information at both the mini-company and top management levels in an organized fashion, we should clarify key control points, or management points, at each work station as well. By equipping each work station, with a scoreboard and other key management tools, we can make clear to everybody the key ideas of goal setting, control points, and PDCA cycles. Thus, from operator to top management level, all of us can function as mini-companies and practice glass wall management. The only difference among them is the scope of responsibility.

Exhibit 9.20 illustrates a number of ways to organize an efficient work station. The numbers in the exhibit refer to the following:

1. Name and description of work station
2. Name and picture of operator

Exhibit 9.19. Example of a Scoreboard at the Top Management Level

Courtesy Glass Master Control

3. Standard operating procedure
4. Andon (trouble light to call for supervisor's help)
5. Line stop button (to call supervisor with andon)
6. Sample board (to check the quality of product)
7. Explanation of poka-yoke, i.e., fail-safe mechanism, installed
8. Machine checklist for self-maintenance (checkpoints and lubrication points are numbered)
9. Machine downtime log
10. Safety checkpoint
11. Description of recent improvement (with before-and-after pictures)
12. Layout of the area
13. SPC chart
14. QC process table
15. Sample product
16. Production control board
17. Marking of floor (a place for everything)

Exhibit 9.20. Organizing Our Work Station

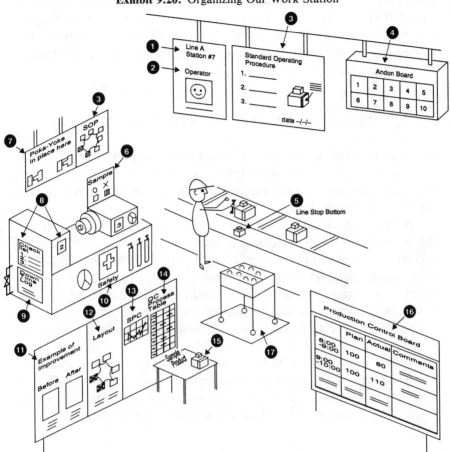

As shown in the exhibit, we may have a scoreboard with a number of control points for each operation as described by the SOP or QC process table. Or these scoreboards may include such items as SPC chart, production control board, machine downtime log, or setup chart. Check items for operators may take such forms as a checklist, SOP, sample board, oil lubrication point, and poka-yoke (fail-safe mechanism).

As a person's responsibility or span of control increases, checking, analyzing, and updating the control points become a crucial part of his or her job. And the person who can run a mini-company well is a good candidate for promotion.

Another point here is that if we can practice the idea of control points using glass wall management, everyone in the whole organization will be able to see how the company is running and be able to contribute ideas much more freely. Again, this situation needs to be contrasted to black box or brick wall management where there is no sharing of information.

LEARNING TO USE CONTROL POINTS

One way to think about control points is to compare them to brain cells. In order to accomplish sophisticated control at a higher level of intelligence, we need to have more brain cells with a good network established among them.

As more and more jobs need to be controlled on the shop floor, there should be a higher density of control points in our shop floor. In fact, if we extend the idea of control points to include the intelligence in machines—that is, control mechanisms to assure the quality of each operation—we may understand that the number of control points in the organization should increase as we delegate our ability to machines, tools, poka-yoke, color-coding, standard operating procedures, and the like.

Yet we know that on the shop floor, no theory will work by itself. So, while we want to establish a network of control points similar to the human nervous system, how can we do this effectively? Let us learn how to use control points in three different phases:

Introduction phase. This is the period when we find that starting something new is interesting. Yet we may do so without knowing why. Selling the ideas and developing ownership, therefore, are essential. The number of control points that we can deal with will be limited according to our capability and the complexity of the jobs. A rough estimate may be as follows:

- Operators: 1 to 10
- Supervisors: 5 to 15
- Managers: 10 to 50

Critical phase. At some point we may become tired of using control points. Like any other improvement project, if the benefits are not clear or if there is no feedback, we will lose the incentive to collect information, update the progress, and review control points. This period is, therefore, critical for influencing the future outcome. Sharing the progress among the group, reaffirming the vision, and addressing the problem directly are keys for success.

Stabilization phase. Success starts to breed more successes, and with experience, we will better understand the meaning of the PDCA cycle, control points, standards, the involvement process, and use of problem-solving skills. As we begin to taste success, the whole organization starts to internalize the idea and to move forward in a coherent fashion.

As illustrated here, the organization's control level will ultimately be as good as the ability of the people who practice these ideas. Therefore, effective managers should use the concept of control points as a means to upgrade people's abilities and vice versa. Also, as we scrutinize the mission and function of the organization—whether it is production, maintenance, sales, or administration—and update the control points of these functions accordingly, we should find that there is no end to improvement.

Control points may also be viewed as a summary of key management indices for an organization. Especially when there are many different type of indices, it is important to develop a framework such that each person or each level of the organization can focus on a few important ones.

DEVELOPING THE NETWORK
OF CONTROL POINTS

Since control points at the top level of the company and those of each unit are related in terms of objectives and the means to achieve them, coordinating all of them becomes a very important task for top management (see Exhibit 9.21).

The control points for the car journey described in Exhibit 9.10 may be represented here as follows:

- Leader plans to arrive at the destination and monitor the progress on the map. (Item A)

Exhibit 9.21. Control Points Reflect Cause-and-Effect Relationships in the Company

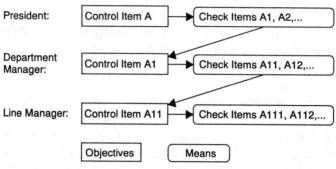

- Leader checks the location of the car according to the map, etc. (Item A1, A2, . . .)
- Navigator monitors the location of the car and updates the leader. (Item A1)
- Navigator checks the speed of the car, etc. (Item A11, A12, . . .)
- Driver monitors the speed of the car and updates the navigator. (Item A11)
- Driver checks the fuel level, oil pressure, etc. (Item A111, A112, . . .)

In a company setting, the following may be an example:

- President plans to reduce defects in order for company to survive and, therefore, monitors the defect rate. (Item A)
- President checks the defect rate of assembly line, etc. (Item A1, A2, . . .)
- Assembly line manager monitors the defect rate and updates the president. (Item A1)
- Assembly line manager checks the defect rate at station A, etc. (Item A11, A12, . . .)
- Station A operator monitors the defect rate and updates the manager. (Item A11)
- Station A operator checks the machine conditions, e.g., temperature, pressure, etc. (Item A111, A112, . . .)

Note that in addition to these hierarchical steps to monitor the process, top management may audit the process at lower levels of the organization in a presidential audit. (See Chapter 11.)

As you see in Exhibit 9.21, these control points form cause-and-effect relationships among themselves. For better coordination, therefore, effective leaders need to have a broad understanding of how different factors interrelate and how the control points concept can be used to (1) tie things together in a network, (2) expose problems, and (3) take action as needed. Exhibit 9.22 shows an example of deployment of control points at one company. (See the section on policy management in Chapter 11 for more detailed discussion of deployment of goals throughout the organization.)

In contrast to developing a vertical framework of the company's structure, picking an item such as the quality of one product and linking it to all related processes in the organization, that is, horizontally across the company's structure, also produces a cause-and-effect diagram (see Exhibit 9.23). (See the section on cross-functional management in Chapter 11 for a more detailed discussion.)

Like practicing the PDCA cycle, as more people understand and practice the concept of control points, the company's management

Exhibit 9.22. Control Points at Matsushita. As you see here, the scoreboard is clearly defined across the company assuring the congruence of goals.

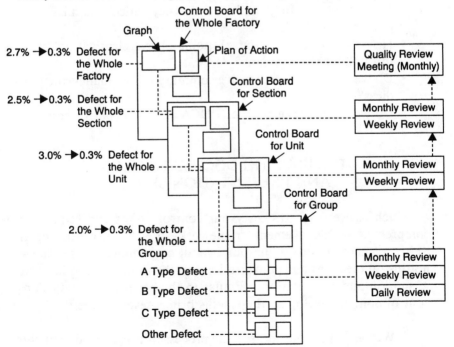

Courtesy Matsushita Electronic Parts

Exhibit 9.23. Control Points as Viewed Horizontally (Example: Quality)

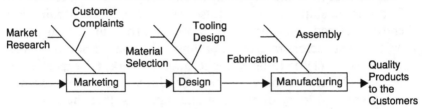

structure will become stronger. At the same time, communication throughout the company will be vastly enhanced and teamwork will be more closely coordinated. Like anything else, however, until a certain critical mass of people are exposed to the idea and a certain level of success is achieved, there will not be significant improvement. Thus, education and feedback of progress to people remain very important. Since this topic is important in tying SFM to the total company business, we will discuss these methods further in Chapters 10 and 11. For now, however, let us ask ourselves:

- Have we applied control point concepts in our organization?
- If so, what are they, and how do they reflect the mission of our organization?
- Has a network of control points been clearly established throughout the company?
- Do we have a comprehensive summary of key management indices?
- Do we practice the cycle of PDCA for each control point?

DEVELOPING DOCUMENTATION AND PRESENTATION SKILLS

As much as we need to clarify our control points and establish a comprehensive management framework to achieve excellence in SFM, we need to streamline our overall communication process— not just in meetings and conversations on the floor but also in documentation and presentations. Similar to the benefits of establishing control points, developing these skills brings several benefits:

- We can clarify our ideas in the process of preparing documents or presentations. This helps to reduce the clutter of information. Of course, objectivity, accuracy, and clear logic should be respected.

- With effective communication skills, points are made clear, delivery is efficient, timely, and smooth, and the presentation is interesting to hear or read.
- Knowledge, know-how, and ideas are transferred effectively for the benefit of others.
- By using a standardized problem-solving process such as the QC story, communication becomes more streamlined.

So, we may understand that quality, cost, and delivery (QCD) apply to effective communication. Understanding the importance of effective delivery of messages, let us next review the major points of making an effective presentation. The key is for the presenter to put him- or herself in the shoes of the customers—the audience (see Exhibits 9.24 and 9.25).

Similar guidelines should be applied to writing documents. Especially for communication on the shop floor, conciseness, clarity, and simplicity are the key. As much as shop floor (genba) oriented thinking prefers immediate understanding of real things (genbutsu) with real facts (genjitsu), we also need to reflect these ideas by using real parts, pictures, charts, and exhibits in delivering the message. And ideally, these exhibits should, in effect, be talking to us by themselves.

Further, in order to involve more people in making effective presentations and documentation, special consideration should be given to keeping things simple and to the point (see Exhibit 9.26).

As each of us gets used to making presentations and writing documents, communication within the organization will be streamlined. In fact, the organization may develop its own terminology or vocab-

Exhibit 9.24. Key Points of Making Presentation

- Know the purpose of the presentation
- Identify the main ideas
- Know your audience's level of understanding and interest in the subject matter
- Develop the story of the presentation; follow logical steps
- Pick out interesting points to catch the audience's attention
- Practice with dry runs as appropriate
- Use visual aids effectively, yet keep them simple and to the point
- Time the presentation and stick to the schedule

Exhibit 9.25. Use of Cartoons to Make a Point

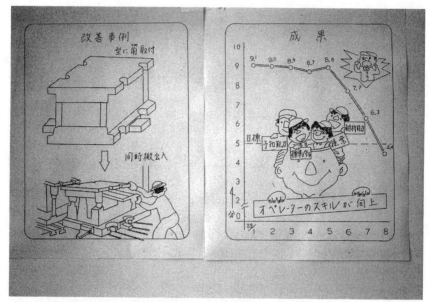

Note: Here, members of a quality circle use cartoons to get their message across to the audience. They have also followed the steps of the QC story, making it easy for presenters and audience to follow logical steps in conveying the message.

Courtesy Daihatsu

ulary for getting the message across quickly, such as wai-gaya, glass wall management, mini-companies, and scoreboards. On the other hand, if we are disorganized or self-centered, communication can be exhaustive and time consuming. Here again, we should be customer oriented and discipline ourselves to keep communication to the point.

REVIEWING THE PROGRESS
OF IMPROVEMENT ACTIVITIES

Along with clear documentation and presentations, a periodic review of improvement activities is an important checkpoint in our management cycle. For example, refer again to Appendix 7.3 for a checklist of typical team improvement activities. Since an organization's vitality depends on how interested people are in their jobs, and how their creativity is utilized, as we identify problems by going through this

Exhibit 9.26. Examples of Effective Communication Techniques at the Shop Floor

Means	Description	Comments
Three-Minute Presentation	This is the executive briefing taking place at the shop floor where people report on improvement activities to managers	Quick and concise process makes it possible for quick review
One-Minute Talk	In daily floor meeting, a team member is asked to talk about anything he or she wants. As each one does so, people get to know each other and become comfortable speaking in front of others	Breaking the psychological barrier is important for each individual's development
One-Page Progress Report	This may be a daily, weekly, or monthly report on key tasks or QCDSM indicators for management review	Summary report forces people to think in an organized manner
Use of Story Board	As a scoreboard helps make management information visible, flip charts and story boards, etc. may be used for people to write ideas on	Boards represent idea notebooks of all team members on display

checklist, we should think of ways to address these points, repeating the PDCA cycle over and over.

Even if we call a team self-managed, it does not mean that its members have a free hand. As much as teams will check their performance themselves by use of checklists and so on, there are also the equivalent of bankers or venture capitalists providing resources for the team and keeping an eye on their investment. Consequently, each mini-company needs to make sure that bankers or managers are properly informed about the progress by such means as periodic meetings as well as reports such as monthly reports, quarterly reports, or annual reports.

Even though some bankers may not require a detailed progress report, it should be considered an important duty of the mini-company president to prepare proper documentation for his or her own sake. This habit will help us to see clearly how we are progressing. When reports are well organized with proper support data, logic, analysis, and evaluation of benefits, managers will develop

Exhibit 9.27. Display of Improvement Project Status. A display board is provided to show the status of each team's progress. Here, each step of the QC story corresponds to each column, enabling people to see how they stand in relation to other teams. As the team progresses, the token on the display moves to the right one step at a time. And as teams complete projects, the number of completed projects are tallied in the far right-hand column, like some of the score cards for games that we play.

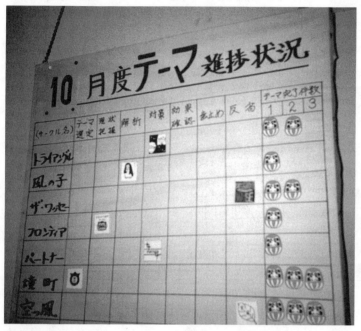

Courtesy Daiwa Seiko

much more confidence, just as bankers develop confidence in those with good credit records.

In other words, becoming accustomed to such practices will not only help us organize our thoughts but it will also help us develop good management discipline. As skills are developed, an informal exchange of ideas may prove to be enough in some cases, but until we can master such a skill, the discipline of good documentation and presentation should never be taken lightly.

SUMMARY

- Leadership needs to be supported by a comprehensive management framework.

- As our free market system encourages the notion of survival of the fittest, assessing the level of competitiveness by such means as benchmarking will bring a new insight to focus our efforts.
- For us to improve our performance, there are different stages in the development of people's goal-setting skills. There are also different stages of development in people's skills for managing the continuous improvement process using the PDCA cycle.
- Developing these skills is like exercising and developing muscles. As in any team sport, however, it requires everybody's cooperation and discipline to follow through.
- If we study the way a supervisor spends time, he or she performs a multitude of tasks, each representing a PDCA cycle. The more we can upgrade the abilities on the shop floor through practicing the PDCA cycle collectively, the greater the competitiveness of the whole organization.
- Practicing control points throughout the organization will help to clarify the key management points of the organization.
- Even though it may take time and skill to utilize the concept of control points, their effective use will help to identify problems and help us to use our creativity in a more focused and organized fashion.
- As our organization grows, we also need to develop effective communication skills, e.g., documentation and presentation skills. This will enable our organization to function smoothly just as our body functions with an autonomous nervous system.
- As our communication skills increase, we can not only check our own performance effectively but we can also inform our bankers of our progress. Accordingly, problems and opportunities will be identified and addressed in a timely and effective fashion.

Chapter Ten

TYING SHOP FLOOR MANAGEMENT TO THE TOTAL COMPANY BUSINESS

In order to manage our company better and make it more competitive, we have studied developing core values, orienting each person and the organization to customers, upgrading skills, and developing leadership necessary to move forward. And in the last chapter we studied the basics of managing shop floor improvement activities. Expanding on these, we will now tie the company-wide management system to support shop floor management (SFM).

COMPANY-WIDE PLANNING

We have learned that in order to thrive in today's business world, we need to be able to control the process closest to where the action is: the shop floor. The company's strategy development and deployment process should reflect such thinking. Yet by putting ourselves in other people's shoes, and looking at the business from different levels within the organization, we will find that each individual—whether in top management, middle management, on the support staff, or on the shop floor—does certain things better than others.

This then reflects the idea that each individual should be viewed as president of his or her own area of responsibility or, as discussed before, as president of his or her mini-company. If we can develop a support system for better coordination, cooperation, and communication among different groups within the company, therefore, we can make shop floor management tie in with the total company's business, making it an important part of a totally integrated business

262

system. To do this, however, an important step is the planning process in which priorities are set for the whole company.

In traditional organizations, a top-driven policy and strategic direction were considered keys to success (remember the spindle model in Exhibit 1.8). While direction from the top may still be important, a better use of all creative resources within an organization may shift the power structure to differ from that of the traditional company.

In other words, instead of a belief that strategy should be developed from the top, our organization may need to be flexible enough to coordinate top-down, bottom-up, as well as cross-functional management processes to search for the best use of people's talent within the company. Especially when we recognize the limitations of traditionally run organizations, such an orientation should become an important strategic direction for the company, as well as the people within it.

BUSINESS PLANNING FOR SELF-MANAGEMENT

As mentioned in Chapter 7, the plan-do-check-act management cycle may look like the diagram in Exhibit 10.1, where each unit of the organization is practicing PDCA cycles to continuously move forward.

Here, the first criterion for better planning is the ability to ana-

Exhibit 10.1. Practicing the PDCA Cycle Throughout the Organization

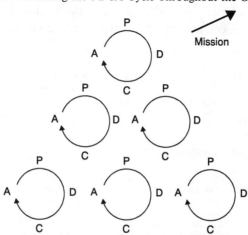

lyze a situation and come up with solutions. These correspond to the check and act steps of the PDCA cycle. As discussed before, when people develop problem-solving skills both as individuals and as a team, and go through the PDCA cycle over and over, their planning capability should improve. Naturally, our aim here is analyzing a situation and coming up with a solution to develop a persuasive plan with a high probability of success.

DEVELOPING A MINI-COMPANY BUSINESS PLAN

As in the case of a business startup situation, the ability to produce a good business plan with sufficient backup data and analysis is an important criterion to run any business. Whether we propose our business plan internally to the company or to external organizations such as bankers or venture capitalists, the process is very similar. Even though there are various ways to develop a business plan, I have found the format in Exhibit 10.2 to be effective.

As you may have noticed, this is essentially the same format as described in Exhibit 3.4 when we first studied the mini-company concept. A short review of each item, however, may help:

1. *A name for the mini-company* is developed with team members or people in the same unit of the organization. This will help develop an identity for the group.
2. *A mission statement* is developed by thinking about why the group exists, why they come to work, etc. Reflecting the concerns of people in the mini-company, this may differ from the mission statement for the whole company. Yet, as long

Exhibit 10.2. Contents of Mini-Company Business Plan

1. Name of the company (i.e., mini-company)
2. Mission statement
3. Company profile
4. Customer-supplier relationships
5. Major objectives
6. Analysis to achieve objectives
7. Plans of action
8. Measurements and reporting methods

as people have ownership, this should help promote team-work to get things done. (For examples, see Exhibit 3.8.)

3. *The company profile* lists the team members and describes their skills, including the machines they use and a description of products or services produced. The processes may be described in the form of a process flow diagram. By doing this, people may be surprised to learn that they deal with complex processes and use varieties of equipment, tools, and fixtures, and that they represent a very skillful team.

4. *The customer-supplier relationship* describes the relationship with internal and external parties providing or receiving products, parts, or information. Describing this on paper will help people to realize the importance of a customer orientation (For example, see Exhibit 2.3 and 3.3). As we do this, we may find that we have not listened to our customers as much as we should have.

5. *Major objectives* are key items that the team wants to achieve in this planning period. These may be tied to the mission and function of the company. Quality, cost, delivery, safety, and morale (QCDSM) may be the key ingredients (for example, see Exhibit 4.3).

6. *Analysis* is where problem-solving tools are used objectively to assess the situation and logically come up with recommendations. Cause-and-effect diagrams and pareto principles may be used by the team to come up with countermeasures to achieve objectives. Objectivity, clarity, and persuasiveness are the keys.

7. When countermeasures are developed, they are summarized as *plans of action* using 5W2H (who is doing what, when, where, why, how, and how much). Here, the resource constraints need to be considered carefully.

8. In order to clarify the control points and monitor the progress in a comprehensive manner, *measurements and reporting methods* are summarized (for example, see Exhibit 9.14).

As you see here, all the elements of this process have been covered in previous chapters: our vision and mission from Chapter 1, customer orientation and basic mini-company concept from Chapters 2 and 3, involving everyone and upgrading skills from Chapters 4 and 5, acquiring and practicing problem-solving skills from Chapters 6 and 7, practicing leadership skills from Chapter 8, and managing shop floor improvement activities from Chapter 9. Thus, this whole mini-company exercise will provide a comprehensive framework for us to practice Shop Floor Management. (Please note that in conjunction with the business plan and to address specific projects in more detail, a QC story form or simple project summary sheet may be provided as backup material.)

As much as solving a problem requires coordination of efforts, developing a business plan also requires a well-coordinated effort by people from different disciplines. No good business plan can be developed in a vacuum. Unless people from other functions review or examine the plan and their viewpoints are reflected in it, it will not have a solid base.

To illustrate, if customers are not informed of such a plan, their ideas and key concerns may not be addressed appropriately. If suppliers are not involved, their unique views on solving the problems may not be incorporated. If managers or support people are not involved, resources may not be allocated appropriately and the coordination of efforts may be insufficient. In many ways, this is like playing catch with different groups of people. The ball represents coordination, cooperation, and communication. If everybody shares ideas and finds ways to help each other, each plan will be better developed, helping to accomplish the total company goals as well as individual goals.

Clearly, the concept is not difficult to digest, but it is teamwork, analytical skills, and the willingness to run a mini-company that make the process function. When more people are engaged in this process, the power can be phenomenal; we may develop a refined network or nervous system that did not exist before.

We can practice this exercise even in a traditionally managed environment if people are willing to try. In fact, it is more important to practice in such an environment because the need for change is greater. While our tendency is to blame problems on others, we should always try to find our own way into the future.

COORDINATING THE BUSINESS PLAN DEVELOPMENT PROCESS

For the business planning process to be effective, therefore, business plans should be shared in the meeting among colleagues while they are being developed. This has several important benefits as shown in

Exhibit 10.3. Such sharing meetings will provide a setting for checks and balances and ensure that business plans are not developed in a vacuum—that is, not reflecting the voice of customers or not fully utilizing limited resources such as man, material, machine, or money.

To illustrate the process of developing a business plan more in detail, let us look at an example of the business planning process from a midwestern automobile supplier. Traditionally, in this company, the business plan had been developed in a fully top-down mode with the emphasis on financial numbers. People's ideas were not incorporated into the plan development process, resulting in a lack of ownership. Furthermore, driving to achieve the numbers proposed by the top often made people behave counterproductively, emphasizing some people's goals at the expense of others. Some even took the process as nothing more than a ritual.

Consequently people found the mini-company exercise described here quite a change. While the idea of ownership and self-management sounded good, most people who were accustomed to the traditional ways of running a business experienced difficulty in adjusting their thinking, especially at the beginning. Some people were skeptical:

- "This is like going back to school and writing a report. . . ."

- "Let's wait and see if the management is really serious about this."

- "This sounds good but I feel uncomfortable speaking up in the group."

Exhibit 10.3. Benefits of Exchanging Business Plans Among Mini-Company Presidents

- Each president can see how others are proceeding.
- Being customers or suppliers to one another, each president can ask questions if the other mini-company's business plan does not address key concerns.
- Each president can identify constraints and try to resolve them by sharing resources early on.
- Presidents can share ideas or techniques for developing good business plans among themselves.
- Each president can help others, and in turn receive help from others.
- By helping each other, team spirit will develop.

Yet, others had a different attitude:

- "Let's do it. If we do what we've always done, we get what we've always got."

- "If we fail to do this, then all we have to do is to go back to the old way—nothing to lose by trying it."

- "I understand why we have to do this. Even if I don't know how well we can do it, I think it is important to try."

Then, all the managers decided to go through this new business planning process while maintaining the traditional number crunching one. After going through the process for a few weeks, there were more opinions. Some commented:

- "I am too busy to do this. I have so many other things to do."

- "It is easier to do it myself than to involve my people and take away their time."

- "Show me an example of how other people did this. Then I can do it easily."

But again, others had a different attitude:

- "I am happy that people are enthusiastic about this. We have never worked like this before."

- "Let me share what we did so other people can benefit from my experience."

- "I explained this to my subordinates, and they, themselves, want to develop mini-companies. So it's snowballing."

The management met every week to compare notes on how the process was moving in each of the mini-companies. Some were progressing further than others. Occasionally, a few people showed up without much preparation. But there were no negative comments from other managers because the whole orientation of this exercise was "self-management." In fact, many offered encouraging comments and assistance so that everybody could move forward as a group.

As people shared this experience, assisted each other, and gave each other guidance, things started to snowball. Internal customers and suppliers were sharing concerns and trying to come up with plans of attack, sometimes jointly. In one instance, a customer survey was conducted by one mini-company to better understand the needs of its customers. And as this approach was shared in a weekly update meeting, several more customer surveys were taken by other mini-companies benefiting from such a good idea.

In another instance, someone came up with a new way of presenting materials using better graphics. Then another person found an effective way to use computer software for charting. Almost instantly, these ideas were shared and people started to help each other. So everybody benefited from such an exchange of ideas.

People also found that customer-supplier relationships were working more like a network (remember Exhibit 2.6). They were beginning to realize that if one helps the other, then the other may also help back. In a larger sense, it is almost like all the members of a team helping each other.

As an example, the maintenance group identified production as a customer. So, they met together to share concerns, analyze the situation, and prioritize the plan of action. As much as the maintenance group wanted to do effective preventive maintenance, the production group wanted the same but with minimum schedule disruption. So they figured out a new way of scheduling preventive maintenance to prioritize certain critical machines. Also, a plan was developed to train operators on maintenance so that production people could follow correct procedures in running machines and to assist in maintenance work.

In another instance, as a mini-company idea and its business plan were shared and implemented, more and more people showed interest and started to develop their own mini-companies or mini-mini-companies. As this process went on, more people realized the importance and fun of working together. They were surprised to find that by helping others—that is, their customers—they got help from others as well. So, when people became aware of these new interrelationships, it was like light bulbs coming on here and there and, finally, across the whole organization. To me, this is best described as "organizational enlightenment."

Needless to say, with enhanced communication among the people, this business plan became much more thorough than the one the traditional approach had accomplished. It reflected many people's creativity and ownership as opposed to bureaucracy and power politics. Accordingly, top management gave full authorization to the plans people developed.

EXECUTING THE BUSINESS PLAN

Once business plans are developed, the next step is to implement them following the PDCA cycle. As discussed before, in order to review the progress, certain areas may be designated as mini-company "board rooms" where people can conduct meetings and with space to post key information describing progress and comparing the plan and actual performance.

Simply by visiting this area, any person can see what projects are being worked on and their levels of progress. People can also see that these activities relate to achieving the key objectives, and hence, achieving the mission of the mini-company. Combining these activities across the company, then, will help to achieve the objectives and mission of the entire company. Here again, the measurements may be compared to a baseball scoreboard, reflecting the team performance, as opposed to "numbers" which do not reflect people's pride and ownership.

As in the company's board meetings, the exchange of ideas in the mini-company meeting along with the mini-company scoreboard will help identify ways to accomplish the business plan. As the need arises, plans may be adjusted, yet the principle of PDCA will be maintained. (Exhibit 10.4 shows an example of such a scoreboard. Here, along with the scores of key items on QCDSM, the focus subjects of the month are described at the bottom of the board. For this month, they are quality, total productive maintenance, and reduction of overtime.)

SHARING THE PROGRESS

A point to remember in the execution stage of the business plan is that it should be considered natural for the mini-company president to report to his or her "bankers" or "venture capitalists" at certain intervals. This follows typical business practice where most bankers request periodic progress reports from presidents. Bankers don't like surprises. They like objectivity, clear-cut point-to-point discussion

Exhibit 10.4. Mini-Company Scoreboard Used at Matsushita

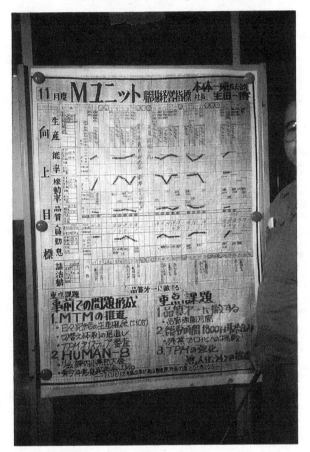

Courtesy Matsushita

with good analysis and supporting data. Of course, many are bottom-line oriented, but a good progress report should include analysis, descriptions of specific key activities, and, future forecasts, so that they get an immediate sense of what is going on.

Exhibit 10.5 shows such a progress report developed by a department of Sparling Instruments, a small California company. Notice that this report corresponds to a mini-company scoreboard on QCDSM. The president of the company reviews these reports every month and gives feedback. Also, depending on the content, he gives a department-of-the-month award in his monthly all-employee meetings.

In the beginning, some people were reluctant to fill out the report

Exhibit 10.5. Monthly Progress Report

SCOREBOARD

DEPARTMENT OF THE MONTH
Due by 12:00 on the first Friday of each month

Department   <u>Machine Shop</u>   Month <u>February</u>   19 <u>92</u>

Team Leader <u>Lambert De Vera</u>   Completed by: <u>Lambert De Vera & Ray Bolin</u>

Quality (Rejection rate improvement, process improvement)

- Redesigned the 625 housing; reduced both machining time by 75% and material cost by $1.5 per housing.
- Modified the drill & tap fixture of the collar P/N 121244 and reduced cycle time by 10%.
- 10 hrs CNC training (Jesse Casillas), 10 hrs slab mill training (William Garcia)

Cost (Productivity improvement, cost reductions)
- Acquisition of a CNC station (Part program management system); allows operator to instantly program and edit part program estimated saving:
  - a.) Machine Shop 168 hrs/yr.
  - b.) Engineering Dept. 45 hrs/yr.
- Creation of a problem solving team to improve the fabrication process of the Mag Meter which will increase productivity, reduce labor cost and also improve quality.
- Fabrication of jaw, milling and aligning fixtures for the vertical shaft, 239 collars, prop plug & 6" & 8" Mag Meter and reduced machining time by 10 20%.   (OVER)

Delivery (On time orders, paperwork, reports)

- 82% completion of the production "Hot List", 43 out of 52 work orders

- New work orders issued = 74

- Work order completed = 89

Safety (Improvements, training done, etc.)

- No accidents or injury reported. Implemented a weekly safety inspection within the Machine Shop Dept.

- During safety meeting, we discussed about proper actions to be taken in the event of chemical eye splash.

Morale

a. Number of people in team __18__ b. Number of suggestions __50__	B/A	277%
c. Number of people with suggestions __6__	C/A	33%
d. Number of unplanned absences· __5__	D/A	27%

Courtesy Sparling Instruments

form. But because the president regularly provided comments on each department's report with a red pen, people gradually accepted the idea and found it useful.

Exhibit 10.6 shows a progress report developed by a Japanese sporting goods company. As you see here, measurable goals are tracked, reflecting the extensive use of control points. Also, color coding is used for ease of practicing management by exception.

When a report is made to the bankers, it also makes sense to share progress among peers, that is, a group of mini-company presidents. Since they played an important role as customers or suppliers providing comments in developing the business plan, periodic updates will keep them informed, and provide a check-and-balance mechanism among mini-company presidents. While bosses may be viewed as bankers, other presidents may be considered as board members of the mini-companies.

Reporting on progress in such sharing meetings may be done by every mini-company president. But since plans of action typically require a few months or more to implement, it is recommended that a few presidents make more detailed reports at each meeting in a round robin style. In this way, the presenters can prepare better to share progress in more detail and pinpoint a few focused items.

Also, this will avoid getting into a ritual, numbers-reading type of meeting. In addition, we can display these progress reports for everybody to see. As obvious as it may be, the more glass wall management we practice, the more opportunities we can provide for people to be involved.

SUMMARIZING THE PROGRESS IN AN ANNUAL REPORT

At the end of the year, or every six months, each mini-company president may submit an annual or semi-annual report to his or her bankers, and share this with peers (i.e, board members) and team members. Such reports represent the performance appraisal of the mini-company. They describe the way problems are analyzed and objectives and plans of action are developed and executed, along with a summary of accomplishments and future issues. In fact, when accumulated over time, these documents may even serve as a basis for "appraisal," or "resume," of each president's performance.

Exhibit 10.6. Monthly Progress Report of a Japanese Sporting Goods Company

Category	Control Points	Responsibility	Month 1	2	3	4 5 6 7 8 9 ...	Check & Act Problem	Countermeasures
Quality	• Engineering Changes	KS	65	70	...	... ...	Unclear documentation	...
	• Percent of Resolution for Process Problem	HS	77	80	...	... ...	...	...
Cost	• Parts Commonality & Value Analysis	FD	92	...	...	... ...	...	...
	• Reduction of Overtime	HS	92	...	...	... ...	...	...
Delivery	• New Product Introduction	FD	...	...	...	... ...	...	...
Morale	• Number of suggestion	FD	...	...	...	... ...	...	...
...	...	...						

Check & Act		1	2	3	4 5 6 7 8 9 ...	Total Evaluation
	Total %	90	89	97	... ...	• Need more comprehensive design review procedure. . .
	Judgment	○	○	○	... ...	
	Problems	...			... ...	
	Counter-measures	...			... ...	

• Control Level = > 80%

• Total % = $\dfrac{\text{\# items met the plan}}{\text{\# total items}}$

Note: Judgment "○" column is color coded either green >80%; blue >70%; or red <70%.

Exhibit 10.7. Picture of Progress Report Posted in Cafeteria

Courtesy Sparling Instruments

In this day and age when things change so rapidly, developing business plans and summarizing reports on a semi-annual basis may be more appropriate than waiting to do it at year end. Also, in this way, plans are updated more frequently.

Exhibit 10.8 lists the contents of such a report which may prove useful. Items 1 through 6 are the same as in the business plan. Then, item 7 shows the results of the business plan. Especially for supervisors, I recommend posting pictures that reflect the improvement since pictures can communicate more than a thousand words in one

Exhibit 10.8. Contents of Mini-Company Annual Report

1. Name of the company (i.e., mini-company)
2. Mission statement
3. Company profile
4. Customer-supplier relationships
5. Major objectives
6. Analysis to achieve objectives
7. Achievements
8. Existing problems

glance. They also make the report more interesting for readers (see Exhibit 10.9, pages 276 through 278, for examples). Item 8 describes the existing problems that people feel need to be addressed. (See Exhibit 10.10 for examples of such problems summarized in an annual report.)

As you see in these examples, people effectively used charts and pictures to share accomplishments made during the year, even though they previously did not have shop floor meetings, an organized workplace, or charts on the shop floor, and many people were inexperienced in reading the graphs.

To summarize the points covered above, Exhibit 10.11 shows the benefits of setting aside some time and writing down such mini-company annual reports.

One supervisor at Fireplace Manufacturers, Inc. in California once shared with me, "When I am emotionally down at work, I open my annual report from the past year. Then I remember that the progress we have made was not smooth. By recognizing what it took to

Exhibit 10.9. Examples of Achievements Shown in the Annual Report

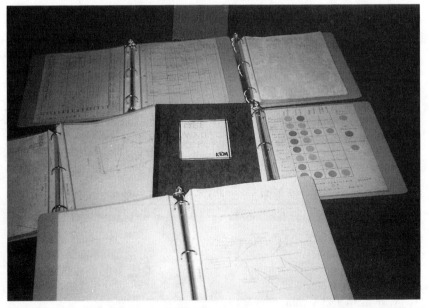

a. This exhibit shows examples of the first annual report produced by supervisors who are all young immigrants to the United States.

Courtesy Fireplace Manufacturers, Inc.

Exhibit 10.9. Continued

Started using this new Camoga splitter in Dec 1990. Currently located in cutting dept.

This punch press machine, which was used for wallet, was converted for the use of clicking of tabs & belt tips. It is still not operating in a reliable manner.

b. This exhibit shows a portion of a very comprehensive annual report with effective use of pictures to show dozens of accomplishments.

Courtesy Leegin Creative Leather Products

Exhibit 10.9. Continued

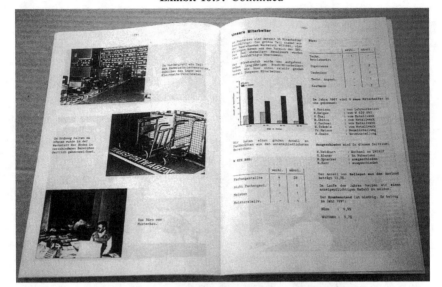

c. This exhibit shows the first annual report of a mini-company published in a large company in Europe to explore the potential of people's self-managing capability.

overcome those hurdles and accomplish our many improvements with everybody working together, I bring my smile back and I'm refreshed to go back to work.''

At Rapid-Line, a manufacturer in Michigan, people prepared an annual report on videotape. By having operators from different areas share the examples of improvements made at the shop floor, everyone became aware that there were many improvements that contributed to the progress of the company. Because this tape involved many people with many interesting stories, it was run repeatedly in the cafeteria for everybody to watch. Some people even watched it several times.

Another idea for first timers who are preparing business plans and annual reports is that just as the PDCA cycle may work better if we start with the check and act steps, it may be better to summarize achievements and existing problems in the annual report first. Then, these can be used as a base to develop a business plan, instead of writing the business plan first without carefully reviewing the past performance.

Exhibit 10.10. Examples of Existing Problems Listed in an Annual Report

Existing Problems :-

- Operator unwilling to do different operation, eg. from braiding to sewing
- Braiders only like to braid the regular 7 & 9 strand braids
- Daily meeting is not conducted; To hold group meeting every two weeks
- Graphs are not updated on a regular basis
- To improve communication between dept. & inspection
- Coordination between this dept & other depts eg Fabtab for buckle
- Housekeeping is not satisfactory, eg accumulating boxes in the rack
- To locate areas for inspector, assistant's desk, & time card slot
- Inconsistent flow of work; there is no Kanban system between Warehouse & dept.
- Buckle system is not followed diligently, eg. order over a month old is not placed in the white box
- Tremendous verification in calculating the group rate of the cell as tickets are not used for braiding & colortoning
- Pay scale of employees in a cell eg. 6 mos vs 2 yrs.
- Only 1 sewer in each cell
- Too much overtime in the cutting group
- Punch press machine keeps breaking down

- Daily morning meeting is not conducted.
- Graphs are not updated.
- Housekeeping is not well practiced.
- New inventory control system is not functioning well, etc.

Note: An important point here is that this list represents the consensus of people. So, even though these items represent shortcomings, it is still wonderful that people were not afraid to draw attention to them. In other words, people are thinking about ways to improve rather than pointing a finger at others.

Courtesy Leegin Creative Leather Products

Exhibit 10.11. Benefits of Publishing a Mini-Company Annual Report

- The process of writing will help organize thoughts objectively.
- People receive feedback on their work—i.e., if the progress was good, the pleasure is shared; if progress was less than satisfactory, the pain is shared—so that they can be more creative.
- By sharing the progress, people tend to develop pride and ownership in what they do.
- This process will help identifying weakness and addressing the problem as a team as opposed to trying to address it on an individual basis.
- An understanding of what happened and why will guide the way into the future.
- Going through this process at regular intervals, we develop a discipline in establishing the rhythm of PDCA.
- This exercise will help developing a framework to discuss the problems jointly as a group.

LEARNING FROM THE BUSINESS PLANNING PROCESS

A number of companies have gone through this process with me in Japan, the United States, and Europe. Some went through it in more detail than others. Some tied this process with an award program very effectively. Others used it as a part of performance appraisals. Just as repetition and perseverance are the key to accomplishing anything, the same is true in this process as well.

Reviewing the lessons learned from business planning, Exhibit 10.12 summarizes the comments of people in one company in the Midwest. The vice president of manufacturing also shared with me the words of reformer Jacob Riis, reflecting the experience he gained in this process: "When nothing seems to help, I go and look at a stonecutter hammering away at his rock perhaps a hundred times without as much as a crack showing in it. Yet at the hundred and first blow it will split in two, and I know it was not that blow that did it—but all that had gone before."

Whether the company is small or large, going through this process with management leadership and people's ownership will establish strong self-managing capabilities. In the case of the business plan as described here, the link to the upper level of the organization is achieved through the manager's guidance. Top management, acting as bankers or venture capitalists, may guide or influence the process

Exhibit 10.12. Learning from the Business Planning Process

Ownership	Baring soul	Measurement
Barrier elimination	Participation	Common sense
Focus on objectives	Attainment of goal	Consensus
Identify customers	congruence	Reconciliation process
Identify needed	Teamwork	Group dynamics
resources	Communication	Clear objectives
Openness/honesty	Checks and balances	Process oriented
Respecting others'	Constancy of purpose	Documentation
opinions	Better utilization of	Flexibility
Can adopt externally	existing resources	Ongoing
imposed goals	Reduces fear	Continual improvement
Commitment	Leap of faith	Reduced redundancy
Cross-functional	Visual demonstration	Resolve
integration	De-emphasis on	Evolutionary
Linkages	financial	Exposing weakness
No right or wrong	Bottom up	Interdependency
Pain, pain	Gain	Comprehensive
Revolutionary	Time-consuming	

Process more in sawtooth fashion

Identification and quantification of critical success factors

PDCA process can be used in everyday life

Expand to all levels/areas of organization

This is such a good idea, it should have come from corporate

Brings honesty and participation, reduces fear

Ability to expand new themes to lowest possible level of organization as well as
to highest (vertical and horizontal)

as it seems appropriate without taking away people's ownership, creativity, or chance to grow with the company.

We know, however, that in some cases managers may be dictatorial and unsupportive. If that is the case we should remember: "We cannot direct the wind, but we can adjust the sails to go where we want to go." Even a dictatorial boss would like to accomplish something anyway. So, if you and your group can show the benefits of the business planning process by successfully executing the plan and producing objective support data and analysis, perhaps you, the shop floor entrepreneurs, can convince your boss about the benefits of this process.

After all, banks and venture capitalists like a great performing company. At the same time, we need to remind ourselves that when we develop a business plan we are not doing it for the sake of following the procedures. Ultimately, we should be responsible for the outcome. These ideas are a means to accomplish that outcome, and not the end unto itself.

TYING THE BUSINESS PLAN WITH THE BUDGET

Depending on our role in the organization, we may not have budgetary responsibility. Yet at home, as major income earners for our families, we have somehow learned to manage the family budget—at least in most cases.

Self-managing without budgetary responsibility may not be called self-managing, by definition. So to gain more self-managing ability, every person needs to learn the financial aspects of the operation as well. By better understanding the accounting data and the financial implications of our business plan, we are much closer to running our own company. Also, we may be able to better make a case to our bankers as to why our ideas are a sound investment for the company.

In many companies, however, missions, plans, objectives, and budgets are not well linked. So, let us understand how to develop that linkage:

- First, we have a mission (to describe the reasons for our existence).
- Objectives of our plan support this mission.
- Next, a plan of action is necessary to achieve these objectives.
- Then, we need to define resource allocation (who is going to do what, when, where, why, how, and how much) for plans to be executed successfully.
- Finally, as plans are successfully implemented, we need to develop standards so that we can further move forward.

If we express this with graphics, it may look like Exhibit 10.13, where QCDSM are major objectives and "a," "b," and "c" indicate different plans developed to accomplish objectives. For example, plan "a" may correspond to education on shop floor management. The

Exhibit 10.13. Linkage Between Mission, Objectives, Plan of Action, and Budget

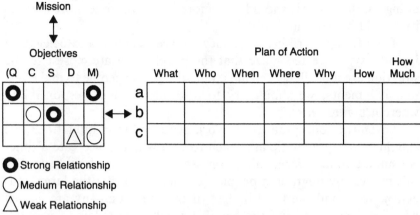

matrix on the left shows the cross-relationships. For example, if plan "a" may accomplish "quality" and "morale," the marks in the matrix indicate such relationships.

The matrix on the right shows the summary of plans so that it is easy to see what is going on and who is involved. The column "How Much" corresponds with budget, or resource allocation in terms of money, manpower, and so on. In other words, the total of this column should correspond to the total budget. Or, when we add up the budget figures that we need to carry out our plans, we need to check this figure with our banker (i.e., our boss). If he or she disagrees, we need to rescrutinize plans and continue to negotiate with our bankers as appropriate.

Using this table for budgetary purposes, we can see how much money and other resources are used on what project, which in turn will help accomplish the objectives, which in turn will help accomplish our mission.

To practice this idea, however, we need to pay attention to a few points. Since detailed accounting procedures tend to be controlled from the top, while adding administrative burden and stifling people's creativity on the shop floor, if we are not careful, the budgeting procedure may do the same.

As most bankers will not go into the details of an operation unless it is necessary, our bankers or venture capitalists (i.e., our bosses) should make sure not to micro-manage the shop floor by overcomplicating the budgetary process. In other words, if we have good mechanisms to control the total budget and gain confidence in doing so, then people should take more initiative while more authority should be delegated to them.

Even though striking a balance between control and delegation is not easy, if we recognize that the people who are closest to the situation are most likely the most knowledgeable people to make certain judgments, we should try to delegate financial responsibility where it makes sense.

Given the conceptual framework described in Exhibit 10.13, we should find a pragmatic approach to follow and not create a time-consuming number-crunching exercise. Instead, we should simplify this process by upgrading people's capability so that the large budgetary items and the total budget of the mini-company are agreed upon with bankers, and the detailed breakdown is left to people's judgment.

Also, as standards should reflect mission, objectives, and the level of shop floor management, detailed accounting controls should be replaced by execution of standards at the shop floor as much as practically possible.

POLICY MANAGEMENT (MANAGEMENT OF THE COMPANY'S STRATEGIC DIRECTION)*

Let us next study how top management's thinking on strategic direction and policy can be linked with the business planning and execution process described above. In our competitive world, it is simply a must to have clear, coherent strategy and a mission that is bought in by the people.

As the company's overall strategic direction is set more clearly at the top and then disseminated and bought into by the people, everyone will have a clear understanding as to where the whole company is going and how to get there. Figuratively, what we are trying to accomplish with policy management is to move from the model on the left to the one on the right in Exhibit 10.14.

Traditionally, however, the corporate strategy developed by

*The term policy management as used here is a translation of the Japanese term *hoshin kanri. Hoshin* refers to a company's policy or strategic direction; *kanri* means management or control. Policy management, then, is the deployment of policy throughout the company. In a broader sense, however, this represents a process for accomplishing a company's mission.

Exhibit 10.14. Sharing Company Policy Within the Organization

Policy Not Shared   Policy Shared

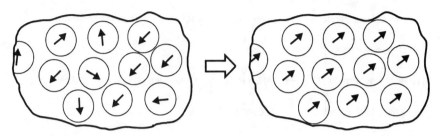

those at the top of the organization has not been shared with many people. As we discussed before, this limits the potential of the organization. When the shop floor becomes a collection of seemingly insurmountable problems and inefficiencies, the capabilities of the people on the shop floor become a major issue for the company's future.

Rather than changing the direction of a company from the top simply to respond to the stock price, companies need to satisfy their customers with minimum waste. If they do so, I believe that in the long run, the stock price will reflect the company's performance. If instead top managers are concerned only with making money from their stock options and the people on the shop floor are changing jobs to obtain slight pay increases, there may be nothing to attract people to such a company except monetary rewards. The corporate mission then means very little to people compared with their financial interest. Even though financial concerns are important in running the business, these are ideally a means to accomplish our mission but not the mission itself.

In order to address the mission of the company and involvement of its people in the policy and strategy development process, therefore, we need to develop a comprehensive process that everybody understands. Exhibit 10.15 illustrates such an effort. The steps of policy development may follow the steps below. The numbers correspond to those in the exhibit.

1. Review of performance from the past period by the department. Any major problems remaining to be addressed are continued to the current period. Also, evaluate major concerns of the organization for the future.

Exhibit 10.15. Process of Policy Management

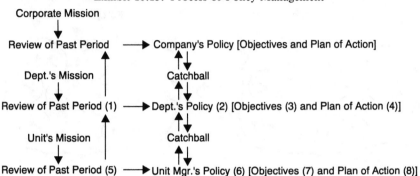

Note: Policy here refers to the strategic direction of the company with objectives and approaches for achieving such objectives. Of course, strategic direction should reflect the mission of the company.

2. Accommodating the company's policy, the department manager develops departmental policy. The policy has two parts, objectives and plans of action.

3. Departmental objectives for the period are developed. If considered critical for the company, some objectives and approaches for achieving them may be suggested from the corporate level. (Catchball in the exhibit indicates the coordination process between department and company.)

4. Plans of action to achieve objectives are developed for the department.

5. The unit manager reviews performance from the prior period. Major problems that still need to be addressed are brought forward to the current period. Also, major concerns of the organization for the future are evaluated.

6. Accommodating the department's policy, the unit manager develops the unit's policy. Again, the policy has two parts, objectives and plans of action.

7. Objectives for the period are developed. If considered critical for the company and/or department, some objectives and approaches to achieving them may be suggested from the corporate or departmental levels. (Catchball in the exhibit here indicates the coordination process between unit and department.)

8. Plans of action are developed to achieve objectives for the unit.

In the process of deploying such a policy, points in Exhibit 10.16 should be considered when selecting the plans of action. Here again, we need to focus on important items of the organization, follow through the PDCA cycle, and use control points (i.e., plan items) on a company-wide scale.

Just as the business planning process at the mini-company level was shared with employees, customers, suppliers, and bankers, this policy management process has similar aims with a stronger emphasis on deploying the company's primary policy, that is, its objectives and plans of action throughout the company. In effect, this is a way of putting a backbone into the organization.

Some may think that policy management is similar to management by objectives (MBO). The difference, however, is important (see Exhibit 10.17). As you see in the exhibit, MBO is more in line with a traditional organization in which results are all that count regardless of approach. Policy management addresses a broader scope of issues in a progressive manner, trying to raise the creativity of people to the maximum.

When we practice policy management, the total picture may look like the one in Exhibit 10.18, which shows the framework of Komatsu's policy management, developed back in the 1960s. As we can see here, the company's goals and approaches are shared and deployed throughout the organization utilizing cause-and-effect relationships and the pareto principle.

At Matsushita's vacuum cleaner division, policy management is displayed on a big board on the shop floor as shown in Exhibit 10.19, where QCD or quality, cost, and delivery (they call it quick delivery, or QD) performance is shared. These QCD measurements are broken

Exhibit 10.16. Key Considerations in Selecting the Plans of Action

- If a department is responsible for a certain policy, that department manager will be responsible for deploying such policy in the organization.
- Another department manager who is not directly responsible for that policy can still support or contribute to the successful execution of the policy, and use judgment about including it in his or her department's plan.
- If plan items selected above become too much to handle, they should be narrowed down to the most important ones.
- If it is not appropriate to execute a certain plan at the department level but it would work at the unit level, assign that item to the unit's plan.
- Plans that are important for the department should be included in the department's plans even if they are not a part of the company's plans.

Exhibit 10.17. Comparison of Management by Objectives and Policy Management

	Management by Objective	Policy Management
Major Orientation	Results oriented (often financially oriented)	Process and results oriented (more strategically oriented)
Strategic Focus	Short to medium term	Short to long term
Responsibility	Individually oriented	Team oriented
Management Style	Delegate; control is tight	Participative, with control (everybody is responsible)
Involvement of People	Top down (one direction)	Top down and bottom up (two directions: catchball)
Process of Change	Breakthrough, innovation	Breakthrough, innovation, plus continuous improvement (PDCA cycle)
Management Process	Bureaucratic	Less bureaucratic, tied in with people's ownership
Satisfying Needs of People	Financial Compensation	Financial and Humanistic needs

down by department and project so that cause-and-effect relationships, for meeting the plant goals are clear to everybody. The progress of implementation plans is then shared by the plant manager with all employees every month. Also, each unit will have a daily floor meeting to update the progress with their scoreboards (see Exhibit 10.4).

To summarize, a comparison of traditional and progressive strategy development processes is shown in Exhibit 10.20.

As you see, a traditional Tayloristic company tends to function more as a deal-making organization where power is centralized (treating people more as tools), whereas a progressive one tends to be people-oriented with a decentralized power base. The values in a progressive organization are more on customer satisfaction, long-term prosperity of people, build-up of people skills as supported by proper leadership, and a comprehensive management support system.

Exhibit 10.18. Policy Management at Komatsu

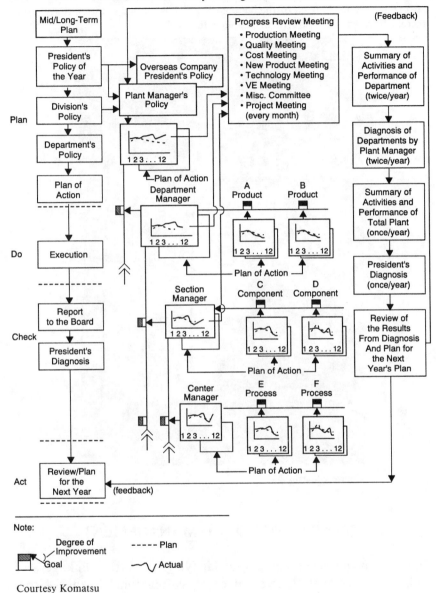

Note:

Degree of Improvement / Goal   ----- Plan   ～∨ Actual

Courtesy Komatsu

Exhibit 10.19. Display of Policy Management at Matsushita. The plant manager, Jiro Izumi, stands in front of the big board, which is located at the entrance of the factory floor where the traffic of people is the busiest.

Courtesy Matsushita

CROSS-FUNCTIONAL MANAGEMENT

In addition to strengthening and clarifying the vertical linkage with policy management, horizontal or cross-functional linkage—from product planning to design to production preparation to purchasing to production to sales—needs to be strengthened as well. In order to assure a customer orientation while promoting company-wide teamwork and breaking departmental barriers, cross-functional management provides an important management support system. (See Ex-

Exhibit 10.20. Traditional vs. Progressive Strategy Development Processes

	Traditional Organization	Progressive Organization
Style of Decision Making	Autocratic; little coordination among people	More democratic; better coordination among people
Number of People Involved	Few specialists and managers	Many; by going through PDCA cycle, people's skill level develops at the same time
People's Buy-in	None; tends to optimize the interest of small number of people	Yes; tends to optimize the interest of larger number of people
Time to Make Decision	Relatively short	Relatively long when organization's skill is limited
Nature of Decision	Often radical; can change direction rather quickly	More fundamental than radical; not easy to change direction when organization's skill is limited
Decision Criteria	Often financial; short-term gain of few people	More holistic; long-term prosperity of whole organization
Implementation	May require coordination of people	Continuously addressing the key concerns of organization

hibit 10.21 as an example for a Japanese automobile parts manufacturer.)

As in the case of weaving, our cloth will not be functional without both vertical and horizontal threads. While quality, cost, delivery, and new product development are examples of items for cross-functional management as shown in the exhibit, other concerns of the organization, such as personnel and education, technology, and administration may also be included in cross-functional management.

Typical cross-functional management may be practiced by developing a committee to (1) clarify the system, rules, roles, and responsibilities, and (2) investigate problems and make recommendations to address the problems. The committee functions somewhat as an

Exhibit 10.21. Relationship Between Vertical and Horizontal Threads of an Organization

	Product Planning	Design	Production Support	Purchasing	Production	Sales	
Quality	●	●	●	●	●	●	→
Cost	○	●	●	●	○	○	→
Delivery	△	○	●	○	●	△	→
New Product	●	●	○	○	○	○	→

Horizontal Linkage (Cross-Functional Management)

Vertical Linkage (Functional / Line Management)

● Strong Relationship   ○ Medium Relationship   △ Weak Relationship

intelligence center and serves as an active nervous system collecting key information from different functions to help in making decisions and executing plans. Typically, the execution is done by the department in charge.

As in the case of policy management, where the PDCA cycle is practiced at all levels, we can practice cross-functional management at different levels and focus on different areas of the organization with the PDCA cycle in mind. There may be corporate-wide committees, as well as divisional, plant, and departmental committees, as appropriate.

A word of caution: Since people are so accustomed to thinking in terms of their own function, it typically requires more than a year for people to absorb the idea of cross-functional management and practice it effectively. For this reason, the first step in getting people used to this idea is to have cross-functional meetings on a regular basis.

COORDINATING APPROACHES
FOR CONTINUOUS IMPROVEMENT

As you may have found from the discussion on policy management and cross-functional management, typically the degree of integration of the management processes varies by company. This is similar to playing baseball with differing degrees of teamwork.

In some cases, a team may win because of luck or a home-run hitter. But over the long run, the team is not likely to have a winning record without good teamwork. In this sense, policy management and cross-functional management are tools that help (and, in a way, force) people to develop teamwork to accomplish common goals.

Implementing these concepts, given proper guidance, typically takes one or two years for a medium-sized organization of, say, five hundred to a thousand people. This takes top management's commitment, well-informed support people's skills, and everybody's willingness to work together.

There are different ways to implement policy management and cross-functional management. For example, one can start at the top, or at the mini-company level. But the point is, if people on the shop floor do not have the skills to go through the PDCA cycle or the ability to self-manage, there will be a limit to what a company can accomplish.

To conclude, let us list in Exhibit 10.22 the different approaches for continuous improvement we have discussed in this book. As we see here, the higher the level the organization, the more coordinating work becomes important to tie these pieces together. In other words, as an organization, a number of approaches may be combined in our journey of continuous improvement. From the people's point of view, they can explore their potential by choosing approaches that match their talents.

Even though the improvement potential will vary depending on the specific situation, Exhibit 10.23 may help us to evaluate these approaches in perspective. Here, the vertical scale corresponds to improvement per each project such as each suggestion or each team project; the horizontal scale corresponds to the time required for implementation of each project. In evaluating the contribution from different activities, a company needs to find a good balance between these approaches so that the contribution from people can be maximized.

Exhibit 10.22. Utilizing Different Approaches for Continuous Improvement

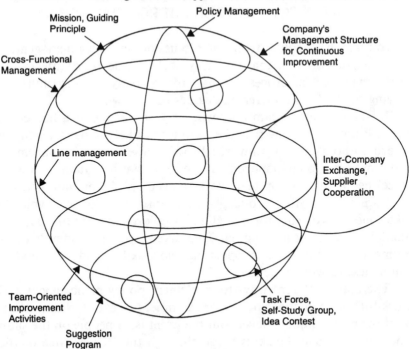

Exhibit 10.23. Potential of Different Approaches for Continuous Improvement

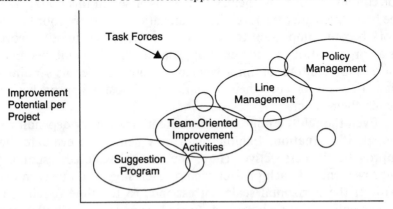

SUMMARY

- In order to utilize the best resources we have in the company, we need to develop a management support system for coordinating, cooperating, and communicating better among different groups within the organization.
- Just as a biologic organism has well-coordinated nerves and muscles, we need to coordinate top-down, bottom-up, and cross-functional planning along with its execution mechanisms.
- Given the proper support, people on the shop floor may function as shop floor entrepreneurs, each running his or her own mini-company. Their bosses may function more as bankers or venture capitalists, providing appropriate guidance to the people.
- As in the case of a business startup, the ability to produce a good business plan is critical. Such a plan should include company name, mission statement, company profile, customer-supplier relationship (description of business environment), major objectives, analysis to achieve objectives, plans of action, measurements and reporting methods.
- Sharing business plans, monitoring the progress, and developing annual reports as a group will help people manage themselves better. Developing healthy competition among group members will also contribute to organizational and personal growth.
- Even if the boss does not help people to develop their skills for self-management, we should learn to practice the mini-company concept so that we can chart our course into the future.
- In order to develop a strong tie between shop floor management and the total company operation, we need to practice the concept of policy management and cross-functional management. By doing so, we can make the whole organization function more as a single team working together to accomplish the company's mission while promoting people to self-manage themselves.

Chapter Eleven

LOOKING AT OURSELVES IN THE MIRROR

So far, we have studied the key elements of shop floor management. Summarizing these, we will study how these elements can be tied together to produce its power. We will also find ways to evaluate how we are doing using a process called a presidential audit. Further, we will study ways to achieve a critical mass of people and accelerate the process of improvement.

TYING THINGS TOGETHER

Reflecting on key areas we have discussed so far, Exhibit 11.1 shows the major elements of shop floor management. In order to maximize the benefits of shop floor management, we need to excel in each of these major elements. Using them as a base, Exhibit 11.2 summarizes the difference between a traditional and a progressive organization.

While addressing the problems within each element is important, the linkages between these factors needs to be strengthened at the same time. For example, core values are linked to the five other major elements. The same is true for each of the other five elements. In other words, each of these elements needs to support each other.

Exhibit 11.3 attempts to describe these linkages. The exhibit is meant to trigger our thinking of SFM from a holistic viewpoint, but should not make us think that this is the complete picture. If we were to explain the essence of this book with this exhibit, however, it might be done as follows:

- First, we need to establish core values and a vision that people in the organization can share (Chapter 1).

Exhibit 11.1. Major Elements of Shop Floor Management

Exhibit 11.2. Difference Between Traditional and Progressive Organizations

Elements of Shop Floor Management	Traditional Organization	Progressive Organization
Core Values (Vision)	- Not shared with people - Emphasis on financials	- Shared with people - Emphasis on respect for people
Customer Orientation	- Driven by self-interest - Do not understand who the customer is	- Driven to satisfy customers - Next process is the customer
Involvement of Everybody	- Labor as extension of machine - Narrow skill base	- Vital element for continuous improvement - Multiple skill base
Problem Solving	- Periodic breakthroughs - Problem solving by few specialist/professionals	- Continuous improvement - Problem solving by everyone
Leadership for Continuous Improvement	- Professional manager - Power-driven	- Leader, educator, catalyst, mentor - People-driven
Management Support System	- Centralized planning - Driven by financial result	- Centralized and decentralized planning - Driven by shared values, vision, objectives and means to achieve them

Exhibit 11.3. Major Elements of Shop Floor Management and Their Linkages

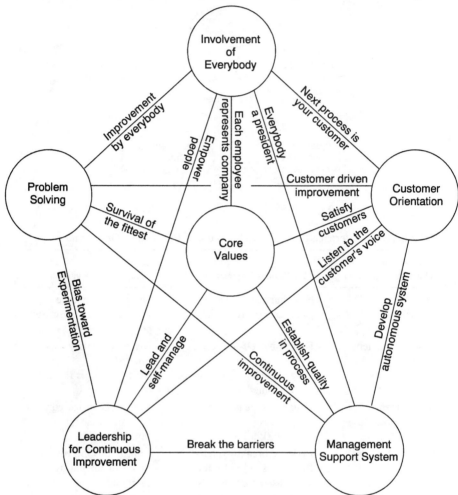

- One of the values should relate to customer orientation (Chapters 2 and 3).
- In order to satisfy customers, whether internal or external, we need to practice the notion that "the next process is your customer," and understand the customer's requirements.
- Since everybody has customers, we need the involvement of everybody (Chapters 4 and 5).
- Yet involvement of everybody is not enough. We need to develop problem-solving skills (Chapters 6 and 7).
- To practice this, we need "improvement by everybody."

- Next, we need to have leadership in having people work together and practice problem solving in the right direction (Chapter 8).
- Leaders then need to encourage people by practicing "a bias toward experimentation" on their own as opposed to having someone else do the work for them.
- Leadership itself, however, cannot guarantee success in today's business. We still need a reliable and comprehensive management support system (Chapters 9 and 10).
- In order to support good leadership, this management support system needs to help "break the barriers" to get things done.

In order to become competitive while benefiting all stakeholders of the company—management, employees, customers, suppliers, shareholders, and the community—we need to focus not just on one or two areas but on all of the elements of shop floor management. In doing so, we need to understand the vital linkage among these key elements and address the weak areas while capitalizing on the strengths of the organization.

EVALUATING THE LEVEL OF SHOP FLOOR MANAGEMENT

Experimenting with the ideas presented in Exhibit 11.3, I conducted quick evaluations of three companies. I scored each characteristic on a scale of 0 (worst) to 10 (best) (see Exhibit 11.4). As you can see in the exhibit, each company has its own peculiar characteristics. Here are some brief comments:

Exhibit 11.4. Evaluation of Shop Floor Management in Three Companies

	Company A	Company B	Company C
Core Values (Vision)	9	9	5
Customer Orientation	7	8	9
Involvement of Everybody	8	9	4
Problem Solving	3	9	4
Leadership	9	8	3
Management Support System	5	7	4
Total Points	41	50	29

- Company A has strong leadership at the top. People are excited about getting involved. Yet the problem lies in a lack of problem-solving tools and experience in utilizing them.
- Company B has the best score of all three companies. Yet its management system is weak, especially at the top. While flexibility has proven to be the strength of this company, a little more formal structure may help to practice the PDCA cycle throughout the company.
- Company C is the weakest of the three. Here, the problem is associated with its success. The company was successful in introducing the right product to the market. But the competition is catching up, while the company has not invested its resources wisely. Unless top management refocuses the company's strategy, serious problems lie ahead.

As a footnote here, Exhibit 11.5 shows an example of such an evaluation done for Company A described above. While this type of audit is important in helping top management understand the health of the

Exhibit 11.5. Evaluation of Shop Floor Management in Company A

Category	Score	Comments
Core Value (Clarity of Vision)	9	Top management's vision is shared among people and well accepted.
Customer Orientation	7	No clear concept of customer orientation exists except that everybody seems to be concerned about their products.
Involvement of Everybody	8	There is an open atmosphere with people sharing ideas and complaints. Union people seem to have developed trust with management.
Problem-Solving Capability	3	Analytical ability to solve problems is weak. Not much training is offered yet. There is a lack of sharing of ideas among people.
Leadership for Continuous Improvement	9	The new top manager is liked by most people. He is dedicated, thinking of the best for the organization. He considers problems challenges.
Management Support System	5	It is close to a seat-of-the-pants operation. Because of the long history of the plant and its previous management style, no new thought has been introduced to upgrade the management system.

organization, from the shop floor people's point of view, we should check our health not because the president is concerned about it, but because this is what we should be doing anyway. In other words, as presidents of mini-companies, we need to be prepared to answer the questions shown in Exhibit 11.6. Also, for those who evaluated the level of SFM using Exhibit 1.12, it may be meaningful to reevaluate by using the checklist described here.

Exhibit 11.6. Checklist to Evaluate the Level of Shop Floor Management

Core Values

- Does our organization, i.e., mini-company, have a clear mission which may be distinct from the company's mission?
- Do our people take ownership in our organization's mission and measure their behavior against it?
- Is there a clear understanding of how our organization's mission ties to the company's mission?

Customer Orientation

- Do people know who their customers are, both internal and external?
- Do people frequently talk with customers?
- Do people monitor the level of customer satisfaction?
- Are customer satisfaction indices improving?
- Do people have clear goals to aim for?
- Is there a clear understanding as to:
  - Who are the customers, suppliers, bankers, etc?
  - What are the individual's roles and responsibilities in achieving the organization's mission?
  - What skills are needed to accomplish the organization's mission
- Have comprehensive communication channels been developed in the organization?
- Do our people understand the roles and responsibilities of other organizations?

Involvement of Everybody

- Do people have a sense of running their own mini-companies?
- Is there shared understanding among the people regarding the direction of the organization and each person's contribution to achieving goals?
- Are there measurable levels of people's involvement, e.g., absenteeism, number of suggestions, etc.
- Is our shop floor organized in such a way that it is easy even for strangers to understand what is going on? (If not, is it a sign that "glass wall management" is lacking)?

(continued)

Exhibit 11.6. Continued

Involvement of Everybody (continued)

- Are standards upheld by everyone? Have people been creative in making standards easy to use even by new employees?
- Are main steps and key items clearly stated in the standards?
- Are standards updated frequently with the records of revision clearly displayed?
- Are there procedures to take corrective action if the standards are not met?
- Are there education and training programs at each level of the organization, according to people's skill needs?
- How do you monitor the effectiveness of such programs?
- What kind of actions are taken if effectiveness is not realized?

Problem Solving

- Is there a process for prioritizing the major concerns of the organization at regular intervals and following through with the PDCA cycle?
- Are problem-solving skills used without difficulty?
- Are there team-based problem-solving activities as well as individual activities?
- Is data collection adequate, e.g., frequency, sampling size, etc.
- Is data effectively utilized close to where the action is?
- Are the problem-solving steps logically followed?
- Are problem-solving steps like the QC story format shared by people?
- Do problem-solving activities contribute to the performance of the organization effectively?

Leadership

- Is there a shared understanding of the company's mission, or is the mission statement merely a few sentences about which nobody seems to care?
- Is there a spirit to challenge conventional wisdom?
- Are people sharing and discussing ideas as a team, or are they too insecure to share, or discuss openly?
- Does the leader empathize with people's growth?
- Does the leader enjoy winning as a team, and share the fruits?
- Does the leader spend time on the shop floor, talking with people and caring about how things are going?

Management Process:

- Is the PDCA cycle practiced throughout the whole organization's management process?
- Are control points used effectively in the organization?
- Is there a proper information gathering and analysis process established, e.g., measure of customer satisfaction, status of plan execution?

Exhibit 11.6. Continued

- Is there a comprehensive reporting procedure that everyone understands?
- Is the reporting process accurate and responsive?
- Are problem-solving tools such as pareto and cause-and-effect diagrams used in analyzing and taking action to meet the major concerns in the organization?
- Is there sufficient cooperation with other organizations in getting or providing support?
- Does the plan match with the company's direction/strategy?
- Does the plan cover the 5W2H principle (who is doing, what, when, where, why, how, and how much)?
- Do our people take ownership in developing and executing the plan?
- Is review of progress carried out in an appropriate manner?
- Is there a clear check/audit and follow-up cycle?

As we can see, these questions are tough and rigorous. Some people may be turned off because there are too many things to think about. Also, even if we know we need to be able to answer each of these questions, we often get busy in fire fighting and forget about doing the important jobs. Nevertheless, if we are to improve continuously, we need to look ourselves in the mirror every now and then, and keep working on these points.

THE PRESIDENTIAL AUDIT

Going through this self-checklist is important, but because we are busy with day-to-day tasks, an audit can provide a more objective view and remind us also to do the important jobs. It is similar to having someone holding a mirror for us to look into.

In addition to the checklist mentioned above, the basic questions listed in Exhibit 11.7 may be asked. To be objective, and to gain insight into how well things are going from the total company point

Exhibit 11.7. Basic Questions for Internal Audit

1. What are our roles and responsibilities? (e.g., mission, policy (objectives and approaches), delegation of responsibilities)
2. What are our key concerns? (e.g., quality, cost, delivery, safety, morale)
3. How are we addressing those concerns? (e.g., approaches to solving problems, use of tools, human relation issues)

of view, our management (i.e., the bankers of our mini-companies) may ask these questions. This process may be called an internal audit. When the president of the company conducts such an audit, we call it a *presidential audit*. (For the sake of discussion in this section, we will call the person doing the audit the president. This may also refer to the president of a mini-company, i.e., top management of a division, or a plant manager and his or her staff people.)

The term presidential audit sounds a little formal, but as long as we take a positive and objective stance to such an audit, everyone in the organization can benefit. In other words, to make such an audit meaningful, the "president" (the person(s) doing the audit) should not search for flaws in people, or assess blame. The purpose is to give guidance to people and encourage them to move forward.

Also, those receiving the audit should not hide problems, or show only the good practices. The purpose is to receive honest, objective opinions and gain insight from management to find ways to do things better. In other words, we are simply taking a good look at ourselves, trying to be humble and objective, and to find ways to further improve.

If we conduct such an audit well, management will have a better understanding of the following:

- The nature of the policy- or mission-deployment process, shared values, communication processes and organizational responsibilities
- The strengths and weaknesses of the organization
- The problems and opportunities related to the organization's cross-functional and hierarchical issues

An important part of the audit, then, is for the president to provide adequate response to the people. As obvious as it may seem, depending on the feedback, people's reactions will differ.

For example, if the president cannot identify any areas to make meaningful comments, people receiving the audit may be disappointed or they may become complacent. But if the president identifies good practices as well as areas that people can improve or where the president could help support the improvement, then the response of people may be quite positive.

For an audit to be meaningful, therefore, the president needs to have not just "people" skills, but a broad knowledge of operations and insight into key basic disciplines, from quality control to industrial engineering or from maintenance to team problem-solving activities. From the side that receives the audit, people need to provide a comprehensive view and "educate" the president so that the president can develop a balanced view of the reality at the shop floor.

THE AUDIT PROCESS

Let us then look at the specifics of the audit process. Typically, there are two parts to it. The first part may be done in the office. People involved in the audit may make presentations and reports or discuss issues related to shop improvement and its linkage to the company's success.

Here, the president will check people's awareness of the problems on the shop floor. After the presentation is made, the president should probe into the problems in detail by asking pointed questions. A general familiarity with the situation is not enough. Rather than having superficial discussions, the president needs to be able to quickly diagnose the situation, search for the essence of the problem, and provide adequate guidance.

The second part is to go out to the shop floor and check the health of the company by touring the area. This is called on-site diagnosis. This may be done by going through the shop floor tour checklist provided in Appendix 11.1.

As we have been emphasizing the importance of addressing the problems at the shop floor throughout this book, and as doctors need to see the patient in person to make an accurate diagnosis, the president needs to see genba, genbutsu, and genjitsu (the Three Reals—real scene, real thing, and real fact) to diagnose the situation properly.

During the tour, persons responsible for the area may point out the improvements that have been made or discuss items they have been working on. Here, the president may ask several questions:

- What are your key areas of concern?
- What do you think of these problems?
- What has been done to improve the situation?
- What are the plans of action?
- How will you assure the effective implementation of those plans?
- How can I help to accelerate the pace of improvement?

Occasionally, people may give ambiguous answers. If so, the president should question further to get to the core of the problem in an objective and logical manner, and see if the person really grasps the problem or is trying to gloss over it. In other cases, people may try to blame another organization for the problem. Yet, all of us should realize that we are concerned about the core of the problem—that is, why the problem exists and how to establish countermeasures—but not *who* is to blame.

To aid the president in the audit process, Exhibit 11.8 provides a list of detailed questions. (Please note, however, that Exhibit 11.6 may be also combined with this. The two exhibits illustrate different ways of asking questions to find the core issues.)

Exhibit 11.8. Topics for a Presidential Audit

Topics Related to Organization's Hierarchical Issues

From Top Management Down

- If mission, roles and responsibilities, key areas of focus, and plan of action are clearly explained not in words but with documents, charts, etc., ask if they are clearly organized, i.e., who is doing what, when, where, why, how, and how different units of the organization relate with each other. Then, further probe how the key ideas are shared and worked on, by whom, when, where, why, and how.
- If there are unclear points, visit the shop floor, clarify the process, and assess the situation with facts and specific examples.

From Shop Floor Up

- Observe how the place is organized, standards are used, key information is shared, data is collected and analyzed, and accomplishments are shared.
- Discuss with people on the shop floor the mission, their roles and responsibilities, key areas of focus, and plans of action. Check if the management process is clear to everyone, e.g., how goals and responsibilities are set. Then clarify the issues and assess the situation by talking with managers. For example, talk about the goal-setting process, plan development, plan execution, feedback of accomplishment, information-sharing process, and performance appraisal process.

Topics Related to Cross-functional Issues

- Review the flow of information and flow of material from suppliers to end users to get the job done. Also, check if there is a closed loop to this customer-supplier relationship so that there is continuous improvement process functioning with the PDCA cycle in mind.
- Review if customer orientation is shared by people. Check if customer-supplier

Exhibit 11.8. Continued

relationship and the specific flow of materials or information are clear to everyone and make logical sense.

Questions Related to the People on the Shop Floor

- How do you monitor performance? (What are the targets and how do you know if you are on target or not?)
- How do you collect data? Where do you collect it?
- How do you share information on your team's performance?
- What document do you use to communicate performance?
- How often do you meet with your customers? What do you discuss? How about with your suppliers?
- How do you get feedback from your customers? How about from your suppliers?
- How often do you meet with your managers? How often do you meet with your people? What do you discuss?
- How do you get feedback from your managers about your performance? How do you give feedback to your people?
- How do you know if everything is in control or not? What is the basis of decision making?
- What do you do if something is out of control? Is there a clear procedure?
- Could you show me some examples of standard operating procedures?
- When did you last update the procedures?
- How do you know if people are following these standards?
- How do you conduct job rotation?
- What kind of problem are you addressing?
- How do you address the problem?
- When is the last time you completed a team-project or contributed ideas for improvement?
- What was the project and who was involved in the project? What kind of tools were used? How effective was that problem-solving process?
- Are there recurring problems?
- Do you think things are improving in general? Why or why not?
- What do you think needs to be improved?
- Are you happy with your job? Why or why not?
- How are you doing against your competitors?

In addition, it is a good idea to use a Polaroid camera to take pictures that support the audit. Such pictures may be later posted for display and convey the point to the people in an effective fashion. (See Exhibit 11.9.) In the exhibit, good and bad practices of SFM

Exhibit 11.9. Polaroid Pictures Used to Display the Points of On-Site Diagnosis

Courtesy Borg-Warner

are listed with brief comments in such a way that people in the plant can see the points clearly, and address the problems later. If people are not accustomed to such a practice, someone, who is experienced in this process, may demonstrate it for the first few audits.

LEARNING FROM A PRESIDENTIAL AUDIT

Just as doctors conduct various tests when diagnosing patients' illnesses, we should ask these questions to probe the health of the organization. Even by checking to see if people can answer these questions without hesitation can give an indication of the problems of the organization.

If people can answer only a small fraction of these questions, it should indicate a big gap in expectations between the president and those on the shop floor. Yet, if people can answer almost all of the questions quickly it may indicate the low level of the president's problem-identification skills.

Naturally, both situations should be considered bad. In an ideal situation, the president should be able to identify areas where people made significant progress and praise those efforts while identifying a few areas for people to further investigate and improve. (This is like receiving a one-point lesson in tennis or golf from the pro.)

When the presidential audit is over, and proper feedback has been given to people, there may be subsequent visits with follow-up questions such as:

- Is the PDCA cycle being practiced to address key problems?
- What happened to the key follow-up items?
- What kind of difficulties have been experienced in moving forward since the last visit?
- What are key targets, and plans of action from here?

As described here, the presidential audit requires a degree of effort from both the president's side and the people's side. Also, it should be noted that the audit may be done not just by the president, but also by mini-company presidents such as the vice-president or a plant manager.

The point is to guide people by following the PDCA cycle while addressing problems on the shop floor and developing people to become self-sufficient. In other words, such an audit can bring benefits as shown in Exhibit 11.10.

To show how such audits may be conducted, an example of a presidential audit schedule in a Japanese sporting goods company, Daiwa Seiko, is shown in Exhibit 11.11.

This company has an annual sales volume of $300 million with a thousand employees in three factories. Some audit presentations followed the QC story form, describing the process, results, current concerns, and future approaches. Schedule, agenda, minutes, and other administrative matters were coordinated by support staff—by the quality assurance department in this case.

Here, reviewing the presentation from the people on the shop floor and providing recognition, encouragement, and advice are con-

Exhibit 11.10. Benefits of Audit

- Top management can check the health of the organization by directly taking the pulse of the company.
- Top management can check on how the company's policy is shared and how plans are carried out before waiting for the results.
- Top management can educate themselves as to how the company needs to be run through direct interaction with people.
- People feel that top management cares about what they do.
- People can share their concerns directly with top management.
- People can confirm the direction of the company and the need for everyone to work together.
- The audit can provide a strong stimulus to everyone. It also serves the function of review, recognition, and reward for the whole organization.

Exhibit 11.11. Schedule of Presidential Audit

1. Preparation of document describing the current situation of operations for top management (sent to the president before his visit)
2. Factory visit (total of two hours)
   a. Tour of shop floor (30 min.)
   b. Update of operations (5 min.)
   c. Review of semi-annual plan (10 min.)
   d. Quality improvement at suppliers—case examples (15 min.)
   e. Productivity improvement—case examples (15 min.)
   f. Lead time reduction—case examples (15 min.)
   g. Question and answer, informal discussion (30 min.)
3. Report of audit and minutes of the discussion (sent to the factory after the visit)

sidered a critical part of top management's job. Just as supervisors may listen to the concerns of their people regularly and operators may listen to the sounds of their machines in going through their daily checklist, the presidential audit should be an indispensable element of shop floor management for top managers themselves in assuring the integrity of the company's operations.

LEARNING TO CONDUCT AN EFFECTIVE PRESIDENTIAL AUDIT

In reality, however, due to lack of knowledge and interest in shop floor activities, only a limited number of senior managers may be able to practice these audits effectively. Nevertheless, top management should enhance their skills to provide pointed questions, comments, or advice during the audit with the assistance of support staff.

Also, remember that merely checking on progress without following up does not contribute much. Thus, if top management learns more about shop floor activities, and at the same time people on the shop floor try to make shop floor activities easy for others to understand, such efforts will help utilize the talent of people while reducing the barrier between the shop floor and the corporate office.

We should note here that even if the understanding of top management may be low initially, one way to spark their interest is to have shop floor people make presentations at the presidential audit, or at a board of directors' meeting. Even if the time is limited, sharing ideas in such a setting will increase understanding of broader issues for all involved. In fact, this may be more of an education for top management than for the shop floor personnel.

In my experience, with a little guidance people generally do a great job in sharing their thoughts. They may have confidence that they know more about their job than anyone else in the world. Also, they may be very open and straightforward in sharing their concerns because they may not have had their voices heard before. If top management or the board has been educated to look at the organization from the viewpoint of the shop floor, this setting will help in effectively cross-checking the organization's operation.

Also, even without a formal audit, a three-minute speech delivered to top management by, say, each of a dozen teams from the shop floor may help develop an understanding of the rate of progress made on the shop floor. Even regularly scheduled breakfast meetings with employees may help facilitate needed communication and prevent potential problems early on. If orchestrated well, we may all be surprised at the degree of stimulation or encouragement this type of activity can generate throughout the company.

By trying out these ideas, we may be able to emphasize our orientation towards the shop floor, remembering the importance of genba (real scene), genbutsu (real things), and genjitsu (real fact). Also, when things are organized clearly for everybody, we know that the organization is customer friendly enough to involve people in the process of continuous improvement.

THE EXTERNAL AUDIT

In addition to the internal review/audit process, external audits can benefit the organization. A supplier audit may be done by an original equipment manufacturer (OEM) such as an automobile or consumer appliance company. As in the case of an internal audit, given the proper diagnosis, recommendations, and follow-up, these suppliers may grow with the OEMs.

Clearly, auditors need skills in order to make an effective diagnosis. Otherwise, the audit may simply become a ritual of checking charts and performance data without providing proper recommendations to address the key problems. The organization that receives the audit also needs to think of it as an opportunity to stimulate the people in the organization.

Another example of an external audit is a quality award, which rewards companies that excel in quality achievement and quality management. For example, there are the Malcolm Baldrige National Quality Award in the U.S., the Deming Award in Japan and the European Quality Award in Europe. Exhibit 11.12 lists the Baldrige Award examination criteria. Again, since everyone in the organization may be viewed as the president of a mini-company, the Baldrige award criteria may also be used as the standard of excellence for organizations seeking the highest levels of overall quality performance.

Exhibit 11.13 describes the relationship between shop floor management and Baldrige National Quality Award examination categories. Since shop floor management may be considered analogous to running a mini-company, all students of shop floor management or shop floor entrepreneurs should be able to examine their own performance against all items described in the Baldrige Award.

A comment from one company president in Japan may summarize the feeling of accomplishment in competing for the Deming Prize:

> I have been president of this company for over twenty years, yet I had never had the kind of experience that I had while applying for the

Exhibit 11.12. Key Concepts in the Baldrige Award Examination Criteria

* Quality is defined by the customer.
* The senior leadership of the business needs to create clear quality values and build the values into the way the company operates.
* Quality excellence derives from well-designed and well-executed systems and processes.
* Continuous improvement must be a part of the management of all systems and processes.
* Companies need to develop goals, as well as strategic and operational plans to achieve quality leadership.
* Shortening the response time of all operations and processes of the company needs to be part of the quality improvement effort.
* Operations and decisions of the company need to be based upon facts and data.
* All employees must be suitably trained and involved in quality activities.
* Design quality and defect and error prevention should be major elements of the quality system.
* Companies need to communicate quality requirements to suppliers and work to elevate supplier quality performance.

From the U.S. Department of Commerce, National Institute of Standards and Technology, Application Guidelines for Malcolm Baldrige National Quality Award, 1991.

Exhibit 11.13. Shop Floor Management and the Malcolm Baldrige National Quality Award

Category/Item	Corresponding Chapters in this Book									
	1	2	3	4	5	6	7	8	9	10
Leadership										
Senior executive leadership	X							X		
Quality values	X	X						X		
Management for quality		X						X	X	X
Public responsibility	X	X						X		
Information and Analysis										
Scope and management of quality data and information			X	X			X		X	
Competitive comparisons and benchmarks									X	X
Analysis of quality data and information						X	X			
Strategic Quality Planning										
Strategic quality planning process									X	X
Quality goals and plans				X					X	X
Human Resource Utilization										
Human resource management			X	X	X					
Employee involvement			X	X	X					
Quality education and training				X	X	X	X			
Employee recognition and performance measurement								X		X
Employee well-being and morale	X	X	X	X				X	X	X
Quality Assurance of Products and Services										
Design & introduction of quality products & services			X						X	
Process and quality control						X	X			
Continuous improvement of process						X	X			
Quality assessment									X	X
Documentation									X	
Business process and support service quality			X		X	X				
Supplier quality							X		X	X
Quality Results										
Product and service quality results									X	X
Business process, operational, and support		X							X	X

(continued)

Exhibit 11.13. Continued

Category/Item	1	2	3	4	5	6	7	8	9	10
Quality Results (*continued*)										
Service quality results									x	x
Supplier quality results									x	x
Customer Satisfaction										
Determining customer require- ments and expectations		x		x						
Customer relationship management		x	x	x					x	x
Customer service standards		x							x	
Commitment to customers	x	x								
Complaints resolution for qual- ity improvement			x			x			x	x
Determining customer satis- faction		x	x							
Customer satisfaction results		x					x		x	x
Customer satisfaction com- parison		x							x	

Note: The categories of Baldrige criteria were taken from the 1991 application guidelines.

Deming prize. It was during that time that all of my employees became aware of what I expected of them. They understood the goals I set for the company. They became dedicated workers, and all of them, acting as one body, tried to reach the same goals.
    —*What Is Total Quality Control?* by Kaoru Ishikawa, p. 192.

AWARD AND REWARD SYSTEMS

When handled well, award programs such as the Baldrige National Quality Award, president's award, supplier award, plant manager's award, suggestion award, or awards for department of the month, supervisor of the month, improvement of the month, housekeeping, safety, or attendance can stimulate people to work together toward a common goal. In the process, such efforts can expand the company's horizon as well as that of the people.

    Work can be regarded as something one has to do to earn money, but at the same time it can be seen as an enjoyable experience, like playing sports or games. Just as people have different tastes in recreational activities, the same is true of competing for different types of awards. People will participate in different ways (see Exhibit 11.14).

However if management abruptly starts, changes direction, or stops these programs frequently, they will lose credibility with people. In many companies, inattention to the minds or feelings of people on the shop floor has already caused them to stop buying in to what management says.

This is unfortunate, but if this is the situation management has to start with, they need to show commitment and perseverance in their actions in order to create a new atmosphere. Managers may wonder "How do we empower people and increase morale while contributing to the success of the organization?"

By providing appropriate feedback to people consistently, many companies have found that energy for further improvement can be fed back into the system, thus generating improvement continuously. Each action may be viewed as a small step, but collectively the organization will move forward.

So, let us ask:

- How have the company's award programs evolved up to now?
- How effective are they?
- How can we improve? Is it rewards, administrative process, sharing, or lack of recognition that we need to work on?

Exhibit 11.14. Continuous Improvements and Rewards and Recognition

As we recognize the shop floor as one of the critical battlegrounds in today's business, we may provide awards such as "mini-company of the month" award for front line supervisors and the crew, and at the end of the year, give the "mini-company of the year" award. Not just the people at the factory floor, but all functions—sales, marketing, design, R&D, human resources, accounting, finance, management information system, production, administration, and so on—will be competing for the award.

For a small company, mini-companies may represent sections or departments with about five to twenty people as a unit. For a large company, each division or plant may have its own mini-companies or mini-mini-companies; again the smallest mini-company may be five to twenty people.

If there is strong consensus, a company-wide mini-company award may be provided, with each division or plant nominating a mini-company from its area for final selection for the president's mini-company of the year award. Perhaps gold, silver, and bronze awards can be provided.

The award criteria may follow the checklist shown in Exhibit 11.6 and/or the Baldrige criteria. The business plan and annual report of these mini-companies may be used as application documents. An award ceremony may be held, the president announces the award and makes a short speech about the selection procedure and what this means for the company. The recipients—the president and crew of the mini-company—may find this most gratifying, perhaps even offering a chance for promotion.

FINDING THE TREASURES OF THE COMPANY

There is an old Japanese saying, "Those who light up corners of the world—they are the national treasures." The point is that we should never forget those who are making our society better. Collectively, they are shedding the light that makes our society bright. When we talk about looking at ourselves in the mirror and instituting award and reward systems to recognize good behavior, perhaps we need to think of these words.

In most countries, there are many sports events, from local competitions to a major national championship game such as the Super Bowl. In these events, we have seen how people can be excited about winning. Also, many seem to be happy just to have the opportunity to participate to see how they might do.

Award programs in our business can have a similar effect. People can experience the feeling of working together and accomplishing something—winning feelings need not be monopolized at the top.

But since these events can become so attractive to many people, management should be very careful that once a company starts an award program it does not stop haphazardly. This has a demoralizing effect on people. If the program seems not to be working well, we simply need to review it and think of ways to improve it, following the PDCA cycle. Don't just drop it—instead of giving up easily, keep working on it. Just as we have seasons in nature, heartbeats in our body, and rhythm in music, business needs to establish rhythm to build upon the past and keep moving forward.

SUMMARY

- We need to address six major elements to make our shop floor management successful. They are: core values, customer orientation, involvement of everybody, problem solving, leadership for continuous improvement, and management support system.
- There are significant differences in how each of these elements is practiced between traditional and progressive organizations.
- We need to develop close linkages among each of these elements in order to develop an excellence in shop floor management.
- The implementation process for shop floor management will vary depending on the organization's historical background and its business environment.
- Rather than asking outside experts to implement shop floor management for the company, the company (or mini-company) needs to develop its own skills to "self-manage."
- One important technique to assess the health of the organization is a presidential audit. Yet to conduct one effectively, top management may need to learn skills to make it most productive.
- External audits such as national quality award applications may provide additional stimulation for the organization to im-

prove. Effective use of these awards and rewards may help people working together toward a common goal.

- Even though awards and rewards may provide occasional recognition, we should not forget to acknowledge all those who work hard in lighting up the corners of our world in as many ways and as often as we can.

Chapter Twelve

WHERE DO WE GO FROM HERE?

After coming this far, I hope we have confirmed the importance of shop floor management that puts people at the center of activities. Yet in reality we may still observe people coming to work and simply repeating their jobs, day in and day out. And some managers may still have very traditional attitudes toward work. But if even a small percentage of people begin to use their own initiative in making improvements, I believe it will make a difference.

As individuals, we may find greater meaning in what we do by making an effort to improve our work and utilizing our talent with our own initiative. Whether our work is related to making things, selling things, delivering things, processing information, or providing services—it will be most desirable for all of us to grow with our own work and experience enjoyment in the process.

FROM A FRAGILE TO A ROBUST SYSTEM

As discussed in the previous chapters, all elements of core values, customer orientation, involvement of people, upgrading of skills, leadership, and the management support system need to be tied together to utilize everybody's talent better. Also, as much as these linkages need to be developed as a company, we need to develop them for each mini-company as well.

If any of these elements are missing, our system will not function well. Consequently, shop floor management (SFM) may be viewed as a people-dependent, fragile system when compared to a more traditional one. Since a changing business environment and employee turnover are more common now than before, our shop floor management may be even more fragile.

However, we should remember that this is the very reason why we should make SFM work, so that we can place ourselves in the driver's seat. We studied the difference between traditional and progressive organizations such as in Exhibit 1.8, where the narrower spindle indicated a traditional power structure. In such situations, people's destinies are more in the control of top management. Also, Exhibits 2.4 and 3.13 showed the difference between local and total optimization, where our self-interest builds up barriers which prevent us from helping each other or having a broader viewpoint.

We know that in traditional organizations, people were used more as tools or machines in such a way that their values were not respected. And if things did not work well, they were disposed of without much consideration for them as individuals. From their viewpoint on the other hand, they often lost the initiative to utilize their creativity after being conditioned by the environment in which they worked for so long.

Such situations are wasteful. As much as management needs to find better ways to utilize people's talent, people need to find ways to contribute their talent in a meaningful way for their own benefit as well. Neither side should waste time complaining to the other. Rather, a type of customer and supplier relationship should be developed. Each person should help others regardless of hierarchical or functional disciplines.

If everybody takes ownership and tries to eliminate his or her own job in order for all of us to improve, the organization's capabilities will also increase. In other words, it is everyone's responsibility to make the total organization integrated and competitive and to maximize our performance, while respecting our own humanistic values.

The whole system may be fragile during its process of development, but perhaps that is meant to be. As much as our competitive environment forces us to improve by reducing waste, shortening delivery time, improving quality, and reducing cost, our own management and the organizations themselves need to change accordingly, even if they become vulnerable in the process. Yet, as we work as a team with everybody taking initiative and developing a customer orientation, barriers can be broken.

Following Henry Ford's precept that "What is desirable and right is not impossible," we need faith and determination to make things work. Our task has become so complex that no single person nor powerful top manager can do the job. We need to have all of our people helping each other to make it happen, each addressing the key steps of the company's operation.

EXPOSING PROBLEMS BEFORE IT'S TOO LATE

As our society progresses, therefore, each person's role will become more and more important. If we are not prepared, however, problems on the shop floor may cause dysfunction in the total organization. Yet, the organization cannot afford to have too much waste, in terms of resources such as extra people, machines, material, and overdesign. Instead, the organization needs to learn to protect itself from potential failure through standardization, education, and eliminating its own waste.

Using an analogy of water level and rocks, the more we reduce the water, that is, extra margin, the more we expose the rocks, or problems. (Remember Exhibits 6.14 and 6.15.) In the production world, the water represents inventory levels, and reducing inventory will expose problems. Then, people can work together to chip away at the rocks—i.e., problems—so that our work becomes streamlined. Then, we can further reduce our inventory in order to continuously improve the situation. The same idea can apply for streamlining information processing.

In the area of quality, we can improve the process by reducing the variations. The more we do so, making our processes more stable, the more we can assure better quality in our products or services. But if the progress slows down, we can experiment to make variations intentionally big so that we can expose areas for further improvement.

Our free market system is in a way a mechanism to reduce the water level continuously. Sometimes it seems to hinder our efforts to survive and achieve prosperity in such an environment. Yet such is the world we live in. And this mechanism has brought many good things to society as well. Since the competition today may come at any time from anywhere in the world, however, we need to intentionally reduce the water level within our organization by ourselves before it is too late.

ACHIEVING A CRITICAL MASS

If the foregoing is a realistic view of our business world, what can we do? In my view, each company needs to set a policy so that its direction and approach are clear to all of its people. Shop floor management will be an important strategic direction by itself. Then, we need to go through the steps shown in Exhibit 12.1 (as discussed in Chapter 4). Some of the specific ideas we have been studying in this book are as follows:

Provide atmosphere for improvement

- Clapping hands at the sharing rally
- Providing a display of improvements
- Awareness of increased competition

Provide tools to make improvements

- Painting floors and machines
- Following discipline of PDCA
- Providing education and training

Provide adequate feedback

- Reward and recognition
- Company picnic
- People having fun at team presentations

At the beginning, progress may be perceived as slow, but once we attain a certain momentum and achieve a critical mass, we can convert a traditional organization into a progressive one quite rapidly. To make it happen, however, we need to keep working on the cycle in Exhibit 12.1. In the process, we need to keep using our creativity and implementing ideas while suppressing potential negativism.

IDEAS FOR IMPLEMENTATION

In order to implement shop floor management, we need to practice the PDCA cycle. Starting with "check," and using the audit process

Exhibit 12.1. Cycle of Continuous Improvement

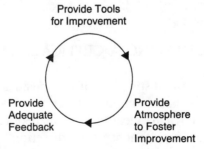

we studied in the Chapter 11, we should be able to identify areas for improvement, then develop plans and implement them. Then, we can go through the PDCA cycle of continuous improvement to get things moving.

At any point in time, different companies are in different phases of evolution, reflecting both their history and their current environment. Some have a clear mission and vision of the future that is shared with their people, others may not. Some have a clear customer orientation, while others may be weak in this area. Some have clear leadership but may lack problems-solving skills to put the vision into practice.

For this reason, even though some outside companies may offer to implement programs for you, it is still important to maintain a self-management orientation. Ultimately, the people at the shop floor should control the situation as much as possible, rather than blindly following the idea of division of labor and having specialists do the job for us. Since nobody can do self-managing for us, everybody's continuous learning is crucial. In this sense, the role of an outside company may be that of catalyst, guide, counselor, advisor, educator, and stimulator.

Having said that, let us summarize key ideas for successful implementation of shop floor management (Exhibit 12.2). As you see, Exhibit 12.2 follows a PDCA cycle. Or we may say that this follows the QC story format where the theme is the implementation of SFM. There is no magic to it. Just like making improvements and learning

Exhibit 12.2. Key Ideas for Implementing Shop Floor Management

- Understand key elements of shop floor management, their interrelationships, and the total picture.
- Practice the PDCA cycle, starting with ''check.''
- Analyze the situation by constraints and potential, and cause-and-effect relationships.
- Address the key areas first.
- Remember that the wind may shift, but we can trim the sails to get where we want to go.
- As we succeed, share the experience, share the reward, provide recognition, standardize the process, and move forward by attacking the untouched problems.
- When we fail, do not give up. Analyze the situation, learn, and try again. Perseverance is key. When things are going well, everybody looks good without much effort. But the true skills of an individual may be demonstrated by how he or she handles an unfavorable situation.

problem-solving skills, we need to experience the process and internalize it one step at a time. And we need to do this both as individuals and as a team, company, or organization.

In the case of team problem solving, a group of individuals can get together, each doing his or her part yet contributing to the whole, and all work together to accomplish a common goal. After the team is formed, they will identify their concerns, get the training they need, and learn to use tools for making improvements. In time they will develop a common language, implement ideas, accomplish results, standardize procedures, work on the next project, and thus expand the whole team problem-solving process.

IMPLEMENTING SHOP FLOOR MANAGEMENT COMPANY-WIDE

In the case of company-wide implementation, the larger the size of the organization, the more complex it becomes. The essence, however, will remain the same. Following the PDCA cycle starting from the check step, we should be able to assess the situation of the organization, clarify weaknesses and strengths, analyze the reasons why, and develop a plan of action. Then we continue with the PDCA cycle, utilizing techniques and ideas such as those described in this book.

In principle this sounds simple, yet as in many situations, in reality it may not be so easy, especially when we are inside the trenches fighting the battle and going after many problems. So let us review examples of how some companies have made major strides in implementing SFM.

Similar to establishing programs such as a suggestion program, the SFM implementation process typically goes through different stages. Exhibit 12.3 shows typical examples, both successful and unsuccessful. As shown in the exhibit, there are four different stages:

1. Introduction Stage. People become acquainted with the idea of shop floor management and develop an understanding about SFM in relation to other programs. At this stage, SFM may be interpreted as empowering people to practice self-management for continuous improvement.

2. Promotion Stage. At this stage the emphasis is on practice. Ideas such as a suggestion program, self-study groups, task forces, and line-based management (mini-companies) are put into practice

Exhibit 12.3. Implementation Process of Shop Floor Management

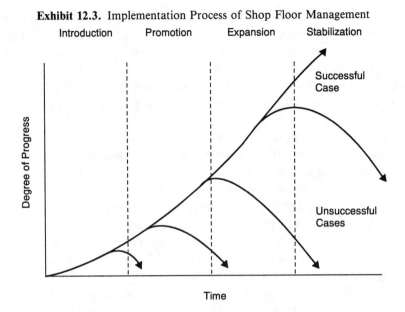

and PDCA cycling is begun. People's ownership and top management's leadership need to be well meshed at the middle management level. Middle management's understanding of SFM and its ability to manage this process is crucial during this fragile phase.

3. Expansion Stage. As people's self-managing activities show positive results, people start to develop confidence. Those who were not certain about SFM may start to understand its potential as well. In order to expand further, however, proper recognition and reward may be necessary. Also, going through a presidential audit, benchmarking world class companies, or aiming for a national quality award may promote this stage of expansion.

4. Stabilization Stage. Everybody in the company internalizes the idea. SFM and its benefits are obvious to all. Concepts of SFM that were foreign at the beginning are now woven into everyday routines. However, as the company grows and more new people join and more new products and markets are explored, there is a continuous need to maintain and deepen these efforts to improve. As we move forward, we will find that many tedious and mundane jobs will be done by tools, machines, and computers in such a way that people can continuously grow into the future.

As shown in Exhibit 12.3, the change process is "S" shaped. In other words, at the beginning, the rate of change is slow. Then, the rate of change increases as time passes and more people digest the idea and get involved. Eventually the rate slows down and stabilizes. This phenomenon is common in nature as well. For example, when changing the direction of a boat or car, we find how external force impacts the position of the object. Similarly, we should remember that it takes time to gain momentum to impact the organization's direction.

Of course, as more people are involved, it requires more energy to change the direction of the organization's thinking. So, it is natural to try to do things by oneself rather than involving others. Yet, as explained before, since our organization requires everyone's cooperation as well as the upgrading of people's skills, unless we involve people, we won't achieve much as an organization.

As a footnote here, if people become more responsible and require less supervision, should they be paid more? My answer is yes, if everything else is the same. But if competitors are moving much farther ahead, following our market economy principle, the pay may not increase. In terms of a company's position and an individual's skill level in the industry, both of these should be increasing if we are doing a good job. Ideally, the company, customers, suppliers, employees, shareholders, community, and society as a whole can benefit.

MAKING IT WORK

Now, let us study the typical reasons why things may or may not work as expected by looking at four different levels of organization corresponding to each phase of the implementation (see Exhibit 12.4). Please note the category labeled "machines, tools, systems, and environment." This is to help us look at the picture objectively from their point of view.

Exhibit 12.4. Why Things May or May Not Work as Expected

Stage	Why Things May Not Work	Why Things May Work
1. Introduction Stage		
• Top management:	- There is no leadership or commitment. - Needs are not clear.	- There is leadership, and commitment. - There is a strong feeling that the subject is important.

Exhibit 12.4. Continued

Stage	Why Things May Not Work	Why Things May Work
• Middle management	- Think this is additional work. - Think this is just another program of the month.	- Are willing to try to improve even if the subject is a little difficult to understand at the beginning. - Think the learning will help not just the company but individuals as well.
• Employees	- Suspicious as to whether this new idea will take hold. - We'll do what we're told, and no more.	- Nothing to lose in trying. If we do what we have always done, we will get what we have always gotten. - What can I do to contribute and seek ways to improve?
• Machines, tools, systems, environment	- People should treat us with more respect. - There is a lack of coordination among us, or between people and us.	- We could be better utilized. - All of us can help with each other.

2. Promotion Stage

Stage	Why Things May Not Work	Why Things May Work
• Top management	- Give lip service, but take no action. - Show frustration when the progress is slow.	- In whatever way I will be supportive and contribute. - Think of ways to help share the progress, even small strides.
• Middle management	- Find excuses why something does not work. - Instead of trying to accomplish something with initiative, wait for others to take action first.	- Find ways to make it work. Think positively. Ask not what company (people) can do for us; ask what we can do for the company (people). - Wherever I can contribute, I will start to do so.
• Employees	- Bosses have to show us that this will work for us. - If we do this, you should pay us more.	- What do you think of my idea? - This will improve my skills and my value to the company. Though my

(continued)

Exhibit 12.4. Continued

Stage	Why Things May Not Work	Why Things May Work
2. Promotion Stage (continued)		
		pay scale depends on the competitiveness of the company, I will develop more marketable skills.
• Machines, tools, systems, environment	- If things are not organized, people cannot use us. - Instead of thinking only about themselves, people need to think of others.	- As they care for us, we can be of more help to them. - We can help each other.
3. Expansion Stage		
• Top management	- Think it takes too much time; patience wears out. - Cannot understand that seemingly little things may mean a great deal.	- It may take time, but patience will pay off in the end. - Each little step is an important contribution towards moving ahead. With everybody's help we can make it.
• Middle management	- Theory and practice are different. - Results are what counts, not process.	- What is desirable and right is not impossible. - If we create a process that generates results, they will show up.
• Employees	- We would rather do our work than use our brains. - Managers are the problem, not us.	- Using the talent that we have been born with can be fun. After all, we are responsible for our family budget. - In order for us to improve continuously, we need to work together, utilizing collective wisdom.
• Machines, tools, systems, environment	- People need to clarify things and share ideas among themselves better. - Machines systems, people, procedures need to be integrated.	- We should be able to share what each of us can contribute and learn from each other. - As we cooperate and respect everyone's roles, we can develop a strong entity that all of us can be proud of.

Exhibit 12.4. Continued

Stage	Why Things May Not Work	Why Things May Work
4. Stabilization Stage		
• Top management	- Does not understand the importance of doing the basics right and continuously. - Does not believe in managing the process of improvement activities; conviction is not there.	- There is no end to our progress. The history of the human race proves this. But, even if we are on the right track, we will get run over if we just sit there. - To manage the process of continuous improvement, we need to practice the PDCA cycle. We need a vision, and approaches to accomplish the vision with a comprehensive management system.
• Middle management	- If I eliminate my job and delegate my work to my people, I will have nothing to work on. - I would rather work on my own than with others.	- We need people's help. The more they update their abilities, the more we can delegate. Accordingly, we can all move forward.
• Employees	- I do not know if I am capable of continuing to do this. - Management is trying to eliminate our jobs.	- The sky is the limit. If we can dream it, we can make it. - We should eliminate the job we are doing now. Then, we can learn more jobs. For those who want to continue to do the same jobs, hopefully we can accommodate their desire or find some job that they like.
• Machines, tools, systems, environment	- People should learn to prevent problems rather than fixing them after the fact. - We should be self-managing. There should be more intelligence put on us so that we can do our jobs without much help from people.	- People can delegate many of their jobs to us. If we can represent people's ingenuity, we can contribute to people's lives in a friendly way. - As people learn to use us effectively and learn to maximize our potential, better harmony will develop.

In most companies, the situation is a mixture of the attributes listed in Exhibit 12.4. So our efforts should be directed at building on the strengths of the organization while minimizing the impact of the weaknesses. For example, it may not be productive to expend energy on those who are not willing to try or cooperate. On the other hand, if an employee has a success story to share and inspires others, we should find a way to communicate that message.

To avoid problems or recover from them, Exhibit 12.5 summarizes hints for successful implementation of SFM:

Exhibit 12.5. Hints for Successful SFM Implementation

1. Introduction Stage

- Study books, review videos, attend seminars, attend conventions where other companies' case studies are shared.
- Visit companies with experience, tour the facilities, and study their stories.
- Exchange ideas with other companies who are interested in or working on continuous improvement.
- Receive visits from people who are experienced in the subject matter and share ideas.
- Remember nobody can do this for you, you have to find your own solution. Guidance from experts may help. But true experts may not provide "step-by-step how-to" solutions for you or your own growth.
- The situation for every company is different.
- Company cultures are different. People are different. Hurdles to implementation and potential gain are different.
- Develop long-term vision and program as much as possible. This is more like a journey than a short trip.
- Confirm commitment. Convince yourself that this is the last and the only attempt to get people involved. Recognize that the journey is not going to be easy. But gain the vision and faith that it will work out—not because of one person, but because of everyone's wisdom. Do not look for home runs, or miracles.

2. Promotion Stage

- Continue to practice items mentioned above as appropriate.
- Develop and execute an internal education or training program as appropriate. Make it flexible, thus reflecting the needs of people where possible.
- Use an internal facilitator, educator, or trainer when possible. The more you teach, the more you will learn. Also, those who teach should have hands-on implementation experience with the people on-line.
- Balance theory and practice so that classroom education and training and use of techniques in real life settings are well integrated.

Exhibit 12.5. Continued

- Realize that each small improvement is important. Believe that improvements can be made by everybody contributing his or her idea.
- As ideas are implemented, conduct show-and-tell sessions at the floor. Invite top management where possible.
- Conduct a sharing rally to review progress. Utilize pictures, videos, and displays to share successes.
- Publicize success in a company newsletter, or by posting case examples, pictures, or slogans as appropriate.
- Conduct a presidential audit, supported by experts as appropriate.
- Be patient, don't expect miracles. There is no overnight cure. This is an especially hard lesson for those who have advanced in their careers without involving people.

3. Expansion Stage

- Continue to practice items mentioned above as appropriate. As you do, follow through with your PDCA cycle. Capitalize on experience to promote learning and sharing, for example, with a trip report, summary of improvement, or mini-company annual report.
- Provide more settings for people to share successes and failures, exchange ideas, and compare performance with world-class companies.
- Emphasize openness to share information. Take a good look in the mirror; learn objectivity.
- Develop an atmosphere of healthy internal competition so that people gain the taste of success.
- Provide more awards and recognition as appropriate.
- Better organize the management information within the company, such as score-boards in a meeting area.
- Practice Glass Wall Management as much as practically possible.
- Conduct the presidential audit on a more formal and larger scale.
- Aim for recognized awards such as a national quality award.
- Find "fire" in people's eyes. Appreciate those who are trying hard, believing that this will work. You are not the only one trying hard. Once, you develop a critical mass of people, it will be easier to get more people to buy in.

4. Stabilization Stage

- Continue to practice the items mentioned above as appropriate. Check effectiveness of different approaches and take proper action.
- Make sure that everyone keeps practicing PDCA diligently throughout the company.
- Introduce stimulation such as special task forces, visitation by experts, or application for recognized awards.

Exhibit 12.5. Continued

* Further improve the quality of work, programs, education and training, and management processes.
* Go back to the basics to reassess the vision, mission, goals and approaches, customer orientation, problem-solving skills, culture, leadership, and management support system. Then set a new vision for further improvement.
* Provide further challenges for people. Share the experience with people outside of the company, so that they too may benefit
* When everything seems to be going well, be cautious and humble. Remember hard times. There are many companies who failed because of their success.

Note: To support this table, Appendix 12.1 presents the voices of people who are engaged in the practice of the new shop floor management.

FACILITATOR'S ROLE

In addition to the points listed in Exhibit 12.5, we need to understand the role of facilitators. Depending on the situation, they can be a great help in getting things done quickly and lubricating the process so that the implementation takes place smoothly. Since people's ownership is key to the success of these activities, facilitators need to have special skills at persuading people to buy in as opposed to pushing their own ideas too forcefully or taking the credit for successes away from the people.

Ideally, facilitators need to be invisible. They need to let people take the initiative and develop feelings of ownership, and accomplishment. Naturally, this means that the facilitator will see people as customers.

To convey the importance of such thinking there is a famous Japanese saying about the role of facilitators: "We should become people who are not needed in the organization. Yet, we should become people who are indispensable to the organization." Even though it is difficult for us to assume such a selfless posture, facilitators need to know that if people don't feel true ownership, they will not show strong initiative. And without people's initiative and their help, progress will be very limited.

In Chapter 8, we learned that leadership is not determined simply by title or position, but is situational. The facilitator's position is very similar. For example, facilitators can be internal champions to spearhead improvement activities at the top, or they may be in middle management, support staff, or at the front line depending on the setting. Whatever the position is, key characteristics of effective facilitators are summarized in Exhibit 12.6:

Exhibit 12.6. Key Characteristics of Facilitators

- Have people skills
- Objective; not narrow minded
- Persuasive and convincing with honesty, logic, and genuine concern for people
- Flexible to accommodate different opinions of people
- Energy to convey the idea, vision, and techniques
- Patient
- Experienced on shop floor
- Not satisfied with current situation
- Positive
- Interested in the change process
- Understand the basic tools of problem solving as shown in Exhibit 6.7
- Basic knowledge about overall operations
- Basic knowledge about managerial system of the company
- Results oriented as well as process oriented
- Healthy and able to bear a certain degree of stress
- Politically skilled in getting things done
- Self-starting, not a quitter

Even though facilitation approaches will differ depending on the setting, it is often useful to identify a certain person (or persons) as facilitator and promoter for the company. In a large organization, there may be a dedicated person who plays such a role, perhaps supported by high level management. He or she may have a separate office—an "SFM promotion office," or a promotion office for total quality management, just-in-time, or total productive maintenance. The role of facilitator may also be performed by a committee. In smaller organizations it may be done by one person on a part-time basis.

While the process of promotion may differ depending on the specific needs of the company, the role of promoter is summarized in Exhibit 12.7.

MAPPING OUT THE IMPLEMENTATION PROCESS

Actual implementation processes may differ by company or unit within the company, depending on their situation. Exhibit 12.8 indi-

Exhibit 12.7. Key Roles of Promoters

- Development of company-wide implementation plan: Coordinate the assessment of the company's strengths and weaknesses. Clarify mission. Identify the function of promoters and develop plans accordingly.

- Investigation, research and development: Provide knowledge base for people to benefit from by investigating books, videos, seminars, education and training courses, visits to other companies, etc. Develop education and training courses. Circulate or loan books, videos, and other educational materials.

- Education and training: Identify the needs of the organization, develop an education plan, and conduct and/or coordinate education and training involving top management as needed. Share success stories from inside and outside the company.

- Information sharing: As an information center, monitor, provide, or exchange information by such means as progress reports, newsletters, memos, displays, handbooks, sharing rallies, or show-and-tell tours. Cross-pollinate ideas or success stories company-wide.

- Counseling, guidance, and audit: Provide resources for counseling, guidance, or audit as needed. Provide recommendations to management. Coordinate activities with top management's business review cycle as appropriate.

- Standardization: Standardize documentation, manuals, operating procedures, education process, terminology, and other aspects as appropriate.

cates different patterns. In case A, the speed of implementation is different by company or unit within the company. The impact from specific business circumstances and internal resistance to the change may affect the rate of progress. Case B shows declining progress similar to that represented in Exhibit 12.3. Case C shows companies going through ups and downs, indicating the variety of influences absorbed along the way.

Exhibit 12.8. Different Patterns of Implementation

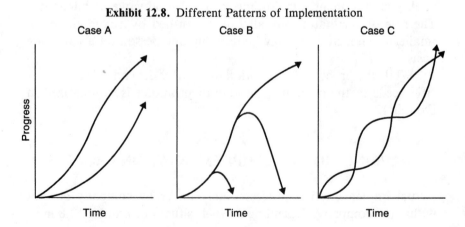

As you see here, continuously improving performance and people development takes patience, tenacity, and consistency. Because of this, and because it is important not to lose sight of the overall improvement processes, it is helpful to summarize the change process in a simple table (see Exhibit 12.9). In essence, the summary is a condensation of the annual reports over time that we mentioned before. Naturally, we may do this for the company overall as well as for mini-companies and individuals.

Even though the contents of a table like this may differ depending upon the company's focus, this type of table has a number of benefits:

- The fact that the organization can develop such a table indicates the level of people's teamwork, objectivity, honesty, and commitment to continuous improvement.
- People will recognize the effort made in the past and think of the future. Even though there is employee turnover, this type of effort will help people to think in terms of PDCA as opposed to PDPD (plan-do-plan-do).
- It serves as a tool to practice glass wall management and encourages others to do so at the mini-company level.
- It is organized in such a way that each year's progress represents the PDCA cycle as a basic wheel of continuous improvement.

As you see, a PDCA cycle is practiced at this company year after year, every time key focus items are identified and addressed. As the situation improves, new processes are standardized to assure the gain. Then, more problem areas are identified to keep the cycle going continuously.

Producing these charts will help expose problem areas as well. By looking candidly and carefully at them, it should become clear that there is always room for improvement. Also, by meeting people, visiting other companies, and reading books, the solution for the next step will be found. Furthermore, since many people have shared in compiling this chart, the solution for the next step should reflect the consensus, or collective wisdom of people.

Depending on the specific situation, the implementation process will vary. Even though no one can plan ahead for all possible situations, collectively, people should be able to come up with answers.

Exhibit 12.9. The Company's Continuous Improvement Process (Example)

	Year 1	Year 2	Year 3
Environment	Increased competition, Increased customer demand	Trend is to smaller, lighter, and more varieties of product	Shorter lead time, flexibility to meet customers' changing demands
Company-wide Focus	Improve cost	Improve quality	Improve lead time new product development capability
Key Activities			
Management	Improve communication, share vision, involve people	Introduce mini-company concept, practice "Next process is customer" concept; conduct presidential audit	Clarify management support system, introduce team problem-solving; conduct presidential audit
Quality	Conduct inspection at the line, make people responsible for quality	Introduce clear procedures, train everybody on quality	Refine procedures, eliminate inspectors, train suppliers
Cost	Implement cell concept, cross-train people	Focus on reducing reworks, rejects	Complete cell arrangement, dedicate machines, consider second shift operation
Delivery	Reduce work-in-process inventory, improve supplier management	Further reduce inventory, improve communication	Refine kanban system, clarify procedures, train people
Personal Development	Conduct new employee training, introduce award program	Modify incentive program, reactivate suggestion program	Use award, recognition and bonus system, conduct employee presentation
Results	Cost target met, lead time reduced by 50%, morale and safety records up	Quality target met, People developed more identity with company	Lead time reduction not satisfactory, problem with space and increased volume
Existing Problems/ Opportunities	Problem with incentive system, key is to change people's mindset	Lead time can be reduced further, rapidly increased demand caused strains	Development of people, potential for overseas production

QUESTIONS AND ANSWERS ON IMPLEMENTATION

There may still be unresolved questions. In order to respond to some typical ones, the following suggestions are provided:

Question 1. I am in a middle management position and top managers are not giving us a clear direction about what to do or where to start, and are even reluctant to do anything. What can I do without top management support or direction?

Suggestion. Determine what is controllable and what is not, then focus your energy on controllable items. Establish your mini-company's mission and values, focus on customer satisfaction, involve people, work on problem solving, lead and guide people for continuous improvement, and clarify and refine the management support system. Develop your mini-company's business plans and follow through with PDCA.

Question 2. I am always busy and have no time or budget to do any of these things that we are talking about. What should I do?

Suggestion. There are important jobs and urgent jobs. If we only do urgent fire-fighting jobs, we may have to do the same thing for the next twenty years, if we are lucky. But if we are to improve, we simply must find time to work on important jobs. This should reduce the number of urgent jobs and the whole situation should become more controllable. It may be easier to find excuses not to do anything about it. But the question is, "Will this job guarantee the success of the organization as well as its individuals?" We need to ask ourselves the right questions.

Question 3. As ideas of shop floor management were implemented, keeping the momentum up became difficult. Initially, many people thought that this was a good idea. But now, after our busy season, a change in management, a big customer claim problem, and employee turnover, we have lost enthusiasm. What can we do?

Suggestion. Instead of looking for a quick fix, I suggest going back to the basics. Revisit the core beliefs and what people take pride in. If there is no clear leader, perhaps you can become the leader. Or, at least, try to speak up and discuss with people what went right or wrong. Think of the cases that were successful. And work out the solution as a group. Progress may be two steps forward and one step backward—or sometimes even three steps backward. Yet isn't it better if we at least try?

Question 4. Somehow, people's interest and the discipline of following up on basic things are not there. For example, the suggestion program is not going anywhere, the charts on the wall are now old and nobody seems to be updating them, and the company newsletter is already three weeks overdue. Even the award program and the education course on problem solving and shop floor management do not seem to be followed up well. I am frustrated. But what can we do now?

Suggestion. It may in fact be better to start small and expand at a controllable rate as opposed to introducing many ideas and not following through. This comes back to people issues. The key is to develop a critical mass of people who will go the extra mile with you. Also, you need to show examples of improvements to others. There is no guarantee that things will work out. The key is whether or not you and your people have truly bought into the process. If you think the situation has overexpanded, go back to the basics and build up people's credibility, confidence, and capability.

Question 5. How do you deal with a person with a negative attitude?

Suggestion. Positively. But if it is going to consume too much energy to explain time after time, it may be more effective to focus on other people first. Once I tried to convince a maintenance manager to develop a maintenance checklist for each machine. Even after several discussions, he was not convinced that this would help. So I redirected my efforts to get more people involved in other areas.

As things started to happen, I found one day that this maintenance manager had implemented the daily checklist without telling me. When I saw him on the shop floor, all I needed to do to communicate was to show my wide grin. I am optimistic that by developing the right environment, such negative attitudes can be redirected. If this still doesn't work, then the person may have to be relocated.

Question 6. How do we deal with cumbersome policies on union-management issues, or pay structure?

Suggestion. Unfortunately, it may take some time to resolve these issues. While we need to work on issues of fairness, and develop a long-term win-win situation, we also need to work on things that are obvious to all. Hopefully, we can be open and trusting as opposed to closed minded and defensive. If we need to deal with most problems at the top level of union and management, it is the same as a planned economy. We need to address the issues in a self-managing manner at the source.

Question 7. What all of this means is that there is no easy solution to square things out, doesn't it?

Suggestion. Most likely, the answer is yes. But I would like to encourage you that it is worth the effort. For example, one company that was practicing SFM increased its sales volume from $6 million to $28 million in six years while improving its profitability multifold. Suddenly, the young president fired a top key executive, saying that the progress was not good enough. Naturally, the morale on the shop floor suffered a great deal. Nevertheless, people felt that they had done their best and learned something wonderful that cannot be taken away from them.

Question 8. Can you tell in one sentence how to implement this? Or better yet, can you do this for me?

Suggestion. I am sorry, but I cannot answer those questions. Often, we may read a book, watch a video, attend a seminar, or receive a diagnosis by some expert, and feel that we learned a lot, but we still do nothing. To me, the desire to improve needs to come from within—no one can implement it for you. It is more the practice of basics than further learning of sophisticated theory. We ask where the solution is. I think it is inside us. Or I may say that I can do it for you if you are committed. But if you are really committed, you probably don't need me as much.

SHOP FLOOR MANAGEMENT IN PERSPECTIVE

As we practice SFM, we can continuously improve by going through the PDCA cycle, using a checklist such as the one shown in Exhibit 11.6, by delegating responsibilities from the top, utilizing the collective wisdom of people, and constantly practicing customer orientation. The organization as a whole becomes creative and it will find its course toward the future.

Yet, top management needs to set a clear strategic direction and lead the whole company. Here, policy management and cross-functional management may be practiced so that the voices of the people are heard and monitored. Then, the strengths, weaknesses, opportunities, and problems are addressed on a company-wide basis. In other words, as much as individuals, mini-companies, and divisions will try to self-manage, the company as a whole needs to coordinate all of these activities.

To illustrate top management leadership, the Tokyo Electric Company (TEC) of Japan had a once-in-a-lifetime opportunity to introduce electronic cash registers when the mechanical cash register still prevailed. The decision to convert to them was a strategic one, made at the top by a few key individuals. Most people were against such a move. Many people in the factory were trained to make the mechanical types, and there was tremendous resistance to the change because it basically nullified these people's skill base.

Yet the hard decision was made. With top management's strong leadership, the company could turn its course and enjoy the benefit of capturing the large market share from its competitors, who were still working on traditional mechanical registers. The introduction by 3M of the "Post it Notes," a pad of memo slips that stick and peel off easily, is a different example where people at the front line came up with an idea and made it a success. As discussed in Chapter 5, the operator who thought of a way to significantly reduce defects is yet an other example of success.

Whether such innovative ideas come from shop floor personnel, middle management, or from top management, the company needs to have the ability to maximize the benefits of such an idea. While this is a major area of study by itself, the point is that SFM and a company's strategy development will require continuous coordination. As our businesses become more complex and the pace of change accelerates, we need to develop a broader view to benefit from such ideas.

In other words, as the customer-supplier relationship grows in importance, we need to grasp the overall picture of how intelligent information can flow throughout our company to maximize its benefits. Any major bottleneck will cause the whole system to malfunction. Whether such linkage is horizontal or vertical, we need to develop an efficient network and practice glass wall management company-wide.

In fact, if we expand our vision, the vertical linkages among individuals, departments, and the company will also expand to include community, nation, and the world. Each of these units of the organization contributes to the others as suppliers and at the same time receives benefits as customers. So, as we develop a better perspective, we should be able to find opportunities to eliminate bottlenecks between any units in the system.

BENEFITS OF SHOP FLOOR MANAGEMENT

We have not summarized the benefits of SFM up to this point mainly because we are to do the things we need to do anyway and benefits are the results of our action. Yet, if we were to summarize, Exhibit 12.10 explains the major categories of benefits.

WHERE DO WE GO FROM HERE?

We have almost completed this book, yet our learning should not stop here. Furthermore, "book learning" is not true learning until these ideas are put into use and the skills internalized. Remember from our discussion of the behavioral change model that we need to

Exhibit 12.10. Benefits of Shop Floor Management

In General Terms

- Accomplishment of vision, mission
- Progress in customer satisfaction, involvement of people, upgrading skills for self-managing, leadership, and management support system
- Improvement of QCDSM, market share, profitability, etc.
- Improvement of competitive strength

More Specifically

- Education ("making people before making product")
- More discipline at the shop floor; better standardization
- Improved teamwork and coordination
- People can provide stimulation with each other for self-improvement
- Improved sharing of information, communication
- Practicing the basics of management
- Activated suggestion program, team improvement, mini-companies', and inter-company activities

process information or stimuli to change our mind, attitude, behavior, and habits, leading to changes in our destiny.

In today's business environment, unforeseen events may unfold in front of our eyes. New management concepts will arise and new techniques for problem solving will be brought to our attention. Constant change has become the norm. Yet, if we have gained the essence of shop floor management, we may be able to find a clear path under even very difficult circumstances. If we can imagine this, I believe we can do it.

Just as a young sailor needs to gain skills before going out on the ocean, our self-managing skills will help us in the course of our journey. As we become seasoned sailors in our own environment, we may teach our followers that learning the basics is really important.

DEW AND MOON

Whether you are a president, manager, support staff, supervisor, or operator, and whether we have worked together before or not, somewhere in our hearts, I believe we all share something in common. Whether it is our willpower or creativity or something else, just like our orientation to genba, as soon as we try to describe "such a thing" with words and models, we may lose the essence of it. Since logic and words are only an interpretation of reality, we can only try, refine, and share these thoughts. This may be the core of shop floor management.

Still, after trying to convey the essence of shop floor management in this book, the analogy that comes to my mind is the moon shining in the sky and the dew on the grass reflecting the moon in each drop. The moon represents the core value; the dewdrops represent the people sharing that core value. Since each human being is valuable, regardless of his fate, each of us is a dewdrop. Within each of us, we have something that is the core of our being. And perhaps, if we are attentive and our minds are not preoccupied, we might see evidence of this on our shop floor, too.

Looking at the light reflecting from machines, talking with people and feeling their energy, and perceiving things that have gone into running our shop floor, I hope we can find the beauty, truth, and spirit of the people in these.

TRAINING OUR MINDS IN A TURBULENT WORLD

We started this book by looking at our business environment. We found many changes and unknowns. Yet, we kept searching for a foundation. We found that we need skills, strength, and spirit, just as we do to maneuver a ship in troubled waters.

If the moon is the solution and a finger is pointing to the moon, indicating that there is a solution, we should look at the moon, not at the finger. Yet because of our upbringing and the various influences that are brought to bear on our organization, we may look at the wrong place if we are not careful. Therefore, we need to *train ourselves* to develop disciplined minds, attitudes, behaviors, and habits, as opposed to intellectualizing them. That, to me, is shop floor management with self-managing discipline that we need.

In closing, and thinking of where each of us may go from here, I would like each of us to search for his or her own shop floor management. And as we move forward, even if we find the rapids in the water, we may still find the moon quietly reflecting on it.

The shop floor is where the action is. The shop floor is where the reality is. The world in which we live may be turbulent. But in this turbulence I believe that the solution always exists. With vision, and with a never-ending quest for this solution, I am sure that we can find a solid foundation within ourselves.

SUMMARY

- Shop floor management may be viewed as a fragile, people-dependent system. Yet it is similar to our democratic society where the collective wisdom of our people decides the future course of action. Whether SFM works or not will be ultimately determined by the people.
- For SFM to be effective, therefore, the success depends on people's ability to identify and be able to solve problems effectively on the shop floor. If such attempt does not work, we may revert to a traditional (Taylor-type) organization.
- As we need to build up the capability of people to be powerful in making this fragile system robust, developing a critical mass of people becomes important.
- In order to implement SFM, we will follow the basics of PDCA cycle. Just like making improvements or learning problem solving skills, we need to experience the process and internalize the capability one step at a time.
- The implementation process may include introduction, promotion, expansion, and stabilization stages. There are many reasons why SFM will not work at every stage before it finally stabilizes. In other words, there are many areas that need everybody's attention.
- In order to successfully implement SFM company-wide, facilitators and promoters are important in mapping out the course and monitoring progress. Also, they will play the role of providing guidance to coordinate overall activities.
- Even if the world we live in seems turbulent, as we develop skills, strength, and spirit, we should find a clear path in it.

Appendix 1.1

EMPLOYEE SURVEY

The following are the results of a survey conducted in 1990 by management in a U.S. plant that employed about 200. The survey was confidential and conducted by a third party so that people's identities were not revealed. Forty percent of the employees responded. The survey results illustrate the nature of the hurdles faced by a typical medium-sized plant in the United States.

In a way, this is a scorecard for management to measure how they have involved people and developed pride in their work. It may be advisable to conduct this type of survey at certain intervals. Realizing how the survey result compares against those of another plant—such as this one—may be meaningful, especially for management.

A. Plant Management

	YES	NO
1. Do you know who the plant manager is?	94%	6%
2. Should there be more personal contact between employees and manager?	85%	15%
3. Do we need regular employee meetings to allow you to voice your opinions.	92%	8%
4. Are our company rules and policies fair?	67%	33%
5. Do we need rules and policies?	96%	4%
6. Do you know who your supervisor is?	98%	2%
7. Is your supervisor fair?	82%	18%
8. Does your supervisor know what he/she is doing?	95%	5%
9. Do you respect your supervisor?	93%	7%
10. Does your supervisor respect you?	88%	12%

(continued)

A. *Plant Management* Continued

	YES	NO
11. Do you have good lead people in your area?	87%	13%
12. Do we need lead people?	92%	8%
13. Do you know what the goals are for your department?	77%	23%
14. Would you like to know these goals?	94%	6%
15. Do you have a desire to be promoted to management at some point?	70%	30%

COMMENTS: _____

_____

B. *Your Job*

	YES	NO
1. Do you understand what your job is?	98%	2%
2. Do you know ways to improve your job?	74%	26%
3. Have you made suggestions to supervisors about ways to improve your job?	50%	50%
4. Did they respond in a positive manner?	53%	47%
5. Did they implement your suggestion?	53%	47%
6. Would you like to work in a team with other employees?	88%	12%

7. How would you rate working conditions in your area?

Excellent:	14%
Good:	39%
Fair:	31%
Poor:	6%
Disgusting:	10%

	YES	NO
8. Do working conditions affect your work?	67%	33%
9. Can the company improve these conditions?	92%	8%

COMMENTS: _____

_____

C. *The Company*

	YES	NO
1. Are you proud of the company?	87%	13%
2. Would you like to be?	91%	9%
3. Are you ashamed of the company?	7%	93%
4. Do you know who we are and what we do?	90%	10%
5. Would you like to have input directly in matters of quality, productivity, rules, etc.?	84%	16%
6. Should we form a committee to represent employee interests other than the union?	91%	9%
7. Should we hold meetings where anyone can voice their opinions?	95%	5%
8. Should supervisors hold departmental meetings?	94%	6%
9. Do you participate in union meetings?	39%	61%

COMMENTS: _____

D. *You*

	YES	NO
1. Are you treated fairly?	74%	26%
2. Are you discriminated against for any reason?	24%	76%
3. Are you respected?	80%	20%
4. Do you have something to offer this company that we are not using?	43%	57%
5. Does this company care about you?	61%	39%
6. Do you care about this company?	98%	2%

(Note: This appendix is referred to on page 33 in the text.)

Appendix 2.1

CUSTOMER SURVEY

This quarterly customer survey form is taken from the *Hourly Associate Handbook* used at the Worthington plant of the Toledo Scale Corporation. As you can see, each individual in the plant is instructed to satisfy the needs of both internal and external customers. The form is developed to receive constructive feedback from people in the customers' position so that their comments can be refelcted in the drive for continuous improvement.

Instructions for Quarterly Customer Ratings

Each employee at the Worthington Plant should know who his or her customer(s) and supplier(s) are. This information is posted in each work cell.

The work cells, as a group, solicit customer ratings on a quarterly basis. A standard form for this rating is to be used and some helpful hints on how to complete the rating have been established.

The work cells will also rate their immediate suport group via the customer rating sheet on a quarterly basis. In the event of a low rating, specifics need to be given so that improvements can take place.

Worthington Plant—Quarterly Customer Rating
Period: _____ Quarter, 19_____

NAME OF CUSTOMER: _____

Dear Customer:

My goal is to be the best possible supplier of goods and services to you. As my customer, your constructive comments would be greatly appreciated in order to help me continuously improve my service to you.

Please rate my services on a scale of 0 to 10, with the higher number representing more satisfaction and "10" being fully satisfied, and the lower numbers representing relatively little satisfaction, and "0" meaning no satisfaction.

1. Timeliness and Reliability of Delivery: _____ (Rating)

2. Quality of Products/Service: _____

3. Responsiveness to Customer Needs: _____

4. Communication with Customer: _____

OVERALL SUPPLIER RATING: _____

Comments by Customer:

_____

_____

Name of Supplier/Work Group	Individuals Making up Work Group
_____	_____ _____
	_____ _____
	_____ _____

Helpful Hints to Assist You in Completing the Customer Rating Sheets.

1. Timeliness and Reliability of Delivery.　　(Circle one)　　Totals

    A. Understands your needs.　　　　　　0　1　2　___

    B. Responds promptly.　　　　　　　　0　1　2　___

    C. Provides accurate info/parts/service.　0　1　2　___

    D. Service is there when needed.　　　　0　1　2　___

    E. Informs you of upcoming changes.　　0　1　2　___

                                                 ___

2. Quality of products and services

    A. Provides 100% quality parts/service.　0　1　2　___

    B. Accepts responsibility for quality work.　0　1　2　___

    C. Request constructive improvements.　0　1　2　___

    D. Positive feedback.　　　　　　　　0　1　2　___

    E. Helps you make your product better.　0　1　2　___

                                                 ___

3. Responsiveness to Customer Needs.

    A. Good listener.　　　　　　　　　　0　1　2　___

    B. Delivers to point of use.　　　　　　0　1　2　___

    C. Reviews changes with customer.　　　0　1　2　___

    D. Is always there when needed.　　　　0　1　2　___

    E. Goes the extra mile to help.　　　　　0　1　2　___

                                                 ___

(*continued*)

4. Communication with Customer.

    A. Communicates clearly.   0   1   2   __

    B. Positive attitude.   0   1   2   __

    C. Understands customer needs.   0   1   2   __

    D. Develops new ideas with customer.   0   1   2   __

    E. Maintains regular communications.   0   1   2   __

$$\text{Overall rating} = \frac{\text{Sum of } 1+2+3+4}{4}$$

Courtesy Toledo Scale

(Note: This appendix is referred to on page 56 in the text.)

Appendix 3.1

CHECKLIST FOR SUPERVISOR'S ROLES AND RESPONSIBILITIES

Score each item from 0 to 10 with 0 being the worst, 10 being the best. This checklist can apply to all mini-company presidents, not only supervisors.

1. Responsibilities Toward Individual Operators   Score

  1.1 Understands the ability and characteristics of individual   ____

  1.2 In assigning the job, considers ability and characteristics of individual   ____

  1.3 Measures the individual's achievement   ____

  1.4 In assessing operators for performance appraisal, considers tasks for his/her future growth   ____

  1.5 Provides training   ____

  1.6 Makes effort to create good relationship with each individual   ____

  1.7 Processes administrative matters without problems   ____

                              Total (   ) $\div 7 =$ ____

2. Responsibilities Toward Team

  2.1 Conveys messages from the management   ____

  2.2 Conveys messages from the team to the management   ____

  2.3 Has good interpersonal relationships   ____

  2.4 Morale of people is high   ____

  2.5 Promotes suggestions and self-management   ____

  2.6 Behaves as leader of his or her area of responsibility   ____

                              Total (   ) $\div 6 =$ ____

3. Promoting Teamwork with Other Departments

  3.1 Exchanges ideas and information to get job done as a group   ____

(continued)

351

3. Promoting Teamwork with Other Departments *Continued*   Score

3.2 Exchanges ideas and information to stimulate each other even
if the subject is not related to the other supervisor   ____

3.3 Has good interpersonal skills   ____

3.4 Actively helps others when there is a problem in other departments   ____

Total (   ) ÷ 4 = ____

4. Promoting Better Relationship with Managers

4.1 Understands the messages from managers, digests and conveys
the message to the operators in his/her own words   ____

4.2 Provides information or opinions which are generated during
the course of work to the manager without hesitation   ____

4.3 When cooperation from other departments is needed, enlists
support of those managers effectively   ____

Total (   ) ÷ 3 = ____

5. Management of Work

5.1 Knows the work in the responsible area better than anyone else   ____

5.2 Clearly indicates work assignments and key items for the day   ____

5.3 Observes the shop floor activities well with regard to delay, mistakes, or quality problems   ____

5.4 Reports and analyzes the performance on production volume,
cost, and quality   ____

5.5 When there are abnormalities such as machine problems or
quality problems, takes action quickly and reports to the appropriate section(s)   ____

5.6 Takes initiative in daily improvement activities   ____

5.7 Makes suggestions on managerial as well as technical issues to
upper management or related units   ____

Total (   ) ÷ 7 = ____

6. Management of Material

6.1 For receiving materials, there are clear criteria and efforts are
made to reduce the inventory as appropriate   ____

6.2 Makes sure that there is a place for everything and everything
is in its place   ____

6.3 Supervises the appropriate storage and use of goods   ____

6.4 Pays attention and makes improvements even for supplemen-
tary supplies   ____

Total (   ) ÷ 4 = ____

7. Management of Machines

7.1 Conducts daily maintenance activities   ____

7.2 Seeks abnormalities of machine condition from inspection items   ____

7.3 Operates machines following the right operating procedures   ____

7.4 When abnormalities are observed, takes appropriate action and informs appropriate section(s)   ____

7.5 Makes suggestions to maintenance section or management on improvement of machine capability   ____

Total (   ) $\div 5 =$ ____

8. Management of Safety

8.1 Has clear understanding on safety at the shop floor in relation to equipment, work procedure, etc.   ____

8.2 Inspects equipment frequently from safety point of view   ____

8.3 Inspects the arrangement and location of material, oil, etc.   ____

8.4 Inspects the method of work for machine operation and material handling, etc.   ____

8.5 Inspects the area outside of his/her own area as well   ____

8.6 Conducts safety education when there are new employees in the area   ____

8.7 Prepares to follow through procedures for safety-related incidents   ____

8.8 Posts safety signs, procedures, etc.   ____

8.9 Educates about safety procedures   ____

Total (   ) $\div 9 =$ ____

9. Management of Environment

9.1 Provides criteria for housekeeping and workplace organization   ____

9.2 Provides criteria for such items as noise, smoke, exhaust gas, dust, heat, etc.   ____

9.3 Instructs people to meet such criteria   ____

Total (   ) $\div 3 =$ ____

10. Other

10.1 Pays attention to union relationship even if there is no responsibility to interface with them   ____

10.2 Following the company guidance, conducts work, completes administrative work smoothly   ____

Total (   ) $\div 2 =$ ____

Summarize the findings on a radar chart such as shown here. Here, the total score of each item is plotted on a corresponding scale in the chart. Then all ten plots are connected by lines such that the larger the area inside the line, the better the evaluation result.

Exhibit 3.1.1. Radar Chart Used to Summarize the Findings

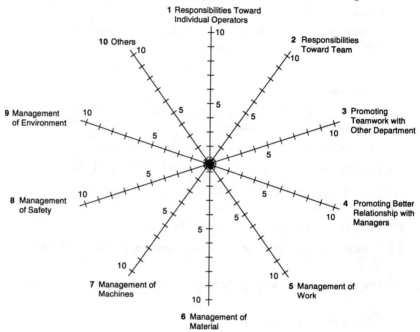

(Note: This appendix is referred to on page 71 in the text.)

Appendix 3.2

DEVELOPING
A MISSION STATEMENT

This appendix shows an example of steps in developing a mission statement, taken from a four-hundred-employee factory of Borg-Warner in Wales. This plant's mission was first developed by a group of about a dozen people from different disciplines including top management and union representatives, and was later conveyed to the rest of the people for comments.

Step 1. Describe the Vision

As a first step, the group listed the elements of the mission by describing the vision of the future people wanted to achieve. They included:

- Drive out fear
- Trust
- Customer satisfaction
- Leadership
- Communicate success
- Happy employees
- Job security
- Happy customer
- High wages
- High productivity
- Best product
- Honesty
- Good process
- Good environment
- Safety
- Training
- Stability
- Teamwork
- Continuous improvement
- Consistency of purpose
- Break down barriers
- Job security
- Full employment
- Working together
- Systematic process
- United leadership
- Making a profit
- Trust
- Good communication
- Good machinery
- Good material
- Healthy
- Capable employees
- Equality of people

Step 2. Categorize by Characteristics

Because the list was long, items were categorized by similar characteristics, using a small card for each item and putting similar items together in groups. Then, a major heading was given to each category:

Continuous Improvement
- Best product
- Good process
- Good machine
- Good material
- Training
- Systematic process
- Good communication
- Stability

Consistency of purpose
- Working together
- Leadership . . .
- Etc., etc.

Other major headings were "Customer Delight" and "Trust, Honesty, and Rewards."

Step 3. Develop a Sentence Utilizing the Major Headings

The assumption here is that major heading should encompass most of the meaning of the items in the original list:

> "To ensure our long term future, we believe in giving customer delight through continuous improvement achieved through trust, honesty, and consistency of purpose."

Step 4. Recognize the Meaning of the Mission, Making Sure All Concerns Are Reflected

There was discussion on the use of specific words, relative importance of words, and so on, before the final mission statement was developed. For example, the term job security was dropped after some discussion since it was viewed as an outcome of the vision rather than the vision itself. Also, people did not want to see them becoming complacent by having a guaranteed job.

Step 5. Develop a Mechanism to Carry
Through the Message of the Mission

At this stage the mission statement is introduced to the rest of the people. Below are several action items.

- Type up mission statement and hand out, and explain personally to people.
- Develop a small plastic card that people can carry with them. (See Exhibit 3.2.1)
  Card should carry significance that this mission is to measure our behavior against.
- Share by visual means:
  Scoreboard—to assure "customer delight" and see how we are doing
  Show improvement process—to assure "continuous improvement" and make the process visible to people by use of pictures, storyboard, etc.
  Pictures of people—to assure "trust, honesty, and leadership" and see how people are practicing such events as award ceremonies, meetings, company picnics, etc.
- Display mission statement as a part of person-to-person communication, in meetings, etc.
- Explain the meaning of the mission statement in the training of employees.
- Develop a mini-company mission statement, and practice the same as a means of developing shared vision.
- Introduce awards and recognition programs to support the mission, for positive reinforcement.

Stage 6. Prepare for the Future

Thinking ahead, as time passes and people get busy, it is expected that there will be a gradual decline in people practicing the mission. So as not to let the intent of the mission wither away, our mission needs to be revisited so that the idea is reflected in our behavior. The sketch in Exhibit 3.2.2. indicates the decay of vision that starts with coherency at the beginning and eventually ends up as scattered ideas.

Exhibit 3.2.1. A Four-Page Summary Card Distributed to Each Employee

<u>Working Together (mission statement)</u>

"To ensure our long term future, we believe in giving *customer delight* (1) through *continuous improvement* (2) achieved through *trust, honesty, and consistency of purpose* (3)."

Customer Satisfaction (1)

• Quality (Q)
• Cost (C)
• Delivery (D)
• Safety (S)
• Morale (M)

Continuous Improvement (2)

Problem-solving steps

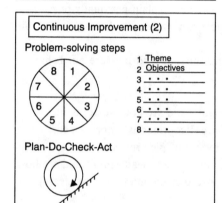

1 Theme
2 Objectives
3 · · ·
4 · · ·
5 · · ·
6 · · ·
7 · · ·
8 · · ·

Plan-Do-Check-Act

Trust, Honesty, and Constancy of Purpose (3)

• Encourage ideas
• Be positive
• Lead by examples
• Be open
• Break down barrier
• Drive out the fear. . . .

Exhibit 3.2.2. Even a Coherent Vision Will Decay If It is not Reinforced

Stage 1 ⟶ Stage 2 ⟶ Stage 3

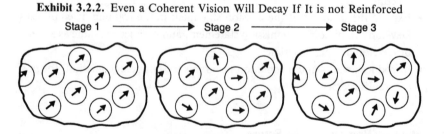

To make our organization coherent, as shown in stage 1 in the sketch, the mission needs to be lived by example, awards, success stories, and positive reinforcement. Also, a mission statement needs to be reviewed, updated, consciously practiced, and lived by. Otherwise, it will quickly lose its meaning and become a mere slogan hanging on the wall.

In a book on children's growth called *Children: The Challenge* by Rudolf Dreikurs, M.D. (Hawthorn Books, 1964), one sentence applies especially to all of us who are in positions of leadership, "We must realize that we no longer live in an autocratic society that can 'control' children but in a democratic society that needs to 'guide' them." Here we can replace the word "children" with "people on the shop floor." We must stimulate people to achieve certain behavior. We cannot enforce any more.

(Note: This appendix is referred to on page 76 in the text.)

CHECKLIST FOR ASSURING THE BASICS OF JUST-IN-TIME PRODUCTION

This checklist was developed by one of the most advanced Japanese car assembly plants for the purpose of assuring the basics of just-in-time production. As you will notice here, very detailed checks are made to assure the integrity of shop floor operations.

Item	Check Items	Comments
Method		
SOP[1]	1. SOP (standard operating procedure) exists	_____
	2. Key points of operation clearly marked	_____
	3. Work done according to the SOP*	_____
	4. SOP used as a tool for improvement*	_____
Work Combination Chart[2]	1. Work combination chart exists	_____
	2. Work is broken down in enough detail	_____
	3. Timing of work adequate	_____
	4. Line balance is adequate*	_____
QC Process Table[3]	1. QC process table exists	_____
	2. Quality checkpoint clearly marked	_____
	3. Quality criteria are clear and effectively practiced*	_____
Checklist[2]	1. Checklists exist	_____
	2. Checklists clearly organized and easy to use by everybody	_____
	3. Checklists used adequately*	_____
Sample Board[4]	1. Sample boards exist	_____
	2. Sample boards clearly organized and easy to practice	_____
Line Stop[5]	1. Line stop concept applied	_____
	2. Line stop concept is easy to use	_____

Items	Check Items	Comments
	3. Line stop concept used effectively by everybody*	_____
Andon[5] (Trouble Light)	1. Andon exists	_____
	2. Andon is clear to everybody, e.g., location and nature of problem	_____
	3. Andon functions without trouble	_____
	4. People use andon effectively*	_____
Rework	1. Rework materials are marked and stored in a clearly defined area	_____
	2. Rules and procedures are clear when rework is needed	_____
	3. Rules are followed adequately*	_____
	4. Countermeasures to problems are done effectively*	_____
Poka-yoke[6] (Fail-Safe System)	1. Display of Poka-yoke exists	
	2. Procedures are clear to check and use poka-yoke	_____
	3. Poka-yoke application is shared effectively*	_____
Production Leveling/ Cycle Time Control[2]	1. Clear rule exists for production leveling	_____
	2. Cycle time control exists	_____
	3. Line stop and andon are linked to cycle time control to expose problems and take necessary action*	_____
Production Control Board[5]	1. Production control board exists	_____
	2. Production control board is used effectively*	_____
	3. Electric display of plan and actual production volume is effectively used*	_____
QCDSM Scoreboard[7]	1. QCDSM scoreboard exists	_____
	2. QCDSM scoreboard is easy to use	_____
	3. QCDSM scoreboard is effectively used*	_____
Material		
Inventory Control	1. Parts storage area of inventory identified, e.g., shelves labeled	_____
	2. Size of inventory not too much, e.g., lot size, kanban quantity*	_____
	3. No discrepancy between the number of parts and display information.*	_____
	4. Proper maintenance is provided to adjust the level and storage area of inventory according to schedule changes*	_____

(*continued*)

Items	Check Items	Comments

Machine

	1. Maintenance checklist exists	_____
	2. Machine trouble log exists and is posted at the machine	_____
	3. Daily maintenance conducted, e.g., lubrication, housekeeping*	_____
	4. Preventive maintenance conducted according to the rule*	_____
	5. Machines running without trouble*	_____
Daily Maintenance	6. Countermeasures to problems are done effectively*	_____

Environment

Meeting Areas	1. Meeting areas are provided	_____
	2. Key information is shared	_____
	3. Meetings are conducted effectively*	_____

Note: For purposes of this book, the checklist has been slightly modified from the original form.

*Indicates the level of discipline required by people at the shop floor.

[1]See Appendix 4.2   [5]See Exhibit 6.16
[2]See Appendix 6.2   [6]See Appendix 6.1
[3]See Exhibit 9.13   [7]See Exhibit 9.17
[4]See Exhibit 7.3

(Note: This appendix is referred to on page 93 in the text.)

Appendix 4.2

BASICS OF STANDARD OPERATING PROCEDURE (SOP)

In order for us to deepen our understanding of SOP, we will summarize the key points in this Appendix:

As we go through a do-it-yourself instruction manual for assembly of a child's toy, for example, if we are not careful, we tend to fall into making mistakes. The same is true for operators. Exhibit 4.2.1 lists some typical problems of using SOP.

Exhibit 4.2.1. Typical Problems of Using SOP

- We do not pay attention to specifications
- We do not read instruction carefully
- Inspection manual is not clear
- Specification is missing on the print
- Engineering drawing is separate from written instruction
- Too many papers
- We are not familiar with parts
- We assume if it fits together, it should be OK
- We depend too much on pictures, and don't read instructions
- Subject to different interpretations

In order to avoid these problems, we need to address key points to control the process as shown in Exhibit 4.2.2. However, often our training does not reflect these points. More often than not, it tends to be "watch and practice" and "let them figure out." Instead of taking SOP lightly, therefore, we need to find ways to train people effectively with SOP so that we can accomplish such benefits as:

- Ease of training
- Enhanced confidence
- Ease of trouble shooting
- Enhanced repeatability, consistency, etc.

Exhibit 4.2.2. Key Approaches to Control the Process with SOP

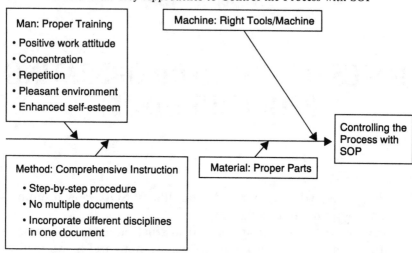

In order to gain benefits, we need to understand the way standard procedures are written. This is especially important when people still tend to take shop floor activity lightly. Steps for developing SOP such as those shown in Exhibit 4.2.3 need to be carefully followed.

Exhibit 4.2.3. Steps of Developing SOP

1. Write major tasks
   Example: Model car assembly
   - Orient floor plate
   - Assemble left front wheel to floor plate
   - Assemble right front wheel to floor plate
     . . . (etc.)
   - Install exhaust tube
   - Perform final QA check
2. Breakdown into detailed instructions
   Example: Orient Floor Plate
   - Pick up floor plate
   - Pick up metal rule in free hand
   - Measure second hole from center to the short edge to be 35 mm (Note: do not say *front* edge because front can be any side)
     . . . (etc.)
3. Write *main steps* by identifying the main action
   - Position floor plate
   - Identify left front wheel hole in the base plate
     . . . (etc.)
4. Write *key checkpoints* by identifying key specification
   - For short edge facing you

Exhibit 4.2.3. Continued

- For distance from hole center to short edge—35 mm
  . . . (etc.)
5. Summarize 3 and 4 above on SOP by:
   - Trying instruction
   - Verbalizing
   - Agreeing on instruction

Illustrating these efforts, Exhibit 4.2.4 shows an example of SOP at Honda of America.

Writing SOP is not an end in itself. We need to train and coach with SOP. (See Appendix 5.1). Also, there are key questions that need to be asked by everyone:

- Why there are still variations, or scatters in the end product?
- How do we choose the standard time?
- Why there are differences by operators?

Then, these questions should lead us to further improvement.

(Note: This appendix is referred to on page 110 in the text.)

Exhibit 4.2.4. Examples of SOP Used at Honda of America Mfg.

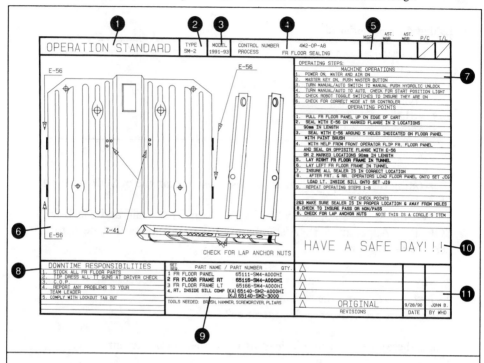

Note: ① Operation standard

② Type

③ Model

④ Control number

⑤ Approval

⑥ Illustration of part to be manufactured (key area marked)

⑦ Operating Steps

   A. Machine operations
    1. Power ON, Water and air ON
    2. Master key ON, push master button
    3. Turn manual/auto switch to...

   B. Main steps (operating points)
    1. Pull floor panel up on edge of cart.
    2. Seal with E–56 on marked flange...
    3. With help from front operator flip...

C. Key Check Points
   2&3. Make sure sealer is in proper location and away from holes
   8. Check for lap anchor nuts...

⑧ Downtown responsibilities
   A. Stock all floor parts
   B. Tip dress all T T guns...
   C. Report any problems to your team leader...

⑨ Part name/# of tool needed:

⑩ Have a safe day!

⑪ Revisions
Date
By (name)

Courtesy of Honda of America, Mfg.

366

Appendix 5.1

JOB TRAINING

Using the case of teaching a new skill to an operator as an example, this appendix describes job training techniques. Please, however, note that this method may be applied not only to job training but also to math, reading, blueprint reading, or problem-solving skills as well. An important point here is that how well we can transfer skills in a short time can determine the competitive strengths of an organization.

Certain knowledge can be acquired through books or lectures, but truly internalized skills will not be obtained without practice. This is like learning to swim. Classroom lecture without practice means little. Also, remember, tools that do not get used often get rusty.

1. Preparation

- Review standard operating procedure (SOP) before beginning the training. Describe the steps of the operation and important points of operation with regard to quality, safety, etc. The SOP can serve as a checklist for proper teaching. If there are no clear steps defined, then come up with one.
- Remember that in the broader context customers, trainers, operators, and the company as a whole will benefit from effective teaching and learning.
- Prepare everything needed for the training, i.e., man, machine, method, material, measurement, and environment (5M1E). (See Exhibit 5.1.1 for checklist.)
- Find out how much trainees already know about the job.
- Assess the ability of the trainees, and provide target for them.
- In order for people to learn new skills, they have to be relaxed, and able to concentrate on learning.
- Trainees should understand the needs for training. For this, trainer needs to create the interest in trainee.
- Conduct training at the actual job site as much as possible.

Exhibit 5.1.1. Checklist to Prepare for Training

	Comments
• Man	
Who	_____
When	_____
To what level	_____
• Machine	
Which job:	
Organization OK?	_____
Condition OK?	_____
• Method	
Try operation before teaching	_____
Are steps of operation correct?	_____
Are key points correct?	_____
• Material	
Jig, tools	_____
Parts	_____
Materials	_____
Gloves, other aids	_____
• Measurement	
Measuring instruments OK?	_____
Standards clear?	_____
Monitor sheet ready?	_____
• Environment	
Noise, temperature, etc. OK?	_____
Safety Hazard?	_____

2. Explanation and Demonstration of Job by Trainer

- Explain what is to be taught—i.e., who, what, when, where, why, how, and how much (5W2H). Indicate key points of the job. Explain the job itself and its relationship to the total picture. Also, teach trainees all necessary terminology related to the job.
- Use standard operating procedure, pictures, exhibits, and charts as much as possible. During training, trainers should ask if these tools are customer (operator) friendly, i.e., if they are helpful in learning the job. Also make sure that all key steps are illustrated correctly.
- Explain the importance of the job. Explain what happens if things do not get done right.
- Explain each step of the job. Demonstrate the procedures slowly so that trainees can easily understand.
- Repeat the procedure, pointing out the main steps and the key points of the

operation with regard to quality, safety, etc. Ask for questions. Check trainees' level of concentration.

- Do not teach more than the trainees can understand.

3. Execution of Job by Trainees

- Let trainees carry out the job at a comfortable pace and see if they can do it as instructed. Correct mistakes as appropriate.
- As trainees perform the job, let them explain the key points of operation. Also, encourage them to ask questions.
- If they cannot conduct the job at a certain point, return to the step they understand and repeat the explanation and/or demonstration again.
- Repeat the procedure until trainees have fully mastered the job. Ask them to restate the reasons why certain points of operation are important. Ask questions from various points of view.
- Provide positive encouragement when trainees do the job well. Also, ask them to come up with ideas for improvement. With fresh eyes, often they can come up with many ideas.

4. Follow-up

- Let trainees understand their responsibility clearly. Even if they can do the steps well at this point, it does not mean that they won't make mistakes in the future.
- Tell trainees who to ask if they have any questions later. Typically, it is the instructor or the trainees' alternates.
- Assign the trainees to the actual job. Encourage them to ask questions whenever necessary. Instructors should answer questions fully and patiently. Especially those who are experienced are often hesitant to ask questions. Yet, if they don't share their concerns, they may develop their own way and break the foundation of standards. Therefore, always encourage questions. Questions often lead to improved SOPs.
- Monitor trainees' work carefully after the instructions have been given. Check not only the end product but also the steps of operation. Also, provide moral support.
- Instructors should take every opportunity to instruct their people. Trainees should learn as much as they can from the instructors. The communication and human relationship between them should become solid.
- As trainees become self-sufficient in their job, reduce the amount of supervi-

sion. Instruction is completed when trainees can conduct the job on a routine basis.

The above training procedure may be simplified as in the Four Steps of Job Training in Exhibit 5.1.2. These instructions are very simple, with each step starting with a verb to clearly indicate the necessary action. We should also note that these steps follow Plan-Do-Check-Act cycle as well.

Exhibit 5.1.2. Four Steps of Job Training

1. Preparation

Review SOP*
Clarify key steps*
Prepare training aids*
Check trainees' existing knowledge
Explain objectives
Put trainees at ease
Create interest in learning

2. Explanation and Demonstration

Explain and show how the job is done
Use SOP and other visual aids
Explain key points of job
Explain each step of job
Repeat the procedure
Instruct clearly, and patiently
Teach as much as trainees can follow

3. Execution by Trainees

Let trainee carry out the job
Correct mistakes as needed
Let trainee explain key points of job
Repeat the procedure

4. Follow-up

Clarify trainees' responsibility
Give name of persons for help
Encourage questions
Provide follow up

*Preparation before meeting trainees

Exhibit 5.1.3. Teaching Is Job # 1

A final note: Many people have commented in my seminars, saying, "It is because they are Japanese that they are so dedicated to practicing excellence in shop floor managment. But we are different from the Japanese." To answer this, here is a quote that many Japanese use to share the difficulty of managing people. The point is that there is nothing inherently different about the Japanese people. People are people everywhere:

> By doing by ourselves,
> by explaining and letting people listen to how it is done,
> by letting them do the work,
> and by encouraging their accomplishment,
> unless we do all of these, people will not take action.

(Note: This appendix is referred to on page 127 in the text.)

Appendix 6.1

ELIMINATING HUMAN ERRORS

Errors occur in different forms. For example, we may skip an operation, locate parts in the wrong direction, use the wrong parts, or forget to tighten bolts. Also, we may assume a machine is doing a job, when in reality there may be a tool failure or inappropriate operation of that machine.

In order to keep us aware of these possible errors, the following checklist can be used to eliminate the most common human errors. We may use this list to help us pay attention in conducting our jobs. Or it may aid us in searching for solutions when we encounter problems.

Exhibit 6.1.1. Checklist to Eliminate Human Error

- Are there any mistakes or forgotten steps in conducting the job?
- Has there been any change of operator?
- Have there been any changes in measurement instruments?
- Is calibration done as needed?
- Have parts been changed?
- Have there been changes in suppliers?
- Changes in plans?
- Changes in design?
- Are instructions ambiguous?
- Are procedures ambiguous?
- Are we day-dreaming, not paying attention?
- Are our jigs and fixtures well prepared?
- Are back-up materials used correctly?

In order to avoid these problems, the ideal solution is to come up with problem-prevention mechanism—a "fail-safe mechanism," or *poka-yoke* in Japanese.

There are two kinds of poka-yoke: One is a mechanism to prevent human error, and the second is a mechanism that catches a person's attention as soon as human error is made. Exhibit 6.1.2 lists specific methods of poka-yoke. Exhibits 6.1.3a to 6.1.3c are examples.

Exhibit 6.1.2. Methods of Eliminating Human Errors

Method	Mechanisms to Prevent Human Error
Design of Product or Parts	• Parts cannot be exchanged by mistake
Tools and Fixtures	• Parts cannot be loaded on machine
Work Procedure	• Work steps are controlled by electric relay

Method	Mechanism to Catch People's Attention
Design of Product or Parts	• Parts are color-coded according to the location of use
Tools and Fixtures	• Use of template
Work Procedure	• When operator passes operation(s) by mistake, relay will detect this and notify operator by turning red light on, or gate will remain closed

Exhibit 6.1.3a. Use of Color Coding

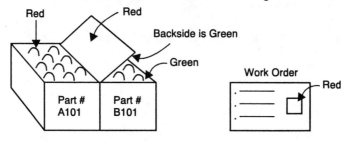

Exhibit 6.1.3b. Fixture Used as Poka-Yoke

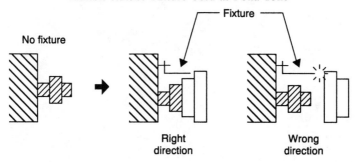

Exhibit 6.1.3c. Gate Used as Poka-Yoke. As operators run many machines to do the welding job, there were a number of defects as a result. A gate was installed and linked to the relay mechanism so that it opens only when the operators conduct the jobs in the right sequence.

Courtesy Kanto Auto Works

(Note: This appendix is referred to on page 156 in the text.)

Appendix 6.2

PROBLEM-SOLVING TOOLS

Although many tools are used at the shop floor, the following are the ones used most often. A key here is whether or not we can use appropriate tools according to the nature of the problem, and be able to communicate the point quickly to others. If experience is limited, it may be best to start out simply by using the pareto chart and cause-and-effect diagram before learning other tools.

1. Histogram
2. Cause-and-effect diagram
3. Check sheet
4. Pareto diagram
5. Graph
6. Control chart
7. Scatter diagram
8. Pie chart
9. Display chart (pictograph)
10. Relations diagram
11. Affinity diagram
12. Tree diagram
13. Matrix diagram
14. Arrow diagram
15. Gantt chart
16. Radar chart
17. Process analysis sheet
18. Cycle time analysis sheet
19. Work combination chart
20. Process flow diagram (flow chart)

If we can articulate (1) the problem and potential causes or (2) the objective and the means to achieve that objective, we are often more than halfway to solving the problem or achieving the objective.

We should be able to use these tools whenever the appropriate situation arises. Yet like learning to use tools for weekend carpentry jobs, it takes practice before we can be qualified. Also, according to our skill level, the tools we use will be different—simpler ones for beginners, and more complex ones for those more advanced. According to Tadasu Fujita, however, the most frequently used tools for QC circles were the pareto diagram and the cause-and-effect diagram. ("Transition of QC Circle in the 1980's" by Fujita, T., *Total Quality Control,* Vol. 40 [December 1989].)

1. Histogram
(Example: Weight)

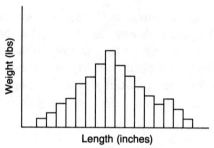

2. Cause-and-effect Diagram
(Example: Quality)

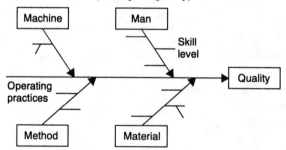

3. Check Sheet
(Example: Defects)

Type	Number of Occurrences	Total
Cracks	⊞⊞ ⊞⊞ ⊞⊞ ‖	17
Discoloring	⊞⊞ ⊞⊞ ⊞⊞ ⊞⊞ ⏐	21
Bends	⊞⊞ ⊞⊞ ⏐	11
Scars	⊞⊞	5
Others	⊞⊞ ⏐	6

4. Pareto Diagram
(Example: Machine Downtime)

Machine downtime (hrs)

Electrical | Mechanical | Pipe | Operator error | Others

5. Graph
(Example: Production Record)

Production units

● Goal

Actual

9/1   9/15   9/30

Date

6. Control Chart
(Example: Dimension)

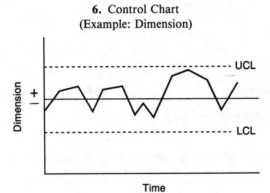

Dimension

+ −

UCL

LCL

Time

7. Scatter Diagram
(Example: Defects—Temperature)

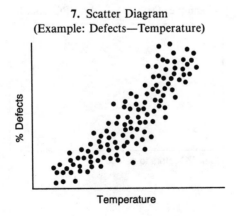

% Defects

Temperature

8. Pie Chart
(Example: Small Group Improvement Activities by Industry in Japan)

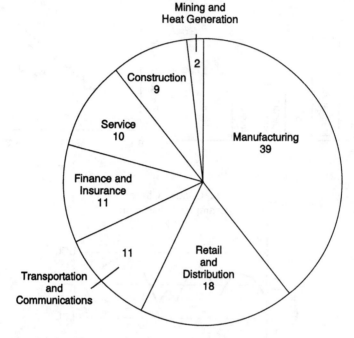

Source: "Transition of QC Circle in 1980's" by Fujita, T., *Total Quality Control*, December 1989, vol. 40.

9. Display Chart (Pictograph)
(Example: Defects found on PC Board)

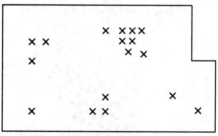

Note: "X" refers to defect.

10. Relations Diagram
(Example: Techniques and Their Relationship Towards Eliminating Waste)

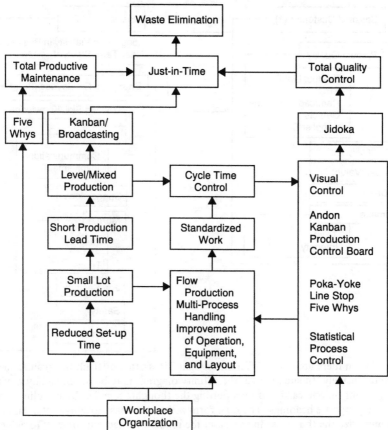

Note: This diagram shows the interrelationship of different techniques to achieve elimination of waste. Compared to the cause-and-effect diagram, however, this diagram makes it easier to describe even a complex relationship. Exhibit 11.3, Major Elements of Shop Floor Management, is another example of a relations diagram.

11. Affinity Diagram
(Example: Mission Statement)

```
┌─────────────────────────────────┐   ┌─────────────────────────────────────┐
│ Satisfied Customer (1)           │   │ Probability (3)                      │
│                                  │→  │ Long Term Viability in Business      │
│  ┌──────────────────────┐        │   │ Near Term Survival                   │
│  │ Product Quality      │        │   └─────────────────────────────────────┘
│  │                      │        │
│  │  Product Liability   │        │   ┌─────────────────────────────────────┐
│  │  SPC                 │        │   │ Energized Employees (2)              │
│  │  Reduced Variations  │ ←      │   │  ┌───────────────────────────┐       │
│  │  Defects             │        │   │  │ Training Skill/Knowledge  │       │
│  │  Supplier Quality    │        │   │  └───────────────────────────┘       │
│  └──────────────────────┘        │   │  ┌──────────┐                        │
│  ┌──────────────────────┐        │   │  │ Team     │                        │
│  │ Reliabilty           │        │   │  │ Communications                    │
│  └──────────────────────┘        │   │  │ Involvement                       │
│  ┌──────────────────────┐        │   │  └──────────┘                        │
│  │ Cost (Value)         │        │   │  ┌───────────┐                       │
│  └──────────────────────┘        │   │  │ Suggestions                       │
│  ┌──────────────────────┐        │   │  └───────────┘                       │
│  │ Delivery             │        │   │  ┌────────┐                           │
│  └──────────────────────┘        │   │  │ Morale │                           │
│  ┌──────────────────────┐        │   │  │ Integrity                         │
│  │ Image                │        │   │  │ Pride                             │
│  │  Trust               │        │   │  │ Trust                             │
│  │  Integrity           │        │   │  └────────┘                           │
│  └──────────────────────┘        │   │  ┌──────────────┐                     │
└─────────────────────────────────┘   │  │ Job Security │                     │
                                       │  └──────────────┘                     │
                                       │  ┌────────┐                           │
                                       │  │ Safety │                           │
                                       │  └────────┘                           │
                                       │  ┌───────────┐                       │
                                       │  │ Community │                       │
                                       │  └───────────┘                       │
                                       └─────────────────────────────────────┘
```

Note: When there are many different thoughts, it is often difficult to organize them comprehensively. In such a case, the affinity diagram may be developed by having one thought on one card and then putting the thoughts together by bundling them under appropriate headings. The final form will make it easy to construct a sentence to summarize the thoughts. In this case, the mission turned out to be: "To achieve long-term viability in business through *satisfied customer(1)* with *energized employees(2)* and accomplishing near term *profitability(3)*"

12. Tree Diagram

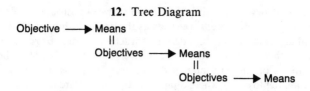

Objective ──▶ Means
‖
Objectives ──▶ Means
‖
Objectives ──▶ Means

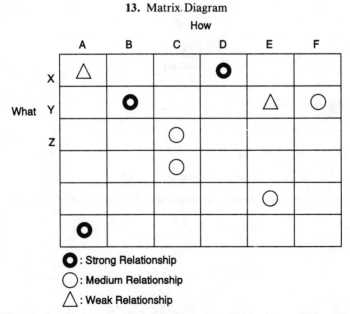

Note: The tree diagram describes the relationship of objectives and means in a cascade fashion. Exhibit 9.21 is an example of such an application.

13. Matrix Diagram

○ : Strong Relationship

○ : Medium Relationship

△ : Weak Relationship

Note: The matrix diagram describes the relationship between two different kinds of characteristics, such as objectives and means to achieve objectives or nature of problems and potential solutions. Or, to relate "what" the customer expects and "how" to meet such expectation, the matrix relates "What" and "How" as shown here. The interrelationships are commonly categorized as strong, medium, and weak.

In the case of developing the relationship between customer needs and design characteristics, a customer needs tree such as the one in Exhibit 2.12 may be represented in "what" column, whereas design characteristics may be represented by the "how" row so that we know that there is clear understanding as to how we can address the needs of the customer in design process. (This matrix is the core of quality function deployment where quality characteristics are translated throughout the company by use of these matrix diagrams.) Exhibits 2.14, 10.13, and 10.21 are examples of such an application.

14. Arrow Diagram
(Example: Project Planning)

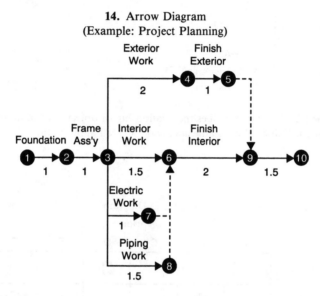

Note: ① : event number

1   : time to finish the job

——▶ : job which takes time

----▶ : indication of interrelationship between jobs

Compared to Gantt chart, arrow diagram describes the interrelation of jobs more clearly.

15. Gantt Chart
(Example: Project Planning)

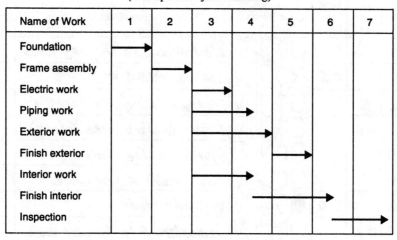

Name of Work	1	2	3	4	5	6	7
Foundation	→						
Frame assembly		→					
Electric work			→				
Piping work			→				
Exterior work			→				
Finish exterior					→		
Interior work			→				
Finish interior				→			
Inspection						→	

16. Radar Chart
(Example: Level of Shop Floor Management)

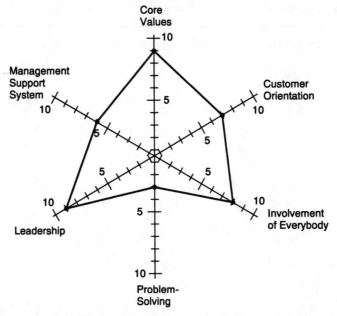

Note: This example corresponds to Company A in Exhibit 11.5 in the text. As you see, this chart makes easy to evaluate which areas are strong or weak as compared to some kinds of standards.

Also notice the exhibit at the end of Appendix 3.1 where evaluation of the supervisor's roles and responsibilities are summarized with a radar chart.

17. Process Analysis Sheet

Step	Dist. In Feet	Time In Mins	Chart Synbols	Process Description	Qty.
40			○⇨□□∨	Electronics awaiting upgrade	
41		0.5	○⇨□□∨	Log in PCBA #s	
42	40		○⇨□□∨	Transfer to upgrade station	
43	40		○⇨□□∨	Return to work area (test)	
44			○⇨□□∨	Storage - Line side	
45			○⇨□□∨	Bds awaiting upgrade	
46		3.0	●⇨□□∨	Upgrade Bds.	
47	32		○⇨□□∨	Transfer Bds to Test area	

○ Operation (non–value added)   ⇨ Transportation   □ Delay

● Operation (Value added)   □ Storage   ∨ Inspection

Note: Process analysis sheet highlights the non-value added work.

18. Cycle Time Analysis Sheet

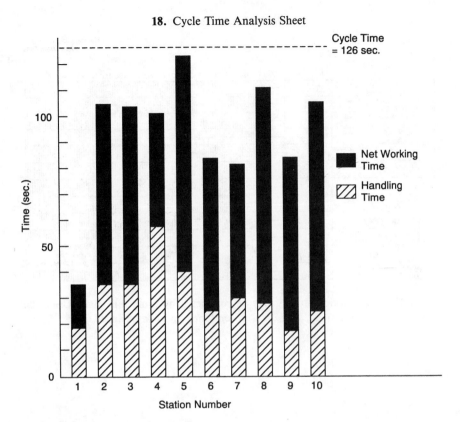

Total handling time = 318 sec. (34%)

Total net working time = 611 sec. (66%)

Total operating time = 929 sec. (100%)

$$\text{Utilization of operator's time} = \frac{\text{Total operating time}}{\text{Cycle time} \times \text{Number of operators}}$$

$$= \frac{929}{126 \times 10} = 74\%$$

Note: Cycle time analysis helps to identify the underutilized time for repetitive operation such as assembly work for line balancing.

19. Work Combination Chart

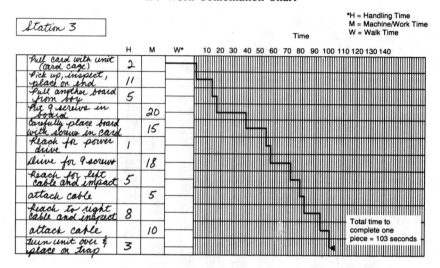

Note: Time and motion studies may be conducted by using this chart. Using the idea of cycle time control, work can be combined and line balanced.

20. Process Flow Diagram
(Example: Quality Improvement Process)

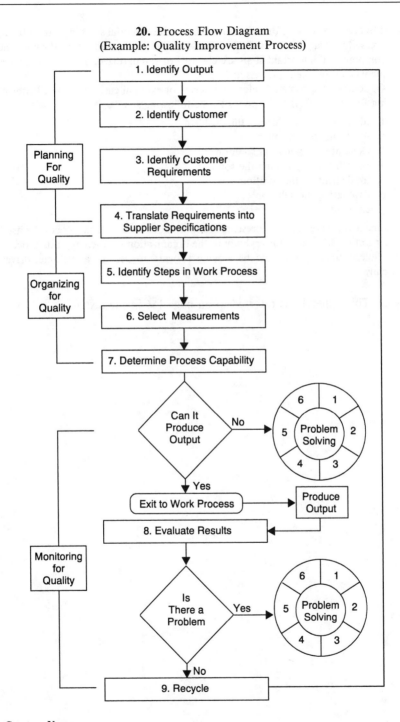

Courtesy Xerox

Note: In order to describe the relationship between sequential steps in a visual form, a process flow diagram is used. By following the arrow, and going through the decision point, all important steps are clarified or standardized. This exhibit shows the quality improvement process at Xerox.

Of course, "customers" refers to internal or external customers. The Problem Solving Process (wheel) corresponds to the following steps:

1. Identifying and selecting the problem
2. Analyzing the problem
3. Generating a potential solution
4. Selecting and planning the solution
5. Implementing the solution
6. Evaluating the solution
(back to step 1.)

As noted here, this example represents the continuous improvement process by itself similar to the QC story. If everybody in the organization is practicing this process, the whole organization should be moving forward to become a customer-driven company.

(Note: This appendix is referred to on page 156 in the text.)

Appendix 6.3

CHECKLIST
FOR IDEA GENERATION

The following list may be used to find a topic to involve people in problem solving. The idea is for people who are close to the situation to be involved in these activities, as opposed to having someone else do the job for them. Here, the 5M1E checklist, the 5W2H checklist, and Osborne's checklist are described as basic idea-generation techniques. Especially when our ideas dry up, these checklists can prompt further thought.

The following 5M1E checklist covers the basics of operation: man, machine, methods, material, measurement, and environment.

Exhibit 6.3.1. 5M1E Checklist

Man

- Can we educate ourselves better in what we do?
- Can we communicate better among ourselves?
- Can we improve the new employee or temporary staff introduction package?
- Can we direct people to the person who is in charge of a certain job without any trouble?
- Can we effectively share work when overloaded?
- Can we do more cross-training and job rotation?
- Can we improve the storage areas for personal belongings?
- Can we improve the condition of the work environment, especially related to health and safety?
- Can we improve the interface with the customer, internal or external?

Machine

- Can we improve the processing method?
- Can we improve the effective use of machines, computers, and other facilities?

(*continued*)

Exhibit 6.3.1. Continued

Machine Continued

- Can we use machines to do the job?
- Can we adequately maintain the service of machines?
- Can we modify, maintain, or upgrade to improve the performance of machines?
- Can we identify the common causes of machine failures and find solutions to prevent them?
- Can we think of improving tools and fixtures to do the work better?
- Can we think of applying the tools in other areas?
- Can we improve the procedures for machine or facility breakdown?

Methods

- Can we simplify, combine, or eliminate our jobs, materials, parts, etc.?
- Can we eliminate the redundant work done at multiple locations?
- Can we do it right the first time?
- Can we clarify the standards better and practice managing by exception?
- Can we change the work method?
- Can we improve the use of SOP so that it is easy to follow?
- Can we improve the training method?
- Can we improve housekeeping and workplace organization for materials, tools, parts, etc.?
- Can we improve the capacity of the operation, machine, or line?
- Can we improve the layout?
- Can we reduce the lot (batch) size of production?
- Can we reduce the setup time?
- Can we stop overproduction?
- Can we reduce inventory?
- Can we reduce unnecessary movement?
- Can we find effective ways of transportation?
- Can we think of improved transportation devices?
- Can we improve the utilization of people's waiting time?

Material

- Can we improve the effective use of resources, such as materials, support people's help, etc.?
- Can we eliminate unnecessary waste in processing?
- Can we reduce scrap and rework?
- Can we find an effective use of materials, e.g., oil, air, steam, paper, gloves, and other consumables?
- Can we improve labeling, color coding, marking systems?

Exhibit 6.3.1. Continued

Measurement (Information)

- Can we improve the organization of information to communicate better? (Are we clear on what information we need and whether we have it?)
- Can we improve the reporting procedure?
- Can we make the best use of the computer system?
- Can we improve visual aids?
- Can we improve the information-gathering procedure?
- Can we reduce the distribution number for reports?
- Can we eliminate generating unnecessary paper?
- Can manual reporting be better than using the computer?
- Can we help the users (customers) of a report to use the information better?
- Can we make the forms simpler to use?
- Can we develop an improved procedure for ease of use?
- Can we speed up information processing?
- Can we improve the storage of records? (Do we have too many or too few records?)
- Can we have key information readily available and updated?
- Can we compare the process or product with that of our competitor's and think of ways to improve?

Environment

- Can we improve the lighting, air, temperature, noise, dust, gas, bad odor, or other work conditions?
- Can we improve safety procedures?
- Can we improve safety equipment?

Another checklist, called 5W2H (what, why, where, when, who, how, and how much), is used for developing the action plan, and is also useful to identify problems.

Exhibit 6.3.2. 5W2H Checklist

What (Object)

What to do?
What is being done?
What should be done?
What else can be done?
What else should be done?
Why can't we eliminate this task, material, etc.?

(*continued*)

Exhibit 6.3.2. Continued

Why (Purpose)

Why does he/she do it?
Why do it?
Why do it there?
Why do it that way?
Why do it then?

Where (Location)

Where to do it?
Where is it being done?
Where should it be done?
Where else can it be done?
Where else should it be done?
Why should it be done there?

When (Timing, Sequence)

When to do it?
When is it done?
When should it be done?
Is it necessary to do it then?

Who (Person)

Who does the task?
Who is doing it?
Who should be doing it?
Who else can do it?
Who else should do it
Why am I (or is he/she) the one to do this?

How (Method)

How to do it?
How is it done?
How should it be done?
Is there any other way to do it?
Is this the best way?

Exhibit 6.3.2. Continued

How Much (Cost)

How much is it?
How much is it costing?
How much should it cost?
How much can we save?

The last checklist is Osborne's Checklist (*Applied Imagination,* A.F. Osborne, New York: Scribner's, 1963).

Exhibit 6.3.3. Osborne's Checklist

Use It Another Way

- Is there another way to use it while keeping the current setup?
- Can anything else be produced?

Borrow an Idea from Something Similar

- Ideas are formed by combining.
- See if ideas used elsewhere can be adapted to your improvement project.

Change or Replace It

- Change the shape, color, sound, smell, movement, location, orientation, power source, and so on.
- Rotate it.
- Remove something that's there.
- Add what's not there.

Expand It

- Add something, spend more time, increase the repetition.
- Make it stronger, longer, or thicker.
- Add some other value.
- Double it, duplicate it, increase it, or exaggerate it.

Reduce It

- Remove something.
- Make it smaller or stronger.
- Divide it.
- Simplify it, reduce it, lighten it.
- Express it in a more subdued way.

(*continued*)

Exhibit 6.3.3. Continued

Use Alternatives

- Use someone or something else.
- Use other elements, ingredients, materials, methods, locations, approaches, or tone of voice.

Replace It

- Use different elements or ingredients, dies, layout, sequence, or arrangement.
- Reverse the cause and effect.
- Change the pace, speed, or schedule.

Reverse It

- Turn it upside down, invert it, reverse the positions, front and back, positive and negative.
- Change the roles, orientation, or setup.

Combine It

- Mix it, make an alloy.
- Assemble it.

Exhibit 6.3.4. Practicing Different Methods of Idea Generation

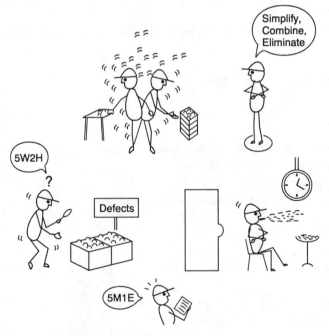

(Note: This appendix is referred to on page 173 in the text.)

Appendix 7.1

ADVICE
ON SUGGESTION PROGRAM

Following are comments from people of Matsushita Electric Industries' Vacuum Cleaner Division answering suggestions on their suggestion programs:

As people contributing suggestions, what do you do to come up with suggestions?

- Take note whenever there is something that does not quite feel right.
- Collect information from the work of other companies or other departments. It may be available from presentations, books, TV, etc.
- Study "idea products" by visiting stores such as a do-it-yourself shop.
- First experiment by cutting, pasting, bending, etc., using such alternative materials as paper.
- Study many examples of improvment.
- Always ask yourself if it is satisfactory the way it is now.
- Always be attentive to what is happening at the shop floor.
- Review improvement ideas of small group improvement activities.

As managers, what do you do to encourage people to contribute suggestions?

- Provide support as much as possible to meet the goal of ten suggestions per person every month.
- As we improve the work by involving our people, link ideas generated by suggestions.
- Provide hints to people so that they can develop the habits, willingness, patience, and confidence within themselves.
- Avoid criticizing ideas generated.
- Always observe people's work, and contribute advice.
- Always generate questions, and ask people to think about them.

- Always demonstrate practicing improvement by management as well.
- In order to develop people's interest in making improvements, help execute ideas to show how things can be improved.
- Encourage people to face reality as opposed to staying at the conceptual level.

As managers and people contributing suggestions, what do you recommend to those who are not practicing a suggestion program effectively?

- It is necessary to incorporate suggestion programs as a part of improvement activities.
- It is necessary to have top management show strong initiative.
- Educate people about the importance of collecting everybody's ideas and the fun of practicing it.
- First, think of making your work easier by making suggestions. And at the same time, be rewarded monetarily in doing it.
- Make the system such that people can make their work easier and make money at the same time.
- By contributing a small idea, experience the nice feeling of making team members happy.

In terms of evaluating the suggestions, points are given according to the following guideline. As examples, Matsushita's and Toyota's evaluation criteria are compared here.

| | Score (Points) | |
	Matsushita	Toyota
Effects/Benefits	0–50	0–40
Idea/Creativity	0–30	0–10
Point of Idea Generation	N.A.	0–10
Efforts	0–10	0–10
Potential for Implementation	0–10	0–5
Adjustments	$-10 \sim +10\%$	$-20\% \sim +20\%$
Total Points	0–100	0–75

Note: Effects/Benefits are divided into tangible (such as reduction of expenses, materials, or manpower), and intangible (such as safety, environment, hygiene, or some types of quality). Points are calculated by combining these. Adjustments are made considering such factors as job responsibility, relation to the main job, etc.

An important point to note, however, is that most of the awards are equivalent to ten dollars or less per suggestion and there is no need to go through the point-calculation shown in the table. They are left to the responsibility of the manager in the area.

To indicate the importance of a suggestion program for the company, it should also be noted that in Toyota's case, the chairman of the suggestion committee is also a vice president of Toyota, and the vice chairman of the committee is a managing director. Realizing the impact to the company's operation, top management of these companies seldom miss the award ceremony and presentations of employee suggestions.

(Note: This appendix is referred to on page 188 in the text.)

Appendix 7.2

BUILDING AN EFFECTIVE TEAM

The following are key characteristics of an effective team. It is recommended that the performance of the team or mini-company be evaluated following the items listed below and that team members exchange ideas to see what can be done to improve. Score each item from 0 to 10, with 0 being the worst and 10 the best.

Key Characteristics	Score
1. Has a clear mission and objectives: Everybody in the team understands, shares, and is commited to accomplishing team's mission, and objectives	____
2. Exhibits strong leadership: Leadership is situational. It may not be the same person who leads each time. Depending on the process or style of people, the leader's role may change. Each person may have special skills or knowledge to contribute.	____
3. Synergy of people is apparent: People's opinions are heard and built on to address the problems and opportunities of the team. One person's idea triggers more ideas from others in a chain reaction.	____
4. Exhibits a good combination of skills and knowledge: Team members contribute in different but complementary manner to achieve synergy.	____
5. Shares information well, and practices glass wall management: There is uninhibited expression of ideas, discussion involves all members, and active listening is taking place at meetings. As a result, they can work flexibly among themselves to accomplish their goals.	____
6. Members support each other: To achieve the mission and enjoy the atmosphere of working as a team, it develops a supportive environment. There is trust, honesty, and consistency of purpose, but no fear.	____
7. Works hard and has fun together: A good team works hard to accomplish the mission and objectives. But the team does not forget to have fun.	____

Key Characteristics	Score

8. Keeps learning as it moves forward: Going through the plan-do-check-act cycle, a good team keeps learning from both successes and failures. ____

9. Individuals feel that they have grown as individuals within the team: It is important for members themselves to feel that they have grown as a whole individual both technically and as a person. ____

10. Team has a good track record of progress: Team's accomplishment is indisputable. As the team sets goals, more often than not, it achieves them. ____

Total score: ____

Note: After the total score is tallied, team members should search for ways to improve their performance.

Exhibit 7.2.1. There is No "I" in the Word "Team'

(Note: This appendix is referred to on page 191 in the text.)

Appendix 7.3

CHECKLIST TO EVALUATE THE KEY STEPS OF TEAM-ORIENTED PROBLEM-SOLVING

The following checklist may be used to (1) plan or review the process of the project by the team members themselves, or (2) evaluate a team project and a team presentation to give awards and appropriate feedback by management.

Exhibit 7.3.1 shows the QC story, which is a standardized form of team problem solving widely used in Japan.

Exhibit 7.3.1. Checklist to Review the Process of Problem Solving (QC Story)

1. Selection of Theme
   - Was the theme discussed thoroughly by all team members?
   - Was the theme selected voluntarily?
   - Are the skills of team members adequate for accomplishing the objectives?
   - Does it reflect the needs of the workplace, mission, and objectives of the company?
   - Was there evaluation of the actual situation vs. the plan, or level of customer satisfaction?
2. Description of Situation
   - Were the Three Reals addressed appropriately?
   - Are problems studied from different viewpoints?
   - Are problem areas narrowed down?
   - Is the use of data appropriate?
   - Was information obtained from managers, staff, customers, or suppliers?
3. Goal Setting
   - Is the process of setting goals appropriate?
   - Is the objective of improvement clearly defined?
   - Are reasons for goals convincing?
   - Are there clear goals of what to do by when and how much?
   - Is there clear plan of action using the 5W2H principle (who is to do what, when, where, why, how, and how much)?
   - Are there sufficient opportunities so that everybody can contribute?

Exhibit 7.3.1. Continued

4. Analysis of Root Cause
   - Is it evident that the team asked why many times?
   - Is a cause-and-effect relationship clear?
   - Is the use of data/information appropriate?
   - Is there good use of proprietary technology and problem-solving techniques?
   - Does everybody help by contributing their ideas?

5. Development of Countermeasures
   - Are there strong relationships between causes and countermeasures?
   - Do countermeasures reflect everyone's creativity, including the opinions of managers, staff, customers, and suppliers?
   - Is the solution unique or original?
   - Are there evaluations of effectiveness, expected benefit, and implementation of countermeasures?
   - Is the plan to implement countermeasures executable?

6. Execution of Countermeasures
   - Are countermeasures implemented using people's ingenuity?
   - Is there evidence of people making extra effort?
   - Does everybody help in executing the plans?
   - Are there considerations on standardization in the future?

7. Evaluation of Accomplishments
   - Are results, both tangible and intangible, monitored appropriately?
   - Are there clear relationships between countermeasures and accomplishments?
   - Does the project move forward as planned?
   - Do other parties buy into the improvement plan as well as the solution?
   - Have the expected results been accomplished?
   - What are the reasons for any difference between planned and actual results?

8. Standardization
   - Does the team establish standards after resolution of the problem?
   - Is there standardization to prevent the same problems from recurring?
   - Is there creative thought in practicing standardization?

9. Lessons Learned and Future Plans
   - Do team members develop confidence and self-esteem as part of the process?
   - Is there adequate education and training for everybody?
   - Is there improvement from how the previous project went?
   - Have many additional suggestions been generated in the process?
   - Was the PDCA cycle practiced during the whole improvement activity?
   - Are there plans to confirm the efforts as a team to continuously move ahead?
   - Following the lessons learned, is there clear direction for the future?

Exhibit 7.3.2 shows the evaluation form used by Xerox for its Team Excellence Award.

Exhibit 7.3.2. Team Evaluation Form Used at Xerox

Rater Name: _____   Date: _____

Team Name: _____   Purpose of Rating: _____

Directions: For each question, circle the appropriate number and add all numbers to attain the final rating.

Scale: 1 = Very Little Evidence; 5 = Very Strong Evidence

RESULTS THROUGH QUALITY (70 points)	INNOVATION (15 points)

1) Relative to its *potential,* did the team have a significant impact on business results? 1 2 3 4 5	1) Did the team come up with a creative or innovative solution? 1 2 3 4 5
2) Did the team's results meet customer requirements as verified by the customer? 1 2 3 4 5	2) Was the team innovative or creative in their process? 1 2 3 4 5
3) Did the team's results support a business objective? 1 2 3 4 5	3) Were several possible approaches to solving the problem identified? 1 2 3 4 5
4) Have the team's results been validated by its Control organization? 1 2 3 4 5	4) Did the team use creative techniques to remove barriers in pursuing their solution? 1 2 3 4 5
5) Have the team's results been able to effectuate long-term change? 1 2 3 4 5	Total _____ × .75 = _____
6) Did the team conduct root cause problem analysis? 1 2 3 4 5	TEAMWORK (15 points)
7) Did the team use analytical/statistical tools and techniques effectively, based on their background? 1 2 3 4 5	1) Did the team demonstrate a good working relationship among team members? 1 2 3 4 5
8) Did the team apply a recognized, systematic process? 1 2 3 4 5	2) Did the team experience contribute to the development of team members' interactive skills? 1 2 3 4 5

Exhibit 7.3.2. Continued

RESULTS THROUGH QUALITY (70 points)	INNOVATION (15 points)
9) Did the team use the process of Competitive Benchmarking, both for functional (how) and output (what) effectively? 1 2 3 4 5	3) Did the team members meet regularly with at least 75% attendance and share in the team's efforts? 1 2 3 4 5
10) Was the team effective in proposing its solution, seeking the necessary approval, and developing a process for tracking the results of the solution? 1 2 3 4 5	4) Did the team have significant constraints or barriers that they overcame to operate as a team? 1 2 3 4 5
Total _____ × 1.4 = _____	Total _____ × .75 = _____

Note: All teams are evaluated using this form and weighting results as follows: quality (70%), teamwork (15%), and innovation (15%).

Exhibit 7.3.3 shows the evaluation form used at Komatsu, Ltd. in Japan as each QC circle completes a project.

Exhibit 7.3.3. Team Evaluation Criteria Used at Komatsu

Subject	Contents	Score*
Contents of Activities	• Did team activity take place as planned?	_____
	• Were proprietary technology, problem-solving techniques, and information used appropriately?	_____
Administration	• Did meetings take place smoothly?	_____
	• Were roles and responsibilities shared by all team members?	_____
Problem Solving	• Was problem solving based on fact, and was the process logical?	_____
	• Was there creative thinking in coming up with a solution?	_____
Efforts for Accomplishment	• Were extra efforts made, and was there a desire for accomplishment?	_____
	• Did the activity address the problems of shop condition and people's mindset?	_____
Effects/Benefits	• Were there valuable accomplishments, either tangible or intangible?	_____

(*continued*)

Exhibit 7.3.3. Continued

Subject	Contents	Score*
Effects/Benefits *Continued* Countermeasures	• Was there consideration given to apply a similar solution in other areas?	_____
	• Are countermeasures expected to be long lasting?	_____
	• Were there improvements made in people's skills or morale?	_____

*In scoring, 5 is the best and 1 is the worst for each subject of evaluation. Also, each QC circle is asked to prepare a one-page summary of team activity using the QC story format when completing the project for evaluation.

Exhibit 7.3.4. Team Improvement Board

Note: As team improvement projects are selected and activities started, profiles of projects are posted on the board with pictures of team members as shown here. Then, there is an annual convention to share the accomplishment of these teams, where awards are given and a small booklet describing each team's activities is also published.

Courtesy Daiwa Seiko

(Note: This appendix is referred to on page 155, 193 and 258 in the text.)

Appendix 7.4

CONTINUOUS IMPROVEMENT STUDY GROUP ACTIVITIES

A group of companies (or divisions or departments of a company) may come together to share the vision of continuous improvement and practice improvement activities. By having seven to ten companies get together and share knowledge, techniques, and experiences at one-month to three-month intervals while rotating the host company, people can see improvement activities of others firsthand. (At Toyota, such activities are conducted internally as well as for supplier companies to deepen the understanding of the Toyota Production System. Emphasizing the self-initiative for improvement, this activity is called the Toyota Production System Self-Study Group.)

The list in Exhibit 7.4.1 is developed to assist people in initiating such group improvement activities for different departments in a company or companies with common interest in continuous improvement.

Exhibit 7.4.1. Description of Continuous Improvement Study Group Activities

---

Objectives

Sharing of expertise, resources
Mutual learning, networking
Effective use of expert/consultant as resource
Continuous improvement

Members' Motivation to Join the Group

Learn what others do
Share common problems and solutions
Eliminate regression to old habits
Discipline to improve
Customers require continuous improvement

(continued)

Exhibit 7.4.1. Continued

Facilitator/Resource Person (one to three people)

Expert: Well versed in subject matter, with vision and high commitment level, well rounded person with facilitation skills

Facilitator: Expert in subject matter, also in charge of administration, facilitation skills

Audience (two to three persons per company)

Top Management: First or second in command

Middle Management: Manager, operations manager

Shop Floor Employee: Supervisor (or operator as appropriate)

Yearly Agenda

Meet every month to three months

One day to two days at a time

Host company will be rotated

Possible field tour to visit world-class companies as a group

Progress report for each meeting and annual summary report at year end

Annual convention to share progress

Topics Covered

Elimination of waste

Housekeeping and workplace organization

Setup time reduction and small lot production

Flow production

Problem-solving processes

Quality improvement

Maintenance

Jidoka—line-stop concept

Kanban

PDCA and management systems

Glass wall management

Empowerment of people

Customer orientation

People involvement

Standards and improvement

Standard operating procedures

Job training

Visual control

Exhibit 7.4.1. Continued

Mini-companies

Policy management, etc.

Typical Day's Agenda

General tour, typically done by three teams—use of checklist

Discussion of general tour, summary of pluses and minuses

Focus topic presentation

Focus tour and preparation for presentation, also concurrent executive breakout session (in Toyota's Self-Study Group, improvement is made on the spot)

Executive report

Executive counseling

Team presentation (5–10 min. per team)

Project tracking and guidance (5–10 min. per company)

Wrap-up discussion

Tools

Polaroid camera and film

Stopwatches

Video monitor and 35 mm slide projector for focus topic and project tracking as prepared by member companies

Overhead projector

Flip charts and stands

Materials Shared

Excerpts of books and video training tapes as appropriate

Other readings on problem-solving, teamwork, presentation, maintenance, etc.

Company-specific information, including layout, suggestion program, examples of procedures, improvement activities as prepared by member companies for the benefits of others

Information and materials are expected to be shared during or outside of the meeting

Feedback and Evaluation

Observations from shop floor tours are presented as pluses and minuses by teams for the benefit of host company. (As appropriate, presentation of team activities are made at the shop floor for the benefit of the employees.)

All pictures taken during the general tour and focus tour will be given to the company for their benefit

In the following meeting, it is expected that host company will give a presentation on the progress they have made

Meeting evaluation is taken at the end of the meeting as a way to improve the process

(continued)

Exhibit 7.4.1. Continued

Administration

Newsletter; distribution of materials shared during the meeting
Distribution of reading material
Preparation of plant visitation: selection of project, review of progress
Budget, food, coordination, etc.

Responsibility of Participants

Make significant improvement for their own sake
Contribution to the team
If there is lack of progress, the member status may be revoked

Some Comments from Members

Use group as resource
Bring in problems for discussion
Jot down any good ideas for later reference
Make time for improvement
Implement ideas within 48 hours
Don't be afraid to fail
Learn from the mistakes
Standardize as improvements are made
Share successes
Celebrate successes
Use visual means of communication, e.g., before and after pictures, exhibits
Spread the words of continuous improvement with others
Initiate internal continuous improvement study group

Exhibit 7.4.1 is a condensation of my experiences with such activities as Toyota's Self-study Group, Continuous Improvement Users' Group (CIUG), The Executive Committee (TEC) and Manufacturing Forum of Southern California's Young Presidents' Organization (YPO). CIUG was founded by Mike Rother, Rick Fleming, and myself with the support of the Industrial Technology Institute to share the continuous improvement efforts with small manufacturers. One member noted, "The Users' Group is like meeting with eight consultants every six weeks; also, it helps us stay on track of continuous improvement." Currently, more than seventy companies from manufacturing and service industries are involved in CIUG in different regions in the United States. In Europe and Asia, there are several similar groups.

In terms of key factors for success of these activities, I believe realization of needs for improvement at the shop floor, sincerity, mutual learning, and faith in the process to be most important. If such an attitude exists among members, methods and techniques may be learned with proper guidance by facilitators. I would like to thank Toyota, Kanto Auto Works, Young Presidents' Organization, Industrial Technology Institute, and many members of these groups for providing me with opportunities to share knowledge and experience.

Exhibit 7.4.2. Scenes of Continuous Improvement Users' Group (CIUG) in Action. A team is making a presentation to employees of a member company. As feedback is given, everybody in the company can understand the group's recommendation for improvement.

Courtesy Continuous Improvement Users' Group

(Note: This appendix is referred to on page 195 in the text.)

Appendix 8.1

EFFECTIVE USE OF VISUAL AIDS

As today's quickly changing environment demands better communication, effective use of visual aids can play an important role at the shop floor. If we can do this effectively, it should help:

- *Sharing the state of progress* without any delay
- *Addressing common concerns* for everyone to see
- *Utilizing everybody's creativity* to attack the common concerns
- *Promoting teamwork* to help with each other
- *Having fun* to join the healthy internal competition
- *Developing pride* in people to see accomplishment, and
- *Recognizing accomplishments* made

The following are examples of such visual aids. As opposed to having an empty wall, we may utilize the space with our ingenuity and spirit of fun. To find effective use of display, the key concept here is to let the display talk to us. People watching the display are the customers.

Ideally, therefore, we want to make it comprehensible even to strangers, who can understand it without having to ask questions. If we post a chart only understandable to the person who made it, or if the chart is too outdated to be posted, we have lost the point of posting charts. Of course, these displays should not be facing toward the executives office if we want people to be involved.

Posting Company-wide Activities on the Wall

The following examples show company-wide activities, describing 5W and 1H (who are doing, what, when, where, why, and how). These visual aids are divided into the following six categories:

1. Progress of Company
2. Awards
3. Improvement Activities and Performance Scoreboard
4. Recent Presentations
5. Status of Team Projects
6. General Information and Pictures of Shop Floor

As we review these, we should realize that similar visual aids may be developed for our mini-companies. Exhibits 8, 9.17, and 9.20 may be also helpful to communicate the message in visual means.

1. Progress of Company

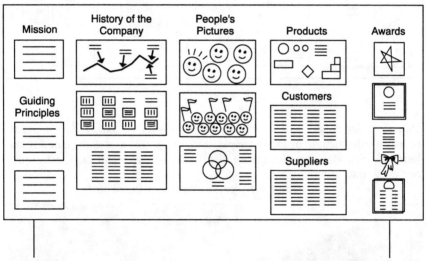

This board illustrates the progress of the company, describing its mission and guiding principles, with descriptions of people, products, customers, suppliers, and major accomplishments.

2. Awards

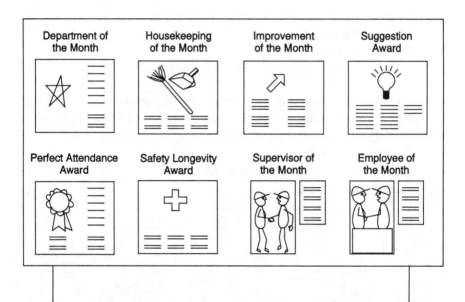

Here are a few examples of award plaques posted with the names of departments or individuals. Pictures of award recipients may be posted as well for monthly and yearly awards. Money earned through work may be important, but these awards add extra stimulation.

Exhibit 8.1.1. Awards Posted on Board

Courtesy Fireplace Manufacturers, Inc.

3. Improvement Activities and Performance (QCDSM) Scoreboard

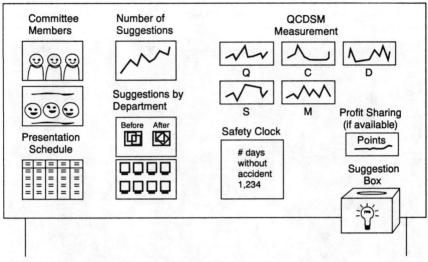

Here are pictures of people working for committees (safety, housekeeping improvement, suggestion, etc.). Also, key measurement of overall improvement activities in QCDSM (quality, cost, delivery, safety, and morale) may be posted.

4. Recent Presentations

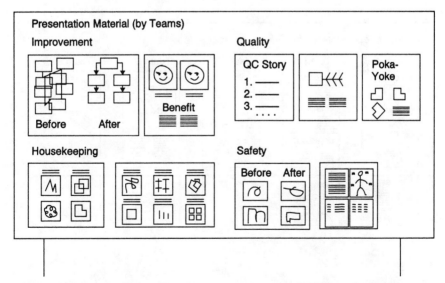

Pictures of group activities show people making presentations to management or to their peers. Posting these photographs communicates many people's efforts and encourages others to move forward.

Exhibit 8.1.2. Information Board Describing the Accomplishments.   Utilizing the empty wall space next to the aisle, a group of people started to post a team's accomplishments on the board. Even though such practice may not be a part of a company to start with, it may eventually become an accepted practice as the self-improvement movement starts to snowball.

Courtesy Borg-Warner

5. Status of Team Project

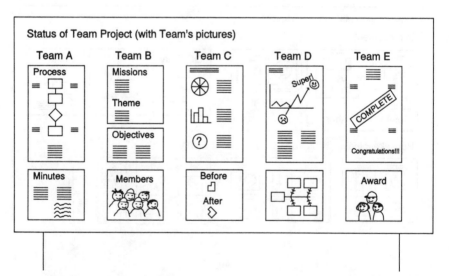

The status of teams' activities may be posted to indicate the level of accomplishment. Examples include supplier development program, setup time reduction, lead time reduction, and quality improvement. The progress of different small group improvement activities, corrective action teams, etc., can be compared.

Exhibit 8.1.3. Information Board Describing the Team's Progress.   This small corrugated board manufacturer has more than a dozen teams working on continuous improvement. Each team is made up of people from customer and supplier sides of the organization and meets every week for one hour to work on the project. To promote awareness on continuous improvement, a sharing rally takes place twice a month to report the progress.

Courtesy Bay Cities Containers

6. General Information and Pictures of Shop Floor

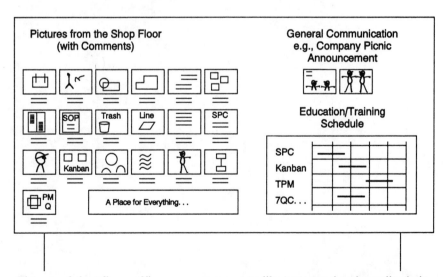

Pictures of shop floor, office or company events like customers' and suppliers' visits, company picnic, etc., may be posted monthly with brief comments. Good and bad housekeeping and organization may also be pointed out. As more pictures of people are posted, people will gather around every time new pictures are posted.

Exhibit 8.1.4. Walls Covered with Hundreds of Pictures. To show progress through people, Grand Rapids Spring & Wire displays hundreds of pictures of people working together. One of the displays reads: "Creating a Quality Culture Takes Time and Good People."

Courtesy Grand Rapids Spring & Wire

As for the posting mini-company activities, or key information at the line, see Exhibits 9.17 and 9.20 in Chapter 9.

(Note: This appendix is referred to on page 215 in the text.)

Appendix 9.1

SUPERVISOR'S DAILY, WEEKLY, MONTHLY, AND YEARLY ACTIVITIES

This appendix describes the activities of supervisors of a company that is advanced in shop floor management. Please note that even though many activities are described here, by upgrading supervisors' skills, over time they should be able to handle most of these. For example, time spent on troubleshooting and meetings will be much reduced as skills improve.

Exhibit 9.1.1. Daily Activities of Supervisors

Preparation for Morning Meeting

- Review prior shift's results.
- Check condition of work area visually.
- Prepare items to share in the meeting, e.g., QCDSM, situation of company and plant, suggestions, feedback from the morning walkthrough, condition of jigs and fixtures, follow-up items from previous meetings.
- Post key agenda items and relevant information on a meeting board so that people can follow agenda easily.

Conduct Morning Meeting

- Share above items. Ask for questions, comments, or suggestions.
- Provide directions as necessary, reminding people of key areas to focus their attention.
- Encourage people's participation in the meeting.
- As appropriate, let one person from the group take a turn and talk about any subject he likes.
- Make sure everybody is attentive.
- If some items need follow-up, take notes for review later. Proper follow-up is a key to successful meetings and developing good relationships.

(continued)

417

Exhibit 9.1.1. Continued

Review of Startup Operation

- Take action on items that require immediate attention, e.g., safety concerns, maintenance, or repairs.
- Walk around the area and check operating conditions (5M1E: men, machines, method of production, material, measurement, and environment).
- Make sure all the checklists and production records are current and properly posted at the designated areas.
- Check that operators are conducting their work as planned. Are they working in accordance with the standard operating procedure? Are standards difficult to follow? Do operators know the importance of standards? Are there any suggestions for improvement of the standard operating procedure? Are they following the safety requirements, production procedure, and other basic rules of operation?
- See if the operators need guidance. Offer help as needed.
- Check if quality assurance is properly enforced.
- Check the results of quality level, production volume, inventory level, levels of housekeeping and workplace organization.

Review of Operation with Manager and Peers

- Meet and report on the status of the operation with manager and peers.
- Discuss broader issues that require a coordination of efforts from different disciplines, e.g., QCDSM in broader terms, personnel and capacity planning, operator allocation.
- Explain necessary countermeasures being taken, review the progress of QCDSM, maintenance and improvement activities, suggestions, attendance, etc.
- Discuss and brainstorm as appropriate, to come up with improvement ideas on any items of concern.

Miscellaneous Jobs (in between meetings)

- Walk around the shop floor and talk with people. Develop a pleasant atmosphere in the workplace. Listen to people's comments or complaints, whether they are related to their work or personal lives. Offer advice and counseling as appropriate.
- In conversations with operators, think of them as your customers enabling you to get the job done.
- Check items as discussed in "Review of startup operation" above.
- If delay of production occurs as indicated by production control board, investigate the reason and take corrective action.
- Review quality information and feed pertinent information back to proper line/

Exhibit 9.1.1. Continued

staff, e.g., review the impact of work when operators are assigned to a new job. Call meetings with related departments depending on the nature of problem.

- Take care of administrative work, miscellaneous paper work, data collection and analysis of problems, review and follow-up of action items and suggestions, preparation for meeting and presentation, etc.
- Conduct line job as needed. Also, try to learn jobs by performing them so that you are familiar with the work. Perhaps new ideas for improvement may be generated while working. Closer working relationships may be developed between supervisors and operators as a result.
- Confirm progress in job training, cross-training. Let people take qualifying tests.

Dealing with Abnormal Conditions

- Deal with problems in safety, quality, scheduled delivery, etc. by taking corrective action.
- In the area of safety, when people are not trained, instruct them to stop operation immediately, ask for help, and wait for further instruction without trying to use their judgment. Always follow instructions as set forth by the company. In case of fire, earthquake, or other emergencies, guide people according to prescribed procedures.
- In the area of quality, instruct operators to take corrective measures so that further problems will be prevented. As appropriate, stop the line and inform your manager about the situation for evaluation of countermeasures. It is very important for operators to feel comfortable enough to report problems.
- In the areas of delayed delivery, or machine breakdown, etc., contact the relevant department (e.g., production control, maintenance, etc.), explain the situation, and take corrective action.
- Whatever the problems, it is imperative for supervisors, managers, and support people to be able to listen to the people reporting the problems with empathy. This is fundamental to developing teamwork.
- When the line is expected to be down for more than 15 minutes or so, instruct operators to work on housekeeping, workplace organization, or have a group meeting on certain problems. If the stoppage is short, operators may focus on working in their immediate areas.

Lunch Time, Break Time, and After-hour Activities

- Check the status of machines, tools, fixtures, and general workplace organization.
- Share time with your people and get to know them better. New employees especially may need extra attention to feel comfortable working with colleagues, and to learn their work areas.

(continued)

Exhibit 9.1.1. Continued

Lunch Time, Break Time, and After-hour Activities Continued

- Take an active part in recreational activities. Develop team spirit, share the excitement of working as a team, and competing for awards, improvement ideas, and better customer satisfaction.

End of Shift

- Check that all shutdown procedures are followed, e.g., housekeeping, workplace organization, status of machines, tools, fixtures, and safety.
- Summarize the day's operation on shift book by recording QCDSM, e.g., qualtiy level, productivity level, delivery (production) performance, safety information, attendance, overtime, machine trouble, material usage, etc. with comments.
- Conduct meeting with operators to share key points of operation. Review what went right and wrong, and reasons why. Share next day's schedule, discuss job assignments, plans for vacation, etc.
- Communicate with the supervisor of next shift. Items for communication may include:
  Production information: planned and actual production volume, inventory status, amount of work in progress, productivity level
  Quality information: corrective actions taken on quality problems, requests to next shift to work on quality problems that could not be resolved during the day shift, defects supplied to the line
  Status of machine maintenance, improvement projects
  Safety problems, near misses
  Job assignment, allocation of work, personnel transfers, etc.
- Plan ahead for the next day

Exhibit 9.1.2. Weekly or Monthly Activities of Supervisors

Participate in Production Schedule Meeting

- Meet with manager and peers.
- Obtain the production plan and evaluate production capacity.
- Review performance of operators, develop plans to provide assistance, education, or training.
- Share the status of inventory of materials, parts, etc.
- Allocate resources to meet the production plan, as appropriate.
- Review job, operators' vacation plans, assignments, job rotation.

Participate in Safety and Housekeeping Tour

- With your manager and peers, walk through the plant to review such areas as:
  Safety practices, e.g., use of safety devices, gloves, masks, goggles, etc., and following safety instructions for safely conducting the job

Exhibit 9.1.2. Continued

Housekeeping practices, e.g., "a place for everything and everything in its place"
Improvements recently implemented, as explained by supervisor or operator who
  came up with suggestion in the area (provide recognition as appropriate)
Operating procedures, layout, etc. if it is difficult to follow
- As walkthrough takes place, generate ideas for improvement and share thoughts.
- At the end of the walk, discuss what has been observed, and share the suggestions generated. Also, vote or select recipient for awards in safety, housekeeping, improvement of the month, as appropriate. (In order to encourage teamwork, the awards may be in the form of something people in the same work area can share.)

Participate in Shop Floor Improvement Meeting

Meet with manager, peers, and support people as appropriate.
- Compare status of QCDSM as contrasted with plans.
- Report objectives and means for achieving them for the next period, e.g., week or month.
- Review the status of different projects on QCDSM and adjust the plans as appropriate.
- Review and discuss suggestions that require coordination across different disciplines.

Participate in Meetings on Engineering Changes, and New Product Introduction

- Meet with engineering staff to go over engineering changes.
- Discuss suggestions made by people on engineering changes, and plan for new product introduction.

Chair or Participate in Team Project and Task Force Meeting

- Review and update the status of projects.
- Contribute ideas and offer support for implementing ideas that advance the projects.

Conduct Education and Training (Use Support People if Appropriate)

- Plan and conduct education and training in such areas as:
  How to follow operating standards for operators
  How kanban works
  How to do maintenance
  How to prevent accidents, take correct procedures when accidents happen
  How to read blueprints, drawings, and specifications
- Conduct tests in order to evaluate learning, as appropriate.

(continued)

Exhibit 9.1.2. Continued

Attend Education and Training Course for Supervisors

- In order to upgrade supervisory skills, attend courses in such areas as:
  Leadership training
  Team-building
  Problem-solving
  How to conduct effective meetings
  How to make presentations
  Specific subjects such as maintenance, quality assurance, economics, business
    planning, etc.
- Practice skills learned and follow-up to review effectiveness of course

Exhibit 9.1.3. Annual or Semi-Annual Activities of Supervisors

Review of past year's performance of the organization

- Develop an "Annual Report" of mini-company to evaluate the past year. Items
  in the report may include:
  1. Mission
  2. Objectives
  3. Profile of organization
  4. Profile of customers and suppliers, internal or external
  5. Plans executed to achieve objectives
  6. Accomplishments
  7. Existing Problems
  8. Lessons learned
  9. Plans for next year
- Make presentation to your manager and peers.

Develop Next Year's Plan for Your Organization

- Develop a "Business Plan" for the next year.
- Coordinate with manager, subordinates, peers, customers, and suppliers of your
  organization so that the business plan addresses the major concerns of the
  organization.
- As plans are developed, share the process of development as appropriate so that
  customers' needs and the company's policy (strategic direction) are reflected in
  your business plan. Also, discuss your concerns with the other parties in this
  process.

Review Past Year's Performance and Develop Next Year's Plan for the Operators

- Review the performance and develop education plan, job assignment plan, career development plans with operators.

Exhibit 9.1.3. Continued

- Assess the need for additional employees.
- Assess pay and bonuses, and discuss with your manager.

The contents of this appendix may seem to be presented in too much detail. A point to note, however, is that not only are many companies practicing these as a natural way of conducting business, but there are also those who are enthused about these ideas in building their future. As an example, I met with the people in a company located deep in the mountains several hours from Jakarta, Indonesia, and I was impressed that they were working hard to digest and practice these ideas, even though the wage of operators there was one dollar per day.

(Note: This appendix is referred to on page 239 in the text.)

Appendix 11.1

SHOP FLOOR TOUR CHECKLIST

This is an exercise to look at the organization's problems from the shop floor point of view. The more we focus our intelligence on where the action is, and address problems and explore opportunities then and there, the better off we will be.

There are two sections here. The first one addresses generic issues. Next, the "Shop Floor Checklist" addresses different subjects with a few representative areas to look at.

Basic Questions to Ask in the Shop Floor Tour

* Is there a place for everything and everything in its place?
* Is everything organized in such a manner that even a stranger can understand what is going on?
* Are work procedures standardized in such a way that even a new person can do the job in three days?
* Are key points of operations clearly identified for everybody to notice?
* Is key management information displayed in such a way that mission, goals, and approaches to achieve goals are easily tracked even by strangers?
* Are there mechanisms to expose problems effectively?
* Is there a clear indication that problem-solving activities are being done by people at the floor?
* Are examples of improvement displayed for others to benefit from?
* Are there clear indications that people are involved?
* Are there designated areas to conduct daily meetings?
* Are people at the floor open and friendly to visitors?
* Is there a sense of goal orientation in people?
* Are techniques/concepts internalized deeply by people for use, or applied superficially by specialists or management?

Shop Floor Tour Checklist

Only three items are listed in each category here. As appropriate, the list should be expanded to accommodate the specific needs of organization.

Housekeeping and workplace organization

Labeling, yellowlining, marks to designate areas

Color coding

Housekeeping and organization checklist

Safety

Clear safety procedure

Unblocked fire extinguisher

Floor uncluttered

People

Big first names on the badge, team members' pictures

Attendance chart, vacation schedule

Cross-training chart

Work procedure

Process chart

Easy-to-read standard operating procedure at the work station

Checklist

Schedule

Production control board

Leveled/mixed production, small lot production

Cycle time control

Inventory

First-in, first-out

Inventory level

Kanban

Exposing problems

   Andon

   Jidoka (line stop concept)

   Charts with control limits

Problem solving

   Suggestion program, small group improvement activities

   Use of problem-solving tools, lending library

   Multiple areas for meeting at the floor, with charts, blackboard

Quality

   Customer feedback

   QC process table, designated control points of quality

   Statistical process control, poka-yoke, sample board

Improvement

   Display of improvement on the shop floor

   Emphasis on small improvements, not just the big ones

   Number of suggestions and projects completed

Management

   Display of mission, goals, plan of action

   Scoreboard to monitor key performance indices (e.g., QCDSM)

   Daily floor meeting

Office

   Open office arrangement

   Clarity of information flow

   Same discipline practiced as in the factory

Pride, ownership, trust, equality

   Cleanliness of rest room, locker room, cafeteria

   Friendliness, openness to visitors

No special treatment of management

Reward and recognition

Awards, newsletters with department news

Show and tell, sharing rally

Applause for achievements

(Note: This appendix is referred to on page 305 in the text.)

Appendix 12.1

VOICES OF PEOPLE WHO ARE ENGAGED IN THE NEW SHOP FLOOR MANAGEMENT

In order to get a firsthand impression of people who are engaged in shop floor management, this appendix offers the comments of some of them. These people range from operators to presidents, and their companies range from electronics to automotive industries, and from $10 million to over $10 billion in sales volume. However, the vision they share is very similar. As we work on our efforts for continuous improvement with everybody involved, it is the author's hope that these people's voices are heard, shared, and digested by many.

All coments are taken from the video education course, *The New Shop Floor Management—Empowering People for Continuous Improvement,* by Kiyoshi Suzaki, distributed from the Society of Manufacturing Engineers, One SME Drive, P.O. Box 930, Dearborn, Michigan 48121.

Rethinking Our Shop Floor

It's like we were saying—on the shop floor, that's where you collect the sins of the whole corporation. You've got the problems from the supplier, you've got design problems, material problems, workmanship problems, but they all come together on the shop floor, and rather than just point your finger and say "It's not my fault," I think that's where it needs to be solved. You need to get together on the shop floor as a team and go back through to whether it's design, supply, or whatever, and solve the problem from there.

—Victor Fitzsimmons,
V.P. Manufacturing,
Printronix

Changing Business Environment

It took us four to five years to design, develop a product, put it into manufacturing, and put it into the field. Our competition was doing that in three. When we moved to three, they went to two, when we went to two they went to one. So you can see the intensification of that entire process.

—Nick Argona, Manager,
Organizational Effectiveness,
Xerox Corporation

It used to be about every ten to twelve years people would change their skills. Now it's becoming every two to three years. In this industry [H.P.] it's very fast because there's quick changes in technology and so forth.

—Stu Winby, Manager,
Factory of the Future,
Hewlett-Packard

Traditional Management

We were never allowed to voice an opinion of our own. We always had to go through channels to be heard, and a lot of times if someone didn't like the idea, they would just kind of forget about it. Nothing would ever come of it.

—Rita Haggerty,
Operations Associate,
Motorola

The key problem with the traditional management style we had here was that it was inflexible. It wasn't able to change rapidly enough to meet the dynamic needs of our market.

—Mel Waite,
Materials Manager,
ALPS

Creating a Vision

We need to create an environment where people feel good about working. Instead of machines, people are positioned in the center of the shop floor.

—Hiromi Kawashima, Center Manager,
Prototype Assembly, Komatsu, Ltd.

When we were discussing about our vision as a lamp factory, we talked about how we would feel if we were a bulb coming into our operation from our glass blowing plant. How would we feel, what would we expect? We would expect a spotlessly clean receiving area, even though the long truck ride might have jarred us, we came into areas with world craftsmen and carefully maintained equipment.

—Pete Machuga,
Plant Manager,
General Electric,
Ohio Lamp Plant

Customer Orientation

Our philosophy is that if one customer buys a car that has one problem on it, as far as that customer is concerned, every car we produce could have the same problem.

—William Ray Wilt,
Assistant Plant Manager,
Honda of America Mfg., Inc.

An employee will come up to you asking you to replace some key element of the process. Even if it's a screwdriver, a wrench, a pair of pliers, or something like that, the only question that is necessary to ask the individual is, "Are these things necessary for the pursuit of the basic goal?" That basic goal being to provide the customer with the highest possible quality. . . . Not "Is it justifiable? Do you really need it?" The question is, "Is it part of the process of providing the customer with quality?"

—John Lucas,
Plant Manager,
Toledo Scale Corporation

In order to make a customer happy we have to understand the language the customer is speaking. In order to make the employees happy, in order to get them to participate in our program, in order to empower them, I have to understand their language.

—Clement Khaw,
Manufacturing Engineer,
Leegin Creative Leather

Collecting the Wisdom of People

Because of the competitive environment we're in—because the industry is changing so rapidly, the economy is changing so rapidly—it isn't possible for any one person or any small group of people to determine the best way to move this business ahead. It requires the brains and involvement of every employee in this company.

—George Kilishek,
V.P. Manufacturing,
ALPS

You like to think you're brilliant. David Packard at Hewlett-Packard is a brilliant man, but he's one guy on the entire staff of fifty thousand or however many employees. If everyone was only ten percent as smart as David Packard, and you multiply ten percent times fifty thousand, that's five thousand times smarter than David is. So I guess that vision is what gets me thinking.

—Jerry Kohl,
President,
Leegin Creative Leather

Teamwork

There is no "I" in the word "team."

—Todd Skelly,
Team Coordinator,
Honda of America Mfg., Inc.

Self-Management

We've always answered them and they have gone and done what we told them to do. Now what we are asking people to do is learn how to make those decisions themselves.

—Gerry Bieber,
Manufacturing Advisor,
Toledo Scale Corporation

It's kind of like letting your kids go off on their own for the first time. You want to be there to help and protect them. And now here I'm watching [my people] do all these things and I have the urge to go in and tell them what to do. And I've got to refrain . . . I've got to hold myself back and let them do it on their own.

—Eileen Nichols,
Production Supervisor,
ALPS

The first thing is, you have to be willing to let go. You can't micro manage—it absolutely will kill you if you micro manage. Two, you've got to have a fundamental belief that people want to do a good job, and given the opportunity, they will work far in excess of your expectations. Three, you understand that when you do this, you're going to be a greater success as a manager, because not only are you getting rid of those things that are not really a lot of fun, but now you can start developing people.

—Donald M. King,
Project Leader,
Motorola

They own their particular process, they own the equipment, they can make changes as far as layout if it's going to improve it. They can make recommendations and they'll be listened to.

> —Jerry Hekker,
> V.P. Manufacturing,
> Steelcase

It was tough to get used to being able to make your own direction, the way you want to go, without someone telling you do it this way or that way. Now you feel more like coming to work because you know you've got more responsibility and you are more involved, and you're proud of what you're putting out for the customer.

> —Raymond Winnans,
> Group Leader,
> G.E. Ohio Lamp Plant

We are part of the solution now; we aren't part of the problem.

> —Michael Witaker,
> Operator, Calsonic

Ownership

They are the owners of their department, they are the ones that really know what is going on. We want to give them the vision, and the values and the direction, but when it really comes to implementing and to really deciding what is an area that can be improved upon, we want them to make those decisions.

> —M.F. Zaldivar,
> Director of Manufacturing,
> Leegin Creative Leather

They are really starting to see themsleves at this [mini-] company that's doing business, and they are starting to think what's the best way, the smartest way for us to do business.

> —Tom Boardman,
> Stockroom Supervisor,
> Printronix

Our plant manager started on the floor. So eventually you could start on the production floor and become the president of Honda of America. Everyone believes in that.

> —William Ray Wilt
> Assistant Plant Manager,
> Honda of America Mfg., Inc.

Roles and Responsibilities of Supervisors and Managers

A manager's job is not to do things himself but to get others to do things successfully; to coach, to guide, to train, to facilitate, to do all those kinds of things to get others to be successful in their jobs.

> —James Martin,
> Production Manager,
> Hewlett-Packard

In your daily communications you must constantly act as an advisor, a facilitator, a friend, and most of all, a very trusted fellow employee. You should never put yourself as a manager in a position of being one notch better than the shop floor employee, because he's the expert.

> —John Lucas,
> Plant Manager,
> Toledo Scale Corporation

I have become much less involved with the day to day running of the operation. I'm looking more into long term. What's the operation going to look like in a year; five years. My planning has changed from week-to-week, month-to-month planning into a yearly five-year planning, or long-range planning.

> —Judith E. Sherrer,
> Team Leader,
> Hewlett-Packard

In our operation, the first-line supervisor is the most important part of our management team. That first-line supervisor has a direct influence and direct control over our manufacturing operation, and manufacturing is our business. So we placed a lot of emphasis on developing the role of the first-line supervisor as the coach, as the leader, as the teacher of the various manufacturing philosophies we are trying to get in place.

> —Mel Waite
> Materials Manager,
> ALPS

It's very important for all of us to understand that one of the big charters for us is probably to work to eliminate our jobs. It's going to be important for us to understand that by doing this it will continue to keep our organization so successful so there will also be opportunities for us to move into after we have done these kind of changes.

> —James Martin,
> Production Manager,
> Hewlett-Packard

Managers don't actually ever lose control. They gain more in the process, in the end, because they've gained better quality, they've gained the respect of the people.

> —Lynn Limbeck,
> Assembler,
> Motorola

Rather than being a policeman, rather than being the bad guy in the organization, our objective has been to turn the manager into a coach, leader, teacher, and to help set the goals and objectives for the organization.

—Mel Waite,
Materials Manger,
ALPS

For me, the role has changed. Instead of being rewarded for my own direct actions, how I feel I'm successful is by making sure that people have the information that they need or the resources they need to get their job done.

—Judith E. Sherrer,
Team Leader,
Hewlett-Packard

Instead of me doing all of the directing, and the controlling, all of the classical things to make things happen, we were able to establish a culture that said, "Hey, the people nearest to what is happening will make the decision and make it happen." And it has turned out far beyond any expectations that I could possibly have.

—Donald M. King,
Project Leader,
Motorola

Suggestions

When an associate turns in an idea and after it has been approved for implementation, [he or she is] the owner and project leader to implement that suggestion.

—William J. Hayes,
Assistant Manager—Technical Training,
Honda of America Mfg., Inc.

Instructing People

He [the Boss] wouldn't tell you the exact answer. What he would do is plant a seed for you to think about and let you decide on your own what the problem is and the best way to solve it. I think that's a good way of teaching someone—not to actually tell them what to do or how to do it, but give them the idea and let them go on their own and try to solve that problem.

—William Ray Wilt,
Assistant Plant Manager,
Honda of America Mfg., Inc.

The easy way in doing something is to tell people just do it, that's the easy way. The hard way is to say what you think.

—Norio Sugahara,
General Manager,
Tokai Rika

That notion of giving them a fish, that's not going to work anymore. We want to teach them how to fish for themselves.

> —Randy Bauder,
> Organization Development Trainer,
> Motorola

I think probably the biggest thing to implementing this environment is learning how to answer questions with a question . . . As a supervisor or manager when people come to you if you always give them the answer, they're never going to evolve.

> —James Martin,
> Production Manager,
> Hewlett-Packard

I give them [operators] the direction to go and get their own answers. In the past whenever they had a problem they would come right to me and say, "How do we do this? How do we fix this?" Now what I'm telling them is we go through a series of questions, and instead of me answering it for them, they come up with their own answer or they find out who they need to talk to get their own answers. So they are taking more ownership.

> —Eileen Nichols,
> Production Supervisor,
> ALPS

Education and Training

I think that education is probably the most important thing we can do, because what we are learning today in the schools probably will be obsolete in five years, and so if we don't renew ourselves to a corporate commitment to the education, I think we'll end up being obsolete.

> —Ted Woods,
> V.P. & Director of Manufacturing & Quality,
> Motorola

We are finding that the more you educate and the more you take it into a personal self-development, the more they want and the more they will develop themselves.

> —Harry Featherstone,
> President, Will-Burt

It's amazing when people say they don't have time to do any training, because if they took the hour or two to do the training, by the time they get done training and get the people involved in the activities, they end up having a week of free time instead of an hour of clutter time.

> —Eileen Nichols,
> Production Supervisor,
> ALPS

You can't empower the people without giving them the adequate tools and things that they need to do. . . . to do some of the things that you've traditionally done. I mean, if you're going to turn over control of something that you did to some other people, you have to make sure that they know how to do it.

—Doug Boone, Team Member,
Design Engineering,
Motorola

I think nothing is impossible to do. If I think I can do, I can do it. I don't know when, I don't know where, but I can do it. . . . I know many people that are fifty or sixty, and they are studying, so it is never too late to begin studying.

—Francisco Leon,
Machine Operator,
DACOR

Don't be afraid to try it. Ask, if you've got problems, whether it's reading, spelling, math, English, ask for help.

—Kenneth R. Reinertsen,
Plywood Blanking Saw Operator,
Simpson Timber Company

Standard Operating Procedure (SOP)

We cover things that are important such as the quality, the safety, the ease of doing it. We identify key points and we illustrate those points in pictorials. This document then, becomes one that we can use to train people with and then we can be assured that the process is being done in a standard manner. When we encounter a problem it's a lot easier to go back and determine what the problem is.

—Robert P. Ganger,
V.P. General Manager,
Glass Master Control

When we come up with an operation standard, we should make it simple enough and describe it well enough that anyone could walk up to that job and be able to complete one cycle with the correct parts. Maybe not in the time frame needed, but they should be able to do the process, even if they've never done it before.

—Rick J. Pfarr, Team Leader,
Honda of America Mfg., Inc.

The operation standards are upgraded by the production associates, with the approval of management. The production associates have the responsibility of keeping them current and changing them as we can improve them.

—Todd Gordon, Coordinator
Honda of America Mfg., Inc.

I think most important is the orientation to detail and how important that is on the shop floor. Being detail oriented, you create a more consistent product.
—Kathy Gietzen, Engineer,
Richard-Allan Medical Industries

Leadership

I think in order to be a good leader or good trainer, you need to show that you care, that the people are learning, that you are interested in their thoughts, and that you are willing to sometimes make a fool of yourself in order to get them involved in something. When they see that you are willing to do that, it kind of breaks the ice and gives them a chance to start the experiment.
—Eileen Nichols,
Production Supervisor,
ALPS

Don't try to do it yourself. Recognize that you're not going to be rewarded for what you do, you're going to be rewarded for what you are able to guide the people that work for you to do.
—James Martin,
Production Manager,
Hewlett-Packard

Decision Making

I find that I have to really literally bite my tongue not to make a decision. I've gotten to where I am because I make decisions, but now you have to think "Don't make that decision if it does not really belong to you."
—Donald King,
Project Leader,
Motorola

Change Process

What I found out is that the operators have a thirst to know. They want to know more information. As managers and as supervisors we have a tendency to back away from giving them too much information because we don't believe they can handle it. When you start to do training with your people you find that the more information you give them, the more enthused they are about what they are doing. They understand better what they are doing and why, and they begin to ask questions that probably never would have come up if you didn't give them that little bit of information.

—Eileen Nichols,
Production Supervisor,
ALPS

I did not trust management, but yet it was not only trusting management, it was trusting your co-workers. You always had the feeling that everyone was after your job. And now they were saying "Go for it," and it's like everybody's trying to do everyone else's job and it's like how can you do this. . . . It worked. It worked by letting go, each individual letting go and contributing what they knew to the next one. It just grew and grew. It was unbelievable, what had happened.

—Lynn Limbeck,
Assembler,
Motorola

The purpose of the meeting was trying to come up with areas of waste that we could tackle and try to improve on. The supervisor that was conducting the meeting was having a really difficult time trying to get the people to cooperate and come up with ideas. And he kept insisting and insisting, "Come on guys, give me ideas of areas we could tackle as areas of waste." Finally, one person said, "The biggest waste is this meeting." And that's just an example. Now it's funny, but at the time we were very concerned, because how do you change that attitude, how do you change the attitude that just because you are sitting down discussing a problem, that you are not wasting your time. It was not easy, not easy at all.

—M.F. Zaldivar,
Director of Manufacturing,
Leegin Creative Leather

Most importantly, the change needs to be self generated, it needs to come from within the organization.

—Mel Waite,
Materials Manager,
ALPS

It takes an enormous amount of emotional input and energy to effect change, and it takes a great deal of consistency and repetition to get anything. It's like trying to turn the Queen Mary or a battleship.

—John Adams,
President,
Sparling Instruments

All of a sudden we asked them for their ideas, their thoughts, their involvement, when about ten years ago we brought them up and said we'll tell you what to do, here's how to do it, here's the tool you'll use, and don't bother telling us how to do it. I think that was very difficult and took at lot of convincing, but once that person or that group gains your confidence and your trust, it was very easy to attain.

—Ann Calahere,
Business Center Manager,
Xerox Corporation

I fed my own ego by being the answer man for everything and going out on the floor and being the sparkplug that made things happen. And I found that with this style of management, what we must do is to turn that around and give that feeling of accomplishment in the hearts of the people on the floor. And surprisingly they take to this like ducks to water, if you give them a chance and the opportunity to do it.

—Robert P. Ganger,
V.P. & General Manager,
Glass Master Control

A lot of people had a denial phase. They didn't want to do it. They just wanted to come in every day, sit down and do their work, and be told what to do every day and then go home. We've since worked through all these problems and it took a long time. It wasn't something that was accomplished overnight.

—Robert Bates,
Manufacturing Advisor,
Toledo Scale Corporation

Implementation

It's like taking that thousand-mile journey, you have to take the first step, and then you have to continually take the next step and the next step and the next step. Each step in itself is not very difficult, but when you look at it in total scope you think it's most difficult. And this process is the same way. You just start doing the things that are necessary to do it.

—Robert P. Ganger,
V.P. & General Manager,
Glass Master Control

Do not start the process without considering the fact that it's something that's going to be continuous.

—John Lucas
Plant Manager,
Toledo Scale Corporation

If you don't have management behind you, get it. Get it and get some little teams, anything, two people, ten people, whatever, get your ideas together and I think you'll find some real improvements.

—David Sweet,
Group Leader,
Xerox Corporation

Be patient, be patient, because it does take a little longer to implement things, but the results are much more rewarding than I used to get when I made that decision myself.

—Ann Calahere,
Business Center Manager,
Xerox Corporation

Don't expect too much too soon. Allow for failures, because those failures can often turn out to be successes.

—Edward Allen,
Warehouse Supervisor,
ALPS

You've heard a lot, you've seen a lot, I think it's time to get off the pot and do something about it.

—Ricky W. Storck,
Setup Operator,
PW Pipe

The big thing is do it. It will work. You've got to be willing to take the chance, but it's not a chance. As a matter of fact, it's the nearest thing to a guarantee that I've ever seen in my years of industry. But you've got to be willing to set broad guidelines as a manager and don't tighten the suckers down. Let and help the people operate within those guidelines.

—Bob Carroll,
Manufacturing Section Manager,
Motorola

There's always going to be stumbling blocks, but that's part of your everyday life. You grow and grow, and the more you grow the more you learn, the more you learn the better off your company will be—and, the better off your product will be.

—Steve Kroner,
Electronic Technician,
Toledo Scale Corporation

There are a lot of variables that influence success, and interestingly, success itself is a key variable. Once the students see the success, then the motivation factors start working in their favor.

—Dr. Dee Tadlock,
Literacy Consultant

It is important to do it until we succeed. Also, if we have such an attitude, I am sure we will succeed.

—Jiro Izumi
Plant Manager,
Matsushita

Reward and Recognition

You start to see progress; you start to see people grow and accomplish things you didn't think they could do. I think probably the biggest reward is seeing the growth of the people in the organization.

—John Adams,
President,
Sparling Instruments

He's been with us now for about a year and a half, and he's never missed a day. He worked in a company for fourteen years before he came to work for us. He told me that in those fourteen years he missed one day, but the sad thing was that nobody ever told him or recognized him or thanked him for doing that for the fourteen years he was there. The company he used to work for at one time employed about five hundred people. Right now they have fifty.

We wanted to tell that story to as many of our people as possible, and they all felt proud of what we were doing. At the same time, I also wanted to remind them that maybe two years ago, we could have been that other company. We could have been the company that did not recognize the operators as much as we should.

—M.F. Zaldivar,
Director of Manufacturing,
Leegin Creative Leather

(Note: This appendix is referred to on page 332 in the text.)

EPILOGUE:
WITHSTANDING THE RAIN

We have now spent time together with this book, sharing ideas on shop floor management. In order to develop a holistic understanding of the subject, we have addressed the subject from different angles, chapter by chapter. I am certainly hopeful that they fit together in the reader's mind.

When I started this manuscript, I thought this work would be similar to trying to put a jig-saw puzzle together. Yet this does not mean that the subject is difficult. It means that it requires more of an intuitive understanding rather than an intellectual bias. Our orientation to the shop floor rather than the office or ivory tower signifies this point. If we go through a process of practicing self-management and self-improvement, readers may develop their own solutions— rather than being told what to do. Since, ultimately, the solution needs to be found by the readers in order for it to be meaningful, their astute insight and practice at the shop floor is ultimately what counts.

In this book, we studied such subjects as our values, the customer, problem solving, and leadership, and examined their linkages. To grasp the essence of shop floor management, we should realize that these ideas produce the power only when we digest them as a whole. As much as our orientation toward local optimization does not bring us a total understanding, we need to go beyond such piecemeal thinking. Instead of digesting just a representation of ideas, we should stretch ourselves so that the essence can be grasped directly, intuitively, and immediately.

Frederick Taylor approached the subject of shop management scientifically, dividing things into pieces, analyzing them, and providing the solution. Logically, such an approach is unassailable. Yet when I think of issues such as people's desire for self-management, or self-improvement I feel an emptiness in Tayloristic thinking that needs to be filled. In his time, these issues may have been considered irrelevant. But today, I see it as our responsibility to go beyond.

It seems that a logical, intellectual thinking process needs to be overcome or at least supplemented by our creativity and intuition. Not argument for the sake of argument, but something beyond the logic which reaches to our consciousness—even to the point that once we grasp it in our minds, we do not need words to communicate because it is just there.

Albert Einstein comments, "Imagination is greater than knowledge." On our shop floor, we can find signs illustrating such a message as well:

- At the shop floor, concepts do not solve the problem by themselves.
- If we are self-centered, our own thinking may prevent us from getting the idea.
- If we depend on specialists or authorities, it may take away the initiative of our self-management drive and our creativity to control our own destiny.

Furthermore, as much as we need to address these points as individuals, we need to do the same as an organization. Otherwise we have the problem illustrated by the example of the blind men and the elephant: each person thinks of the elephant separately, as a tree trunk (leg), a blanket (ear), or a snake (trunk), as opposed to getting the total picture.

Or we may see "elephant" as a conceptual illustration of an elephant, but not the real "ELEPHANT," as a small child might see it, without any prejudice. Or, we may see the finger that points to the moon and investigate the finger, thinking that there is a solution, without looking at the moon (the real solution) in the sky at which the finger is pointing.

For that reason we need to go back to the shop floor where the reality is. We need to practice these ideas, and develop our own capabilities. Then, we may create the critical mass of people—leading to "organizational enlightenment," where empowered people are leading improvement activities continuously and lighting up the corners of the world.

When that happens, it is like liquid crystalizing itself all of a sudden. Whether an individual or an organization, this is similar to an enlightened moment of discovery, or the solving of a jig-saw puzzle with everybody's creativity. In other words, it is the moment that tree "trunks," "blankets," and "snake" turn into an "ELE-PHANT."

Realizing that true creation does not seem to come with self-centered, earthly desire, however, our brains should be free from constraints. Accordingly, management needs to develop an appropriate setting and create a moment of enlightenment if they want to utilize the wisdom of people.

If you have had the joy of sharing some improvement experiences, whether the subject matter is big or small, or if you have seen the eyes of your colleagues shining when sharing excitement at work, you understand what I mean. That is the kind of moment and thought that I ultimately wanted to share in this book. Such moments may come as small incidents at the beginning. But, hopefully, we can find many shining treasures on our shop floor and in our lives!

Self-management may relate to democracy. Without people's ownership, dictatorships may prevail. Certain direction may help. Yet, in order to prevent us from going back, each individual needs to upgrade his or her skills to self-manage better and eliminate the opportunity for dictators to assume authority.

Our sense of ownership, consciousness, and intelligence will be the toughest protection from a centralized power structure or an organization with a myriad of regulations. We need to keep working on these with our self-management drive so that living in a democratic society our conscience will prevail.

Customer orientation is related to the market economy. As opposed to the planned economy, when everybody is self-managing and trying to satisfy his or her customers better, we can collect the wisdom of everyone to contribute to our society at large. Competition will force us to use our creativity for our customers' best interests. It is tough. But at the same time, we are the beneficiaries of such a battle.

In a way, a democracy and a market economy provide a framework for our behavior. But in a larger sense, we should be continuously working towards a society that respects people's identity and initiatives. As human beings we are customers oursleves, and thus we need to satisfy ourselves. Also, we are the customers of the prior generations who expended their efforts in the past. We can also do this from where we are today in whatever we do. Whether it is production, or service, whether it is in the field of politics, environment, school, or philosophy, we can contribute for our own well being.

Creativity means life; we are different from robots, or machines. To appreciate what we have, we need to throw away our fixed mindset, and let fact, reality, ideas, and people on the shop floor speak for themselves. Barriers are something we create by ourselves. Let us listen even to three-year-old children and learn from them. Let us have openness, humbleness, and faith in accomplishing our vision.

Let us work on the quality of our work and the quality of our management. Also, let us work on the quality of our behavior. Then, let us learn from these insights and think that we will succeed. And if we think like that, I am sure we will succeed. Henry Ford said, "What is desirable and right is not impossible." Walt Disney said, "If we can dream it, we can do it." I also believe that if we are prepared for it, we can find the answer in our own hands.

For the people at the shop floor who shed the light to light up the corners of the world, I want to end this book with the words of the Japanese poet, Kenji Miyazawa. While he was a poet, his mind was always with rice farmers in the northeastern part of Japan where natural disasters were common. At the same time, he lived his life in his world of cosmic consciousness or the world with no boundary, saying "Unless the world as a whole can achieve happiness there is no happiness as an individual. . . . The consciousness as a person will progress from individual to group to society to the universe."

The following poem was found after his death in his personal notebook. Later, it was published and awakened many Japanese people's minds. Somehow, I relate this poem to the voice of people at the shop floor.

Withstanding the Rain

Withstanding the rain
Withstanding the wind
Withstanding the snow or the heat of the summer
Having a strong body
Without earthly desire
Always smiling quietly

Eat a liter of rice in one day
with miso* and small amount of vegetables
Facing all affairs
without thinking of myself
See well, listen well, and understand well
and not to forget
Living in a small thatched hut
on the field next to the pine forest
When there is a sick child in the east
visit him to take care
When there is a tired mother in the west
visit her to carry the bundle of rice
When there is a person about to die in the south
visit and assure that there is no need to be afraid
When there is a fight and lawsuit in the north
point out to stop since it is of no use
When there is hot dry weather, shed tears
When there is a cold summer, wonder without any hope
Called a fool by everyone
Without being appreciated
Without being shunned
I want to become such a person

—Kenji Miyazawa (translated by the author from
Poetry of Kenji Miyazawa, edited by
Tetsuzo Tanigawa [Iwanami Shoten, Publishers,
1950], p. 325)

*Miso: Bean paste

BIBLIOGRAPHY

Bounine, J., and Suzaki, K. *Produire Juste a Temps—Les Sources de la Productivité Industrielle Japonaise*. Paris: Masson, 1986.

Imai, M. *Kaizen*. New York: Random House, 1986.

Ishikawa, K. *What Is Total Quality Control?* Englewood Cliffs, NJ: Prentice-Hall, 1985.

Maslow, A. H. *Motivation and Personality*. New York: Harper, 1970.

Matthiessen, P. *Nine-Headed Dragon River*. Boston: Shambhala Publications, 1987.

Osborne, A. F. *Applied Imagination*. New York: Scribner's, 1963.

Peters, T. *Thriving on Chaos*. New York: Alfred A. Knopf, 1987.

Peters, T. and Waterman, R. *In Search of Excellence*. New York: Harper & Row, 1982.

Sekiya, T. *Honda Motor-The Men, The Management, The Machine*. Taipei: Koke-ToSho, 1982.

Suzaki, K. *The New Manufacturing Challenge*. New York: The Free Press, 1987.

Taylor, F. *Shop Management*. New York: Harper & Brothers, 1919.

Womack, J., Jones, D., and Roos, D. *The Machine That Changed the World*. New York: Harper Perennial, 1990.

Japanese Publications

Honda, S. *One Day, One Story*. Kyoto: PHP Institute, 1985.

Karatsu, K. *TQC: Japanese Wisdom*. Tokyo: JUSE, 1981.

Matsushita, K. *Sayings of Konosuke Matsushita*. Kyoto: PHP Institute, 1983.

Ohno, T. *Taiichi Ohno's Workplace Management*. Tokyo: Japan Management Association, 1982.

Suzaki, K. *Just-in-Time Revolution (JIT Kakumei no Shogeki)*. Tokyo: Diamond Publishing Company, 1987.

Suzaki, K. et al. "The New Wave of Toyota Production System." *Factory Management,* May 1985.

Tanigawa, T. *Poetry of Kenji Miyazawa*. Tokyo: Iwanami Shoten, Publishers, 1950.

Tozawa, B. *Kaizen-Teian I & II*. Tokyo: Japan Industrial News, 1989 & 1990.

Yasuda, Y. *Toyota's Suggestion Program*. Tokyo: Japan Management Association, 1989.

Video-Education Courses (With Facilitator's Guide & Workbook)

Suzaki, K. *The New Manufacturing Challenge—Techniques for Continuous Improvement*. Dearborn, MI: Society of Manufacturing Engineers, 1988.

Suzaki, K. *The New Shop Floor Management—Empowering People for Continuous Improvement*. Dearborn, MI: Society of Manufacturing Engineers, 1992.

ACKNOWLEDGMENTS

After meeting many people, and reading many books, I realize that it is not just the men and women in business, but many others as well who have inspired me to write this book. Furthermore, since I have gained my knowledge from so many people, I am not certain if there is any work that is my own. Writing this book is then a process of interpreting all of these people's ideas combined with my own. In that sense, this book is the product of many.

My upbringing in Japan and my work as manager and engineer at Toshiba and as consultant at the Boston Consulting Group in Tokyo provided me with unique experience, not just in looking at things from a Japanese viewpoint but in comparing it with the situation overseas. Later, I traveled extensively and lived in the United States, where my business school studies and work for U.S. firms, and starting my own businesses have brought me a different outlook in my life. Through these experiences, I have been fortunate to visit hundreds of companies in over twenty countries providing seminars and consulting services while my previous books have been read by people in more than eight languages.

All of these encounters are reflected in this book in some form, and many people's ideas are also reflected as I put my thoughts on paper. But the reverse of this process also happens. When I meet people who have read my previous books, for example, I feel that I have already shared ideas with some of them. Even a man in Uzbekistan in Central Asia who had read my previous book several times had given me the impression that I could really share thoughts with him when I first met him. Similar situations have happened with other people from different countries.

These represent the joys of sharing. But now, I am happy to acknowledge those who have encouraged me, given me insight, or shared their ideas and experiences. Similarly, if this book triggers some positive thinking in readers' minds or provides some form of encouragement, I hope my readers can transfer some of these to others for their benefit.

Specifically, however, many people have inspired me through their books, seminars, or in person. They include Messrs. Konosuke Matsushita, Soichiro Honda, Taiichi Ohno, Kaoru Ishikawa, Masakazu Nakayama, Kenichi Ohmae, and Daisetz Suzuki from Japan, and Messrs. Henry Ford, Thomas Edison, Tom Peters, Joseph Juran, and W. Edwards Deming from the United States.

Many others shared their thoughts with me when I entered this field of consulting, education, seminars, and writing. They include, from Toshiba, Messrs. Kazuwo Iwata, Shoichi Saba, Joichi Aoi, Etsuro Ashiwara, Shigekazu Yoshijima, and Tatsuro Ohmura; from Toyota and Toyota's affiliate, Messrs. Masao Nemoto, Tetsuo Kondo, and Shoji Moriya; from Daiwa Seiko, Mr. Shutaro Mori; from General Electric, Messrs. Salomon Levy, Bob Proebstle, and Pat Marriott; from Boston Consulting Group, Messrs. Bruce Henderson, Dick Lochridge, Bob Ching, and George Stalk; from Arthur Young & Company (currently known as Ernst and Young), Messrs. John Schorneck, Deward Watts, and Lee Sage.

More recently, through Suzaki & Company, Eucalyptus Group, Suzaki-Lochridge and Company, Systems Management Group, Continuous Improvement Users' Group, Japan Technology Transfer Association, Bekaeart Consulting (Spain), Productivity and Quality Consultants (Indonesia), and Dymos Consulting (Japan), I have worked with many who shared the beliefs described in this book. They include Chip Land, Dick Lochridge, Mike Rother, Rick Fleming, Eric Gatmaitan, Larry Richert, Luis Mauleon, Jose Luis Martinez, Leon Bronshteyn, Marc Checheonitsky, Sonny Irawan, Kristanto Santosa, Fumio Goto, and Kazuo Moro.

Through my consulting work, I have met and shared ideas with countless numbers of people whom I owe many, many thanks. By facing the problems at the shop floor and by sharing thoughts and going through hard times together, we have made significant progress within those companies as well as individually.

Thinking back, I realize that by attempting to impart some of my energy to others, I may often have seemed too blunt and outspoken. In other instances, I have felt almost guilty speaking up. Yet because as I typically visit companies every month to every year to assess their progress, I knew it was important for someone who did not have a strong personal interest with the company—someone who could be impartial and objective—to be able to say whatever I thought was best for the company.

While I want to apologize for my atypical behavior, I also believe many great friendships were developed as a result of going through the hard times together while sharing beliefs and maintaining openness and honesty with each other. I owe a great deal to these people and appreciate the time we spent together.

Since they are from all levels of the organization—from operators to the president—and they number too many to thank by name, I will list their companies instead.

From the United States: Alcoa, Alps Manufacturing (USA), Amot Control, Apple Computer, Auburn Gear, Bay Cities Container Corp., Blount, Inc., Borg-Warner, Calsonic Climate Control, Inc., Cosmair, CTS Corporation, Cummins Engine, Dacor, Edgewood Tool & Manufacturing Company, Energy Containers (a BFM aerospace company), Fireplace Manufacturers, Inc., Firestone Tire, FMC, Ford, General Electric Company, General Motors, Glass Master Control, Grand Rapids Spring & Wire, Harley-Davidson, Hewlett-Packard, Honda of America Manufacturing, IBM, Industrial Technology Institute, Leegin Creative Leather Products, Inc., Lewis Metal Stamping and Manufacturing Co., Masco, Milliken & Co., Motorola, Inc., Pacific Scientific, Priam, Printronix, Puritan-Bennett, PW Pipe, Richard-Allan Medical Industries, Rockwell International, Sam Blount & Company, Simpson Timber Company, Sparling Instruments, Steelcase, Tech Group, Tektronix, Tokai Rika (USA), Toledo Scale Corporation, TRW, Westvaco, Whittaker, Wil-Burt Company, Worldmark, Xerox Corporation, and scores of member companies in the Continuous Improvement Users' Group, The Executive Committee, and the Young Presidents Organization.

From Japan: Aisin Seiki, Canon, Daihatsu, Daiwa Seiko, Fujitsu, Hitachi, Hitachi Kenki, Honda, Iseki, Isuzu, Kanto Auto Works, Komatsu Ltd., Kubota, Matsushita Electric Industrial Co., Ltd., Mazda, Mitsubishi, NEC, Nippondenso, Ricoh, Sanesu, Sanyo, Sharp, Sony, Suzuki, Tokai Rika, Tokyo Electric Co., Tokyo Juki, Toshiba, Toyota, Toyota Gosei, Yamazaki Machinery, and Yanmar.

From Europe: British Aerospace, Daimler Benz, F.L. Smith, Haviland, L'Oreal, Land Rover, Neuhaus, Plastic Omnium, Robert Bosch, Rover Group, Saab, Siemens, and Tyrolit.

Also, people from many associations have been helpful: American Production and Inventory Control Society, American Society of

Quality Control, American Supplier Institute, Association of Manufacturing Excellence, Diamond Publishing Co., The Executive Committee (TEC), Factory Management, Japan HR Association, Japan Daily Industrial News, Liaison Sociales, Masson, Precision Metal Forming Association, Society of Manufacturing Engineering, and the Young Presidents' Organization (YPO).

A number of professors have given valuable assistance, including: John Banaszak (Rock Valley College), Elwood Buffa (University of California, Los Angeles), Bill Gleeson (Marquette University), Robert Hall (Indiana University), Wald Hancock (University of Michigan), Bob Hayes (Harvard University), Chuck Holloway (Stanford University), Don Kane (Cornell University), Noriaki Kano (Tokyo Science University), Shigeru Mizuno (Tokyo Institute of Technology), Junichiro Nakane (Waseda University), Ahmet Satir (Concordia University), Arthur Swasey (Yale University), Steve Wheelright (Harvard University), Horst Wildermann (Passaw University), and Hajime Yamashina (Kyoto University).

I also wish to thank the following colleagues, friends, and associates:

John Adams	Don Haller
Siegfreid Adler	Ed Heizer
Nick Argona	Harald Helletsberger
Elliot Blank	Heinrich Henkel
Sam Blount	Akiko Heurich
Joachen Burkhart	Mike Joseph
Gordon Burns	Hajime Karatsu
Jim Campbell	Toshiwo Kenmochi
Dick Chandler	Bob Kleist
Fujio Cho	Jerry Kohl
Richard Cohon	Shigeki Kurokawa
Ron Contino	Harry Koltun
Dick Dawson	Joel Kotkin
Jim de Los Reyes	John Lucas
Bill Finn	Pete Machuga
Victor Fitzsimmons	Raimo Makinen
Gary Fukayama	Olivier Mitterand
Tsuneo Funabashi	Scott Moon
Lee Gardner	Jun Mori
Andy Goldfarb	Rick Newhauser
John Grabner	Sam Oshikoji

Oscar Reak
Ed Riedel
Barry Rodger
Todd Root
Chava Sanchez
Michel Semerad-Radulescu
Nori Shimizu
Dick Shonbeger
John Stoll
Ken Stork
Norio Sugahara

Larry Sullivan
Ken Thorpe
Eugine Tokarev
Bunji Tozawa
Steve Uhlmann
Thomas Wagner
Jack Warn
Bill Wilcock
Ted Wood
Micky Zaldivar, and
Jim Zawacki

I also appreciate the cooperation and support of many companies from the United States, Europe, and Asia that were kind enough to let me use photographs and other materials relating to their shop floor management. Without their support, I could not have shared ideas in such a direct fashion. Of course, it is my responsibility if I failed to represent a company well in this book. However, I hope readers will appreciate the help that people in these companies provided. They are: Aisin Seiki, Alps Manufacturing (U.S.A.), Bay Cities Container, Borg-Warner, Clipper Belt Lacer, Continuous Improvement Users' Group, Cosmair, Daihatsu, Daiwa, Seiko, Fireplace Manufacturers, Inc., Glass Master Control, Grand Rapids Spring & Wire, Honda of America, Mfg., Industrial Technology Institute, Japan HR Association, Japan Railway—West Japan, Juki, Kanto Auto Works, Komatsu, Ltd., Leegin Creative Leather Products, Inc., Matsushita Electric Industrial Co., Ltd., Mazda, Motorola, NEC, Nissan, Printronix, Robert Bosch, Society of Manufacturing Engineers, Sony, Sparling Instruments, Co., Inc., Tokai Rika, Tokyo Electric Co., Toledo Scale Corporation, Toshiba, Toyota, UBISA, and Xerox Corporation.

The next group of people are those who helped me come up with ideas or provided support to write, shoot the videos, and so on. They are my parents in Japan, Matsujiro and Fusako Suzaki; my wife Barbara and my son Kenji; people from SME who helped me to develop the video education courses, *New Shop Floor Management* and *The New Manufacturing Challenge,* Tom Drozda, Tim Savage, Bill Masterson, Karen Wilhelm, and John Poswalk; my friends and mentors, Fred Newman, Jim Conner, Bob Miner, Gerald Baker, Lee Gillis, Jean Bounine, Bill Harris, John Hornsby, Don Bowker, and many others.

Whether the contribution is generating ideas, producing pictures, sharing progress editing the manuscript, or delivering the material, it is quite clear that I could not have completed this book without their help. Lastly and most importantly, I would like to extend my deepest appreciation to these who make things happen at the shop floor.

INDEX